· THE ·
BURGER
COURT

THE
BURGER
COURT

Counter-Revolution or Confirmation?

EDITED BY BERNARD SCHWARTZ

New York   Oxford
Oxford University Press
1998

Oxford University Press

Oxford   New York
Athens   Auckland   Bangkok   Bogota   Bombay
Buenos Aires   Calcutta   Cape Town   Dar es Salaam
Delhi   Florence   Hong Kong   Istanbul   Karachi
Kuala Lumpur   Madras   Madrid   Melbourne
Mexico City   Nairobi   Paris   Singapore
Taipei   Tokyo   Toronto   Warsaw

and associated companies in
Berlin   Ibadan

Copyright © 1998 by Bernard Schwartz

Published by Oxford University Press, Inc.
198 Madison Avenue, New York, New York 10016

Oxford is a registered trademark of Oxford University Press

Library of Congress Cataloging-in-Publication Data
The Burger Court : counter-revolution or confirmation? / edited by
Bernard Schwartz.
p.   cm.
"Based upon the papers presented at a major conference in 1996 at
the University of Tulsa College of Law"—Pref.
ISBN 0-19-512259-3
1. Constitutional history—United States.   2. United States.
Supreme Court—History.   I. Schwartz, Bernard, 1923–1997.
KF4541.B855   1998   97-51416
347.73'26—dc21

1 3 5 7 9 8 6 4 2
Printed in the United States of America
on acid-free paper

FOREWORD

Bernard Schwartz, the editor of this volume, died on December 23, 1997, after being struck by a car as he crossed the street. At the time of his death, this book was substantially complete. All of the essays had been written, and he had finished his editing. Ironically, the edited texts had been sent to contributors the very day he died.

Professor Schwartz was the quintessential scholar. Author of more than sixty books and literally hundreds of articles he pursued the lore of the law with a youthful passion. In the last full academic year of his life, he published five books. Yet for him, scholarship was no arid occupation. He ferreted out facts with the zeal of a cub reporter and the energy of a mountain lion. And once he had the facts, he turned them and churned them and analyzed them, and then he thought them over again.

His "personal" jurisprudence was very sympathetic to that of Earl Warren and William Brennan; he was Warren's biographer and Brennan's friend. Yet he loved the Supreme Court so deeply that he never closed his mind to other philosophies. Once a friend made a slighting remark about Chief Justice Burger in Schwartz's presence. "No, no," he interrupted, "Burger has made outstanding contributions." He had a passion for fairness and accuracy and balance.

Bernard Schwartz graduated Phi Beta Kappa from the City College of New York and received his law degree from New York University. Subsequently, he received his masters and doctoral degrees from Harvard. He also received an LL.D from Cambridge University and a *doctorat d'université* from the University of Paris. He joined the N.Y.U. Faculty of Law in 1947 and taught there for 45 years before retiring in 1992 as Edwin D. Webb Professor of Law. Shortly thereafter he became the Chapman Distinguished Professor of Law at the University of Tulsa, the position he held at his death.

While the history and jurisprudence of the Supreme Court was his greatest concern, Professor Schwartz was also a recognized authority on administrative law, a regular object of his contributions to law reviews, particularly to the *University of Tulsa Law Journal* and to the *AdLaw Bulletin*. His article, "A Decade of Administrative Law: 1987–1996," was a tour de force summary of the legal status of regulatory law, with perceptive coverage of issues like delegation of powers, investigatory power, the right to be heard, and adjudicatory procedure. His *Administrative Law: A Casebook* went to its fourth edition in 1994.

But if administrative law was an interest, constitutional law was an obsession. Once again, he was author of a standard textbook as well as a multi-volumed *Commentary on the Constitution of the United States*. His works on the Supreme Court include *A History of the Supreme Court*; *The Warren Court: A Retrospective*; *The Unpublished Opinions of the Warren Court* and its companions on the Burger and Rehnquist eras; and the enduring *Super Chief: Earl Warren and His Supreme Court—A Judicial Biography*.

But Bernard Schwartz, for all the seriousness of his scholarship, had a lighter side, nowhere better in evidence than in *A Book of Legal Lists: The Best and Worst in American Law*. This was his own compilation of the ten best and the ten worst Supreme Court justices, the ten greatest trials, and the ten greatest legal movies. With humor and imagination, Schwartz staunchly defended his choices, although he did admit to a colleague that he had perhaps been too harsh on Chief Justice Salmon P. Chase when he put him on the "ten worst" list. A large audience will also remember Schwartz's trivia quizzes in the *Supreme Court Historical Quarterly*.

Over a decade ago, it was noted of Schwartz that he "has read, and retained, the contents of every constitutional decision of the Supreme Court." Professor Schwartz modestly replied: "It's a little exaggerated, but I know most of them." He did, too. He will be greatly missed.

James B. O'Hara
January 1998

PREFACE

In 1983, a book was published entitled *The Burger Court: The Counterrevolution That Wasn't.* Is the subtitle an accurate summary of the Court headed by Warren E. Burger?

It is now more than ten years since Chief Justice Burger retired—long enough to provide the perspective for an answer. This book, based on the papers presented at a major conference in 1996 at the University of Tulsa College of Law, provides a detailed retrospective on the work of the Burger Court. It examines the Court's jurisprudence and its place in the law and life of the nation. It is hoped that the volume will be a suitable reminder of the Court that, next to its predecessor, may have been the most activist in our history.

Tulsa, Oklahoma   B.S.
1997

CONTENTS

Contributors   xi

1. Introduction   3
   James B. O'Hara
2. My Life on the Court   9
   William J. Brennan, Jr.
3. The Players and the Play   13
   Robert Henry

I. THE CONSTITUTIONAL CORPUS

4. The Burger Court's Place on the Bell Curve of Racial
   Jurisprudence   57
   Derrick Bell
5. Women as Constitutional Equals: The Burger Court's Overdue
   Evolution   66
   Stephanie K. Seymour
6. Liberty and Sexuality   83
   David J. Garrow
7. Freedom of Speech   93
   Bernard Schwartz
8. Freedom of the Press   108
   Anthony Lewis
9. Church and State   119
   Robert F. Drinan, S.J.

10. The Burger Court and Criminal Justice: A Counter-Revolution in Expectations 131
    Martin H. Belsky
11. Economic Rights 147
    Lino A. Graglia
12. Federalism 173
    Shirley S. Abrahamson and Thomas N. Hilbink

II A BROADER PERSPECTIVE

13. Chief Justice Warren E. Burger and the Legal Profession 189
    Jerome J. Shestack
14. The Burger Court in Historical Perspective: The Triumph of Country-Club Republicanism 203
    Mark Tushnet
15. A Journalist's Perspective 216
    Tony Mauro
16. A Public Interest Lawyer's Perspective 222
    Alan B. Morrison
17. The Court and State Constitutional Law 244
    Stewart G. Pollock
18. The Burger Court in Action 261
    Bernard Schwartz
19. International Impact 273
    Finn Backer
20. The Burger Court: A Critique 286
    Joseph M. McLaughlin
21. The Legacy of the Burger Court 305
    John J. Gibbons

CONTRIBUTORS

Shirley Abrahamson, Chief Justice, Supreme Court of Wisconsin

Finn Backer, Justice, Supreme Court of Norway

Derrick Bell, New York University

Martin H. Belsky, University of Tulsa College of Law

William J. Brennan, Jr., Associate Justice, U.S. Supreme Court

Robert Drinan, Georgetown University Law Center

David J. Garrow, Emory University, Pulitzer Prize Winning Author

John J. Gibbons, Seton Hall University Law School, Chief Judge (Retired), Third Circuit United States Court of Appeals

Lino Graglia, University of Texas

Robert Henry, Judge, Tenth Circuit United States Court of Appeals

Anthony Lewis, *New York Times*

Tony Mauro, *USA Today, Legal Times*

Joseph M. McLaughlin, Judge, Second Circuit United States Court of Appeals

Alan Morrison, Public Citizen Litigation Group

Stewart G. Pollock, Justice, Supreme Court of New Jersey

Jerome J. Shestack, President, American Bar Association

Bernard Schwartz, University of Tulsa College of Law

Stephanie Seymour, Chief Judge, Tenth Circuit United States Court of Appeals

Mark Tushnet, Georgetown University Law Center

• THE •
BURGER
COURT

INTRODUCTION

JAMES B. O'HARA

Warren E. Burger served as Chief Justice of the United States for a sometimes tumultuous seventeen-year period from 1969 to 1986, presiding over a Court that wrestled with a set of compelling constitutional issues. *United States v. Nixon* set the stage for the resignation of a President; *Roe v. Wade* created a divisive debate not yet calmed; *Lemon v. Kurtzman* attempted to enunciate a clear standard for vexing church-state issues; a series of criminal cases established often controversial policy for search and seizure, the exclusionary rule, and the death penalty; the "Pentagon Papers" case was a milestone freedom-of-the-press decision.

When Burger came to the Supreme Court, it was widely supposed that he came with a specific agenda: to roll back the energetic activism of the recent past. Many great decisions of the Warren Court—particularly those defining rights of criminal defendants—were anathema to a vocal number of Americans. Other decisions of the Court on civil rights and reapportionment provoked attack not only from out-and-out bigots but also from thoughtful scholars who questioned the policymaking role of the judicial branch. Burger was a known critic of the Warren jurisprudence, and he was appointed by President Nixon, whose concern about activist judges was a feature of his 1968 campaign. The so-called Burger agenda was projected to be, at least by many Court observers, a counterrevolution against the Warren revolution.

The present volume examines the record of the Burger era and its heritage both positive and negative. Judges, practicing lawyers, and academic scholars review the work of the Court from various perspectives, analyzing, applauding, criticizing, and questioning its decisions and directions. They challenge the reader to do the same.

The book's plan is simple and logical. First, there is a brief and eloquent essay by Justice William J. Brennan, Jr., who served on the Court for more than thirty years, including the entire Burger tenure. Second, there is a general "Overview," highlighting the individual Justices who served with Burger, and contrasting the Burger and Warren eras. Next, comes "The Constitutional Corpus"—a detailed examination of the decisions in substantive areas such as race and gender equality,

First Amendment rights, economic issues, and federalism. Finally, the focus shifts to "A Broader Perspective," an effort to assess the work of the Court in a "big picture" sense, with insights from the president of the American Bar Association, then from an historian, a journalist, a public interest lawyer, and distinguished European and American judges.

The opening essay "My Life on the Court" by Justice Brennan, is moving, reflective, and passionate. With obvious pride, the Justice recalls some of the great decisions in which he took part; a legacy, he modestly adds, belonging "not to me" but to the courageous Americans who sought their rights in Court. The passion is directed at the death penalty—"a barbaric and inhuman punishment"—which he confidently predicts the Supreme Court will ultimately outlaw.

Judge Robert Henry's "Overview" is a serious analysis, written in a most engaging, sometimes even lighthearted, style. He begins by sketching briefly the lives and philosophies of the thirteen Justices of the Burger Court—"exceptionally talented jurists." But his primary contribution is a reflection on the nature of judging, and the collective philosophy of the Burger Court in juxtaposition with that of the Warren Court. It is one of the ironies of American judicial history that Burger, popularly regarded as an apostle of judicial restraint and strict construction, led a Court that was arguably more "activist" than the one Warren led. Judicial activism, Judge Henry concludes, "is here to stay." Finally, the Burger Court merged its own activism with the Warren record; adjusting here, modifying there, but leaving the *corpus* intact.

Derrick Bell begins the systematic examination of the major "Constitutional Corpus" section with an intuitive and focused look at the Court's record in racial equality cases. Drawing on Lewis Steel's 1968 article "Nine Men in Black Who Think White," Bell notes that both the Warren and the Burger Courts were far more prepared to overturn blatantly racial classifications than to tackle racism in its subtler forms. In his view, the Burger Court tended to perpetuate, rather than ameliorate, racism. Bell's bluntness does not distort his insight. He is quick to praise where praise is due but is pessimistic about any change in the pattern of race decisions.

Chief Judge Stephanie Seymour speaks on gender issues, noting that the Burger Court was markedly more sensitive to women's rights than any previous Court in history. Judge Seymour recognizes that the Court may have been mirroring societal changes because similar sensitivities are also recognizable in contemporary legislation. Yet, during Burger's tenure, and not always with his sympathy, the Court applied the Equal Protection Clause of the Fourteenth Amendment to women, subjected gender challenges of legislation to a "heightened" scrutiny, and forbade peremptory challenges in jury empanelment based on gender. All this was, of course, in addition to the landmark *Roe v. Wade*.

A more detailed analysis of *Roe* comes from Pulitzer Prize historian David Garrow in his essay on liberty and sexuality. Garrow traces the right of privacy doctrine from its initial expression by Justice Douglas in the 1965 case of *Griswold v. Connecticut*. In *Roe* itself, the initial 7–2 decision was revolutionary, particularly so because Justice White's dissent also seemed to favor at least some abortion rights. Only after the original decision did opposition grow within the Court. A later effort to extend privacy to homosexual activity failed in *Bowers v. Hardwicke* by a 5–4 vote, but Garrow believes this decision is not the final word on the subject.

Bernard Schwartz addresses freedom-of-speech issues, beginning with the Court's most unique and notable contribution: the protection of commercial speech, announced in *Virginia State Board of Pharmacy v. Virginia Consumer Council* and later extended in other cases. Next, he addresses issues of political speech, symbolic speech, and "public forum speech." Schwartz's essay is particularly vivid because of his use of internal memoranda among the Justices as he traces the ongoing processes of decision making.

Anthony Lewis of *The New York Times* addresses the Court's approach to freedom-of-the-press issues. The Burger Court heard more than twenty significant press cases, but the results, in the aggregate, present no comprehensive theme or philosophy. Quoting Churchill, Lewis concludes that the handling of press issues was "a pudding without a theme." Yet the issues raised were themselves significant: the Pentagon Papers dispute; government precensorship of a Central Intelligence Agency agent's book; fair trial "gag" orders, and laws prohibiting publication of the names of rape victims or juvenile defendants. While criticizing the rationale behind some of the decisions, the author finds freedom of the press "intact" and secure at the end of the Burger era.

Reverend Robert F. Drinan, S.J., a former member of Congress, focuses his attention on church-state issues. It had been widely assumed that the Nixon appointees to the Court (Burger, Blackmum, Powell, Rehnquist) would attempt a fundamental change in freedom of religion jurisprudence. Yet, there were no radical shifts. The Court rejected a challenge to tax exemption for church property in *Walz v. Tax Commission* and rejected some state efforts to provide direct financial aid to church-related schools, but it did permit federal grants for building construction at religious colleges. In short, the Court tended to avoid absolutism, sometimes at the expense of a consistent legal norm. The so-called *Lemon* test enunciated in *Lemon v. Kurtzman* was an effort to set a rational standard for deciding financial aid issues. But often the test itself was difficult to apply, and even Chief Justice Burger, its author, sometimes found himself in dissent when the Court applied it.

Martin H. Belsky draws on his considerable experience as a prosecutor to look at the criminal law and procedure cases. Contrasting the Burger and Warren eras, Dean Belsky finds the Burger emphasis more sympathetic to the concerns of police and prosecutors; by contrast, the Warren emphasis stressed the constitutional rights of the accused. Yet there was no Burger "revolution"; what occurred was a pragmatic shift in the paradigm.

Lino Graglia speaks to the issue of economic rights. Professor Graglia looks at cases under three constitutional headings: economic substantive due process, the Contract Clause, and the Takings Clause. He then addresses antitrust issues arising from statutes. The resulting essay is sharply critical of the fifty-year pattern of the federal courts, with, Graglia insists, an antibusiness bias often founded on mistaken economic principles and based on shoddy constitutional analysis. But the Burger Court made dramatic and positive contributions in the antitrust area, restoring the original purpose of the Sherman and Clayton Acts by removing, not imposing, restraints on commerce and trade.

Chief Justice Shirley S. Abrahamson and Thomas N. Hilbink provide a carefully researched summary of federalism—"a notoriously slippery concept." Fine lines are often extraordinarily difficult to draw in constitutional cases, and a clear line of demarcation in the relationship between the federal government and the states has eluded many generations of jurists. This essay contains two major sections: First, an analysis of the possible limitations by the Tenth Amendment on congressional powers under the Commerce Clause and second, the potential limitations on federal judicial power under the Eleventh Amendment. It concludes with a detailed look at the personal contribution of Chief Justice Burger to the understanding of federalism in his extrajudicial writings and speeches and in his work to improve state courts, particularly by encouragement of the State Justice Institute, state-federal judicial councils in the circuits, and the National Center for State Courts.

The final segment of the book, "A Broader Perspective," is a series of essays attempting to place the Burger Court, and the Chief Justice himself, in a wider context by looking at the Court's work outside the narrow range of specific constitutional issues.

The president of the American Bar Association, Jerome J. Shestack, speaks warmly of Chief Justice Burger's work for the legal profession. From the first years of his tenure, Burger maintained a thoughtful and cordial relationship with the ABA, symbolized by his State of the Judiciary messages at its annual meetings. The Chief Justice understood the symbiotic relationship between the Court and the Bar, and each enlisted the help of the other in addressing the problems of judicial reform, public dissatisfaction with the legal structure, correctional institutions, and establishment of professional standards.

Mark Tushnet provides an insightful analysis of the Court's historical setting. The Burger Justices—even those appointed as conservatives—tended to be pragmatic rather than dogmatic. The shift to the right was, therefore, not dramatic. A most interesting facet of Tushnet's essay is his thumbnail sketch of the interplay among the Justices in key cases, coupled with examples of what he calls Chief Justice Burger's "ineptitude" in trying to lead the Court to results the majority was unwilling to embrace.

Tony Mauro, a respected veteran member of the press corps covering the Supreme Court, argues that the Court needs the press if its decisions are to be understood and accepted by the public. Yet he is able to chronicle a number of episodes in which Warren Burger evidenced his distrust of the press by an exaggerated concern about coverage of judicial activities, and especially by his opposition, shared by other Justices, to television in the courtroom. Yet for all the hostility the press felt for Burger, and he for them, the First Amendment fared well at the hands of the Burger Court. In retrospect, Mauro observes, the press now seems willing to adopt a revisionist attitude and perhaps is even willing to offer Burger a reluctant salute.

Defining public interest law as the use of the courts to effect policy change, Alan Morrison traces the response of the Burger Court in major policy areas: access to the courts, standing, class action suits, separation of powers, and access to public records. His overall judgment is that public interest law fared much better than could have been predicted at the beginning of the Burger era in 1969.

Justice Stewart G. Pollock of the New Jersey Supreme Court credits the Burger Court with stimulating a renaissance in state constitutional law. A long-abiding standard precludes Supreme Court review of the actions of state courts in their interpretation of state law when those courts rely solely on state legal grounds. As a legacy of *Michigan v. Long*, state courts now include a "plain statement" when their decisions are based on adequate and independent state grounds. The result of this doctrine has been to wean state supreme courts from excessive reliance on federal law and to encourage them to develop a body of state constitutional law. Justice Pollock then contrasts the difference in emphasis within the Burger Court on questions relating to the good-faith exception to the exclusionary rule, with Chief Justice Burger stressing a law-and-order approach, and Justice Brennan placing more emphasis on the rights of defendants. At Brennan's urging, a number of states expanded their own law to provide protection beyond that granted by the Supreme Court's interpretation of the United States Constitution. This trend continues. The far-ranging effects of Burger Court jurisprudence on federalism cannot yet be completely measured. Only time, and continued state constitutional development, will give a measuring standard.

Bernard Schwartz addresses "The Burger Court in Action," which was the subtitle of his book *The Ascent of Pragmatism* (1990). A major characteristic of the Burger tenure was the absence of any common understanding of mission held by all the Justices. A centrist bloc tended to be pragmatic, resisting consistent adherence to either the right (Burger and Rehnquist) or the left (Brennan and Marshall). But Schwartz sees Burger himself as miscast, despite his diligent concern for the justice system and his personal warmth and charm. Although the Chief Justice began his tenure with an expressed desire to strike at the Warren decisions in many areas, his Court tended to confirm them. Indeed, in its way, the Burger Court was more activist than the Warren Court, if the number of federal and state laws struck down is a reasonable measure of activism. However, Schwartz finds the activism "rootless," a direct consequence of the philosophical divisions among the Justices.

Justice Finn Backer of the Supreme Court of Norway admits special difficulty in dealing with the international implications of Burger Court decisions. Judicial review is not universal, yet in some countries, it antedates *Marbury v. Madison*. The judicial traditions vary from place to place; some nations, Norway, for example, are kingdoms. The effects of American decisions are therefore subtle. They sometimes are felt slowly; sometimes not at all. One interesting issue raised by Justice Backer is the different standard in abortion law found in most European countries. In Europe, abortion rights are guaranteed by statute, not by constitutional interpretation.

This book concludes with two final essays, both by appellate judges. The first is a critique, albeit an objective, even friendly one, by Joseph M. McLaughlin. Judge McLaughlin discusses in detail several major areas of special interest: racial discrimination, religion, and criminal procedure. This last area of criminal procedure provides a springboard for a very focused examination of the Burger Court's efforts, often unsatisfactory, to balance a defendant's constitutional right to confront witnesses with common law and statute rules on admission of hearsay evidence in criminal trials. He goes on to highlight two other persistent themes of Burger era decisions: separation of powers and federalism. Burger himself will be remembered for his opinions in *Chadha*, which struck down one-house veto provisions in scores of statutes, and in *United States v. Nixon*, when the Court held that executive privilege was not open-ended, and that President Nixon was required to turn over to the Special Prosecutor the Oval Office tapes which ultimately brought his presidency to an end.

The final essay in this analysis of the seventeen-year period during which Warren Burger presided over the Supreme Court is John J. Gibbons's summary of the Burger legacy. Judge Gibbons notes that the legacy of the Burger Court was not necessarily the personal legacy of Warren Burger. Three recurring themes arise from Judge Gibbons's analysis. First, the Commerce Clause jurisprudence of the Burger era helped to revive the dual sovereignty implicit in the Constitution. Next, federal judicial power was somewhat curtailed by limitations on federal injunctive relief in criminal cases. Finally, it was the tendency of the Burger Court to encourage the increase of executive power. Judge Gibbons sees all these tendencies as flawed.

This collection is the first truly systematic review of the work of the Court during the tenure of Chief Justice Burger. After more than a decade, review of individual cases and of trends can now be more sharply focused, and comprehensive judgments can be more accurately made. No doubt, this era will be of continuing interest to practitioners and to academic scholars for years to come. This book is a major contribution to the beginning of that dialogue.

Note

This introduction is based on O'Hara, "The Burger Court: Counter-Revolution or Confirmation—The 1996 Tulsa Conference," 17 *The Supreme Court Historical Society Quarterly* 1 (No. 4, 1996).

MY LIFE ON THE COURT

WILLIAM J. BRENNAN, JR.

I can scarcely admit to myself that more than forty years have passed since President Eisenhower appointed me to the Supreme Court of the United States, and more than six have passed since I retired. It has been observed that my thirty-four years on the Court nearly broke the record, but those exhilarating years passed in a twinkle of an eye. I was startled when others pointed out that I served with 22 of the 108 Justices who ever served on the Court. I never considered them en masse; I counted each, individually, as a cherished friend who taught me about law and life.

When you get to be ninety; you learn to stay away from numbers. But I cannot resist a comment on what my dear, dear friend David Souter calls "the gravitational pull of the Brennan total."

David tallies up "the sheer number, the mass of opinions" that bear my name. Gazing up from my desk at the forty-odd shelf feet of my judicial opinions, all bound neatly in red, I reluctantly acknowledge that "mass" is apt description. The 461 majority opinions. The 425 dissents and 474 other opinions. Yet each opinion must also be viewed independently. For each was shaped by the heroic efforts of litigants and judges, the profound insights of scholars, countless hours of impassioned debate among my colleagues on the bench and my law clerks in chambers, and, I admit, quite a bit of hand-wringing on my own.

This last point underscores what I will, at the risk of sounding ungracious, declare to be the fundamental flaw of those who credit me with some of the Court's strides. The truth, which I cannot stress strongly enough, is that I served on a Court of nine. The strides we made on the Court during my tenure we made as a team. The majority opinions that bear my name could not have been without my colleagues' input and votes. I was never alone, except occasionally in dissent. And there is no "Brennan legacy" that can be teased out and considered on its own merits.

I am often asked to identify my favorite opinion from those red volumes. I have steadfastly refused, for that would be almost as impossible as picking a favorite child. I will, however, say that high on the list of the Court's accomplishments during my tenure were a panoply of opinions protecting and promoting individual rights and human dignity.

As I have said many times and in many ways, our Constitution is a charter of human rights and human dignity. It is a bold commitment by a people to the ideal of dignity protected through law. The vision is deeply moving. It inspires our own citizens and countless millions abroad. Just as notions of dignity have changed with time, so too has our charter. Some disagree with my perspective, but I approached my responsibility to interpret the Constitution in the only way I could—as a twentieth-century American concerned about what the Constitution and the Bill of Rights mean to us in our time. The genius of the Constitution rests not in any static meaning it may have had in a world that is dead and gone but in the adaptability of its great principles to cope with current problems and present needs. As Justice Benjamin Cardozo expressed it in his classic book *The Nature of the Judicial Process,* "a *constitution* states or ought to state not rules for the passing hour, but principles for an expanding future." To be "true to its function," he continued, it must never lose "its power of adaptation, its suppleness, its play."

Only from this perspective was the Court able to erect some of liberty's most enduring monuments, such as the classic *Brown* decision, shortly before I took the bench, that a public school cannot slam its doors on pupils based on their skin color. Thanks to the evolving understanding of the Constitution, no future child is likely to confront the same first view of the Supreme Court that Judge Robert Carter poignantly described—a view of a Justice, quite literally, "turning [his] back on black people and manifesting indifference to their needs and aspirations."[1]

In my time, it was the "living" Constitution, infused with a vision of human dignity, that prohibited local police from ransacking a home without a warrant (in 1961) and forbade state prosecutors to compel an accused to convict himself with his own words (in 1964). Only the freedom to reinterpret constitutional language enabled us to make the leap in our ruling (in 1962 and 1964) that each American should have an equal vote. Only with the faith in a malleable Constitution could we have conceived of developing the string of cases (beginning in the 1970s) in which we ruled that laws could not treat men and women differently. The same essential vision girded our enduring ruling, that the press must have protection to report on matters of public concern (in 1964). It was the Constitution's "suppleness" that allowed us to conclude (in 1970) that the government may not cut a welfare recipient's lifeline without first holding a hearing, a ruling so rich that different commentators could see in it many different meanings.

These rulings emerged out of everyday human dramas. Consider the picture of the Cleveland police breaking down Dollree Mapp's door, ransacking her home, and then violently twisting her arm and handcuffing her because she dared to examine their phony warrant. Or think of Esther Lett and her four nieces, who were rushed to the emergency room after eating putrid food out of garbage cans—all because the welfare agency cut off their benefits before they had a chance to prove the agency had made a grievous mistake. Imagine Sharron Frontiero, who worked just as hard as her male counterparts in the Air Force but received inferior benefits. Or what about Charles Baker and thousands of other citizens of Tennessee cities who seethed about having twenty-four times less voting power than their rural neighbors? At the heart of each drama was a person who cried out for nothing more than common human dignity. In each case, our Constitution intervened to provide the cloak of dignity.

If my years left a coherent legacy, it belongs not to me but to these courageous Americans who dared to fight so others would not have to.

That is not to say that this string of cases achieved a comprehensive definition of the constitutional ideal of human dignity. We do not yet have justice for all who do not partake in the abundance of American life. We are still striving toward that goal, and doubtless it will be an eternal quest.

One area of Supreme Court law more than any other besmirches the constitutional vision of human dignity. My old friend and colleague Harry Blackmun called it the "machinery of death": It is the death penalty.

Although the Court was unmoved by the evidence presented to it in 1987, it was then, and it remains today, an uncontroverted fact that the races of a capital defendant and the victim are among the most powerful predictors of whether the defendant lives or dies. The statistics, some of which I reviewed in my dissent, paint a chilling portrait of racial discrimination. Yet racial disparity is but one of a host of inequalities that inhere in the death penalty. Another is the stunning lack of counsel adequately equipped to afford capital defendants a fair opportunity to defend their lives in the courtroom, and the puzzling move to defund the most effective defenders. Equally disconcerting is the growing pressure to dispense with independent judicial review of death sentences, even though, by conservative estimates, the reversal rate of capital convictions and sentences is 45 percent.

Yet the ultimate problem is more fundamental. I have long believed that the death penalty is in all circumstances a barbaric and inhuman punishment that violates our Constitution. Even the most vile murderer does not release the state from its constitutional obligation to respect human dignity, for the state does not honor the victim by emulating the murderer who took his life. The fatal infirmity of capital punishment is that it treats members of the human race as nonhumans, as objects to be toyed with and discarded.

The machinery chugs on unabated, belching out its dehumanizing product. It is distressing. But I refuse to despair. I know, one day, the Supreme Court will outlaw the death penalty. Permanently. I hope I will live to celebrate the day, but I am supremely confident the day *will* come.

If our free society is to endure, and I know it will, those who govern must recognize that the framers of the Constitution limited their power in order to preserve human dignity and the air of freedom, which is our proudest heritage. The task of protecting these principles does not rest solely with nine Supreme Court Justices, or even with the cadre of state and federal judges. We all share the burden.

It may be too early to know how history will judge what we tried to do while I served on the Court. But we must not await history's verdict. Too much work remains. Too many injustices persist. Too many wrongs cry out to be righted. These are obligations we cannot ignore and dare not neglect.

Perhaps my ultimate reflection is unremarkable: Continuous hard work is needed if we are to realize the true potential of our Constitution and its Bill of Rights. To paraphrase Thomas Jefferson, eternal vigilance is the price of liberty and dignity—two of the true measures of freedom.

If I have drawn one lesson in my ninety years it is this: To strike another blow for freedom allows a man to walk a little taller and raise his head a little higher. And while he can, he must.

Notes

Adapted from *Reason and Passion: Justice Brennan's Enduring Influence* 15 (Rosenkranz and Schwartz eds., 1997).

1. The reference is to what happened when Charles Houston, the African American NAACP counsel, began his argument in a 1938 civil rights case. Justice McReynolds then turned his chair around and presented his back to counsel.

· 3 ·

THE PLAYERS AND THE PLAY

ROBERT HENRY

The Warren Court was a hard act to follow. As Bernard Schwartz observed:

> The Warren Court led the movement to remake the law in the image of the evolving society. Such change required the Justices to perform the originative role that the jurist is not normally called upon to exercise in more stable times—a role usually considered more appropriate for the legislator than for the judge. In terms of creative impact on the law, the Warren tenure can be compared only with that of Marshall himself.[1]

The great legacies of this remarkable Court were cases that answered the defaults of political systems unwilling to deal with segregation and political disenfranchisement; further, the Warren Court explored the ranges of individual rights of the accused, trying to measure the proper balance between individual rights and communal well-being on the constitutional scale. *Brown v. Board of Education*[2] and its progeny in civil rights; *Reynolds*[3] and *Baker*[4] in apportionment; *Gideon*,[5] *Miranda*,[6] *Mapp*,[7] and the other great criminal law cases—these Warren Court precedents made history and still more or less define the parameters of modern constitutional law.

But the scope and pace of the Warren Court's activism were not without critics. The approach of that Court was instrumentalist—actively using the law to reach for social justice and to favor *individual* rights over the interests of the government in several criminal law contexts. Many argued that the Court exceeded the bounds suggested by our Founders. Others, though reluctant to challenge the results in desegregation and reapportionment, viewed the expansion of Bill of Rights protections to accused defendants as handcuffing the police in a time of rising crime.

The Court that succeeded the Warren Court experienced great pressure to roll back this almost unprecedented activism. Some of the pressure was improperly motivated, fostered by racism or fear of the loss of political power. Some was properly motivated by the fear that Alexander Hamilton's "least dangerous branch"[8] had thwarted his prophecy by seizing the roles of both lawmaker and law interpreter.

Whether the concerns about the Court were *immoral* (racist) or *selfish* (the political old guard wanting to retain power) or *theoretical* (the courts were becoming too active, expanding standing and ignoring such prudential concepts as the Article III requirement of a case or controversy) or *practical* (the police were being hamstrung by new rights for the accused as violent crime was rising), the concerns opened up a political opportunity which Richard Nixon quickly seized in the 1968 presidential campaign. The revolutionary activist tide should be stemmed, he argued, and law-and-order Justices were needed to do it. Knowing of a judge on the District of Columbia Court of Appeals who was a "self-made" man who shared these views (and was a good Republican spear carrier besides), Richard Nixon, as President, chose Warren E. Burger to lead the counterrevolution. Candidate Nixon promised that he would nominate "strict constructionists" and created widespread expectations of a more conservative Court.[9]

Measured by this goal—counterrevolution—the Burger Court was certainly a failure. But this goal is not the proper yardstick. For one thing, President Nixon's stated goal may not have been all that genuine. Although some who called for change in the law were principled, thinking the proper balance had been skewed, for Richard Nixon much of his rhetoric represented practical politics: a quest for election using tactics that did not inspire reflection but rather reaction. Further, even if this goal of a counterrevolution was the President's goal or that of his advisers and handlers, it was not necessarily the aspiration of the Court. Certainly Chief Justice Burger and later Justice William H. Rehnquist shared some of the vision. "Holdover" Justices did not, and even later appointees of Presidents Nixon, Ford, and Reagan probably did not have it as their primary goal, if it was a goal at all. Fortunately for American jurisprudence, many Justices simply take the attitude of Justice Byron White who, when asked what was his greatest case, declined to identify any particular case, observing that he did not perceive that it was his job to decide great cases but simply to decide cases.

However, before we evaluate the Burger Court in relation to President Nixon's desires, or any other goal, it might be well to view the drama of this most intriguing Court by recounting its *dramatis personae*. Enough time has passed that some may have forgotten relevant biography of some of the thirteen Justices who served on this Court; new students of the Court may not have been exposed to even a little background of perhaps the most remarkable collection of jurists to sit in the marble palace.

It is difficult to classify the Justices who sat on the Burger Court,[10] even for purposes of a cast of characters. Nevertheless, perhaps for arbitrary and capricious reasons, they can be placed into four categories. First, the "Early Departures," which includes Justices Black and Harlan; second, "Justice Douglas," who was—and who would enjoy being placed—in a class by himself; third, the "Holdovers," the Justices who served on probably the most influential Court in our history,[11] the Warren Court, including Justices Brennan, Stewart, White, and Marshall; and fourth, the "Burger Justices," including Justices Blackmun, Powell, Rehnquist, Stevens, O'Connor, and Chief Justice Burger himself.

I take care throughout this essay to avoid mixing up names, but this Court is particularly nominally confusing. To appreciate the magnitude of the problem consider the following: To begin with Chief Justice *Earl Warren* was replaced by Chief Justice *Warren Earl* Burger. But the complications do not end there. While Justice Black was born in Harlan, Alabama, Justice Harlan was not. And speaking of Justice Harlan his full name was *John Marshall* Harlan II, not to be confused with Chief Justice John Marshall, nor should this Justice Harlan be mistaken for his grandfather, Justice John Marshall Harlan I who was on the Court early in the century. Justice Thurgood Marshall is the only Justice Marshall of recent times. There were three Williams but they are not that easily confused. There was *William* Brennan, who often stood for things diametrically opposite to things his colleague *William* Rehnquist stood for; then, of course, there was *William* O. Douglas, who stood for even more things and found standing for things like trees, which others (e.g., Richard Nixon) had only stood on. The complicated issues that the Warren Earl Burger Court addressed may not seem black and white, although there was, of course, a Justice Black and a Justice White, who in the Burger Court were more aligned than opposed, seeing many issues in the same shades of gray—except for penumbras which Justice Black did not see at all.

I. The Players

The Early Departures

Hugo Lafayette Black was born in Harlan, Alabama, in 1886. The son of a store-keeper in rural Clay County, his two-year undergraduate law program and short stint as a Birmingham police court judge gave little evidence of the greatness he would later achieve. Chief Justice Rehnquist ranked Black as the "most influential" of Justices with whom he sat,[12] while Chief Justice Warren himself once admitted that he was primarily a disciple of Black.[13] Though a member of the Burger Court for only a term, his deep influence remained, jurisprudentially and personally—as it does to this day.

Scholars as intellectually diverse as these Chief Justices had similar views of Justice Black: Judge Richard A. Posner lists Black with John Marshall, Oliver Wendell Holmes, and Louis D. Brandeis, as both a great judge and a major figure in the history of American political liberalism,[14] while John Hart Ely suggests that the growing intellectual appreciation of Black during the Burger Court years was itself a reason for the popularity of interpretivism—the idea that constitutional issues should be resolved by enforcing norms that are stated or clearly implicit in the text. Dean Ely observes of Black:

> His soft-spoken charm was always apparent to those who were not his rivals, and that he stood where a person had to stand when it counted has been apparent for some time. But there seems to be something new, a growing intellectual appreciation of Hugo Black: people are discovering what to the perceptive was obvious all along, that behind his "backward country fellow" philosophy, with its obviously overstated faith that the language of the Constitution would show the way, there lay a fully elaborated (though surely debatable) theory of the limits of legitimate judicial discretion and the hortatory use of principle.[15]

Justice Black's ascent to the marble palace was not an easy climb. A self-proclaimed "country lawyer," he was a populist U.S. senator for two terms, and a devout supporter of the New Deal. President Roosevelt appointed him to the Court in 1937. Black's confirmation to the Court was surprisingly difficult for a member of the Senate. First, the virulent anti–New Dealers fought him tooth and nail. Further, strong rumors persisted that he was once a member of the Ku Klux Klan. But the combination of senatorial courtesy, that age-old tradition of faith that fellow senators (and then it *was* fellow) have for and in each other, and the equally powerful desire to adjourn, allowed Senator Black to don the ermine.[16]

Subsequently the rumors were shown to be true, and Black directly admitted what he previously refused to deny: he had been a member of the Klan. The Gallup poll revealed that a majority of Americans thought Black should resign from his seat if he had been a Klan member. It is difficult to imagine what shape modern constitutional law would have taken had Black been forced to resign to atone for his past mistake. History will determine whether Justice Black kept the pledge he made in an early draft of the radio address: "As God is my witness, so long as I sit upon the Supreme Court I shall administer equal justice towards all."[17]

Black's prominent place in constitutional law and history is secured by two views that are always associated with his name. First, he was an *absolutist* with respect to the First Amendment. He argued that when the text related that "Congress shall make no law" abridging First Amendment freedoms, particularly speech, it had to be interpreted literally. Thus, he opposed the various First Amendment balancing tests, even Justice Holmes's famous "clear and present danger" test. Likewise, he opposed controls over libel, obscenity, and "subversive" speech, writing powerful dissents whose grace and lyric beauty are as compelling as their reasoning. Indeed, a portion of his dissent in *In re Anastaplo*, read at his funeral, merits quotation:

> Too many men are being driven to become government-fearing and time-serving because the Government is being permitted to strike out at those who are fearless enough to think as they please and say what they think. This trend must be halted if we are to keep faith with the Founders of our Nation and pass on to future generations of Americans the great heritage of freedom which they sacrificed so much to leave to us. The choice is clear to me. If we are to pass on that great heritage of freedom, we must return to the original language of the Bill of Rights. We must not be afraid to be free.[18]

Black was also known for his advocacy of the doctrine of "incorporation." In *Adamson v. California*[19] he explained his view that the framers of the Fourteenth Amendment had intended in the Due Process Clause (with perhaps some assistance from the Equal Protection Clause) to "incorporate" all the protections of the Bill of Rights. Thus read, the Amendment would in essence say "nor shall any *state* deprive any person of the rights guaranteed by the Bill of Rights." Although this total incorporation doctrine was never adopted, Black's essential quest was accomplished because virtually all the protections of the Bill of Rights were selectively incorporated.[20]

In his last years on the Court, Justice Black seemed to move rightward. Perhaps his literalism had accomplished what it needed to, but in any event, he found himself more at odds with his colleagues, even his old friends. After a minor stroke, suffered while playing his beloved tennis, he developed partial memory loss. His perceptive recent biographer said that Black "was losing the marked sense of knowing when not to write," and that "no longer was he the artist."[21] He resigned from the Court on September 17, 1971, the one hundred eighty-second anniversary of the signing of the Constitution. He died a week later.

Justice John Marshall Harlan II[22] was born in Chicago in 1899 and died in Washington, D.C. in 1971. He was an Associate Justice from 1955 to 1971. His father was a lawyer and a Chicago alderman and raised him, in the words of several scholars, as a "patrician." He attended Princeton University, where he was president of the student newspaper and was selected as a Rhodes Scholar. After completing his British education, he enrolled in New York Law School, completing a two-year program in one year.[23] He was retained by a prominent New York City law firm, eventually becoming the leader of the firm's litigation team. He briefly served on the Court of Appeals for the Second Circuit, having been appointed by President Eisenhower, who later appointed him to succeed Justice Robert H. Jackson in 1954.

Harlan has been called the "paradigm of the true conservative" judge.[24] As Anthony Lewis observed:

> [Conservative judges] should respect a precedent once established even though they opposed that result during the process of decision. For such true conservatives as Justice John Marshall Harlan, that consideration was certainly a factor; he might warn and dissent against what he foresaw as the baleful effects of a decision, but he would hesitate thereafter to subject it to constant relitigation. He valued stability over perfection.[25]

In fact, stability might have described Justice Harlan himself. As Judge Henry Friendly noted, "There's never been a justice of the Supreme Court who has so consistently maintained the high quality of performance or, despite differences in views, has enjoyed such nearly uniform respect from his colleagues, the inferior bench, the bar, and the academy."[26]

Justice Harlan's paradigmatic conservatism was clearly demonstrated by the two judicial values he most often advocated: federalism and proceduralism. He valued the "experimental social laboratories," borrowing Brandeis's term, represented by the state governments. His belief in federalism as "a bulwark of freedom"[27] was so strong that he saw federalism as the *equivalent* of the Bill of Rights and the Fourteenth Amendment as a guarantee of personal liberty.

With respect to proceduralism, Justice Harlan took a narrow view of both due process and judicial power. He dissented in *Reynolds v. Sims*,[28] the Warren Court's landmark reapportionment decision, saying that he rejected the following view:

> [t]hat every major social ill in this country can find its cure in some constitutional "principle," and that this Court should "take the lead" in promoting reform when other branches of government fail to act. The Constitution is not a panacea for every blot upon the public welfare, nor should this Court, ordained as a judicial body, be thought of as a general haven for reform movements.[29]

Justice Black, who both tangled and tangoed with Justice Harlan, once observed that Justice Harlan proves that there "is such a thing as a good Republican."[30] Coming from the populist prophet, it was high praise. Harlan was truly a lawyer's lawyer.

Today, Justice Harlan is remembered for his marvelously crafted opinions, his consistent and principled judicial conservatism, and the patrician traditionalism that was, at the same time, remarkably sensitive to other views. Upon learning that he had terminal cancer, he delayed the announcement of his own resignation to avoid interfering with the accolades accompanying the retirement of his seriously ill confrere Justice Black (who proved there can be such a thing as a good Democrat).

Though Justice Harlan represents the best of the judicial "conservative" tradition, he did concur in some of the "liberal" activism of the Warren Court.[31] In his dissent in *Poe v. Ullman*,[32] he noted that Fourteenth Amendment due process is informed by history and tradition and that "tradition is a living thing."[33] Harlan's language describing the method of construing his holy writ is perhaps the most eloquent defense of nonliteralism ever written by a conservative:

> [T]he basis of judgment as to the Constitutionality of state action must be a rational one, approaching the text [of the Constitution] which is the only commission for our power not in a literalistic way, as if we had a tax statute before us, but as the basic charter of our society, setting out in spare but meaningful terms the principles of government.[34]

He went on in *Poe* to suggest a constitutional right of privacy several years before the majority reached the same conclusion.[35] Perhaps the best summary of his character was presented by his former clerk, Norman Dorsen:

> [I]t fell to John Marshall Harlan, by nature a patrician traditionalist, to serve on a Supreme Court that, for most of his years, was rapidly revising and liberalizing constitutional law. In these circumstances, it is not surprising that Harlan would protest the direction of the Court and the speed with which it was traveling. He did this in a remarkably forceful and principled manner, thereby providing balance to the institution and the law it generated. Despite this role, Harlan joined civil liberties rulings on the Court during his tenure to the degree that his overall jurisprudence can fairly be characterized as moderate, or conservative primarily in the sense that it evinced caution, a fear of centralized authority, and a respect for process.[36]

In noting the departures of these two great jurists, one cannot help but wonder what effects their continued presence on the Court would have had. It is ironic to speculate that the once great "liberal" Black and the "paradigmatic conservative" Harlan might have changed ideological positions on the most controversial case of modern times, *Roe v. Wade*.[37] Black, dissenting in *Griswold v. Connecticut*,[38] could not see a constitutional right to privacy in a penumbra of substantive due process or anywhere else. Harlan, joining *Griswold* and echoing his instructive concurrence in *United States v. Katz*,[39] might very well have gone the other way, adopting the *Roe* balance.[40]

Interestingly, the Justices who replaced Black and Harlan voted contrary to their predecessors' probable votes: Lewis Powell concurred in *Roe*, and William Rehnquist dissented.[41]

Justice Douglas

William Orville Douglas was born in 1889 and died in January 1980, having served longer than any other member in the history of the Supreme Court. He was a rugged individualist, an outdoorsman, and certainly a loner—"a lover of humanity who did not like people."[42] Though Justice Douglas was crippled by polio in his youth, he climbed mountain peaks in his seventies. Douglas attended Columbia Law School and briefly practiced at a Wall Street firm before teaching at Yale Law School as one of its youngest tenured professors. Like many young legal intellectuals, he went to Washington to work in Franklin D. Roosevelt's New Deal government; he became a member and later chairman of the Securities and Exchange Commission. He had the good sense to engage in that endeavor so important to Washington advancement—poker. He had the further good sense to play with Harold Ickes, FDR's influential Secretary of the Interior. Perhaps drawing to an inside straight, he was appointed to the Court at the early age of 41, though he was bettered here by the brilliant Joseph Story, who was appointed at 32, and William Johnson, the first great dissenter, appointed at 33. Justice Douglas was a fairly conventional Justice at first, but seemed, perhaps, restless.[43]

After Justice Douglas became "bored," his opinions and actions tended to be more colorful. He would often walk out of conference when Justice Felix Frankfurter began one of his tirades—which Justice Douglas warned would last about fifty minutes, the same amount of time as one of Frankfurter's Harvard law classes. Some suggest that his restlessness even occurred in his personal life: He was remarried three times, the last time at the age of 66 to a woman of 22. Whether finding penumbras, extending standing to trees, or issuing a dramatic last-minute stay of an execution, Justice Douglas seemed to want to be in the controversial middle of things.

Douglas's lifestyle, his eccentric manners on the bench (he often seemed to be writing personal letters during oral argument), and his penchant for provocation led, in April 1970, to a call for his impeachment by House Minority Leader Gerald R. Ford. It seemed for a while that the impeachment might proceed. Indeed, one day while the Court was in session, Justice Black passed his old friend a note which read, "Dear Bill: If they try to impeach you, I'll resign and be your lawyer. I have one more hard trial left in me. Hugo."[44] According to Justice Black's recent biographer, Justice Brennan said, "Hugo was serious."[45] Now *that* would have been the trial of the century!

Though Justice Douglas was a brilliant jurist, his law was not theory driven; he left no great jurisprudential legacy but is remembered primarily for his individualism and his devout belief in environmental causes. Few Justices have inspired so much antagonism and, at the same time, so many accolades.

The Holdovers

William Joseph Brennan, Jr., was born in Newark, New Jersey, in 1906 and was an Associate Justice from 1956 to 1990. An Irish Catholic Democrat, Brennan was appointed by President Dwight D. Eisenhower in the midst of the 1956 reelection campaign. Although it is uncertain how many Irish Catholic Democrat votes Justice Brennan may have brought the President, it is certain the President later considered Brennan one of his worst mistakes, although with Earl Warren on the Court it is doubtful that Brennan's appointment would ever have made Ike's number-one spot. Justice Brennan's father was a coal shoveler at a local brewery (remember Horace Greely: I didn't say all Democrats were saloonkeepers; I said all saloonkeepers were Democrats) and later became a prominent labor leader and reformer in New Jersey's restless political environment. Justice Brennan attended Harvard Law School and progressed to the state trial bench and then to the state Supreme Court. The lone dissenting vote cast against him in the Senate was by Senator Joseph R. McCarthy, who quite possibly remembered that Brennan publicly, eloquently, and often compared the McCarthy Era hearings to the Salem witch trials.

Justice Brennan's accomplishments on the Warren, Burger, and Rehnquist Courts were legion. A review of the case names he authored indicate his influence: *Texas v. Johnson*,[46] *Craig v. Boren*,[47] *Goldberg v. Kelly*,[48] *New York Times v. Sullivan*,[49] and *Baker v. Carr*.[50] Indeed, his activism on the Warren Court led Dennis J. Hutchinson, an editor of the *Supreme Court Review*, to say that the use of the term "Warren Court" was a misnomer: "It was 'the Brennan Court.'"[51] Though it is an overstatement to rename the Warren Court, it is certainly clear that the Chief Justice and Justice Brennan had a remarkable relationship, probably equaling that of Chief Justice John Marshall and Justice Joseph Story. Warren often turned to Brennan to build the consensus necessary to structure a Court opinion, and the two often met before weekly Court conferences to discuss cases and plan strategy.

In the Burger Court, Brennan was clearly no longer at the right hand of the throne. But his intellect and persuasive ability often decreed that the de facto leadership of the Court was in his hands. To his critics, "he epitomized an unrestrained federal judiciary that had abrogated unto itself the ultimate control over virtually every facet of daily life, thus demeaning the right of citizens to govern themselves through representative democracy. . . . "[52] More favorable observers would simply note that to Brennan, "the meaning of the Constitution is to be found in today's needs, not in the search for what was intended by its eighteenth-century draftsmen."[53]

As Bernard Schwartz noted in an article discussing Supreme Court superstars:

> [T]he Brennan jurisprudence was based upon what he termed "the constitutional ideal of human dignity." This ideal led him to his constant battle against the death penalty, which he considered a violation of the ban against cruel and unusual punishment. His battle to outlaw capital punishment was a losing one for Brennan, but it was the only major battle he lost in his effort to ensure what he said was "the ceaseless pursuit of the constitutional ideal." The ultimate Brennan legacy was that no important decision of the Warren Court was overruled while the Justice sat on the Burger and Rehnquist Courts.[54]

The Italian composer Gioacchino Rossini composed a number of noteworthy operas, including the famous *Barber of Seville* and numerous other works. However, despite these accomplishments and his European fame, he seems to be known in America today, if at all, for only one piece of music: The *William Tell Overture*, which is variously referred to as the Lone Ranger Theme or the music accompanying an explicit scene in the movie *A Clockwork Orange*. One wonders how Mr. Rossini would feel about this. Perhaps Justice Potter Stewart could tell us, because despite a number of very important opinions, Stewart's immortal fame comes from a *bon mot* in *Jacobellis v. Ohio*,[55] where the Justice explained that he would not attempt to define hard-core pornography, "[b]ut I know it when I see it, and [this] is not that."[56] Justice Stewart later lamented that this might become his epitaph.[57]

Justice Stewart was born in 1915 and died in 1985. He was an Associate Justice from 1958 to 1981. After graduation from Yale Law School, he joined a Wall Street firm and then served as a Navy officer during World War II. After the war, he again practiced law, which led him into politics. He was elected to the Cincinnati city council twice and then as vice mayor. Perhaps this was his first contact with vice so that he would later know it when he saw it. President Eisenhower appointed him to the Court of Appeals for the Sixth Circuit in 1954 and, when Justice Harold H. Burton retired in 1958, Ike appointed Justice Stewart to his seat.

Justice Stewart was a capable player in the middle of the Court. He would neither a liberal nor a conservative be, defining himself by saying, "I am a lawyer . . . I have some difficulty understanding what those terms mean even in the field of political life. . . . And I find it impossible to know what they mean when they are carried over to judicial work."[58] His primary legacy is that of stability and moderation and not his contributions to constitutional theory.

Justice Byron R. White is one of the most interesting Justices to occupy the "stable middle" of the Burger Court. Born in Colorado in 1917, he became an Associate Justice in 1962, retiring in 1990—a brilliant student as well as a fabled athlete, he graduated first in his high school class, first in his undergraduate college, and first in his class at Yale Law School. In addition to his academic feats, he was a legendary athlete, earning the nickname "Whizzer" for his accomplishments on the football field, both in college and in the pros. He also played a mean game of basketball on the "Highest Court in the Land," the basketball court in the gym on the top floor of the Supreme Court building.

He clerked for Chief Justice Fred M. Vinson in 1946 and 1947 and then returned to his native Colorado to practice law with a Denver law firm. White became active in President John F. Kennedy's campaign and became close friends with the President's younger brother, Robert, the young lawyer whom JFK appointed Attorney General to give "Bobby a little experience before he starts to practice law."[59] As Assistant Attorney General, White was given difficult assignments in many areas, including civil rights, and always acquitted himself admirably. His qualifications were so outstanding that his nomination was confirmed in the Senate by a voice vote.

Justice White's performance on the Court is also difficult to categorize. He adopted positions that seem both liberal and conservative but was always known for no-nonsense, clear opinions, among the most terse on the Court. Although progressive on civil rights, Justice White tended to find himself on the conservative side in the criminal law area. He therefore held a particularly important role in the Burger Court as a swing vote and as a Justice capable of writing narrow, precise opinions.

Though he is remarkably humble in light of his tremendous accomplishments, as well as extremely polite, Justice White was known to mutter sotto voce on the bench during a particularly bad argument, "[T]his is unbelievable."[60]

Justice Thurgood Marshall was born in Maryland in 1908 and died in January 1993. He was termed by President Clinton "a giant in the quest for human rights," and noted constitutional law scholar Lawrence Tribe hailed him as "the greatest lawyer in the 20th Century."[61]

The great-grandson of a slave and the son of a dining car waiter and a school teacher, Thurgood Marshall took his bachelor's degree from Lincoln University and graduated at the top of his class at Howard University Law School. He became director of the NAACP Legal Defense and Education Fund and was responsible for a number of Supreme Court victories, including landmark cases such as *Sipuel v. Regents of the University of Oklahoma,*[62] *Shelley v. Kraemer,*[63] and *Brown v. Board of Education* .[64] A remarkable advocate, this lawyer who was denied admission into a state law school handled as many as 450 cases at a time covering voting rights, restrictive covenants, segregation, and educational opportunity. As a judge on the Court of Appeals for the Second Circuit, he authored more than 150 opinions and was later appointed Solicitor General, where he continued to achieve an impressive record in his litigation before the Court.

Justice Marshall agonized over capital punishment cases. As the only Supreme Court Justice in modern times to have defended a man charged with murder, when Marshall spoke on the topic it was with authority and experience. He related that his belief in America in general, and the Constitution in particular, came from a unique source. Claiming to have been something of a "hell-raiser" as a youth, Marshall said that one of his teachers, for discipline, sent him to the basement to learn parts of the Constitution. He thus made his way "through every paragraph" of the Constitution. That creative punishment inured to the benefit of all Americans.

I hope I may be forgiven for making a few Oklahoma-specific comments about Justice Marshall. As the lawyer for my dear friend, the late Dr. Ada Lois Sipuel Fisher, the plaintiff in *Sipuel v. Regents of the University of Oklahoma*, he made trips to Norman, Oklahoma City, and Washington, D.C. on her behalf. In his first appearance in the district courthouse in Cleveland County, where the "sundown town"[65] of Norman was located, the great lawyer, later destined to become a circuit judge, Solicitor General, and Justice of the Supreme Court, lunched on peanuts from the courthouse vending machine, as no restaurant in the town would serve him. His efforts on behalf of Ada Lois Sipuel, a self-described "guinea pig," led to the first unanimous decision by the Supreme Court condemning segregation. It also briefly led to the creation of Oklahoma's segregated law school, which "held classes" in the state capitol, having two professors and one student—Ada Lois Sipuel. Again with Marshall's help, that fiasco was ended and Fisher entered and graduated from the University of Oklahoma Law School. Remarkably, toward the end of her life, she was named to the Board of Regents of the University that would not admit her as a student—until Thurgood Marshall forced their hand.[66]

Burger Justices

Harry Andrew Blackmun was born in November 1908 and served from 1971 to 1994. An undergraduate mathematics major, he left the queen of sciences to attend Harvard Law School. He had a successful law practice, later becoming counsel to the

Mayo Clinic, a task that perhaps forever changed his life. He was appointed by President Eisenhower to the Court of Appeals for the Eighth Circuit and later appointed by President Nixon as the famous "third man." This was after the failure of the nominations of Clement Haynesworth and G. Harold Carswell. (Senator Roman Hruska, the floor manager of Harold Carswell, in attempting to defend Mr. Carswell from the often-leveled charge that Carswell gave mediocrity an exalted status, uttered the immortal phrase which did not help his candidate's flagging chances, that "even the mediocre are entitled to a little representation.")[67]

Well, *this* third man's theme was certainly not mediocrity. Thought at first to be a Burger clone and the other half of the so-called "Minnesota Twins," Justice Blackmun's evolution—and perhaps that of the Court—caused him to move from the right to the middle, and, finally, to end firmly on the liberal wing of the Court. As one scholar observed, "His service on the Court signifies the possibility, and actuality, that a justice can change views when confronted with situations that call deeply held beliefs into question."[68]

Justice Blackmun, professionally extremely demanding of his clerks but publicly gentle and kind, centrist and compassionate, became one of the most controversial Justices to occupy a chair on the Court. His position on *Roe v. Wade*[69] and *Doe v. Bolton*,[70] opinions assigned to him partially because of his expertise in things medical acquired as Mayo Clinic's attorney, guaranteed him lasting friends and eternal enemies. His powerful, literary opposition to the death penalty at the last of his term showed that age had intensified rather than diminished his passion.

Lewis Franklin Powell, Jr., born in 1907, was Associate Justice from 1972 to 1987. Justice Powell is universally respected and admired. He was a former president of the American Bar Association and the American College of Trial Lawyers. Though considered a member of the Virginia *aristoi*, Powell was certainly not a segregationist, opposing the state's policy of massive resistance to integration and successfully presiding as a school board member over the integration of the Richmond Public Schools. When nominated by President Nixon to succeed Justice Hugo Black, he was confirmed by a vote of 89–1.

Although he frequently cast pro–civil rights votes, endearing him to progressives, he also was frequently in the middle and often the swing vote on the Court. His influence is perhaps best shown in *Regents of the University of California v. Bakke*,[71] where his opinion was required to make a 5–4 vote majority to strike down rigid racial quotas in university admissions. (The opinion also upheld a limited kind of affirmative action that would allow consideration of race as part of an overall application process.)[72]

Justice William Hubbs Rehnquist was born in 1924 and served as an Associate Justice from 1972 to 1986 and is the current Chief Justice. He was appointed by President Richard Nixon concurrently with the appointment of Lewis Powell. Nixon selected him for his conservative views on criminal justice, his advocacy of judicial restraint, and his legal support for Republican causes.

Justice Rehnquist graduated first in his class at the Stanford Law School and is recognized as perhaps the most forcefully intellectual member of the current Court. In this vein, notes Anthony Lewis: "On the [Burger] Supreme Court, only

Justice William Rehnquist really goes back to first premises in his opinions and is willing to rethink doctrines in terms of a personal constitutional idealogy. He is today's equivalent of Hugo Black—at the other end of the judicial spectrum."[73] Although frequently alone in dissent in his initial days, he has seen his views on federalism and restricted rights of criminal appeal to the Supreme Court move more and more to the mainstream. Outspokenly conservative on a number of issues, it is fair to say that he has moved toward the center, though not very close to it perhaps, as Chief Justice. Compared to his predecessor, Rehnquist is clearly more at the helm. Thurgood Marshall noted, "[H]e has no problems, wishy-washy, back and forth. He knows exactly what he wants to do and that is very important as Chief Justice."[74]

Well prepared at conference, considerate of other views, capable of terse and concise opinions, yet also possessing a literary flair,[75] Chief Justice Rehnquist has certainly been one of the most influential Justices of this century. In a 1996 speech, the Chief Justice showed that his polemic skills could be effectively raised on behalf of the courts as he diplomatically but forcefully defended the independence of the judiciary as one of the "crown jewels of the American system."[76]

Justice John Paul Stevens was born in 1920 and appointed an Associate Justice in 1975. He was President Gerald Ford's only nominee to the Supreme Court and is perhaps the Court's most frequent dissenter in modern times. He had a distinguished academic career at Northwestern University Law School and clerked for Supreme Court Justice Wiley B. Rutledge before entering a law practice in the antitrust area. There must be something unique about antitrust law. At least three great Justices specialized in it: Justices Harlan, Douglas, and Stevens. Perhaps it was their desire to leave this field that led to their greatness on the Court.

Noted for his omnipresent bow tie, Justice Stevens not only writes marvelously researched opinions but also has a ready wit. When it was proposed that lawyers representing the judiciary on a salary dispute be given a generous legal fee due to their courage in defending the unpopular concept that judges should receive a pay raise, Justice Stevens suggested that it was not all that courageous, saying, "It's not quite like a march on Selma."[77]

A legal academician who is a friend of mine recently told me that if you just read the facts in a Supreme Court case and decide what you *really* think ought to be done—what is both fair and right and comports with the law—then you can probably look at Justice Stevens's opinions and see the result you envisioned in print. Perhaps Stevens's popularity in the academy is because of his independence; an unconventional legal thinker, Stevens often goes his own way—even to the point of not participating in the "cert pool" with other Justices.[78]

The "first sister," Justice Sandra Day O'Connor, was born in 1930 and has served on the Supreme Court since 1981. A graduate of Stanford University, she was third in the class in which Chief Justice Rehnquist was first; yet, upon her graduation with such a distinguished record from such a distinguished law school, she was unable to find a decent job in the private sector. Indeed, William French Smith, later the Attorney General who recommended her for the Supreme Court, was a partner in a firm that refused to hire her as an associate.[79] She became a deputy county attorney, later serving as an assistant attorney general, state senator, and finally a trial judge and judge of the Arizona State Court of Appeals.

Justice White suggested a short time before her appointment that the Court should drop the customary salutation "Mr. Justice." He was, of course, prescient, and the Court was at least forewarned when President Reagan appointed Justice O'Connor as the first woman to serve on the high bench in 1981. Though generally conservative, Justice O'Connor is also independent. She has moved cautiously in the area of abortion rights and recently accomplished the unique task of writing a concurring opinion to her own majority opinion.[80]

Justice O'Connor's influence has continued to grow in the Rehnquist Court, as she and Justice Anthony Kennedy often control the Court's middle. Her influence was recognized by the American Bar Association, whose *Journal* in 1993 called her "arguably the most influential woman official in the United States."[81] Her prestige has even been popularly noted. In a 1996 issue of *Time*, she ranked as one of the twenty-five most influential Americans.[82]

Finally we come to the Chief Justice of this Court, Warren Earl Burger, born on September 17, Constitution Day, in 1907. He served as Chief Justice for seventeen years, from 1969 to 1986, longer than any Chief Justice of this century.

Chief Justice Burger was in many ways a self-made man. He was one of seven children who lived on a twenty-acre truck farm on the outskirts of St. Paul, Minnesota. In high school he was president of the student council and lettered in four sports. Coming from a family of modest means, he sold insurance in the day and attended night school for two years at the University of Minnesota and four years (again at night) at the St. Paul College of Law, now William Mitchell College of Law.

Both teaching and practicing in a local law firm, Burger also became active in Republican politics, assisting progressive Republican Harold Stassen, a former Minnesota governor, in his bid for the presidency. At a critical time in the 1952 Republican Convention, Burger helped to swing crucial Minnesota votes to Dwight Eisenhower; he was rewarded with a job as Assistant Attorney General in charge of the Civil Division of the Justice Department.[83]

President Eisenhower appointed Burger to the Court of Appeals for the District of Columbia Circuit, where he served from 1956–1969, and attracted the attention of President Nixon, offering Nixon the opportunity to keep his campaign promise to put "political conservatives" and "strict constructionists" on the bench.[84]

Chief Justice Burger's accomplishments as a Justice or jurist have not been widely praised. Most observers would agree with the following account:

> [Chief Justice Burger's] intellectual contribution to the Court's jurisprudence—the center of his activity—has been contradictory or negligible. Those who have portrayed him in recent days as an apostle of judicial restraint have been forced to wince at the expansion of judicial power over which he presided, from abortion to due process to free speech."[85]

The reason for this "contradictory or negligible" contribution may stem from several sources. First, the Chief Justice seems not to have been a "people person." One standard and objective source, *The Oxford Companion to The Supreme Court of the United States*, states that he was "less successful in guiding the other justices to jurisprudential results that he favored than either Earl Warren or William

Howard Taft," and that, within the Court, "he appears to have been more pugnacious than conciliatory."[86] The *Companion* contends that in his tenure, "there were leaks to the press—some clearly from his colleagues—indicating dissatisfaction with his leadership."[87] Noting that the Chief Justice did not seem to be able to effectively manage the conference and that he was unwilling to suppress his own dissent to preserve the appearance of harmony, the *Companion* concludes that "as a judge Burger was not of the first rank, but his work was much better than contemporary critics allowed and not recognizably different in craftsmanship from that of most of his colleagues."[88] Some critics were not even that kind with respect to his "judging" function, revealing that the Chief Justice's two most famous opinions, *Swann v. Charlotte-Mecklenburg Board of Education*[89] and *United States v. Nixon*,[90] were the work of a "committee of the whole."[91]

The Chief Justice may indeed have had trouble with that somewhat elusively described trait of judicial temperament. (I do know it when I see it and Burger did not have it.) Indeed, a word frequently used to describe him is "pompous." For example, Leonard Levy says, "I have never met a more starchy person than Burger. Pomposity enshrouded him like a miasma that blanketed him with his own sense of self-importance."[92] Or, again from the *National Law Journal*: "Publicly, he struck many as pompous and prickly, which bruised his image, if not his effectiveness."[93] Roger Newman, in his biography of Justice Black, may render the cruelest cut of all:

> Sitting at the center of the bench was a man of self-aggrandizing tendencies who strutted around like a peacock and acted like the anointed. Warren Burger wanted a carpet from his chambers to the bench. More chief housekeeper than chief justice, he regularly went around the building checking on the potted palms.[94]

Other possibilities may have contributed to the Chief Justice's alleged juridical shortcomings. His administrative accomplishments, which were surely outstanding (and which will be reviewed in a moment) must have taken valuable time away from the judicial task. He certainly did not seem to be highly prepared for the conferences.[95]

Further, as *The New York Times* indicated in its Burger obituary, he seemed to assign relatively straightforward cases to himself, which meant that "his personal imprint on the Court's jurisprudence was not always readily identifiable."[96] Thus, his personality, his lack of preparation, and his own assignment practice may have conspired to diminish his judicial role.

I feel uncomfortable about seeming so critical about the nominally central figure of this volume. However, most objective Court watchers would agree that my assessment is not an unfair summary of the large body of criticism of the Chief Justice's "judging." Let me hasten to add a few complimentary thoughts.

First, as shown later, the Chief's judicial abilities must be evaluated in light of one of the strongest group of Justices to ever sit on the High Court. Second, it is probably true that most constitutional scholars are to the left of the Chief Justice and their evaluations may suffer from a lack of objectivity. The words "probably" and "may" are used for two reasons: (1) because the Chief Justice was not the constitutional right-wing monolith that some have suggested,[97] and (2) many of these commentators, though clearly to the left of the Chief, nevertheless try to be objective and may in fact succeed.

My own view is that the Chief Justice's considerable abilities, although not those of a Black or a Rehnquist, were diminished by his constant attention to administrative detail, civic contributions, and symbolic functions. Also, by being "judged" *both* in relationship to this most talented cast *and* in relationship to the unachievable Nixonian goal of a counterrevolution, he is difficult to evaluate objectively.

What are clearly substantial accomplishments by the Chief Justice are his administrative and civic contributions. His administrative legacy begins with his memo announcing that the Court would enter the modern technological age: "The necessary steps are now being taken toward acquiring a Xerox machine in the building."[98] (This statement brings to mind that old Xerox commercial picturing medieval monks laboriously hand copying their work, just as described in Umberto Eco's *The Name of the Rose*. One can envision the scribes in the marble palace frantically carrying their typed carbon-copy papyri from chamber to chamber as the information age whizzed on outside the forbidden city. Traditions die hard, but some must be interred.)[99]

The same sources quoted earlier that were juristically critical are full of administrative praise: "[Warren Burger] did more to professionalize the operation of the federal judiciary than anyone since Chief Justice William H. Taft and worked more aggressively and effectively with Congress than any of his predecessors."[100] His administrative duties led him to represent the courts before Congress in a manner Justice White considered to be better than under Chief Justice Warren.[101] Indeed, when one reviews the legacy of his administrative work, one wonders how the Chief Justice could do any judging as well as finding occasional time for his hobbies of gardening and œnology. During his term, the following institutions were created: the National Center for State Courts, the Institute for Court Management, and the Institute for Corrections. The Federal Judicial Center was transformed into a major research and publishing center for American courts. He urged new training programs for Court personnel, fully computerized the Supreme Court, and assiduously lobbied Congress on behalf of judicial needs. Again, the *Oxford Companion*: "The nonjudicial aspects of the office of chief justice were well suited to Burger's abilities and temperament, and to this dimension of his role he brought enormous energy, forcefulness, tenacity, and the willingness to risk controversy."[102] Further, as Chief Justice Abrahamson explains later in this volume, Burger's respect for state courts and federalism was warmly received and his public support for state courts was profitably utilized by state judges.

Finally, Chief Justice Burger's civic volunteerism should certainly be recalled. As an extremely active member of the American Bar Association and as the congressionally designated chairman of the Commission of the Bicentennial of the United States Constitution, Burger unquestionably performed a leonine labor of love. These biographical notes on the Chief can conclude with a quotation from his eloquent foreword to the pocket-sized copy of the Constitution that his commission issued, one that I keep on my desk and distribute wherever I can:

This Constitution was not perfect; it is not perfect today even with amendments, but it has continued longer than any other written form of government. It sought to fulfill the promises of the Declaration of Independence of 1776, which expressed peoples' yearning to be free and to develop the talents given them by their Creator.

For 200 years this Constitution's ordered liberty has unleashed the energies and talents of people to create a good life.[103]

A Talented Cast

It can certainly be said that,

Seldom, if ever, in the Court's history has there been a period when the pivotal Justices were as intelligent, open-minded, and dedicated as Potter Stewart, Byron White, Harry Blackmun, Lewis Powell, and John Paul Stevens. An advocate faced with the challenge of changing judicial minds with sound arguments would do better to attempt the task in front of that group than almost any other that has in the past held the balance of power on the Court.[104]

This group of "pivotal" Justices was considered the ideological center of the Court and seemed to hold the balance of power during the Burger years. It was, by any fair evaluation, an exceptionally strong team (any team with "Whizzer" White on it would be exceptionally strong). All these Justices were stable, intelligent, and noted for integrity, and all were capable lawyers.

Nevertheless, the Burger Court was criticized, I think unfairly, as possessing "a weakness on the wings."[105] The liberal and conservative wings were each occupied by two Justices throughout the Burger years. On the left, Justices Brennan and Marshall fought to preserve the legacy of the Warren Court and even to extend its vision of individual rights and dignity. On the right, first Justice Harlan and Chief Justice Burger battled to restore federalism to its "proper" balance and then, when Justice Rehnquist replaced Justice Harlan, he and the Chief Justice sought, as Justice Rehnquist himself observed, "a halt to . . . the sweeping rules made in the days of the Warren Court."[106]

The criticism of the "wings" seems overstated. Certainly, the principal Justice on each side, Justice Brennan on the left, and Justice Harlan (later Justice Rehnquist) on the right, was an outstanding Justice. Brennan's ability to persuade—and to coax, cajole, even charm—without doubt carried his clear agenda forward. As a commentator notes, "If we look at Justices in terms of their role in the *decision process*, William J. Brennan, Jr., was actually the most influential Associate Justice in Supreme Court history."[107] He continues: "It is true that, after Chief Justice Warren's retirement, Justice Brennan was no longer the trusted insider. Yet, even under Chief Justice Burger, Brennan was able to secure the votes for his position in many important cases."[108]

Although Justice Marshall is not usually credited with Brennan's style of consensus building, because he was an effective and extraordinary advocate, his vote was authoritative as well as consistent. His persona, that of the greatest constitutional practitioner of his day, added force to his own advocacy within the Court.

Though perhaps neither of these Justices had the literary flair of a Holmes or even a Douglas "when the spirit was upon him," their work clearly insured the continuation and even confirmation of the Warren Court legacy.

Likewise, on the right, Justices Harlan and Rehnquist definitely had their visions. Harlan exercised great influence in his last two years on the Court. Indeed, the "paradigmatic conservative" Justice is enjoying something of a renaissance today. His well-crafted opinions and eloquent and restrained dissents (one can imagine that the Justice would be horrified at the ad hominem tone of some of today's dissents) are models of the jurist's craft. Further, his skill translates into success in later generations: One scholar suggested that Justice Harlan's opinions were overruled considerably less than those of his conservative compatriot, the combative and non–verbally restrained Felix Frankfurter, whose opinions were overruled in remarkable numbers.[109]

Justice Rehnquist, far from being only a voice crying in the wilderness, quickly came to be a respected advocate of positions eloquently and even elegantly stated. A 1993 study by two political scientists, based on a survey sent to lawyers, judges, scholars, and students, placed both Chief Justice Rehnquist and Justice Brennan on the list of the greatest Supreme Court Justices.[110] Although it is suggested that Justice Rehnquist is unworthy of "greatness" because he has not been able to "persuade a court to give effect to his judicial agenda,"[111] the battle is not yet over, and his influence is exceptionally strong. In fact, the strident writing of some recent Justices, compared with a moderation in Rehnquist's own tone, suggests that Rehnquist may be seen as more of a craftsman and gentleman in the Harlan mold as time moves on.

Chief Justice Burger, like Justice Marshall, was a certain vote in line with his own vision, although his vision was often the opposite of Marshall's. His own opinions, although they reflect no underlying comprehensive jurisprudence, are, by and large, solid examples of his adherence to "moderate" conservative thought.

Perhaps these "wings" may be better envisioned as flying buttresses that kept the roof on the cathedral while the center worked things out.[112] The mere fact that neither won a clear victory is not a reflection of the ability of the antagonists but, rather, a function of both the times and the magnitude of the task. In summary, the Justices of this Court were indeed a strong group of jurists. Somewhat ironically, as many scholars noted and some of his colleagues intimated, the Chief Justice was possibly the weakest judge of the lot, and that may be part of the reason that no compelling theme emerged from the Court he could not quite lead.

II. The Play's the Thing

Having reviewed the cast, what can we say of the play itself? What generalities or "strands and patterns" can we extract from or even impose on the Burger Court's production?

Let us start with the bad news: No pattern can be detected. Indeed, as Christopher Wolfe observed of the Burger Court:

> [T]he appointment of new justices by Republican presidents who claimed to be looking for "strict constructionists" created widespread expectations of a more con-

servative Court. While this was borne out in some respects, the actual results were much more complex and mixed, and very difficult to characterize simply.[113]

Vincent Blasi agrees: "[T]he Burger Court's work does not lend itself to any concise, comprehensive characterization. In certain areas, the recent Court has consolidated the landmark advances of the Warren years. In other areas, a mild retrenchment has taken place. Much of the time, the Court seems to have been drifting."[114] Also, Carolyn Graglia, a former clerk to then-Judge Burger, provides further consensus: "[T]he ideological ethos of Earl Warren's Court continued to prevail; the Court would not be turned around by its new chief, under whose leadership it overruled none of the major decisions of his predecessor."[115] Given that the Burger Court cannot be put into any paradigm or model, what, if any, generalizations do emerge?

Several are suggested. First, as already stressed, the Burger Court was a Court of exceptionally talented jurists; indeed, that is a significant cause of the difficulty in forcing it into a unified model. Second, the Burger Court was unquestionably an activist Court. Admittedly, that activism was pragmatic, balanced, ad hoc — indeed rootless — or perhaps we might say that the activism was not grounded in any kind of common vision. Third, the "counterrevolution" indeed "wasn't"; that is, the Warren Court, as John Adams said of the deceased Thomas Jefferson, "still lives." Finally, though "inferior" federal court judges (that word always stings a bit) can and should say, "We are all Holmesians now," activism in the marble palace — of one sort or another — is likely to stay.

Activism

Gerald Gunther has remarked that

> judicial activism was allegedly the hallmark of the Warren Court. Greater judicial restraint was one of the refrains of Richard Nixon in his campaigns and, supposedly, in his selection process. Yet, if anything can be said of the Burger Court, it is that activism is still very much a dominant strand in the Court's institutional performance. True, it is a more rootless activism — a more centrist, ad hoc activism — than that of the Warren Court, but it is activism nonetheless."[116]

Gunther opens his argument with his strongest point: the trumping example of an activist decision, *Roe v. Wade*.[117] Underscoring his jurisprudentially principled objection to such activism, he relates that his then dean at Stanford, John Hart Ely, termed *Roe* an even worse, more unjustified judicial performance than *Lochner v. New York*,[118] and that he agrees with his dean (a rare thing, especially among constitutional law professors and deans).[119]

One is tempted to almost rest the case on activism by citing *Roe*. *Roe's* substantive due process foundations, flowing back through *Griswold* even to *Lochner*, are discussed and criticized by scholars with so little in common as Robert Bork ("either substantive due process all the way or not at all. If we want *Griswold* and *Roe*, then *Lochner* and *Adkins*[120] come with them")[121] and, as mentioned, John Hart Ely (*Lochner* cases "universally acknowledged to have been constitutionally improper").[122]

Before we get too far into this topic we should perhaps define activism. (I suppose I cannot get away with again saying, "I know it when I see it," as that epitaph is clearly taken.)

Judicial activism is not, despite Richard Nixon's clouding of the waters, a generic liberal trait. Activism can be urged on behalf of both the right and left.[123] Perhaps there is even an activism on behalf of flaming moderation. It is fair to say that, according to Justice Oliver Wendell Holmes—who claimed, persuasively, to know—that a primary tenet of judicial restraint, the opposite of judicial activism, is deference by the judge to the legislature. Echoing his famous dissent in *Lochner v. New York*, Holmes observed, "There is nothing I more deprecate" than judicial use of the Fourteenth Amendment "to prevent the making of social experiments that an important part of the community desires. . . ."[124]

Judges who are activist, like Justice Holmes's majority colleagues in *Lochner*, tend not to defer to legislative determinations, whether those of state legislatures or Congress. And legislatures often tend to alternate between so-called conservative and liberal goals. Whereas substantive due process used by activist judges in *Lochner* was considered pro-business and hence conservative (very broadly speaking), substantive due process used by judges in *Griswold*[125] was pro-privacy and hence liberal (again very broadly speaking—besides, sex was involved). The point is that a hallmark of restraint is *deference to legislatures*; activism violating this hallmark can be either liberal or conservative or perhaps neither. Activism in opposition to this cardinal tenet of restraint occurs, as Justice Black said, "when Courts used the Due Process Clause 'to strike down [state] laws . . . because they may be unwise, improvident, or out of harmony with a particular school of thought.'"[126]

Activists also tend to look at constitutional grants of rights very broadly; activists see new rights or new emanations from old rights, and they are willing for courts "to assume a prominent role in the resolution of constitutional crises."[127] (They like "fairness" and "rightness" seen from various vantage points and get very concerned when "justice" and "the law" take divergent paths.) Restraintists suggest that the courts are not directly accountable to the public and should therefore take special care to defer in these controversies, even those of cosmic importance. (Some really testy restraintists, like Andrew Jackson, might suggest that the courts have inherent enforcement problems on really controversial stuff.)

Finally, to activists, the all important English doctrine of precedent—*stare decisis*—is not sacrosanct. In short, law tends to be seen by activists as "an instrument of politics rather than a self-perfecting, autonomous conceptual structure."[128]

Given these traits of activism, let us look at the evidence. While the Warren Court in its 16 turbulent and admittedly activist years struck down 21 federal and 150 state statutes, the Burger Court struck down 31 federal and 288 state laws in roughly the same period.[129]

Further, the statutes the Burger Court decapitated were certainly significant: Stricken federal laws included the legislative veto,[130] in an extremely important "activist" decision authored by Nixon restraintist Chief Justice Burger himself, and the Gramm-Rudman Act, which sought to deal with the growing budget deficit, in an opinion also written by the Chief Justice.[131] Other invalidated acts covered elections, judicial salaries, voting, gender classifications in the military, and social security programs. "If deference to Congress be the acid test of judicial restraint, the litmus of the Burger Court comes out much the same color as that of its predecessor."[132]

With respect to activism in resolution of constitutional crises, the Warren Court's great interventions were in school desegregation and reapportionment. The Burger Court likewise boldly went "where no one had gone before" in resolving *United States v. Nixon*,[133] which "represents nothing less than a bold and stunningly successful instance of judicial activism."[134] Other examples of Burger Court activism in the constitutional sphere include the Pentagon Papers case, *New York Times v. United States*[135] (in which the Court both limited the power of the President and arguably expanded the power of Congress); *Nixon v. Administrator of General Services*,[136] (the second Nixon tapes case, which reigned in or rained on the doctrine of executive privilege), and *Buckley v. Valeo*,[137] (which among other important things was a separation of powers case that protected the President's power of appointment).

As to the activist's willingness to define new rights or expand old ones, I already discussed the Burger Court's decision in *Roe*; I could also add *Furman v. Georgia*[138] (holding unconstitutional a state death penalty as "cruel and unusual" as administered). Bernard Schwartz argues:

> [T]he hallmark of the activist Court is the *Roe*-type decision that creates a new right not previously recognized in law. The Burger Court recognized new rights for women and those dependent on public largess. During the Burger years the law on sexual classification was completely changed.[139]

As Chief Judge Seymour both experienced and now explains later in this volume, the change in gender law was remarkable indeed.

Note, however, the Burger Court's activism *qua* disrespect for *stare decisis*. In many cases this is activism in reverse, or perhaps "restraintist activism." This is discussed further at a later point.

In conclusion, although the Chief Justice was wont to say, borrowing from Learned Hand, "The Constitution does not constitute us as 'Platonic Guardians,'"[140] the activism of his Court, in words the great Greek Geometer would embrace, is "intuitively obvious to even the most casual observer."[141]

Pragmatic, Rootless, or Ad Hoc Activism

Having identified this activism, and still avoiding Plato, can we do the Aristotelian thing and classify it? Dean Ely asks the question and answers it (rare enough for a dean, but he was a *professor* then):

> What outlook does underlie the Burger Court's constitutional jurisprudence? The safest answer, and in this case probably the most accurate, is what Winston Churchill is reported to have said . . . [while sending back to the kitchen] a pudding someone served him: it seems to lack a theme."[142]

Another observer notes of the Burger Court:

> There have been a few definite conservative shifts, which involved the overruling of Warren Court precedents. There have been even more areas in which the new

Court has nibbled away at the fringes of precedents, refusing to accept their logical extension or application to different factual situations or "distinguishing" them away on weak grounds. At the same time, there are various areas in which the Burger Court has pushed further in liberal directions than the Warren Court did, and in many other areas the results have been either moderate or a mixture of liberal and conservative policies.[143]

Noting again the counterrevolutionary goal and the sometimes heated rhetoric of the President and Chief Justice, many scholars agree that the Burger Court was clearly activist but conclude that the activism was "rootless." Thus, the unparalleled rights-creating activism of *Roe* was not rooted in a consistent rights-creating theory. Further, in criminal law—the one area in which rooted activism (though perhaps an activism of returning to pre-Warren Court days) was most clearly expected—the Court, though moving to the right, did not repeal the great triumvirate of *Miranda*,[144] *Mapp*,[145] and *Gideon*[146] and even extended defendants' rights in a few areas.

The area of criminal law shows this rootless activism most clearly; let me offer a few cases that seem to suggest this ad hoc, balancing, or rootless decision making. Admittedly, scholars argue that the Warren Court was not as liberal as is often thought (or even that there were two Warren Courts).[147] For example, consider these cases that the "impeach Earl Warren" crowd seldom mentioned: (1)*Draper v. United States*[148] (holding that there was probable cause to arrest without a warrant based on an informant's tip—really an allegation—that Draper would have drugs on him one day or the next and based on corroboration of completely innocent detail—his appearance and travel schedule); (2) *Hoffa v. United States*[149] (the court held that Fourth, Fifth, and Sixth Amendment rights were not violated by a planted government informant who heard conversations between the defendant and associates relative to jury tampering); (3) *Lewis v. United States*[150] (a warrant was not required for the undercover entry into a home to purchase marijuana, opinion by Earl Warren); and (4) *Terry v. Ohio*[151] (probable cause is unnecessary for Fourth Amendment search and seizure if there is a reasonable suspicion that criminal activity is afoot and that the suspect is armed and dangerous—this justifies a stop and frisk, this opinion is also by Warren).

Nevertheless, the Warren Court's criminal law legacy is primarily thought of as three cases: *Miranda v. Arizona* (the well-known *Miranda* rights to remain silent, have counsel, etc.), *Mapp v. Ohio* (the Fourth Amendment exclusionary rule), and *Gideon v. Wainwright* (right to trial counsel for indigent defendant in felony case).

The Burger Court, though clearly moving to the right, did not flatly overrule any of the triumvirate. In fact, the Court extended *Gideon's* right to trial counsel to preliminary hearings in *Coleman v. Alabama*[152] and also extended the right to any offense involving imprisonment in *Argersinger v. Hamlin*.[153]

Further Burger Court cases compound the difficulties of classification: (1) *Vale v. Louisiana*[154] (the search of a house was held to be impermissible even though a drug transaction was seen in the driveway and arrestee's relatives were in the home where they presumably could destroy evidence); (2) *Brown v. Texas*[155] (the court overturned a conviction for refusing to identify oneself when lawfully stopped; there was no reasonable suspicion to lawfully stop a person simply because it was a high drug traffic area); (3) *Welsh v. Wisconsin*[156] (holding that although the right circumstances may justify warrantless entry to make an arrest in the home, it is difficult to conceive of a warrantless home arrest that would not be unreasonable under the Fourth Amendment when the underlying offense is extremely minor and no exigent circumstances existed—in this case a drunk driving offense); (4) *Payton v. New York*[157] (a routine felony arrest in a home violates Fourth Amendment in the absence of an arrest warrant—in this case the arrests for armed robberies and murder); (5) *Steagall v. United States*[158] (holding that even if the police have an arrest warrant, they need a search warrant to enter a third-party home in order to make the arrest).

That you can point to "conservative" Warren cases and "liberal" Burger cases is not the point. In the overall context of these two Courts, the Warren agenda seems to be motivated by a concern for due process "rights" whereas the Burger Court agenda seems to balance those rights with the needs of the community, with at least some Justices remembering their presidentially voiced goal to reign in the Warren Court. Thus, it may be the *role* the Burger Court was placed in—that of counter-revolutionist—that makes it appear more different from its predecessor than it actually was.[159]

Perhaps, in addition to this at least partially unfulfilled expectation of counter-revolution, the Courts did differ in their views of the goals of criminal law and the proper procedural functions.[160] The Warren Court was more interested in "rights" and the Burger Court (and its successor) more clearly interested in crime control.

Given the entire corpus of cases of both Courts, those who argue that the Burger Court's work was rootless and more difficult to clarify are correct. As Schwartz writes:

> The Warren Justices saw themselves as present-day Chancellors, who secured fairness and equity in individual cases, fired above all by a vision of the equal dignity of man, to be furthered by the Court's value-laden decisions.
>
> No similar vision inspired the activism of the Burger Court. Instead of consciously using the law to change the society and its values, it rode the wave, letting itself be swept along by the consensus it perceived in the social arena—moving, for example, on gender discrimination when it became "fashionable" to be for women's rights. From this point of view, the Burger Court's activism has been well termed a "rootless activism," which dealt with cases on an essentially ad hoc basis inspired less by moral vision than by pragmatic considerations.[161]

The Warren Court Lives

One of the most ironic stories of our Founders is that of the relationship of John Adams, the "obnoxious and disliked . . . lawyer for the revolution" from Braintree, Massachusetts, and Thomas Jefferson, the soft-spoken Virginia Renaissance Man with a "peculiar felicity of expression."[162] At an early point in their lives, at the Continental Congress in 1776, they were firm allies. Adams was perhaps the sine qua non of the Declaration of Independence; Jefferson of course, penned most of its ringing natural law-based phrases. In Washington's Cabinet, these friends became implacable foes, a state that did not improve when they ran against each other for President. Adams was a good loser in perhaps only one sense: He was good at keeping his cronies in office, although not good enough, or at least fast enough, to get the commission to Mr. Marbury.

After these old foes retired, they became friends again. The two developed a lively exchange and correspondence—an exchange that ended, amazingly, when they both died—on July 4, 1826, fifty years to the day after the signing of their greatest collaboration.

Although Jefferson in fact predeceased Adams by a few hours, the author of some of "the most influential dull works ever published"[163] uttered as his last words, "Jefferson lives." Although historians debate the exact meaning of those words, we cannot really effectively look to the text for any lasting import. I believe the great lawyer meant that the legacy of the friend with whom he had achieved rapprochement still lived.

The analogy is not strained at all in reference to the Warren and Burger Courts. Despite Chief Justice Burger's professed goals, at the end of the Burger Court, it was clear the "Warren Court lives." Indeed, as Schwartz concluded: "In historical terms, indeed, the Burger Court's main significance was its consolidation and continuation of the Warren heritage."[164]

Although the Warren Court's jurisprudence encompassed many important subjects, its greatest legacy is in three areas: desegregation, reapportionment, and rights of the accused. Although this list ignores some bellwether cases (one hesitates to fail to mention the expanded rights given the press in *New York Times v. Sullivan*,[165] especially as Anthony Lewis is contributing to this volume),[166] these three areas constitute the major legacy in the view of historians, the part of the general public that knows that there was a Warren Court, and many lawyers as well. These precedents—although among the most activist judicial decisions ever made—fared very well in the Burger years. And they succeeded despite "a solid six-member majority of appointees made by three presidents who had harshly criticized liberal judicial activism and [who had also] vowed to change the Court's direction."[167]

This is not to say that the Burger Court did not veer to the starboard. With the notable exception of a few areas that the Warren Court only tangentially addressed (abortion rights being the most notable example), the Burger Court did indeed move to the right. But this movement was, as Kenneth W. Starr described it, a strategy of "Don't overrule, but don't extend beyond the case. . . . Devise exceptions . . . and prune off any excesses."[168] Let us look at the specifics.

Segregation

Brown v. Board of Education[169] stands as the universally hailed most important decision of the Warren Court. The case was a vindication of the great dissent of the first Justice John Harlan in *Plessy v. Ferguson*,[170] and held essentially that "separate" was inherently unequal. This decision was rendered, remarkably, by a unanimous Court (and it was extremely difficult to get Justices Black and Frankfurter to sing from the same hymnal, unless FDR was the choir director) at a time the nation was far from unanimous on the topic.[171]

Although a very few southern politicians, including Oklahoma's governor, Raymond Gary (and we have little to be proud of in this area other than some remarkable plaintiffs), supported the decision, in other states federal troops were called forth to enforce the Court's bold rule. (It was during this time that one of Robert Kennedy's young assistant attorneys general named Byron White stood almost alone and toe-to-toe against the recalcitrant governor of Alabama and his state troopers. Haughtily asked where all the freedom riders were, the once great athlete and future great Justice replied, "They were in the hospitals to which the Governor's men had sent them.")[172]

Though the *Brown* decision was certainly an example of liberal activism, it is now considered mainstream (particularly after some Burger Court decisions extending it).[173] It is seldom meaningfully attacked, and then only by a few academics who can do so safely—and benignly[174]—from the Ivory Tower. Even "originalists" like former Reagan Attorney General Edwin Meese and former Court of Appeals Judge Robert Bork support the decision. The *Brown* legacy not only survived the Burger Court[175] but is now a part of both the jurisprudential and political frameworks of modern America, "securely rooted in our public law."[176]

Reapportionment

Chief Justice Warren thought that the reapportionment decisions, particularly *Reynolds v. Sims*, were his Court's greatest legacy.[177] In thinking about the changes those decisions promoted in the South and particularly in Oklahoma,[178] I am tempted to agree with the Chief Justice's evaluation.

But these decisions were unquestionably activist. They were opposed by two of the greatest conservative Justices ever to sit on the Court: Justice Frankfurter, who termed the whole political question-laden area of apportionment a "political thicket,"[179] and Justice Harlan, who patiently noted in dissent that the Equal Protection Clause of the Fourteenth Amendment had nothing to do with voting.[180] But Earl Warren was undeterred. When he decided "that the Constitution required an equal population apportionment standard for all legislative chambers except the United States Senate, the fact that no American legislature had followed the new requirement did not deter him from uniformly applying the standard."[181]

The rhetoric against this activism heated as the full play of "one person, one vote" became apparent. Justices Clark and Stewart dissented in a later reapportionment decision, which rejected a non–population-based system selected by the voters in a popular referendum, saying that the Court's theory was without support "in the words of the Constitution, in any prior decision of this Court, or in the 175-year political history of our Federal Union."[182]

Despite these objections, sincere and jurisprudentially defensible, the reapportionment cases were popular and complied with relatively quickly. The eminent sense of Justice Douglas's simple phrase, "One person, one vote,"[183] summarized popular sentiment. As one originalist phrased it:

> The stark simplicity of the "pure" democratic principle makes it very powerful in a country that is ideologically committed to democracy. More traditional and nuanced views of democracy are relatively complicated and difficult for the average

person to understand, and are also at a disadvantage among intellectual elites who are suspicious of political arrangements that seem to favor the status quo and prevent programmatic change."[184]

These decisions, among the most activist in the Court's history because they overturned established precedent and were not based on a specific constitutional text (indeed they were contrary to the "Great Compromise"), remain intact. The Burger Court sounded no retreat here.

Rights of Accused

Considering the now exalted places these cases hold—*Brown* with its repeal of "separate but equal," and *Reynolds* and *Baker*, with their constitutionalizing of "one person, one vote"—the young student of the law might inquire about all the fuss surrounding this activist Warren Court. We should, however, remind those who did not live in the 1960s that segregation—apart from being intrinsically insidious—resulted in the worst domestic violence this country has ever seen. And, the *ancien régimes* of state legislatures, called on to give up the political power that gross malapportionment provided them, frequently responded with less than civic republican altruism.

But even if the controversy of Warren Court jurisprudence cannot be easily understood by those who did not live through the era, the Warren Court criminal law decisions, with perhaps the exception of *Gideon v. Wainwright*, remain as controversial as ever. A complete discussion of these cases and their progeny is beyond this paper. Let me just observe that *Miranda* and *Mapp* have been significantly scaled back, whereas *Gideon* was extended. Some of these criminal law cases were dealt with earlier. An additional word should, nevertheless, be said here.

The most famous of the criminal law cases is probably *Miranda v. Arizona*. Thanks to actor Jack Webb, most of us know that *Miranda* held that suspects must be informed of their rights, including the right to remain silent and to have a retained or appointed lawyer present before being subjected to "custodial interrogation." Yale Kamisar termed *Miranda* "a most welcome, and . . . most ambitious, effort to seize the police interrogation-confessions problem by the throat."[185] He goes on to note, "The prize for ingenuity [in applying the Fifth and Sixth Amendment protections to 'in custody' questioning] . . . should not go to the Warren Court for doing so but to those who had managed for so long to devise rationales for not doing so."[186]

Initially, in *Rhode Island v. Innis*,[187] the Burger Court took an expansive reading of the term "interrogation," holding basically that words or actions that the police should know are likely to elicit an incriminating response trigger *Miranda*'s safeguards. Later, in *Edwards v. Arizona*,[188] the Court held that once a suspect asserts his or her right to counsel (as opposed to his or her right to remain silent) the police cannot "try again."

Yet, in what Kamisar calls the "third Burger Court"[189] (the first being critical of Warren Court criminal procedure cases and the second a "significantly less police-oriented Court"),[190] the Court resumed its initial hostility to Warren Court decisions. Let us see what new "rationales for not doing so" the Burger Court devised.[191] In *Harris v. New York*,[192] a closely divided Court held that statements obtained in violation of *Miranda* could be used to impeach the petitioner's testimony at trial. Further, not only did the Court create a "public safety" exception to *Miranda* warnings in *New York v. Quarles*,[193] it also held in *Moran v. Burbine*[194] that failure to inform a suspect of events occurring outside his presence did not vitiate an otherwise valid waiver. The "event" was the information that a public defender's services were arranged by his sister. Finally, having earlier described the warnings in *Michigan v. Tucker* as "prophylactic safeguards,"[195] in *Oregon v. Elstad*, Justice O'Connor, for the Court, held: "Though *Miranda* requires that the unwarned admission must be suppressed, the admissibility of any subsequent statement should turn in these circumstances solely on whether it is knowingly and voluntarily made."[196]

Miranda has survived, but the foundation for its demise may have been laid. Supporters of *Miranda* must take comfort that its most seemingly implacable foe, Chief Justice Burger, in a 1980 statement in *Rhode Island v. Innis*, somewhat rootlessly observed: "I would neither overrule *Miranda*, disparage it, nor extend it at this late date."[197]

Mapp v. Ohio, the exclusionary rule opinion that Justice Fortas once termed "the most radical decision in recent times . . ."[198] suffered even more mangling than *Miranda*. Though in *Bivens v. Six Unknown Named Agents*, the Burger Court, in its activist mode, created a new cause of action against federal agents (a sort of federal 42 U.S.C. § 1983 action), the Chief Justice used his dissent to term the exclusionary rule "as an anomalous and ineffective mechanism with which to regulate law enforcement. . . ." He further argued that the Court should not be "clinging to an unworkable and irrational concept of law."[199] Before long, his position gained ground. In *United States v. Leon*,[200] the Court adopted a good faith exception to the rule, which was explained in *Massachusetts v. Sheppard*: "The exclusionary rule should not be applied when the officer conducting the search acted in objectively reasonable reliance on a warrant issued by a detached and neutral magistrate that subsequently is determined to be invalid."[201] Finally, in *INS v. Lopez-Mendoza*,[202] the Court used a cost-benefit analysis to decide whether to apply the exclusionary rule in a deportation case. Schwartz criticizes cost-benefit analysis, suggesting that it can result in not "objective analysis" but "Benthamism in modern dress—and with a subjective vengeance."[203]

Mapp was so intensively subjected to a cost-benefit analysis that its future is perilous. This reflects an important difference in the Burger and Warren Court resolution of criminal law issues. The Warren Court tended to think in terms of whether an important procedural right was violated; cost-benefit analysis as used by the Burger Court suggests that we balance the violated right against the costs to society.[204] Bentham lives.

Gideon v. Wainwright fared best of the Warren Court trilogy. *Argersinger v. Hamlin*[205] extended the right of counsel to any offense involving imprisonment, *Coleman v. Alabama*[206] extended the right to preliminary hearings, and *Faretta v. California*,[207] to the chagrin of many of us who have to look at the records involved, confirms the right of self-representation—going it alone without a lawyer. So *Gideon*, if anything, was expanded.

In short, though a strong retrenchment[208] occurred, none of the trilogy cases was overruled. However, with the current crime problems brought about by drugs, the use of cost-benefit analysis suggests that *Mapp* may be vulnerable indeed.

III. Is Activism[209] Here to Stay?

In 1968, when President Richard Nixon began his campaign assault on Earl Warren and his Court,[210] perhaps the central plank was the decrying of "activist judges," although judges being "soft on crime" would be a close second. In fact, Warren Burger's writing of a few articles on these themes (coupled with his Republican credentials) probably caused President Nixon to select Judge Burger as his Chief Justice nominee.[211]

Frankly, some of the attacks on judicial activism (although I do not think this was true of President Nixon's attack) had racist foundations. Certainly, those opposed to integration, long successful at using southern legislative seniority to freeze or slow integration and equality, were galled to see the courts lead, often with unanimity, in a revolution that forever changed our country. Local leaders argued that activist judges intervening in local schools destroyed "local control" of schools. These concerns were exacerbated when courts ordered busing of schoolchildren across town and integration of faculties as well as facilities. And, following *Brown*'s lead, federal courts began to deal with a host of suspect governmental hiring practices.

Activist judges, President Nixon and his partisans argued, had also intervened in criminal areas allowing the "criminal to go free because the constable blundered."[212] Blackstone's famous ratio of 10:1[213] never caught hold with the American public; indeed, it is amazing that more judges were not personally harmed as a result of the withering fire that was directed at them, which most felt they were ethically prohibited from answering.[214]

Though President Nixon appointed Chief Justice Burger, and later Justices Powell, Rehnquist, and Blackmun were added to stem the Warren activist tide, Nixon's concern with things judicial soon turned to other more immediate concerns (such as *United States v. Nixon*). Largely falling into disuse during President Ford's term, the antiactivism mantle later fell to President Reagan's Attorney General, Edwin Meese III. Meese vilified and excoriated activism, but his arguments had a bit of a hollow ring. Basing his constitutional theory on what Judge Posner describes in other contexts as the "clever disguise"[215] of *originalism*, the actual positions that the Attorney General and his associates took before the Court clearly expose the accuracy of Judge Posner's observations about that theory.[216]

One of the cardinal principles of restraint, as discussed earlier, is deference to Congress. However, the Reagan administration, as led by Attorney General Meese, clearly had a mixed record here, frequently arguing against congressional acts, as in the Gramm-Rudman case.[217] The *Congressional Quarterly* concluded:

> [D]espite its stated opposition to judicial activism, the Reagan administration has engaged in an unprecedented degree of legal activism before the Supreme Court. Since President Reagan took office in 1981, the Solicitor General—who speaks for

the government before the high court—has volunteered that administrations' views to the justices more often than any of his predecessors.[218]

This observation may not hit the bull's eye. The mere fact that the Reagan administration was legally active does not mean that it encouraged legal activism. Further evaluation of the positions taken would be required. Admittedly, the possibility of tension between the Attorney General's restraint rhetoric and the Department of Justice's record before the Court is real.[219]

The shibboleth of restraint is still very strong, despite its patchy record with both conservatives and liberals on the Court. At a discussion at New York University for the Institute for Judicial Advocacy, I advocated the view that, with respect to federal court of appeals judges, "We're all Holmesians now." I did not mean that cynically—I believe that most courts of appeals and district court judges do begin their careers feeling restrained by the Constitution, Congress, precedent, and the very inertia of the system. By and large, that restraint continues throughout most judicial careers and *appropriately so*.[220] The rule of law should not be like the Dow-Jones average.

But the prescient Justices of the Supreme Court know that the shibboleth cannot be allowed to become a mantra. Great Justices as diverse as Douglas and Rehnquist have been activist in one way or another when they felt the situation demanded it. Conservative justices such as Felix Frankfurter, Holmes's principal disciple, stifled by adherence to "his master's voice," may have missed the chance to be placed in the first tier of Justices by following too rigid a role of restraint.[221]

Some sort of "activism" will always be with us. Founders Alexander Hamilton and Chief Justice John Marshall[222] have certainly vindicated an instrumentalist and hence activist view of *some* of the "spare but meaningful terms" that govern us.[223] Hamilton even defended his activist views with the compelling logic of scripture, "For the letter killeth, but the spirit givith life."[224] If Hamilton's and Marshall's instrumentalism has not shown us the vitality of well-placed activism, perhaps, then, *Brown v. Board of Education* and *Baker v. Carr*[225] have. And Judge Posner, the most provocative and influential jurist since Holmes, argues that the pragmatic judge should be "practical, instrumental, forward-looking, *activist*, empirical, skeptical, antidogmatic, experimental. . . ."[226]

Though activism in interpreting the Constitution is a tool that should be rarely used, if history is our guide, it will be used.[227] Though he was speaking of *originalism*, Judge Posner's remarks are again relevant to activism as well:

> "The Court's survival and flourishing depend on the political acceptability of its results rather than on its adherence to an esoteric philosophy of interpretation. The Court has never been consistently originalist, yet has survived. Maybe the justices know more about survival than their critics do; we economist types believe that people generally know more about how to protect their own interests than a kibitzer does."[228]

It is argued here that the Burger Court was a Court of exceptional talent and considerable activism. That its activism was theme-less, like Churchill's trifle, makes it difficult to analyze. The strands and patterns of this Court's tapestry do not tell a coherent story.

But maybe they do in a unique way. That a Court could be, at least partially, constructed with the express goal of elimination of activism and fail, even miserably fail, to do so may prove something indeed.

Vincent Blasi suggests that judicial review—and he implies activist judicial review—can be seen as a "corrective, an antidote to other forces that threaten the political system."[229] He suggests that the 1970s were *destined* to be an activist decade for the Court, a decade that suggested or required the application of the judicial corrective. He argues that two destabilizing forces promoted the need, or at least the yearning, for this corrective.

First, there is the rampant growth of government bureaucracy. Citizens are overwhelmed by the size of government and, as one recent bestseller suggests in its title,[230] the demise of judgment and common sense that seems to come with this vast bureaucratic growth. Courts can simplify this Byzantine labyrinth. They allow a single citizen or a group of citizens to have access to the power and the grandeur of the marble palace, where these modern-day Davids can aim a pebble at the Goliath of their choice. (Goliath may not always be government; he may be a vast multinational corporate conglomerate, or he may even be a snail darter.) Courts allow a more fair fight (though this oversimplifies economic disparities of the parties); they create a "more manageable world where human choice seems to matter . . . and value judgments are within . . . comprehension."[231]

Courts simplify these complex battles into a series of binary resolutions: It is either a taking or it is not; we will preserve the species' habitat, or we will not; the defendant gets a new trial or he goes to prison for a very long time. As Blasi concludes:

> [T]he greatest contribution the Supreme Court makes to the political system is through its simplifying function, its role in preserving one arena in an otherwise incomprehensible political domain where the disputes are bilateral and rationally debatable and where the choices are intelligible and explainable.[232]

We can call this the "my day in court" syndrome. The enduring legacy of the television show *The People's Court* may exhibit this syndrome. Judges are often amazed how much better people seem to feel after having had a chance to make their case and to understand, basically, what is going on. Thus, courts may be active in some areas because the people simply want them to be, and they demand it.

Blasi's second force inviting corrective judicial review, perhaps related to the first, is the rise of single-issue politics and its effect on legislatures. Some of these issues are related only to self-interest, for example, How much are welfare benefits or tax deductions going to be? Others are philosophical or religious: Will we allow abortions or euthanasia or how separate will church—or synagogue, temple, tabernacle, mosque, etc.—and state be?

Blasi argues that the growth of the bureaucracy and single-issue politics work together to impoverish the debate that is essential for a deliberative republican government to survive. Viewed through this lens, judicial activism may correct the inequalities of the legislative process. It may reflect disinterested decisions of judges more interested in the commonwealth than the private wealth. It may clarify the constitutional parameters that restrict what may be a temporary legislative majority (or it may protect an area that is best governed by a countermajoritarian rule). Both with respect to the problems of bigness—big government or unequal economic power—and the problems of smallness—excessively parochial politics—the Supreme Court can be seen as a possible republican corrective to malfunctioning political behavior. In this regard, we should remember that Justice Harlan F. Stone, in the famous footnote 4 in *Carolene Products*,[233] suggested a special place for judicial review, not only where constitutional rights embraced within the Fourteenth Amendment are reviewed and in the case of prejudice against discrete and insular minorities but also in cases involving the integrity of the political process itself.

To be sure, all activism is not equally serious, whatever one's perspective. Constitutional activism—adding to our expanding constitutional rights—is much more serious and potentially damaging than filling in a statutory blank when several legitimate choices compete. But statutory activism itself also raises serious concerns: First, the blanks left in Congressional statutes often have Constitutional ramifications—of federalism if nothing else. Second, if courts get in the habit of filling in statutory blanks, will that not encourage the same action on the Constitution itself? Legislatures should consider these ramificiations when they leave gaps in statutes through either haste or inability to decide among competing options.

Public-choice theory,[234] a branch of law and economics, expands and reinforces the Blasi themes. Although a detailed discussion of this theory is beyond the scope of this paper, public-choice theory seems to have two tenets that reinforce the desire—if not the need for judicial activism. First, public choice suggests that the overwhelming desire of (functionally) *all* legislators is to get reelected, or, as one scholar puts it, the actions of federal legislators can be understood by use of the "simple abstract assumption" that representatives are "single-minded seekers of reelection."[235] I must stress that I *do not* agree with this analysis (it is too simplistic and denies the considerable impact of old-fashioned civic republican-style principle), nor *does* the theory mean that seeking reelection is per se bad (e.g., it *may* result in good representation). What I do believe, after a decade of service in a state legislature, is that reelection is probably the primary goal of a significant number of legislators for mixed reasons, including power, prestige, and policy impact. Clearly a major goal such as reelection will affect legislative outcomes.

If reelection is so important, legislators must vote in such a way as to maximize its probability. Because politics is usually a zero-sum game, what you give someone you have to take from someone else. Thus, each time a legislator makes a decision, there are winners and losers. The key, according to this theory, is to balance it so that there are enough winners or so that the winners are powerful enough to get the legislator reelected. Or, if a legislator can avoid making a decision at all, he or she can defer the battle to another day.

One last part of the syllogism: The discrete, unified special interests will seek political benefits that will help them but may hurt the general public. The reason this works is, first, that the "general public" often does not vote generally. Second, the special interest is highly motivated and *will* vote or better yet contribute campaign contributions to their legislative friends. All this can be easily remembered in the old adage my predecessor in the Oklahoma Attorney General's office left me with: "Those whom you generally help, generally forget; those whom you specifically shaft, specifically remember."

If this part of public choice is at all descriptive and predictive, this kind of activism is indeed here to stay. Responding to current political pressures, legislatures will pass more and more specific or "special" legislation that will be challenged in courts, where economic disparities are less decisive. Further, and very significantly, legislatures will often avoid the critical choice, leaving the decision to administrative agencies and the courts, which do not have to face electoral pressures. Thus, Congress may not directly tell us whether there is an implied right of action or whether a bill suggests quotas, or even the effective date of the noncapital provisions of the recent Antiterrorism and Effective Death Penalty Act of 1996.[236] Congress's failure to decide only postpones the decision, for eventually a court will have to make it. Incidentally, some legal scholars *on the right* have argued that the realities of public choice suggest a renewal of judicial activism. These scholars, including Richard Epstein, suggest that the courts should reverse the New Deal course and revive "pre–New Deal constitutional rules dealing with economic liberty, restrictions on federal power, and limits on administrative agencies."[237] *Lochner* lives.

Again, Judge Posner offers a paradigmatic harbor from which the thoughtful may seek republican discourse on the subject of constitutional activism. In an article discussing problems with Judge Bork's views on constitutional doctrine, he notes:

> The idea of the Constitution as a binding contract is an incomplete theory of political legitimacy, not an erroneous one. A contract induces reliance that can make a strong claim for protection; it also frees people from having continually to reexamine and revise the terms of their relationship. These values are independent of whether the original contracting parties are still alive. But a long-term contract is bound eventually to require, if not formal modification (which in the case of the Constitution can be accomplished only through the amendment process), then flexible interpretation, to cope effectively with altered circumstances. Modification and interpretation are reciprocal; the more difficult it is to modify the instrument formally, the more extent is flexible interpretation. Bork is aware of the practical impediments to amending the Constitution but is unwilling to draw the inference that flexible interpretation is therefore necessary to prevent constitutional obsolescence.[238]

In another work, Judge Posner refers to another source of flexibility in our jurisprudential joints, "Our dominantly positivistic discourse has enough natural law play in its joints to give us all the rhetorical flexibility we need."[239]

Even the conservative and restrained Justice Frankfurter would agree with some flexibility, having said that John Marshall was correct: In expounding a constitution, the document is not to be read as "an insurance clause in small type, but a scheme of government . . . intended for the the undefined and unlimited future."[240]

The Burger Court may have conclusively demonstrated one thing: that activism of one sort or another is here to stay.[241] Despite the fact that its Chief Justice and a majority of its members were selected by restraint-advocating Presidents (and, further, other Justices, such as Justice Black—at the end of his tenure—and Justice White, had restraintist leanings), the Burger Court was at least as active as its predecessors. Further, Blasi's "destabilizing forces" of the 1970s continue to exist and were probably exacerbated, as public choice suggests. Finally, there is an inherent problem in being a restraintist if you feel that you have been losing for fifty years—the definition of restraint tends to be hard activism in the opposite direction.[242] Hence, some very conservative scholars suggest not deference to the legislature, that classic hallmark of Holmesian restraint, but revival of the property protecting function of substantive due process or even the expansion of the Takings Clause "as the true center of the legal universe."[243]

The moderate highly principled approach of John Harlan II seems to have few advocates, though many admirers. As Anthony Lewis has said, "[W]e're all activists now . . . activism for what is a different question."[244] Perhaps the real battle of future courts will not be "dignity" versus "deference",[245] originalism versus instrumentalism, or liberalism versus conservativism. The real battle presaged by the Burger Court—perhaps the most activist Court of our history—will be to seek a principled resolution of cases before the Court, a resolution that carefully utilizes Judge Posner's "flexibility in the joints." It must be a resolution free from political control but wary of political restraints; it must properly preserve separation of powers and federalism, and respect constitutional and even common-law restraints, while addressing Justice Harlan's living traditions[246] and Roscoe Pound's prophecy that the "law must be stable and yet it cannot stand still."[247]

Notes

I would like to thank the following for their assistance and comments: Professors Arthur LeFrancois, Janet Levit, Andy Spiropolous, and Rick Tepker; also Alexander Dreier and Suzanne Mitchell; a special thanks to my insightful colleague Judge David Ebel for his comments and critiques; and finally a special thanks to the indefatigable Professor Bernard Schwartz both for his invitation to participate in this conference and for his encouragement and suggestions. Clearly, I did not take all of these jurists' advice; the fault for errors and reasoning is, alas, my own.

1. Schwartz, "Supreme Court Superstars: The Ten Greatest Justices," 31 *Tulsa L.J.* 93, 136 (1995).
2. 347 U.S. 483 (1954).
3. Reynolds v. Sims, 377 U.S. 533 (1964).
4. Baker v. Carr, 369 U.S. 186 (1962).
5. Gideon v. Wainwright, 372 U.S. 335 (1963).
6. Miranda v. Arizona, 384 U.S. 436 (1966).
7. Mapp v. Ohio, 367 U.S. 643 (1961).
8. *The Federalist* No. 78.
9. Wolfe, *The Rise of Modern Judicial Review* 292–93 (1986).
10. I used *The Oxford Companion to the Supreme Court of the United States* (Hall ed., 1992) extensively in these biographical sketches of the Justices. The book is an invaluable general resource for those interested in the Court.
11. Though I later suggest that the Burger Court may have been even more activist than the Warren Court, I believe the Burger Court's "rootless" activism was less influential in shaping public policy and eventually public opinion.
12. Schwartz, supra note 1, at 132.

13. Newman, *Hugo Black* 597 (1994).

14. Posner, *Overcoming Law* 97 (1995).

15. Ely, *Democracy and Distrust* 3 (1980).

16. Newman, supra note 13, at 256–57; Hall supra note 10, at 72.

17. Newsman, supra note 13, at 256, 259. After the radio address, the Gallup poll majority shifted in Black's favor.

18. 366 U.S. 83, 116 (1961). For a brief discussion of the fascinating petitioner in this case see, Henry, "Forward into the Past: Observations Regarding George Anastaplo's 'Lectures for the Student of Law,'" 20 *Oklahoma City University L. Rev.* 1 (1995).

19. 332 U.S. 46 (1947).

20. The exceptions include the Second Amendment's right to keep and bear arms, the Third Amendment's troop quartering protections, the Fifth Amendment's right to indictment by grand jury, and the Seventh Amendment's right to a jury trial in a civil case. See Adamson v. California, 332 U.S. at 68; Duncan v. Louisiana, 391 U.S. 145 (1968), especially at 148–50 & n. 14.

21. Newman, supra note 13, at 588–89.

22. I am specially indebted to Norman Dorsen of the New York University School of Law for his insights about Justice Harlan, for whom he clerked. I have had the privilege of hearing Professor Dorsen speak twice on this subject. Much of my material comes from a lecture he presented at his university and from his remarks at the 1994 Warren Court Symposium at the University of Tulsa. Dorsen, "John Marshall Harlan," in *The Warren Court: A Retrospective* 236 (Schwartz ed., 1996).

23. Bright-eyed law students of today, God bless 'em, may wonder how it is that two such great jurists could rise to the zenith on such little law schooling. As a former law school dean I must tell you that times have changed since then. For one thing, we have all these opinions of Justices Black and Harlan that we have to teach.

24. Schwartz, *A History of the Supreme Court* 375 (1993).

25. Lewis, "Foreword," in *The Burger Court: The Counter-Revolution That Wasn't* viii (Blasi ed., 1983).

26. Dorsen, in Schwartz ed., supra note 22, at 236 (quoting Friendly, "Mr. Justice Harlan: As Seen by a Friend and Judge of an Inferior Court," 85 *Harv. L. Rev.* 382, 384 (1971)).

27. See id. at 238 (citations omitted).

28. 377 U.S. 533 (1964).

29. Id. at 624–25.

30. Newman, supra note 13, at 588.

31. Dorsen, in Schwartz ed., supra note 22, at 236. An intriguing Harlan case is Cohen v. California, 403 U.S. 15 (1971), which, as a precursor to Justice Brennan's New York Times Co. v. Sullivan, 376 U.S. 254 (1964), and also Justice Scalia's R.A.V. v. City of St. Paul, 505 U.S. 377 (1992), promoted a coherent approach to problems of governmental discrimination on viewpoint and message. Is this "liberal" or "absolutist" in the Black/Douglas tradition of "Congress shall make no law means Congress shall make no law" approach?

32. 367 U.S. 497 (1961).

33. But showing his conservatism in building on this Anglo-American tradition, he counsels "judgment and restraint." Id. at 542.

34. Id. The power of this dissent is cogently revealed by Justice Souter's constant appeal to the concurrence in Washington v. Glucksberg, 117S. Ct. 2258–2293 (1997). It is at the least highly debatable that Justice Harlan would endorse this "rational continuum" approach.

35. "[T]his Connecticut legislation . . . violates the Fourteenth Amendment. I believe that a statute making it a criminal offense for married couples to use contraceptives is

an intolerable and unjustifiable invasion of privacy in the conduct of the most intimate concerns of an individual's personal life." Id.

36. Dorsen, in Schwartz ed., supra note 22, at 249.

37. 410 U.S. 113 (1973).

38. 381 U.S. 479 (1965).

39. 389 U.S. 347 (1967).

40. Dorsen, in Schwartz ed., supra note 22, at 243.

41. It is also interesting to note, especially to those who see "liberal" and "conservative" as a simple dichotomy, that Chief Justice Warren himself had doubts on whether the right to privacy included a right to an abortion. At the Griswold conference he stated, "I can't say . . . that the state has no legitimate interest (that could apply to abortion laws.)" B. Schwartz, *The Ascent of Pragmatism* 409 (1990).

42. Id. at 19.

43. Judge Posner observed that "William Douglas, until he became bored with being a Supreme Court Justice, wrote conventional enough opinions." Posner, supra note 14, at 281. Also, note Chief Justice Rehnquist's observation: "[Douglas] had a brilliant legal mind, but by the time I came to know him as a colleague I think he was somewhat bored with the routine functions of the court." Rehnquist, *The Supreme Court: How It Was, How It Is* 255 (1987).

44. Newman, supra note 13, at 600–01.

45. Id. at 601 n. 9.

46. 491 U.S. 397 (1989).

47. 429 U.S. 10 (1976).

48. 397 U.S. 254 (1970).

49. 376 U.S. 254 (1964).

50. 369 U.S. 186 (1962).

51. Schwartz, supra note 1, at 143.

52. Hall ed., supra note 10, at 88.

53. Schwartz, supra note 1, at 149.

54. Id. at 149–50. Another commentator also sees Justice Brennan as primarily concerned with "dignity." "According to Lexis, Brennan used the word 'dignity' in more than thirty opinions." Irons, *Brennan v. Rehnquist: The Battle for the Constitution* xi (1994).

55. 378 U.S. 184 (1964).

56. Id. at 197. The actual quote is, "But I know it when I see it, and the motion picture involved in this case is not that."

57. He was functionally correct: Virtually every news story recounting his death mentioned the phrase. See Schwartz, supra note 41, at 23.

58. Id. at 412.

59. Harris, *The Fine Art of Political Wit* 260 (1964).

60. Schwartz, supra note 41, at 27.

61. See Savage, "Thurgood Marshall, 84, Dies," *L. A. Times*, Jan. 25, 1993, at A1.

62. 332 U.S. 631 (1948).

63. 334 U.S. 1 (1948).

64. 347 U.S. 483 (1954).

65. In sundown towns, African Americans were not allowed out after dark. See Henry, "Foreword," in Fisher, *A Matter of Black and White*, xvi (1995).

66. See generally id.

67. Hall ed., supra note 10, at 128.

68. Id.

69. 410 U.S. 113 (1973).

70. 410 U.S. 1979 (1973).

71. 438 U.S. 265 (1978).

72. A useful critique of this opinion appears in Goldstein, *The Intelligible Constitution* 81–104 (1992).

73. Lewis, in Blasi ed., supra note 25, at ix.

74. Schwartz, supra note 41, at 12.

75. See Rummel v. Estelle, 445 U.S. 263, n. 27 (1980) (referencing Shakespeare's *Hamlet* and *Julius Caesar* in an apt analogy about the varying brutality of similar crimes); Milkovich v. Lorain Journal Co., 497 U.S. 1, 12 (1990) (quoting Shakespeare's *Othello* re reputation).

76. Remarks of the Chief Justice Washington College of Law Centennial Celebration, Panel: "The Future of the Federal Courts," American University, April 9, 1996. Copies available from the Supreme Court.

77. Schwartz, supra note 41, at 44.

78. For an explanation of how the certiorari pool works, see Rehnquist, supra note 43, at 263.

79. Schwartz, supra note 24, at 319.

80. "High Court's Rulings Not Always What They Seem," *The Sunday Oklahoman* (Associated Press), June 30, 1996, at A9.

81. 79 A.B.A. J. 48 (March 1993).

82. "Time's 25 Most Influential Americans," *Time*, June 17, 1996 at 57.

83. Greenhouse, "Warren E. Burger Is Dead at 87; Was Chief Justice for 17 Years," N.Y. *Times*, June 26, 1995, at A1.

84. Howard, "He Was Not What They Expected," *Nat'l L. J.*, July 10, 1995, at A20.

85. Hutchinson, "A Transitional Chief Justice with a Contradictory Record," *Nat'l L. J.*, July 10, 1995, at A20.

86. Hall ed., supra note 10, at 105.

87. Id.

88. Id. at 104–06.

89. 402 U.S. 1 (1971).

90. 413 U.S. 683 (1974).

91. Hutchinson, supra note 85, at A20.

92. Levy, "Anecdotage," 13 *Constitutional Commentary* 3 (1996).

93. Hutchinson, supra note 85, at A20.

94. Newman, supra note 13, at 598.

95. Schwartz, supra note 41, at 12.

96. Greenhouse, supra note 83, at C10.

97. F. Carolyn Graglia, who clerked for then-Judge Burger when he was on the D.C. Circuit, says that Chief Justice Burger himself claimed to be a "liberal." Her excellent tribute, his first law clerk's "Fond Memories of a Gracious Gentleman," appears in 74 *Tex. L. Rev.* 231. The "liberal" quote is at 235, where the "l" word appears at least four times.

98. Schwartz, supra note 41, at 398.

99. Schwartz indicates the downside of this technological triumph. Casual conferencing diminished as copies and computers flourished. Id. at 398–99.

100. Hutchinson, supra note 85, at A20.

101. Schwartz, supra note 41, at 8.

102. Hall ed., supra note 10, at 106.

103. Burger, "Foreword," *The Constitution of the United States* (Washington: Commission on the Bicentennial of the U.S. Constitution, 1986).

104. Blasi, "The Rootless Activism of the Burger Court," supra note 25, at 210–11; see also Schwartz, supra note 41, at 400–01.

105. Blasi ed., supra note 25, at 211.

106. Schwartz, supra note 41, at 400.

107. Schwartz, supra note 1, at 142 (emphasis added). Schwartz explains that the acknowledgement of Oliver Wendell Holmes's greatness was, for the most part, delayed until his dissents were adopted by later courts; in terms of overall influence, Holmes is still paramount. But in terms of influence in the decision process, Brennan prevails.

108. Id. at 143.

109. Dorsen, in Schwartz ed., supra note 22, at 248. I believe that in the oral presentation I heard Dorsen present at New York University he suggested a causal link between hostility of tone and later reversal rates. If so, we can wait a few years and find out if there is any merit to this plausible theory. See, e.g., Garrow, "One Angry Man," N.Y. *Times* (Magazine), Oct. 6, 1996, at 68–69. Garrow raises the obvious comparison of Frankfurter and Justice Scalia. Scalia's brilliance rivals Frankfurter's and his wit and personal charm are probably superior. But his strident dissents may diminish his legacy.

110 Pederson and Provizer, *Great Justices of the U.S. Supreme Court* (1993).

111 Schwartz, supra note 1, at 156.

112 I believe this analogy was made in the 1981 motion picture, *First Monday in October.*

113. Wolfe, supra note 9, at 292–93.

114. Blair ed., supra note 25, "Preface" to 1983 edition.

115. Graglia, supra note 97, at 233.

116. Remarks by Gerald Gunther, *Proceedings of the Forty-sixth Judicial Conference of the District of Columbia Circuit,* 111 F.R.D. 91, 250 (1985).

117. *Roe* is called "the paradigmatic Burger Court case." Schwartz, supra note 41, at 294.

118. 198 U.S. 45 (1905).

119. Gunther, supra note 116, at 250. Schwartz disagrees. His argument is that because only "fundamental rights" receive strict scrutiny under the Due Process Clause, this substantially narrows the revival of substantive due process. Schwartz, supra note 41, at 309.

120. Adkins v. Children's Hosp., 261 U.S. 525 (1923).

121. Bork, *The Tempting of America* 225 (1990). See also Ely, "The Wages of Crying Wolf: A Comment on *Roe v. Wade*," 82 *Yale L.J.* 920 (1973).

122. Ely, supra note 15, at 14–5.

123. In an article criticizing recent attacks on federal judges during the 1996 presidential campaign, Jeffrey Rosen observed that Clinton appointees Ruth Bader Ginsburg and Stephen Breyer adopted judicially restrained views arguing that judges should defer to the decisions of Congress on the constitutionality of federal laws concerning minority set-asides, voting rights, expansion of federal criminal jurisdiction, and federal civil rights protections. Rosen noted that this restraint led these Justices "to conservative as well as liberal results." Rosen, "Benchmarked," *The New Republic,* May 27, 1996, at 12.

124. Schwartz, supra note 41, at 405 (quoting Truax v. Corrigan, 257 U.S. 312, 344 (1921)).

125. Griswold v. Connecticut, 381 U.S. 479 (1965).

126. Ferguson v. Skrupa, 372 U.S. 726, 731–32 (1963) (citations omitted).

127. Blasi ed., supra note 25, at 200.

128. Posner, supra note 14, at 279.

129. Schwartz, supra note 41, at 408. See also Blasi ed., supra note 25, at 200. "The Warren Court struck down, on average, barely more than one federal statute each term; the Burger Court invalidated Federal laws at twice that rate." See also Howard, infra note 132 at 67.

130. INS v. Chadha, 462 U.S. 919 (1983).

131. Bowsher v. Synar, 478 U.S. 714 (1986).

132. Blasi ed., supra note 25, at 200. "Without question, though, it [the Burger Court] was an activist court." See also Howard, "Chief Enigma," *A.B.A. J.*, Oct. 1995, at 66.

133. 418 U.S. 683 (1974).

134. Blasi ed., supra note 25, at 201.

135. 403 U.S. 713 (1971).

136. 433 U.S. 425 (1977).

137. 424 U.S. 1 (1976).

138. 408 U.S. 238 (1972).

139. Schwartz, supra note 41, at 409–10.

140. See Plyler v. Doe, 457 U.S. 202, 242 (1982) (Burger, C.J., dissenting).

141. This was the phrase high school geometry books used to employ when they could not figure out how to explain an assumption. For Plato to value an observation, it would indeed need to be intuitively obvious.

142. Ely, supra note 15, at 248, n. 52.

143. Wolfe, supra note 9, at 293.

144. Miranda v. Arizona, 384 U.S. 436 (1966).

145. Mapp v. Ohio, 367 U.S. 1043 (1961).

146. Gideon v. Wainwright, 372 U.S. 335 (1965).

147. Kamisar, "The Warren Court (Was It Really So Defense-Minded?), The Burger Court (Is It Really So Prosecution-Oriented?), and Police Investigatory Practices," in Blasi ed., supra note 25, at 64.

148. 358 U.S. 307 (1959).

149. 385 U.S. 293 (1966).

150. 383 U.S. 206 (1966).

151. 392 U.S. 1 (1968).

152. 399 U.S. 1 (1970).

153. 407 U.S. 25 (1972).

154. 399 U.S. 30 (1970).

155. 443 U.S. 47 (1979).

156. 466 U.S. 740 (1984).

157. 445 U.S. 573 (1980).

158. 451 U.S. 204 (1981).

159. See Wolfe, supra note 9, at 293 (the general approach to judicial review was the same: both were "balanced," and had modern conceptions of judicial power); Bork, supra note 121, at 101 (both Burger and Rehnquist Courts legislated policy and were more liberal than the American people).

160. Arenella, "Rethinking the Functions of Criminal Procedure: The Warren and Burger Courts' Competing Ideologies," 72 *Geo. L.J.* 185, 186 (1983). Note also Dean Belsky's essay later in this volume. He perceptively and persuasively argues that prosecutors and police felt a difference in the Courts and were encouraged if not assisted by the difference.

161. Schwartz, supra note 41, at 411–12.

162. Schwartz, *Main Currents in American Legal Thought* 8–23, 53–74 (1993). Sherman Edwards's delightful musical "1776" takes some liberties but captivatingly describes the first collaboration of these two great founders (G. Schirmer, Inc., New York).

163. Id. at 17.

164. Schwartz, supra note 41, at 413.

165. 376 U.S. 254 (1964).

166. See Lewis, *Make No Law: The Sullivan Case and the First Amendment* (1991).

167. H. Schwartz, *Introduction to the Burger Years* xii (H. Schwartz ed., 1987). The six were Warren Burger, Harry Blackmun, Lewis Powell, William Rehnquist, John Paul Stevens, and Sandra Day O'Connor.

168. Remarks made at the Institute of Judicial Advocacy breakfast at the American Bar Association Annual Meeting, Aug. 5, 1996, in Orlando, Florida.

169. 347 U.S. 483 (1954).

170. 163 U.S. 537 (1896).

171. See Noonan and Wilson, *The Responsible Judge* 67–82 (1993).

172. Schwartz, *Superchief: Earl Warren and His Supreme Court* 429 (1983).

173. E.g., Swann v. Charlotte-Mecklenburg B. of Educ., 402 U.S. 1 (1971) (allowed busing to achieve racial desegregation); Keyes v. Denver Cent. School Dist. No. 1, 413 U.S. 189 (1973) (first nonsouthern school desegregation case).

174. Perhaps not personally "benignly": Two prominent academics with excellent credentials seem to have been prevented from becoming federal judges because of their views on *Brown:* Lino Graglia and Bernard Siegan. See Posner, supra note 14, at 247, n. 13.

175. The debate over *Brown's* commanded school integration has shifted all the way from whether we should have it (now that affirmative action-like solutions are increasingly suspect) to whether educational goals including diversity and pluralism may survive strict scrutiny as a compelling governmental interest. (This argument may test whether Justice O'Connor was correct in the observation she made in *Adarand* that strict scrutiny is no longer "strict in theory, but fatal in fact." Adarand Constructors, Inc. v. Pena, 115 S. Ct. 2097, 2117 (1995).)

176. Schwartz, supra note 41, at 404.

177. See "Earl Warren: Interview on Justice in America," 19 *The Annals of America* 37 (1974).

178. See, e.g., Morgan, England, and Humphreys, *Oklahoma Politics and Policies* (1957) ("The Old Guard suffered an even greater setback when . . . *Baker v. Carr* . . . finally forced Oklahoma, along with all state legislatures, to reapportion on the basis of 'one man, one vote.'" Also at 81 ("no change has been more important than the reapportionment of the legislature [which] followed . . . *Baker v. Carr.*").

179. See Wolfe, supra note 9, at 266. Harlan also suggested that state models based on factors other than population (e.g., the U.S. Senate) were reasonable.

180. Colegrove v. Green, 328 U.S. 549, 556 (1946).

181. Schwartz, supra note 41, at 407.

182. Lucas v. 44th Gen. Assembly, 377 U.S. 713, 746 (1964) (Clark and Stewart, J.J., dissenting). See also Wolfe, supra note 9, at 267.

183. Gray v. Sanders, 372 U.S. 368, 381 (1963).

184. Wolfe, supra note 9, at 267.

185. Kasmisar wrote an excellent article on the Burger Court in Blasi ed., supra note 25, at 66. See also "The Police Practice Phases of the Criminal Process and the Three Phases of the Burger Court," in Lewis, supra note 166, at 143.

186. Id. at 154.

187. 446 U.S. 291 (1980). See Kamisar, in Blasi ed., supra note 25, at 66.

188. 451 U.S. 477 (1981).

189. Kamisar, in Blasi ed., supra note 25, at 144.

190. Id.

191. Note, however, that Kamisar suggests that the Warren Court in its last two years engaged itself in "a process of reexamination, correction, consolidation, erosion, or retreat. . . ." Kamisar, in Blasi ed., supra note 25, at 67.

192. 401 U.S. 222 (1971).

193. 467 U.S. 649 (1984).

194. 475 U.S. 412 (1986).

195. 417 U.S. 433, 446 (1974).

196. 470 U.S. 298, 309 (1985).

197. 446 U.S. at 304.

198. Schwartz, supra note 41, at 358.

199. 403 U.S. 388, 420 (1971).

200. 468 U.S. 897 (1984).

201. 468 U.S. 981, 987–88 (1984).

202. 468 U.S. 1032 (1984).

203. See Schwartz, supra note 41, at 364.

204. Id. at 362–64.

205. 407 U.S. 25 (1972).

206. 399 U.S. 1 (1970).

207. 422 U.S. 806 (1975).

208. I cannot leave the retrenchment in the criminal law area without noting the changes in habeas corpus. In Stone v. Powell, 428 U.S. 465 (1976), Justice Powell (no relation to the respondent, as you might guess) writing for the Court, held:

> Where the State has provided an opportunity for full and fair litigation of a Fourth Amendment claim, a state prisoner may not be granted federal habeas corpus relief on the ground that the evidence obtained in an unconstitutional search and seizure was introduced at his trial.

The decision again involved a cost-benefit conclusion. Further, in Wainwright v. Sykes, 433 U.S. 72 (1977), Engle v. Isaac, 456 U.S. 107 (1982), and United States v. Frady, 456 U.S. 152 (1982), the Court left no doubt that the so-called "cause-and-prejudice" standard had become the dominant standard for assessing procedural defaults. That meant that adequate and independent state laws that could uphold a conviction would trump federal jurisdiction. The Great Writ was on the way to becoming the (Not So) Great Writ, a process almost completed by the 104th Congress. The explosive growth of prison habeas cases, many clearly frivolous, seems to have tipped the cost-benefit analysis, rendering habeas a most unlikely form of relief.

209. The very term "activism" in any kind of judicial context is a modern-day lightning rod. Of course, activism is of different kinds and is often in the eye of the beholder. Judge Posner's brilliant jurisprudential work on this subject should be more widely read, especially his highly acclaimed recent volume *Overcoming Law*.

Many observers think of judicial activism as an unprincipled and constitutionally unmoored effort to create law in the image of the activist judge whose reach has just exceeded his grasp. That rarely occurs and recently with even less frequency. Grabs (or grasps) such as *Dred Scott*, *Lochner*, and *Brown v. Board* have achieved mixed results. *Dred Scott* is today universally condemned; *Brown* is almost universally praised; *Lochner* is largely disfavored but has some new adherents, as I later discuss.

I seek to briefly discuss the various kinds of activism, some of which I term "constitutional activism," "statutory activism," and "activism in reverse." In fact, the common-law creation function, which still exists in federal law, and in reality must exist, is also perhaps one kind of activism.

My goal is not to defend or attack activism but to analyze it. Paradigm-shifting activism frightens me, but like most observers I see its rare place in our jurisprudence. *Marbury* and *Brown* are good examples of its positive use; *Dred Scott* is a great example of the perils.

Part of the tension of "activism" is lyrically described in Sanford Levinson's revision of Robert McCloskey's *The American Supreme Court* (2nd ed. 1994). Concluding his "Coda," Levinson states, "The Supreme Court will remain fascinating, for good or for ill, so long as there is a United States that tries to resolve the tension between popular sovereignty and adherence to fundamental norms even when the majority would prefer to ignore them." Id. at 222. Thankfully, the majority is not always so obstreperous.

210. President Nixon's hostility toward Chief Justice Warren cannot be explained by his only venture as an advocate before the Court. In that case, Time v. Hill, 385 U.S. 374 (1964), Nixon argued well but lost, though both Chief Justice Warren and perhaps his staunchest critic on the Court, Justice Fortas, voted with him. See Schwartz, *Decision: How the Supreme Court Decides Cases* 174–177 (1996). See also Newman, supra note 13, at 590. This curious figure of modern American politics, at times brilliant, at times base, was perhaps the last President for some time whose resumé will reflect an oral argument before the Court.

211. Howard, supra note 132, at 66.

212. People v. Defore, 150 N.E. 585, 587 (N.Y. 1926).

213. "It is better that ten guilty persons escape than one innocent suffer," 4 Blackstone, *Commentaries.* Voltaire made a similar point in *Zadig* ch. 6 "It is better to risk saving a guilty person than to condemn an innocent one."

214. Several federal judges in the South did experience considerable retribution. See, e.g., Weaver, *Then to the Rock Let Me Fly: Luther Bohanan and Judicial Activism* (1993).

215. See Posner, supra note 14, at 237–55.

216.

> "Judicial Restraint" sounds like the reasonable notion that judges should not intrude on legislative and executive prerogatives. But in practice, Attorney General Edwin Meese III, Chief Justice Rehnquist, and others who share their views have given it a variable content. They support judicial restraint when the judiciary is asked to protect civil rights and civil liberties; while they unabashedly favor an energetic activism when it comes to curtailing such rights and liberties, or to promoting business interests.

Schwartz, supra note 163, at xvii–xviii.

217. Bowsher v. Synar, 478 U.S. 714 (1986); Schwartz, in Schwartz ed., supra note 167, at xviii.

218. 44 *Cong. Q.* 616 (Mar. 15, 1986); Schwartz, in Schwartz ed., supra note 167, at xix–xx.

219. Herman Schwartz criticizes Attorney General Meese as well for his attacks on Chief Justice Taney's decision in Dred Scott v. Sandford, 60 U.S. (19 How.) 393 (U.S. 1857), as inconsistent with the Attorney General's praise for *Brown.* The inconsistency of this analysis—suggesting that Taney's reading of the Constitution as supporting racial distinctions was activist and Warren's overturning of Plessy v. Ferguson, 163 U.S. 537 (1896), was not—is difficult to explain from the originalist point of view. See Schwartz, in Schwartz ed., supra note 163, at xxi.

220. I find that my views on restraint are the same today as those I expressed at my swearing in ceremony:

> Appellate judges are restrained by the Constitution, thank God, whose masterful generalities and important amendments have created the finest government a large populace yet produced.
> Judges are restrained by the legal system in America, by our common law school education, by the Bar, by our friends and especially by those friends of ours

who are judges at the trial level whom we know and respect. Judges are restrained by the law and tradition, as well they should be. But judges, like legislators, executives and citizens, all share a responsibility to keep the courts open, so that the aggrieved, whether multi-national corporations or pro se prisoners, can have their day in court.

If not Elysian, these views are at least Elyian. A transcription of these remarks is available at the Tenth Circuit Library in Denver.

221. Schwartz, supra note 41, at 497–506. However, as noted at 506, Frankfurter's restraintism may be heard more clearly now than then. And, further complicating the analysis of this complicated man, Justice Frankfurter did go to great lengths to support and foster the rule in *Brown v. Board of Education.*

222. Id. at 25. "It was Hamilton who helped lay the groundwork for some essential principles of American public law—notably the doctrine of judicial review and that of implied powers." See also *The Federalist* No. 78. As to Marshall's inestimable contributions, only the same two need be listed to make the point: Marbury v. Madison, 5 U.S. (1 Cranch) 137 (1803); McCulloch v. Maryland, 17 U.S. (4 Wheat.) 316 (1819). Furthermore, Jefferson—critic of judicial activism that he sometimes was—also employed instrumentalist activism, especially in authorizing the Louisiana Purchase, which turns out to have been a good idea as well. See Schwartz, supra note 162 at 53.

223. See Anastaplo, *The Constitution of 1787* (1989). Anastaplo's analysis of the various "constitutions" that have governed us deserves thoughtful consideration. It is ludicrous to dismiss from our culture, politics, and law these great constitutions, including, as he argues, the English language itself. Further, the great historian Leo Strauss emphasized the importance that the Declaration of Independence contributes to our traditions and to the spare but meaningful terms.

224. 2 Corinthians 3:6; 1 *Legal Papers of Alexander Hamilton* 359 (Julius Goebel ed., 1965) (Hamilton's notes from argument in *Rutgers v. Waddington* that "in law as in religion letter kills). See also Horwitz, "Foreword: The Constitution of Change: Legal Foundationalism," 107 *Harv. L. Rev.* 32, 48–51 (1993) (suggesting that differences in constitutional ideas of Jefferson and Marshall may relate to their differing religious backgrounds). See also Henry, "Catching the Jurisprudential Wave: Bernard Schwartz's *Main Currents in American Legal Thought,*" 33 *Tulsa L. J.* 385 (1997).

225. 369 U.S. 186 (1963).

226. Posner, supra note 14, at 11.

227. Ely, supra note 15, at 181, persuasively suggests that activism should be limited to areas of participation. This is in opposition to Professor Bickel's suggestion, discussed id. at 103. Ely's theory would allow for *Brown* and *Baker*; I am not sure it covers *Marbury.*

228. Posner, supra note 14, at 243.

229. Blasi ed., supra note 25, at 209.

230. Howard, *The Death of Common Sense* (1994). Howard might disagree with Blasi that courts currently provide simplified resolution of some complicated issues. However, he would hope, I believe, that restoring more common sense (and common law) judgment in the law would clearly result in simplified resolution of complex issues.

231. Blasi ed., supra note 25, at 209.

232. Id.

233. United States v. Carolene Prods. Co., 304 U.S. 144, 152–53 n. 4, ¶ 2 (1938). See also Ely, supra note 15, at 75–6.

234. Public choice gets complicated fast. One definition often used is that of Mueller in *Public Choice* II (1989): "[T]he economic study of non-market decision making, or simply

the application of economics to political science," quoted in Farber and Frickey, *Law and Public Choice: A Critical Introduction* 7 (1991). Eskridge and Frickey's text, *Cases and Materials on Legislation: Statutes and Their Creation of Public Policy* (1988), has an excellent summary of public choice.

235. Farber and Frickey, supra note 234, at 20 (quoting David Mayhew).

236. Chief Justice Rehnquist recently suggested this very thing. "Congress could simply have assumed that the courts would sort out such questions. . . ." Lindh v. Murphy, 117 S. Ct. 2059, 2069 (1997) (Rehnquist, J., dissenting).

237. Farber and Frickey, supra note 234, at 63.

238. Posner, supra note 14, at 244–45.

239. Posner, *The Problems of Jurisprudence* 238 (1997).

240. Schwartz, supra note 1, at 5.

241. After preparing this essay I noted that Professor Burt Neuborne concluded that the 1995–96 term of the current Court shows "one of the most activist courts you can imagine. . . . It reaches in and defends fundamental values and is not afraid to do that." See "Term Reveals Pragmatic Supreme Court," *Nat'l L. J.*, July 29, 1996, at C2.

242. See Wolfe, supra note 9, at 297–98, adherence to precedent may be misplaced reliance: "The rule of law [in criminal defendant's rights] would seem likely to profit . . . from a willingness to overturn precedents . . . [to return] to the framers' intent. . . ."

243. Schwartz, supra note 162, at 576; that this Takings Clause jurisprudence is clearly activist is suggested by Judge Bork, supra note 121, at 230: "Epstein has written a powerful work of political theory, one eminently worth reading in those terms, but has not convincingly located that political theory in the Constitution."

244. Blasi ed., supra note 25, at ix.

245. Irons, supra note 54, at xi.

246. Alexander Hamilton, during his oral argument in *Rutgers v. Waddington*, also attested it seems, to "living traditions," through his powerful scriptural allusion to the second Letter of St. Paul to the Corinthians, that the letter kills but the spirit gives life. See 2 Corinthians 3:6; 1 *Legal Papers of Alexander Hamilton* 359 (Goebel ed., 1965) (Hamilton's notes from argument in *Rutgers v. Waddington* read "in law as in religion letter kills").

247. Pound, *Interpretations of Legal History* 1 (1923). See also Schwartz, supra note 162, at 164.

· I ·

THE
CONSTITUTIONAL
CORPUS

THE BURGER COURT'S PLACE ON THE BELL CURVE OF RACIAL JURISPRUDENCE

DERRICK BELL

If, as the cynics maintain, no good deed goes unpunished, it may follow that bearers of unwelcome truth cannot expect a just reward this side of Heaven. Lewis Steel, a young lawyer on the NAACP's national legal staff, learned this lesson the hard way when, almost thirty years ago, he wrote an article titled "Nine Men in Black Who Think White."[1]

Chief Justice Earl Warren's imminent retirement in 1968 sparked a national debate regarding the political orientation of his successor. Steel acknowledged that each Justice has some effect on the Court's direction, and that the power struggle over the appointment of a new Chief Justice was not irrelevant to the freedom struggle. He maintained, though, that the pattern of decisions in the racial field indicates that it is not the thinking of individual Justices but the philosophy of the entire Court on civil rights that has not moved out of the shadow of the nineteenth century's racist decisions.

In scathing terms, Steel condemned both the Warren Court's conservative critics and the egalitarians' stale defenses because, he argued, a hard analysis of the Court's race-related decisions reveals "an institution which has not departed from the American tradition of treating Negroes as second-class citizens." While acknowledging the Warren Court's invalidation of the most egregious racial laws, in Steel's view, these decisions actually tracked other American institutions that, inspired by the triumph over Nazi racism in World War II, and embarrassed by the rigidity of racial segregation here at home, were abandoning overtly discriminatory policies in favor of positions that made it appear that racial equality had become part of their public policy.

Citing executive orders banning discrimination to recipients of government contracts, the desegregation of the military forces, and the enactment of antidiscrimination laws in a number of states, Steel maintained that the *Brown* decision[2] and the series of decisions that followed invalidating segregated public facilities did little more than bring the Court up-to-date. By 1954, Steel asserted, the Court could have served notice on the American people that equality was an absolute right, one that came before all other rights, and that its further subversion would not be tolerated. Instead, Steel wrote, the Court delayed any action for a year and then ordered school desegregation in such vague terms as to virtually invite and certainly encourage the entrenched resistance that followed.

Stripped of its rhetoric of judicial prudence, Steel charged that the Court delayed school desegregation because it "considered the potential damage to white Americans resulting from the diminution of privilege" that segregation had provided them, deeming this harm as more critical than continued damage to black people in the educational, economic, and psychological forms the Court itself had acknowledged in the *Brown* decision. Surveying the Warren Court's work in the racial area, Steel found the Court "struck down only the symbols of racism while condoning or overlooking the ingrained practices which have meant the survival of white supremacy in the United States, North and South."

Steel's piece was obviously insightful at the time even if its expression was not politic. In 1968, though, civil rights advocates were hailing the Court's decision in *Green v. New Kent County*[3] rejecting delaying schemes such as freedom-of-choice plans and finally requiring the elimination of segregated schools, "root and branch." With literally hundreds of stalled school cases awaiting application of these long-awaited orders, few of us were ready to publicly find fault with the U.S. Supreme Court. And, absolutely none of the Court's few liberal critics held a seat on the NAACP's national board. Most of them viewed the Supreme Court as the savior of blacks or at least their best hope of eliminating racial discrimination. Unfortunately for Steel and, as it turned out, for the whole civil rights movement, the NAACP's national board met in New York City on the Monday morning following publication of Lewis Steel's article. To put it mildly, they were appalled and outraged. They denounced Steel's article and summarily fired its author.[4]

When then NAACP general counsel, Robert L. Carter, was unable to get the Board to rescind its discharge order, or even give Steel a hearing, Carter and the rest of the legal staff resigned in protest. It is fair to say that the NAACP legal staff was never the same. It is also accurate to note that the uncritical Warren Court worship by the nation's leading civil rights organization, typical of most liberal groups, provided the foundation for a range of criticisms of the Burger Court that were as applicable to many of the actions—and nonactions—of the Warren years.

Of course, both the Warren and Burger Courts were more supportive of blacks seeking racial justice than any of their predecessors and, as it is turning out, their successor, the Rehnquist Court. But, as Steel charged, the Court in both the Warren and Burger eras was far more ready to invalidate overtly discriminatory policies that ended indefensible restrictions on the rights of blacks than it was willing to tackle the more subtle rules that do not create blatant racial classifications but in their racist administration are as pernicious as the most flagrant Jim Crow signs.

This pattern became clear even in the Court's implementation of its *Brown* precedent.

We now know that the Warren Court's "all deliberate speed" standard in *Brown II*[5] actually meant no substantive school desegregation orders for a dozen years. School cases decided during this period, such as *Cooper v. Aaron*[6] and *Griffin v. Prince Edward County*,[7] served more to uphold the Court's authority than to advance the desegregation of the schools. The Court also refused to review a series of conservative appellate court decisions which upheld so-called de facto school segregation in northern cities.[8]

Years earlier, civil rights lawyers decided to attack segregation in the public schools as the weak link in the Jim Crow chain.[9] Their strategy proved effective, but in the wake of the *Brown* decision, the Court, having returned the school cases to the quagmire of lower courts, relied on the precedent in issuing a series of decrees which slowly struck down segregation in public transportation, public facilities, and recreational areas, all overtly discriminatory practices in the southern and border states. Frustrated by the snail pace of desegregation, thousands of civil rights protesters turned to an innovative array of marches, sit-ins, picket lines, and boycotts.

Perhaps the Warren Court's main contribution to the civil rights movement was its reversal on various due process grounds of many of, but far from all, those convictions under disorderly conduct and breach-of-the-peace laws. The Court found these laws too vague or overbroad to sustain convictions of those arrested while peacefully protesting Jim Crow policies in public facilities. The Court's support encouraged those willing to take to the streets in often dangerous confrontations with local forces committed to preserving the status quo, but they also served notice on law enforcement agencies and facilities owners that segregation could not be enforced via peace and order laws.

Recognizing that they could no longer use laws to enforce segregation, and with the presence of television curbing the resort to violence—the traditional means of maintaining the racial order—government officials and business owners negotiated the desegregation of public facilities in cities and towns across the South.

I agree with Lewis Steel, though, that these reversals won the approval of many whites who viewed the blacks and their white supporters as humble supplicants seeking succor from white America. And it must be said that whenever the conviction records contained evidence of disorder by the demonstrators—as opposed to the frequently violent reaction by whites—the Court denied review. In short, while protesting the maintenance of Jim Crow laws including those the Court had invalidated years earlier, the Warren Court required blacks to be peaceful, even submissive, in the face of hostile attacks and hateful provocations.

By the mid-1960s, however, the public's sympathetic view of even peaceful protests changed, and the Court's attitude changed as well. The Court, in *Cox v. Louisiana*, warned demonstrators that the right to protest could be limited, and then in cases involving protests no less peaceful than earlier ones in which convictions were reversed, the Court upheld convictions outside a jail.[10] It also refused to overturn a contempt conviction of Dr. Martin Luther King, Jr., based on King's refusal to obey a state court injunction barring protest marches in Birmingham.[11]

This more harsh approach was consistent with growing anxieties of whites who felt blacks were "moving too fast." In apparent reaction to these concerns, the Court began accepting southern state officials' protestations that they had acted in good faith in halting peaceful protests with arrests and prosecutions. In *Cameron v. Johnson*,[12] for example, the denial of injunctive relief based on this acceptance flew in the face of common experience. The Mississippi legislature enacted a statute to halt voter registration picketing at the courthouse in Hattiesburg, Mississippi.

The very next day, thirty-five to forty persons were arrested, effectively ending the protest.

The loss of support was felt by the NAACP directly when the Court refused to review a huge money judgment awarded against the organization by Georgia courts in a suit seeking damages for picketing.[13] Earlier, the Court had protected the NAACP against the hostility of state entities in landmark decisions, *NAACP v. Alabama*[14] and *NAACP v. Button*,[15] which enhanced First Amendment protections for all citizens.

In the area of property rights, the Court struck down California's famous Proposition 14 intended to repeal existing and bar future enactment of fair housing laws,[16] the Court finding that the referendum was state action that served as an unconstitutional "encouragement" of racial discrimination. The case, along with its famous pre-*Brown* predecessor, *Shelley v. Kraemer*[17] barring judicial enforcement of restrictive covenants, is generally seen as a strong statement of judicial support for racial equality, but it has proven of little actual value to blacks seeking housing in areas wishing to exclude them. Arguably, both cases, like the early twentieth-century decision in *Buchanan v. Warley*,[18] striking down a city ordinance requiring residential segregation based on the majority race living in a particular neighborhood, served the interests of free alienability of land against state interference as much as they did the civil rights interests of blacks.

Jones v. Alfred H. Mayer Co.[19] broadened the rights of individuals seeking relief for housing discrimination. The decision, though, came as Congress was enacting the Fair Housing Act of 1968, and after the Court refused to become involved in cases challenging the use of urban renewal funds to remove blacks from suddenly desirable urban areas and to otherwise perpetuate segregated housing conditions.[20] As Lewis Steel claimed, favorable action in the urban renewal area, where the effect of local, state, and federal action on housing is greater than that of any individual, would have done far more to aid ordinary black people than all the other housing cases put together.

The supersensitive area of interracial sex and marriage provides a final example of how the Warren Court balanced the civil rights of blacks against the prejudices of whites. While promptly applying the *Brown* precedent to segregated public facilities, the Court, during the same term in which it decided *Brown*, refused to review the Alabama conviction of a black man who married a white woman.[21] During the following two terms, in *Naim v. Naim*, the Court shamelessly avoided review of Virginia antimiscegenation law in 1955 and 1956.[22] Finally, a decade after *Brown*, the Court evidently felt that the societal myths, fears, and economic concerns that led to the enactment of miscegenation statutes some three centuries before had abated and struck down a Florida statute setting more severe penalties for interracial than intraracial cohabitation and adultery.[23] Three years later, it declared Virginia's law against racially mixed marriages unconstitutional.[24]

There are more illustrations of this pattern of balancing black rights against white interests in retaining advantages and expectations based at least in part on past and continuing policies of racial discrimination, but these illustrations of the Warren Court's "racial balancing" provide a workable measure for evaluating the Burger Court's racial decisions. Indeed, if a "black value weight" of say one to ten were assigned to each civil rights decision, and then the decisions were arrayed in a line based on this value, the resulting frequency distribution would form a bell curve. My statistical reference is intended as analogy rather than analysis. The Court's decisions do not easily allow themselves to be plotted or weighed, but in rough fashion, the shape of the bell curve of racial decisions is influenced more by the ever-changing concerns of whites than by the continuing quest for racial justice by blacks.

There are similarities in the Warren and Burger Courts' decisions in racial cases in that the early years brought the more liberal decisions. During the Warren Court, as Lewis Steel suggested, the post–World War II desire to eliminate the most blatant forms of racial segregation, and the insistent demands by blacks for its elimination, helped push the Court to *Brown* and the series of desegregation decisions that followed it.

For the Burger Court, a major though unacknowledged influence for its pro–civil rights decisions in the late 1960s and early 1970s were the large number of race riots or urban rebellions that occurred during these years. These were particularly intense following Dr. Martin Luther King, Jr's murder in the spring of 1968 and provided dramatic emphasis to the warning in the 1969 Kerner Commission Report that "our nation is moving toward two societies, one black, one white — separate and unequal."[25]

In addition to a great deal of law-and-order rhetoric condemning riots, most of what we now call affirmative action programs were initiated during this period. And, it is hardly fortuitous that the Burger Court's two most far-reaching civil rights cases, *Griggs v. Duke Power Co.*[26] and *Swann v. Charlotte-Mecklenburg County School District*,[27] were both decided in 1971, with strong opinions in both written by Chief Justice Burger. In *Griggs*, he gave a broad interpretation to Title VII, the fair employment provision of the Civil Rights Act of 1964, finding the Act prohibited job qualifications that had a disparately adverse impact on covered applicants unless the requirements were shown to be closely related to job performance. And in *Swann*, a decade-old school desegregation case, Burger set out standards for eliminating a dual-school system, approving in the process busing and the use of quotas to measure the achievement of racial balance. Two years later, in *Keyes v. School District No. 1, Denver*,[28] the Court applied similar standards to a northern school desegregation case.

Civil rights advocates hailed both decisions, ignoring the tremendous opposition they engendered and the many politicians ready to ride that opposition into office. We were not deterred. Opposition was the norm in school desegregation cases and with the Court's willingness to order busing and to measure progress by the degree to which the percentages of black and white children in the district were represented in each school, we felt we had the formula through which to realize—at last—the promise of *Brown*. It worked in smaller districts and in larger districts, like Charlotte-Mecklenburg, where the boundaries were countywide. But in many urban districts, like Detroit, white flight was swiftly turning majority white districts into mainly black ones. A new tactic was needed.

Multidistrict desegregation plans seemed the answer. In Detroit, both the district court and the court of appeals found the necessary state involvement in what by the early 1970s was a mostly black Detroit, surrounded by fifty or so mainly white suburban districts. In a close 5–4 decision, the Court, speaking through Chief Justice Burger, agreed that the record contained evidence of de jure conditions in Detroit but no significant violations in the suburban districts. State involvement in the discrimination, the Court found, did not justify interdistrict relief.[29] The proponents who believed that racial balance was the best means to desegregate the public schools pushed on, but the tremendous opposition by whites to metropolitanwide plans, the lukewarm enthusiasm of blacks, and the absence of support from the other arms of government, almost certainly influenced the Court's majority.

Two years later, white opposition to granting black rights at the expense of white prerogatives was probably as influential in the more crucial decision in *Washington v. Davis*.[30] Under it, to gain relief against a discriminatory policy, plaintiffs must show a "discriminatory racial purpose." A showing that in practice, the policy has a disparate effect on blacks is insufficient if the policy is race neutral on its face and it serves a legitimate public function. The Court in refusing to extend the disparate impact standard of *Griggs v. Duke Power Co.*, to equal protection claims, effectively raised beyond reach the barriers to relief in a range of cases in housing, criminal justice, and education. But, it explained, a disproportionate impact standard would be far reaching and would raise serious questions about, and perhaps invalidate, a whole range of tax, welfare, public service, regulatory, and licensing statutes.[31]

The slippery-slope argument is significant because lower court cases applying a disproportionate impact test prior to *Davis* were extremely restrained. In addition, policies with overtly discriminatory purposes had virtually disappeared, replaced by a vast array of race-neutral rules intended to advantage whites while excluding or greatly limiting access to blacks. Slowly, but with certainty, the Court was reverting to its nineteenth-century myopia of color blindness in those racial cases in which the policies under review were not so blatant as to embarrass whites as well as discriminate against blacks.

The Burger Court provided some civil rights victories both before and after *Washington v. Davis*, many of them in areas of much political controversy.[32] In *Milliken v. Bradley II*,[33] the Court approved a lower court order requiring a series of "educational components" in the Detroit school desegregation case and requiring the state to pay for many of them. And it rejected an effort by the Mississippi legislature to subsidize private schools that discriminated against blacks.[34] It also responded with a firm "yes" to the question in *Bob Jones University v. United States*[35] whether the Internal Revenue Code could be read to require denial or revocation of tax-exempt status to private religious schools that engage in racial discrimination based on religious belief. To enforce its religious prohibition on interracial marriage, Bob Jones first barred all black students, and later admitted only black students who were married. Later, in *Palmore v. Sidoti*,[36] the Court held that racial considerations could not be the determinative factor in custody cases.

In the voting area, the Burger Court's record is as mixed as its decision in *United Jewish Organizations of Williamsburgh, Inc. v. Carey*[37] was controversial. There it approved the intentional creation of a "safe" black congressional voting district despite the fact that it divided and diluted the vote of a Jewish community.

But four years later, and now committed to the intent standard of *Washington v. Davis* as the appropriate means of balancing the interest of black voters with those urging retention of the political status quo, the Court destroyed the carefully wrought voting standards evolved by lower courts by holding, in *City of Mobile v. Bolden*,[38] that the Voting Rights Act did not authorize judicial relief in vote-dilution cases in the absence of proof that the discrimination alleged was intentionally imposed. The decision prompted a major effort by civil rights advocates for congressional clarification of the Voting Rights Act, a campaign that was finally successful.

In the affirmative action area, the Burger Court's decisions reflected the public's ambivalence. The closely divided *Bakke*[39] case, in 1978, barred racial quotas while permitting the consideration of race in the decision-making process. Later the Court approved a federal government set-aside program in *Fullilove v. Klutznick*[40] but rejected in *Wygant v. Jackson Board of Education*[41] a teachers collective bargaining agreement with a school district providing that layoffs would be accomplished to protect the school's racial balance. With racial history air-brushed out of the picture, the Court's plurality viewed the issue as whether the Equal Protection Clause allowed school boards to extend preferential protection against layoffs to some of its employees because of their race or national origin. Acknowledging that race might have to be considered to carry out the *Brown* mandate, the plurality, nevertheless, rejected a plan agreed to by both the school district and the union because "layoffs impose the entire burden of achieving racial equality on particular individuals, [referred to as "innocent whites"] often resulting in serious disruption of their lives. That burden is too intrusive."[42]

The *Wygant* decision served notice that members of the innocent white majority would become the "discrete and insular" minority entitled to strict scrutiny review. In the Rehnquist Court, this reversal of the traditional equal protection reading has resulted in the rejection of affirmative action–type remedies in education, voting, employment, and set-aside contracts. But the tension between meaningful relief for blacks and the protection of white expectations based in part on the systemic exclusion of blacks—with the usual resolution of that tension in favor of whites—did not begin with the Rehnquist, Burger, or Warren Courts. It has been the unacknowledged assumption of the society from the beginning when the framers ignored petitions urging that slavery be banned in the new government, then recognized and protected it in the nation's basic law. The periodic attempts to correct racial inequities—beginning with the Emancipation Proclamation—are always motivated as much by the expectation that those remedies will benefit whites as that they will alleviate injustices against blacks.

It follows that the availability of relief for racial discrimination is not determined by the character of harm suffered by blacks or the degree of responsibility for that harm proved against whites. Rather, racial remedies are the outward manifestations of unspoken and perhaps unconscious judicial conclusions that the remedies, if granted, will secure or advance societal interests deemed important by the upper classes.

Racial justice or its appearance may, from time to time, be counted among the interests deemed important by a majority of the Court and society's policymakers. Even then, though, opposition can be expected from poorer whites, many of whom view any remedy for blacks as an unfair preference. They can be expected to oppose and challenge even those remedies—like affirmative action—that can and do improve their status as much or more than that of blacks.[43]

My conclusions, like those of Lewis Steel, apply to the Warren and the Burger Court as well as to their predecessors and successors. They each have some potential for providing aid to a still-beleaguered people, but when racial hostility is high, and the sense that blacks are infringing on white prerogatives is great, both history and current experience teach us that the Court is as likely to shield the status quo of the majority as to protect the always fragile equality rights of the nation's black citizens.

I see no basis for predicting any change in this historic pattern of race decisions and a number of signs—particularly the transformation of the economy—indicating that living conditions for a great many blacks and far more whites will worsen over the next several years. American industry and government are replacing jobs with technology at a frightening pace. Black communities, always vulnerable to changes in job patterns, have been suffering the devastating effects of high unemployment for more than two decades. The adverse effect on whites, already real, has not stirred them to action because it has been deflected by racism onto blacks. The opposition to affirmative action is but one example of this transference, but it is an example that has been endorsed by the Supreme Court in this century in a manner little different than when earlier Courts adopted the "separate but equal" standard at a time when the white populace was struggling for status during the upheavals of the late nineteenth century as the nation switched from an agricultural to an industrial economy.

Viewing the Burger Court's record in race cases in this light, I am able to conclude that it was less good or bad for civil rights than, like the Supreme Court throughout its history, a product of its time.

Notes

1. Steel, "Nine Men in Black Who Think White," *N.Y. Times* (Magazine), Oct. 13, 1968, at 53, col. 2.

2. Brown v. Board of Educ., 347 U.S. 483 (1954).

3. 391 U.S. 430 (1968).

4. See *N.Y. Times*, Oct. 29, 1968, at 43, col. 2.

5. 349 U.S. 294 (1955).

6. 358 U.S. 1 (1958).

7. 377 U.S. 218 (1967).

8. See, e.g., Bell v. School City of Gary, Ind., 324 F.2D 209 (7th Cir. 1963), *cert. denied*, 377 U.S. 924 (1964).

9. Tushnet, *The NAACP: Legal Strategy Against Segregated Education 1925–1950* (1987)(a general discussion of the NAACP's strategy leading up to *Brown*); Carter, "The NAACP's Legal Strategy against Segregated Education," 86 *Mich. L. Rev.* 1083 (1988) (discussing the organization's gradual and incremental approach).

10. 379 U.S. 559 (1965) Compare Adderley v. Florida, 385 U.S. 39 (1966) (convictions for trespass on jail grounds upheld) with Edwards v. South Carolina, 372 U.S. 229 (1963) (common-law breach-of-peace convictions for protest on statehouse grounds reversed on due process grounds).

11. Walker v. City of Birmingham, 388 U.S. 307 (1967).

12. 381 U.S. 741 (1965).

13. NAACP v. Overstreet, 221 Ga. 16, 142 S.E.2d 816, *cert. denied as improvidently granted,* 384 U.S. 118 (1966).

14. 357 U.S. 449 (1958).

15. 371 U.S. 415 (1963).

16. Reitman v. Mulkey, 387 U.S. 369 (1967).

17. 334 U.S. 1 (1948).

18. 245 U.S. 60 (1917).

19. 392 U.S. 409 (1968).

20. See Green Street Ass. v. Daley, 373 F.2d 1 (7th Cir. 1967) (project challenged as not a good-faith renewal plan but a Negro removal plan to create a "no-Negro buffer zone" between a shopping area and the surrounding residential community); Nashville I-40 Steering Comm. v. Ellington, 387 F.2d 179 (6th Cir. 1967) (challenge to highway construction which would destroy Nashville's black, business community and erect a physical barrier between the predominantly black area and other parts of the city).

21. Jackson v. State, 37 Ala. App. 519, 72 So. 2d 114, *cert. denied,* 348 U.S. 888 (1954).

22. 350 U.S. 891 (1955) (remanding the case after oral argument for a more complete record), and 350 U.S. 985 (1956) (dismissing the appeal as devoid of a substantial federal question).

23. McLauglin v. Florida, 379 U.S. 184 (1964).

24. Loving v. Virginia, 388 U.S. 1 (1967).

25. *National Commission on the Causes and Prevention of Violence* (Dec. 1969).

26. 401 U.S. 424 (1971).

27. 402 U.S. 1 (1971).

28. 413 U.S. 189 (1973).

29. Milliken v. Bradley I, 418 U.S. 717 (1974).

30. 426 U.S. 229 (1976).

31. Id. at 248.

32. See, e.g., Hunter v. Erickson, 393 U.S. (1969) (invalidating a city ordinance intended to make it more difficult to enact fair housing laws than other legislation); Norwood v. Harrison, 413 U.S. 455 (1973) (barring provision of textbooks to private schools with discriminatory policies).

33. 433 U.S. 267 (1976).

34. Norwood v. Harrison, 413 U.S. 455 (1973).

35. 461 U.S. 574 (1983).

36. 466 U.S. 429 (1984).

37. 430 U.S. 144 (1977).

38. 446 U.S. 55 (1980).

39. Regents of the Univ. of Cal. v. Bakke, 438 U.S. 265 (1978).

40. 448 U.S. 448 (1980).

41. 476 U.S. 267 (1986).

42. Id. at 283.

43. Bell, "*Brown v. Board of Education* and the Interest-Convergence Dilemma," 93 *Harv. L. Rev.* 518, 522–28 (1980).

WOMEN AS CONSTITUTIONAL EQUALS
The Burger Court's Overdue Evolution

STEPHANIE K. SEYMOUR

The Declaration of Independence declared in 1776, "We hold these truths to be self-evident; that all men are created equal."[1] We learned in our civics and political science courses, from our history and our culture, that those ringing words meant just what they said—all *men* are created equal. When the Fourteenth Amendment to our Constitution was ratified in 1868, it declared that "no state shall make or enforce any law which shall abridge the privileges or immunities of citizens of the United States; nor shall any state deprive any person of life, liberty, or property, without due process of law; nor deny to any person within its jurisdiction the equal protection of the laws."[2] "Person" is a seemingly broader word than "man," but the enactment of the Fourteenth Amendment did not make women equal under the law either. In the century that followed its adoption, right through the era of the Warren Court, women were considered inferior to men under our Constitution, except when it came to childrearing and homemaking.

The Burger Court created a defining moment in legal history by recognizing for the first time that the Constitution protects women against gender discrimination. Before 1971, the Court rejected every challenge to legislative enactments that disadvantaged women because of their sex. By 1986, the Court had put in place an approach to gender-based laws that required them to have an exceedingly persuasive justification and a substantial relationship to the achievement of their goals. This dramatic change in our legal history, belated as it was, mirrored an equally dramatic change in the role of women in society, and the political recognition of that change.

Any examination of gender and the law during the Burger Court must recognize the extraordinary contribution to the evolutionary process made by Ruth Bader Ginsburg. Until her appointment to the U.S. Court of Appeals for the District of Columbia in 1980, she filed briefs with the Supreme Court in most of the cases on the path toward constitutional protection, and she argued several of them.[3] She wrote prolifically, providing thoughtful and scholarly insight and perspective on the cases as they came down, and on the effect on them of the times in which they were decided.[4] The quality of her endeavors was itself a refutation of the stereotypical view that women had no place in the world outside the home and could make no meaningful contribution to that world. It is therefore altogether fitting that Justice Ginsburg recently wrote the latest chapter in the Supreme Court's recognition that the Fourteenth Amendment protects against gender discrimination—the *VMI* case.[5]

Before 1971, the Supreme Court never met a gender distinction it did not like. The most egregious examples are by now well-known, but they bear repeating because they are telling indications of how far the law has evolved. In the first gender case decided under the newly ratified Fourteenth Amendment, Myra Bradwell applied unsuccessfully to the Supreme Court of Illinois for a license to practice law. She challenged the denial of her application in the U.S. Supreme Court, which upheld the denial by concluding that admission to the bar of a state is not a privilege or immunity belonging to U.S. citizens.[6] In an oft-quoted concurring opinion, Justice Bradley, joined by two other Justices, said the following:

> [T]he civil law, as well as nature herself, has always recognized a wide difference in the respective spheres and destinies of man and woman. Man is, or should be, woman's protector and defender. The natural and proper timidity and delicacy which belongs to the female sex evidently unfits it for many of the occupations of civil life. The constitution of the family organization, which is founded in the divine ordinance, as well as in the nature of things, indicates the domestic sphere as that which properly belongs to the domain and functions of womanhood. The harmony, not to say identity, of interests and views which belong, or should belong, to the family institution is repugnant to the idea of a woman adopting a distinct and independent career from that of her husband. . . . The paramount destiny and mission of woman are to fulfil the noble and benign offices of wife and mother. This is the law of the Creator.[7]

Mrs. Bradwell's desire to practice law thus violated divine ordinance, the nature of things, and the law of the Creator, all of which were so apparent to Justice Bradley and his brethren that he saw no need to cite authority for these pronouncements.

Things did not improve. Two years later, Virginia Minor challenged as violative of the Fourteenth Amendment a provision of the Missouri state constitution that restricted the right to vote to men only. The Supreme Court rejected the challenge on the ground that voting was not a privilege or immunity of citizenship, and that the states were therefore free to limit the right of suffrage to men alone.[8]

Even the *Lochner*-era Court, which disapproved of nearly every attempted government regulation of the workplace, upheld limitations on working hours for women. The Court took judicial notice "[t]hat woman's physical structure and the performance of maternal functions place her at a disadvantage in the struggle for subsistence" and "that woman has always been dependent upon man."[9] The Court concluded as follows:

> It is impossible to close one's eyes to the fact that [a woman] still looks to her brother and depends on him. Even [if] all restrictions on political, personal, and contractual rights were taken away, and she stood, so far as statutes are concerned, upon an absolutely equal plane with him, it would still be true that she is so constituted that she will rest upon and look to him for protection; that her physical struc-

ture and a proper discharge of her maternal functions—having in view not merely her own health, but the well-being of the race—justify legislation to protect her from the greed as well as the passion of man.[10]

Many years later, a woman unsuccessfully sought an injunction to restrain the enforcement of a Michigan law that restricted her from obtaining a bartender's license unless she was the wife or daughter of the male owner of a licensed liquor establishment.[11] In upholding enforcement of the law, the Supreme Court approved the state's legislative judgment that bartending by women should be limited to prevent moral and social problems.

As recently as 1961, the Warren Court's opinion in *Hoyt v. Florida*[12] stands as discouraging proof that the more things had changed during the ninety years after Mrs. Bradwell tried to practice law, the more they had stayed the same. Gwendolyn Hoyt was convicted of second-degree murder by assaulting her husband with a baseball bat. "As described by the Florida Supreme Court, the affair occurred in the context of a marital upheaval involving . . . the suspected infidelity of [Mrs. Hoyt's] husband, and culminating in the husband's final rejection of his wife's efforts at reconciliation."[13] Mrs. Hoyt claimed that her trial before an all-male jury deprived her of her right to equal protection under the Fourteenth Amendment. The jury was selected under a state statute that allowed women to serve on juries only if they affirmatively requested to be put on the jury list. Few women had done so. In an opinion by Justice Harlan, the Supreme Court upheld the conviction, echoing the words of Justice Bradley:

> Despite the enlightened emancipation of women from the restrictions and protections of bygone years, and their entry into many parts of community life formerly considered to be reserved to men, woman is still regarded as the center of home and family life. We cannot say that it is constitutionally impermissible for a State, acting in pursuit of the general welfare, to conclude that a woman should be relieved from the civic duty of jury service unless she herself determines that such service is consistent with her own special responsibilities.[14]

Chief Justice Warren and Justices Black and Douglas concurred in the result. All the other Justices fully joined the opinion.

Ten years after *Hoyt*, in the seminal case of *Reed v. Reed*,[15] the Burger Court changed the face of equal protection jurisprudence in a case that challenged an Idaho statute providing that as between a man and a woman equally qualified to administer an estate, the man must be preferred. The state defended the statute as a matter of administrative convenience and as a means of avoiding intrafamily controversy. Chief Justice Burger, writing for a unanimous Court, refused to give these reasons dispositive weight, holding instead that the statute established arbitrary preferences in violation of the Equal Protection Clause of the Fourteenth Amendment. This was the first time the Court refused to defer to a state legislature's view of the circumstances in which women should be treated differently from men.

In deciding the *Reed* case, the Court took a fresh and critical look at a statute that had an adverse impact on women. The Court's willingness to assess for itself the legitimacy of a state's reasons for enacting gender discriminatory laws continued during the Burger Court years and beyond and revolutionized the legal status of women. The first question that comes to mind in understanding the evolution of the revolution is, Why? What factors were present in 1971 and the following years to influence and reorder the Court's thinking about a woman's place in the world that were not at work in 1961?

The paternalistic language that the pre-Burger Court cases used in approving gender distinctions reflected the ambiguous nature of society's attitude toward women that was prevalent in those times and unfortunately still persists to some extent today.[16] Women were "'both put on a pedestal and deemed not fully developed persons.'"[17] The concept of women as the weaker sex arose in the dim past when physical strength was often necessary to success in the world beyond the home. Because women were disadvantaged by their role as childbearer and by their relative physical weakness in a world requiring physical strength, they were viewed as unsuited for worldly endeavors and in need of protection. Kept as they were out of the commercial arena, women were seen as both unable to hold their own there and better and more innocent because they were untainted by it. This attitude continued even after women began to become active in commerce and the trades, evidenced by the many cases justifying restrictions on women's activity as necessary to accommodate their position as the weaker sex.

Technology has long since leveled the playing field by eliminating the advantage previously resulting from physical strength. As Ruth Bader Ginsburg observed in 1980, other changes in society were also at work propelling women out of the home, off the pedestal, and out into the workforce.

> In the years 1947 to 1961 . . . there was unprecedented growth in employment outside the home of women from ages forty-five to sixty-four. A steep increase for younger women followed later, coinciding with, and shored up by, a revived feminist movement—a movement caused by, and in turn spotlighting, dramatic alterations in women's lives. Salient factors in the changing work and roles of women include a sharp decline in necessary home-centered activity; few goods we consume at home must be made there nowadays. Coupled with that, expansion of the economy's service sector opened places for women in traditional as well as new occupations. Curtailed population goals, facilitated by more effective means of controlling reproduction, count as well among important ingredients in this social dynamic. Also central to women's increasing opportunity is the phenomenon of vastly extended life spans. The combination of these last two developments creates a setting in which the typical woman, for the first time, is experiencing most of her adult years in a household not dominated by child care requirements. In addition, inflation has boosted attraction to gainful employment for wife as well as husband. These conditions, along with changing marriage patterns, account in significant measure for the prevalence of the two-earner family, a unit increasingly more common than the family in which a man is the sole breadwinner. In fewer than a dozen years, according to mid-1970s Bureau of Labor Statistics projections, two-thirds of all women between ages twenty-five and fifty-four would be gainfully employed.[18]

One dramatic change in the legal landscape during the Burger Court years may have had the greatest impact of all on the legal status of women. When I graduated from law school in 1965, only 4 percent of the law school graduates were women.[19] By 1971, when the *Reed* case was decided, the number of women enrolling in law school was approximately 9 percent.[20] By 1986, the end of the Burger Court era, almost 41 percent of the enrolling law students were women.[21] In addition to graduating from law school, women began to be appointed as judges in increasing numbers. President Carter began the revolution for the federal courts, appointing eleven women to the courts of appeals and twenty-three women to the district bench between 1976 and 1980. President Reagan continued the trend during his eight years in office by appointing Sandra Day O'Connor to the Supreme Court in 1981, six women to the courts of appeals, and twenty-four women as district judges. Similar changes were taking place on the state courts.

The changes in society and the legal field were reflected in the legislative sphere. Prior to the watershed *Reed* decision, Congress passed the Equal Pay Act[22] in 1963 and the Civil Rights Act in 1964, Title VII of which prohibited employment discrimination on the basis of sex.[23] Congressional action after the *Reed* decision continued to enhance the ability of women to enter on an equal footing areas traditionally reserved to men. In 1972, the Equal Rights Amendment was passed by Congress and began its journey to obtain approval among the states, although it ultimately failed. That same year, Congress passed Title IX of the Educational Amendments of 1972,[24] which prohibited sex discrimination in any educational program or facility receiving federal funds and amended Title VII of the Civil Rights Act to extend protection against sex discrimination to federal employees.[25] In 1974, Congress passed the Equal Credit Opportunity Act[26] prohibiting discrimination on the basis of sex or marital status with respect to credit transactions. In 1978, in response to a case in which the Burger Court had detoured from its general trend of recognizing and striking down sex discrimination,[27] Congress again amended Title VII by passing the Pregnancy Discrimination Act.[28] And in 1980, Congress passed the Science and Engineering Equal Opportunities Act,[29] which authorized the National Science Foundation to increase the participation of women in courses of study leading to degrees in science and engineering and to encourage women to pursue careers in those fields.

This then was the social, legal, and political climate during the Burger Court years. The birth of gender equality jurisprudence was less a product of the Court than a product of the times; it was an idea whose time had clearly come. Indeed, given the across-the-board rejection of gender claims by the Court before 1971, the Supreme Court's gender discrimination doctrine had no place to go but forward. Be that as it may, when the Burger Court years were over, the law of sex discrimination had been permanently altered, along with the opportunities available to women to enter professions formerly reserved to men.

The Court accomplished this alteration in a series of cases that developed and applied an intermediate level of judicial scrutiny to statutes that would previously have been approved as within the legislature's prerogative to deal with woman's place in the scheme of things. In the years leading up to the *Reed* decision, most statutory classifications were evaluated for equal protection purposes under the rational-basis test, an extremely deferential standard which required only that the difference in treatment not be "wholly irrelevant to the achievement of the State's objective," and justified by any reasonably conceivable state of facts.[30] Before *Reed*, the rational basis test was used to uphold every law that discriminated against women, the rational-basis being woman's role as mother, caretaker of the home, and a person unfit or incapable of employment in a man's world.

The Court had applied a much more exacting level of scrutiny to those legislative classifications it regarded as "suspect." Footnote four of the *Carolene Products* case[31] is generally regarded to be the origin of the notion of applying strict scrutiny to suspect classifications.[32] The Court indicated there that the presumption of the constitutionality of statutes might not operate so broadly with respect to legislation directed at racial minorities, observing that "prejudice against discrete and insular minorities may be a special condition, which tends seriously to curtail the operation of those political processes ordinarily to be relied upon to protect minorities, and which may call for a correspondingly more searching judicial inquiry."[33] The idea that minorities might need more protection from discriminatory laws than that provided by the rational-basis test was further developed in the *Korematsu* case,[34] in which the Court noted that legal restrictions limiting the civil rights of a single racial group should be viewed as suspect and subjected to strict scrutiny.[35] The rationale underlying application of this standard, as implied in the cases from which it arose, is the belief that suspect classes are not likely to be represented in the legislature, and that the political process therefore could not be relied on to ensure that their interests would be taken into account.[36] Under the strict scrutiny standard, laws must have a compelling objective and must promote that objective by the least restrictive means.[37] Although the wartime restrictions on Japanese Americans at issue in *Korematsu* survived strict scrutiny, virtually all statutes that have since been subjected to that standard have been invalidated.[38]

In the first step toward a new equal protection landscape for women taken in *Reed*, the Court purported to apply the rational-basis test in assessing whether the statute violated the Fourteenth Amendment's equal protection mandate. The Court thus articulated the inquiry as assessing whether the classification was reasonable and had a fair and substantial relationship to the legislation's objective. The outcome, however, was not the one that application of the rational-basis test had always previously produced. Although the Court accepted the statute's objectives as legitimate—that is, to avoid intrafamily fights and to provide administrative convenience in estate administration—it nevertheless concluded that the means chosen were arbitrary rather than reasonable. As Ruth Bader Ginsburg noted in an article, "[T]he *Reed* decision attracted headlines; it marked the first solid break from the Supreme Court's consistent affirmation of governmental authority to classify by sex. The terse *Reed* opinion acknowledged no departure from precedent, but Court-watchers recognized that something new was in the wind."[39]

With the *Reed* decision the genie was out of the bottle, the toothpaste was out of the tube, and there was no turning back. As one commentator notes, "[R]ights, once set loose, are very difficult to contain; rights consciousness—on and off the Court—is a powerful engine of legal mobilization and change."[40] The Burger Court had begun a journey toward recognition of gender equality. As a review of subsequent decisions reveals, however, the train was driven not by an overarching jurisprudential vision but by social and political change and by the views of the Justices about the facts of particular cases.[41]

Two years after the *Reed* decision, the Court issued *Frontiero v. Richardson*,[42] the opinion many consider the high-water mark in the movement toward gender equality.[43] The case challenged military statutes under which families of male soldiers were granted greater benefits than families of female soldiers. A majority of a three-judge district court panel upheld the statutes on the basis of administrative convenience, which was in turn premised on the panel's view that because the husband is generally the "breadwinner" in most families he is rarely a dependent for purposes of receiving benefits for military dependents.[44] Ruth Bader Ginsburg argued the case in the Supreme Court as amicus for the American Civil Liberties Union. After an exchange of views among the Justices concerning the standard of review,[45] Justice Brennan authored a plurality opinion holding that classifications based on sex were suspect and therefore subject to strict scrutiny. Citing the infamous passage from the concurrence in *Bradwell v. Illinois*,[46] Justice Brennan pointed to the nation's long and unfortunate history of sex discrimination, "rationalized by an attitude of 'romantic paternalism' which, in practical effect, put women, not on a pedestal, but in a cage."[47] He noted that women still faced pervasive discrimination in educational institutions, in employment, and in the political arena.[48] Justice Brennan was unable to persuade a majority of the Court to his view that sex is a suspect class. Justice Powell concurred only in the judgment, believing that categorizing sex as suspect would preempt the political process in light of the fact that the Equal Rights Amendment had been passed by Congress and submitted to the states for ratification.[49] Interestingly, Chief Justice Burger, whose opinion in *Reed* had started it all, wrote to Justice Brennan stating that as the author of *Reed*, he had "never remotely contemplated such a broad concept."[50] The Chief Justice joined the concurrence of Justice Powell. Justice Rehnquist was the lone dissenter.

A year later, the Court heard *Kahn v. Shevin*,[51] which challenged a Florida statute providing a tax break to widows but not to widowers. Ruth Bader Ginsburg again argued to the Court, contending that the statute's gender distinction violated equal protection. Justice Douglas disagreed, holding for the Court that because a single woman indisputably faced greater financial difficulties than those facing a single man, the statute undoubtedly met the "substantial relation" requirement of the rational-basis test. He distinguished *Frontiero* as a case in which the gender distinction was justified solely by administrative convenience. Justices Brennan, Marshall, and White dissented on the basis that sex was a suspect class requiring a greater justification than that offered by the state.

Kahn is a revealing case for several reasons. It underscored the fact that Justice Brennan's position on sex as a suspect class was not that of a majority of the Court, and it did so by approving a gender distinction made in an attempt to *benefit* women and to remedy the effects of what the Court referred to as "overt discrimination or . . . the socialization process of a male-dominated culture."[52] The Court used the same rationale in *Schlesinger v. Ballard*[53] to uphold a discriminatory up-or-out military policy favoring women. Indeed, the notion that gender distinctions pass constitutional muster when made to remedy discrimination and provide a special benefit to women is one that surfaced frequently during the Burger Court's struggle with gender issues. It often explained the Court's approval of some classifications drawn on gender lines and not others. This paternalistic view has been challenged as a short-term gain but a long-term loss for women because it perpetuates the notion that women are somehow weaker, less able to compete on their own, and in need of special treatment. To the extent that a statutory benefit favoring women is truly intended and described as a remedy for past discrimination rather than as protection for the weaker sex, however, it is in my judgment a valuable tool to boost women on their way to equality.

After upholding gender distinctions in *Kahn* and *Ballard* on the basis of their protective and remedial purposes, the Court again shifted gears. In *Taylor v. Louisiana*,[54] decided only a week after *Ballard*, the Court struck down a jury selection system identical to that upheld earlier in *Hoyt*. The Court agreed with the male defendant in *Taylor* that the challenged system denied him his Sixth Amendment right to a jury drawn from a fair cross- section of the community. In so doing, the Court rejected the *Hoyt* rationale, stating as follows:

> If it was ever the case that women were unqualified to sit on juries or were so situated that none of them should be required to perform jury service, that time has long since passed. . . . Communities differ at different times and places. What is a fair cross section at one time or place is not necessarily a fair cross section at another time or different place.[55]

Times and the law were changing. The Chief Justice concurred in the result and Justice Rehnquist dissented.

In *Weinberger v. Wiesenfeld*,[56] Ruth Bader Ginsburg again appeared before the Court, arguing that a social security statute denied equal protection by granting benefits to the surviving spouse of a working man while denying benefits to the surviving spouse of a working woman. Justice Brennan held for the Court that the gender distinction at issue was indistinguishable from that struck down in *Frontiero*. While acknowledging that some empirical evidence supported the notion that men were more likely than women to be the primary supporters of their spouses and children, the Court nonetheless held this rationale insufficient to "justify a gender-based distinction which diminishes the protection afforded to women who do work."[57] Justice Brennan hedged his bets in articulating the framework under which the provision was held invalid, drawing parallels with the statute struck down on the basis of strict scrutiny by the plurality in *Frontiero* while relying on language from *Reed* to actually declare the statute unconstitutional. Justice Powell wrote a more narrowly drawn concurrence in which the Chief Justice joined. Once again, Justice Rehnquist dissented.

In 1975, the Court also invalidated a Utah statute under which women attained the age of majority at eighteen and were then no longer eligible for child support, whereas men did not reach majority until age twenty-one. In *Stanton v. Stanton*,[58] a divorced wife sued for support payments for her daughter after the daughter turned eighteen. The Utah Supreme Court sustained the statute against an equal protection challenge, holding that support for male children should continue longer, based on the "'old notions . . . that generally it is the man's primary responsibility to provide a home and its essentials, [and that therefore] it is a salutary thing for him to get a good education and/or training before he undertakes those responsibilities.'"[59] Justice Blackmun, writing for the Court over Justice Rehnquist's lone dissent, concluded that the statute did not survive equal protection attack "under any test—compelling state interest, or rational basis, or something in between."[60] In a blistering rejection of the "old notions" relied on by the state court, Justice Blackmun pointed out:

> Women's activities and responsibilities are increasing and expanding. Coeducation is a fact, not a rarity. The presence of women in business, in the professions, in government and, indeed, in all walks of life where education is a desirable, if not always a necessary, antecedent is apparent and a proper subject of judicial notice. If a specified age of minority is required for the boy in order to assure him parental support while he attains his education and training, so, too, is it for the girl. To distinguish between the two on educational grounds is to be self-serving: if the female is not to be supported so long as the male, she hardly can be expected to attend school as long as he does, and bringing her education to an end earlier coincides with the role-typing society has long imposed.[61]

Thus, approximately 100 years after the Court took judicial notice that under the law of the Creator the paramount destiny of women was the domestic sphere, the Court now was taking judicial notice of women's activities in business, the professions, government, and indeed in all walks of life. Women had made progress not only in changing their place in the world but in the critical area of changing the Court's underlying perception of their place in the world. The Supreme Court was finally getting the message that stereotyping all women did a great injustice to those women who did not fit the stereotype.

This progress was stabilized by the 1976 decision in *Craig v. Boren*,[62] in which the Court for the first time expressly adopted and applied an intermediate level of scrutiny to gender classifications.[63] The case presented a challenge to an Oklahoma statute that discriminated against males in the sale of 3.2 percent beer. Building on language in *Reed*, Justice Brennan stated the standard for the Court as follows: "[C]lassifications by gender must serve important governmental objectives and must be substantially related to achievement of those objectives."[64] The Court pointed out that cases following *Reed* rejected administrative convenience as a sufficiently important objective. Significantly, the Court also recognized that "increasingly outdated misconceptions concerning the role of females in the home rather than in the 'marketplace and world of ideas' were rejected as loose-fitting characterizations incapable of supporting state statutory schemes that were premised upon their accuracy."[65] Justice Powell specially concurred and, in expressing some misgivings about the opinion's discussion of the appropriate standard for equal protection analysis of gender claims, correctly predicted that the opinion would be viewed as adopting a middle-tier approach subjecting such classifications "to a more critical examination than is normally applied when . . . 'suspect classes' are not present."[66] Chief Justice Burger dissented because he was unable to accept the Court's decision to make "gender a disfavored classification."[67]

The Court applied the intermediate level of scrutiny in the 1977 case of *Califano v. Goldfarb*,[68] in which Ruth Bader Ginsburg again appeared before the Court to assert the unconstitutionality of a social security benefits statute that favored widows over widowers. Justice Brennan, writing for plurality, again agreed. He denounced as unconstitutional sex classifications based on archaic and overbroad generalizations about women that are more consistent with stereotypes than with reality.[69] Justice Stevens concurred in the judgment. Chief Justice Burger joined Justice Rehnquist's dissent, along with Justices Stewart and Blackmun.

Three weeks later, in *Califano v. Webster*,[70] the Court upheld another social security benefits statute that permitted female wage earners to exclude three more lower earning years than a similarly situated male, thereby resulting in a higher level of old-age benefits for the retired female wage earner. The Court concluded that the gender classification passed constitutional muster because it actually reduced the "disparity in economic condition between men and women caused by the long history of discrimination against women [which] has been recognized as . . . an important governmental objective."[71] In so doing, the Court cautioned that "'the mere recitation of a benign, compensatory purpose is not an automatic shield which protects against any inquiry into the actual purposes underlying a statutory scheme'" and distinguished cases in which a scheme that purported to remedy past discrimination was not enacted for that purpose or actually penalized women wage earners.[72] The Court upheld the statutory provision because it attempted to account for job discrimination that prevented women from earning as much as men and thereby operated to compensate women for that past discrimination. The Chief Justice and three other Justices concurred for the reasons given in Justice Rehnquist's dissent in *Goldfarb*.

The decision in *Webster*, when contrasted with those in *Goldfarb and Wiesenfeld*, illustrates the flexible manner in which the Court used the intermediate level of scrutiny. The middle-tier approach allowed "the Justices to base their decisions upon their individual perceptions of the reasonableness of the sexual classification and the governmental interest asserted in each case."[73] *Webster* also revealed the enduring appeal of gender classifications that are protective and remedial.

The decisions mentioned are only a fraction of those decided by the Burger Court dealing with gender classifications. This paper has focused on them because they highlight the Court's progress toward recognizing women's changing place in society and its development of a framework for analyzing gender claims that takes that change into account. The standard the Court adopted was probably as stringent as possible given the makeup of the Court and the widespread persistence of sexual stereotyping in the teeth of reality. And, despite the heightened scrutiny, the Court nevertheless persisted for a time in upholding statutes obviously enacted to protect the weaker sex. The outcomes often turned as much on the views of the individual Justices as on subtle factual distinctions. As a result, the Court's steps toward gender equality were uneven, arguably inconsistent, and subject to the charge of being result oriented.[74] Although the Court's treatment of gender was perhaps not ideal, we must remember that the Court was being asked to make rapid changes in an area long ignored. The end result was to acknowledge and give legal force and protection to women's movement out of the home and into the world.

The changing framework within which the Supreme Court evaluated the roles and rights of women in society is manifest even in cases that at least facially did not deal with gender equality. The cases defining the scope of reproductive rights are a good example. In *Griswold v. Connecticut*,[75] the Court held that it is an invasion of privacy for the state to regulate the use of contraceptives by a married couple. Several of the opinions in *Griswold* focused on the privileged place of the marital institution and the importance of protecting decisions relating to the creation and raising of a family from interference by the government. Justice Douglas referred to the privacy surrounding marriage as "older than the Bill of Rights."[76] The Court still perceived reproductive rights to be bound up in the traditional view of womanhood as inside the family, to be given expression only within that specific social and historical context. But successive decisions by the Court gradually eroded the notion of reproductive rights rooted in the social institutions of marriage and family in favor of a notion of privacy rights held by individuals.[77] The theory that a woman has an individual privacy right in making decisions about her own reproduction achieved full expression in the Burger Court's 1973 decision in *Roe v. Wade*.[78]

Whatever one may think of the substance of *Roe* and its progeny, it is clear that the change from a view of women's rights as rooted in and derived from social institutions and history, to a vision of rights possessed by women as aspects of their individual personhood, created the necessary preconditions for broader progress in the treatment of women under the law. To persist in the vision of women's rights as derivative would have been dehumanizing and at odds with the changes sweeping society at large.

Three gender classification cases form a bridge from the Burger Court to the present day. In 1982, the Burger Court heard *Mississippi University for Women v. Hogan*,[79] which presented an equal protection challenge to a state statute that excluded men from a state-supported nursing school. By then, Sandra Day O'Connor had been appointed as the first woman to sit on the Supreme Court. Justice O'Connor authored an opinion for the five Justices who voted to strike down the statute. In so doing, she stated several principles that had emerged from the Court's past equal protection analysis. First, she said that the statute was not exempt from scrutiny or subject to a lesser standard of review merely because it discriminated against males rather than females. She reiterated that the applicable test was the one set out in *Craig v. Boren*, under which a state must show that the classification serves important governmental objectives and that the discriminatory means used are substantially related to the achievement of those objectives. She cautioned that this test must be applied "free of fixed notions concerning the roles and abilities of males and females."[80] She criticized the view that protective and paternalistic objectives were valid, pointing out that "if the statutory objective is to exclude or 'protect' members of one gender because they are presumed to suffer from an inherent handicap or to be innately inferior, the objective itself is illegitimate."[81]

Determining whether the requisite substantial relationship exists must be done "through reasoned analysis rather than through the mechanical application of traditional, often inaccurate, assumptions about the proper roles of men and women."[82] Justice O'Connor recognized that in limited circumstances "a gender-based classification favoring one sex can be justified if it intentionally and directly assists members of the sex that is disproportionately burdened," but she "emphasized that 'the mere recitation of a benign, compensatory purpose is not an automatic shield which protects against any inquiry into the actual purposes underlying a statutory scheme.'"[83] In rejecting the state's argument that excluding males compensated for discrimination against women and constituted educational affirmative action, Justice O'Connor pointed out that the state's policy actually perpetuated the stereotype of nursing as women's work and helped make the assumption that nursing is a field for women a self-fulfilling prophecy.[84] Interestingly, she noted evidence that excluding men from the nursing field depressed wages and observed that the state's policy may thus be penalizing the very class the state purported to benefit.[85] The Chief Justice dissented along with Justices Blackmun, Powell, and Rehnquist.

Twelve years later, in *J.E.B. v. Alabama ex rel. T.B.*,[86] the Rehnquist Court considered whether the Equal Protection Clause prohibits peremptory challenges to potential jurors on the basis of gender. *J.E.B.* was the defendant in a paternity suit which was heard by an all-female jury due to the state's exercise of its peremptory challenges. Justice Blackmun, writing for the Court, began his discussion by observing that because women had been excluded from jury duty for most of the country's existence, gender-based peremptory challenges were a relatively recent occurrence. This historical exclusion of women was derived from the English common law and was framed in this country as "the ostensible need to protect women from the ugliness and depravity of trials. Women were thought to be too fragile and virginal to withstand the polluted courtroom atmosphere."[87] Justice Blackmun pointed out the following:

> [Beginning with *Reed v. Reed*,] this Court consistently has subjected gender-based classifications to heightened scrutiny in recognition of the real danger that government policies that professedly are based on reasonable considerations in fact may be reflective of "archaic and overbroad" generalizations about gender, or based on "outdated misconceptions concerning the role of females in the home rather than in the 'marketplace and world of ideas.'"[88]

The state's proffered justification was based on the perception that men might be more sympathetic to a male defendant in a paternity suit, whereas women might be more sympathetic to the complaining witness, the mother. The Court refused to "accept as a defense to gender-based peremptory challenges 'the very stereotype the law condemns,'"[89] characterizing this rationale as

> reminiscent of the arguments advanced to justify the total exclusion of women from juries. [The state] offers virtually no support for the conclusion that gender alone is an accurate predictor of juror's attitudes; yet it urges the Court to condone the same stereotypes that justified the wholesale exclusion of women from juries and the ballot box.[90]

In addition to the harm to the rights of the litigant, Justice Blackmun emphasized the harm resulting to the community and to the individual juror caused by exercising peremptory challenges on the basis of gender stereotypes.

> The community is harmed by the State's participation in the perpetuation of invidious group stereotypes and the inevitable loss of confidence in our judicial system that state-sanctioned discrimination in the courtroom engenders.
> When state actors exercise peremptory challenges in reliance on gender stereotypes, they ratify and reinforce prejudicial views of the relative abilities of men and women. Because these stereotypes have wreaked injustice in so many other spheres of our country's public life, active discrimination by litigants on the

basis of gender during jury selection "invites cynicism respecting the jury's neutrality and its obligation to adhere to the law."[91]

Individual jurors are harmed because

> [a]ll persons, when granted the opportunity to serve on a jury, have the right not to be excluded summarily because of discriminatory and stereotypical presumptions that reflect and reinforce patterns of historical discrimination. Striking individual jurors on the assumption that they hold particular views simply because of their gender is "practically a brand upon them, affixed by law, an assertion of their inferiority." It denigrates the dignity of the excluded juror, and, for a woman, reinvokes a history of exclusion from political participation.[92]

The *J.E.B.* decision stands as a strong reaffirmation of the principles developed by the Burger Court in rejecting the government's reliance, either implicitly or expressly, on gender stereotypes when defending challenges to gender discrimination.

The most recent application of the Burger Court's gender equity jurisprudence occurred in 1997 in *United States v. Virginia* (*VMI*).[93] In a lovely twist of fate, the opinion was authored by Justice Ruth Bader Ginsburg, named to the Court in 1993, who was given the opportunity to apply the changes in the law that her legal arguments to the Burger Court helped to bring about. In assessing the challenge presented to Virginia's refusal to admit women to the Virginia Military Institute, Justice Ginsburg drew on both *Mississippi University for Women* and *J.E.B.* to restate and reaffirm the legal framework that recognizes and protects a woman's right to share equally in the world beyond the domestic sphere. She emphasized that the proffered justification for gender discrimination must be "'exceedingly persuasive,'" "genuine," "not hypothesized or invented *post hoc*," and not grounded "on overbroad generalizations about the different talents, capacities, or preferences of males and females."[94] She pointed out the following:

> Sex classifications may be used to compensate women "for particular economic disabilities [they have] suffered," to "promot[e] equal employment opportunity," to advance full development of the talent and capacities of our Nation's people. But such classifications may not be used, as they once were, to create or perpetuate the legal, social, and economic inferiority of women.[95]

Applying these principles to VMI's exclusionary policy, Justice Ginsburg rejected VMI's argument that excluding women was proper in light of gender-based developmental differences, observing that "time and again since this Court's turning point decision in [*Reed*], we have cautioned reviewing courts to take a 'hard look' at generalizations or 'tendencies' of the kind pressed by Virginia"[96] and reiterating that "[s]tate actors controlling gates to opportunity . . . may not exclude qualified individuals based on 'fixed notions concerning the roles and abilities of males and females.'"[97] Reviewing women's struggle to enter law schools, medical schools, and federal military academies, she stated as follows:

> The notion that admission of women would downgrade VMI's stature, destroy the adversative system and, with it, even the school, is a judgment hardly proved, a prediction hardly different from other "self-fulfilling prophec[ies]," once routinely used to deny rights or opportunities.[98]

Concluding that Virginia's "notably circular argument" had "bent and bowed" the applicable test,[99] Justice Ginsburg held for the Court that Virginia had fallen far short of establishing the exceedingly persuasive justification which the Court now requires to support any gender-defined classification.[100] Significantly, even Chief Justice Rehnquist joined the judgment of the Court although not its opinion. Justice Scalia dissented and Justice Thomas did not participate.

What the *VMI* case did most effectively was to quash once and for all sex stereotyping as a justification for discrimination against women. While recognizing that "most" women would likely not want to endure the extreme physical and mental discipline and minute regulation of behavior meted out at VMI, the fact that "some" women could meet the rigorous requirements of the school and wanted to was sufficient to persuade a majority of the Court that it was a denial of equal protection for the State of Virginia to provide a VMI education for men and not for women. The *VMI* case thus stands as the most recent articulation of the enduring legacy of the Burger Court in the area of gender discrimination: a refusal to allow gender distinctions based on stereotypical notions of a woman's abilities and her place in the world, a refusal to uphold such distinctions on the basis of purported "benign" justifications that are in fact neither actual or benign, and an exacting level of scrutiny meant to ensure that this country's history of discrimination does not repeat itself.

Interestingly, the Court in both *Mississippi University for Women*[101] and *J.E.B.*[102] went out of its way to note that it did not need to decide whether gender is a suspect class entitled to the highest scrutiny because the gender classifications in those cases did not withstand even intermediate scrutiny. In the *VMI* case, however, the Court simply applied intermediate scrutiny without mentioning the suspect class issue. The reason for this change is clear: There is no longer a need to label gender a suspect class to achieve equality. The congressional enactments referred to earlier, which mandated an end to gender discrimination in employment, education, and the extension of credit, have for the most part been interpreted favorably to women by both the Burger Court and the Rehnquist Court. These statutory mandates have assisted women in their endeavors to compete with men in the working world. A solid majority of the current Supreme Court now views the intermediate level of scrutiny to require the state to demonstrate an "exceedingly persuasive justification" for gender distinctions,[103] with a "'strong presumption that gender classifications are invalid'"[104] Moreover, as more women attain legislative positions in which they are involved in creating the statutes and judicial positions in which they are applying the scrutiny, the intermediate level of scrutiny will function even more effectively to weed out stereotypes and paternalism.

In sum, and in answer to the question posed by this book's title, there was no Warren Court revolution on gender equality for the Burger Court to either confirm or counter. Rather, the Burger Court was swept up in the tide of political and social change wrought by women who entered the workforce by design or by necessity and who objected to being treated as though they should still be at home cooking dinner and doing the laundry. Chief Justice Burger rather innocently started the movement with *Reed v. Reed*, never intending a revolution, and Justice Brennan took up the call to arms. The addition of Justice O'Connor to the Court made it more difficult for the Brethren to continue with a straight face upholding statutes that assumed a woman's place was in the home, dependent on her husband. The ultimate serendipity, of course, was the appointment to the Court of Justice Ginsburg, who had led the charge for gender equality. Her powers of persuasion will undoubtedly ensure that the Fourteenth Amendment's promise of equal protection will be a reality for women.

Notes

The author acknowledges with appreciation the assistance of her law clerk, Nancy L. Vyhnal, in the composition of this essay.

1. Declaration of Independence ¶ 2 (U.S. 1776).
2. U.S. Const. amend. XIV, § 1.
3. See Cavanaugh, "Towards a New Equal Protection: Two Kinds of Equality," 12 *Law and Ineq. J.* 381, and n. 3 (1994).
4. See, e.g., Ginsburg, "The Burger Court's Grapplings with Sex Discrimination," in *The Burger Court—The Counter-Revolution That Wasn't* (Blasi ed., 1983) [hereinafter Ginsburg, "The Burger Court"]; Ginsburg, "Some Thoughts on Autonomy and Equality in Relation to *Roe v. Wade*," 63 *N.C. L. Rev.* 375 (1985) [hereinafter Ginsburg, "Some Thoughts on *Roe v. Wade*"].
5. United States v. Virginia, 116 S. Ct. 2264 (1996).
6. Bradwell v. Illinois, 83 U.S. (16 Wall.) 130 (1872).
7. Id. at 141.
8. Minor v. Happersett, 88 U.S. (21 Wall.) 162 (1874).
9. Muller v. Oregon, 208 U.S. 412, 421 (1908).
10. Id. at 422.
11. Goesaert v. Cleary, 335 U.S. 464 (1948).
12. 368 U.S. 57, (1961).
13. Id. at 59.
14. Id. at 61–2.
15. 404 U.S. 71 (1971).
16. See Galotto, "Note, Strict Scrutiny for Gender, via *Croson*," 93 *Colum. L. Rev.* 508, 538 (1993) [hereinafter Galotto, "Strict Scrutiny"].
17. Id. (quoting Wasserstrom, *Philosophy and Social Issues: Five Studies* 19 (1980)).
18. Ginsburg, "The Burger Court," supra note 4, at 139–40.
19. See *A Review of Legal Education in the United States* (1995 ABA Sec. Legal Educ. and Admissions to the Bar Rep.).
20. Id.
21. Id.
22. 29 U.S.C. § 206(d).
23. 42 U.S.C. §§ 2000e et seq.
24. 20 U.S.C. § 1681.
25. 42 U.S.C. § 2000e-16.
26. 15 U.S.C. § 1691.
27. General Elec. Co. v. Gilbert, 429 U.S. 125 (1976) (disability plan's failure to cover pregnancy-related disabilities does not violate Title VII).
28. 42 U.S.C. § 2000e(k).
29. 42 U.S.C. § 1885a.
30. McGowan v. Maryland, 366 U.S. 420, 425–26 (1961).

31. United States v. Carolene Prods. Co., 304 U.S. 144 (1938).

32. See Galotto, "Strict Scrutiny," supra note 15, at 513.

33. *Carolene Prods.*, 304 U.S. at 152 n. 4.

34. Korematsu v. United States, 323 U.S. 214 (1944).

35. Id. at 216.

36. Schwartz, *The Ascent of Pragmatism* 219 (1990).

37. Ginsburg, "The Burger Court," supra note 4, at 133.

38. Schwartz, supra note 35, at 220.

39. Ginsburg, "The Burger Court," supra note 4, at 133.

40. Grossman, "Constitutional Policymaking in the Burger Years," 86 *Mich. L. Rev.* 1414, 1416 (1988) (reviewing *The Burger Years: Rights and Wrongs in the Supreme Court* (Schwartz ed., 1987)).

41. See Ginsburg, "Some Thoughts on *Roe v. Wade*," supra note 4, at 378; Bender, "Is the Burger Court Really Like the Warren Court," 82 *Mich. L. Rev.* 635, 652–53 (1984) (reviewing *The Burger Court: The Counter-Revolution That Wasn't* (Blasi ed., 1983); Grossman, supra note 39, at 1417–18.

42. 411 U.S. 677 (1973).

43. Galotto, "Strict Scrutiny," supra note 15, at 520.

44. *Frontiero*, 411 U.S. at 681.

45. See Schwartz, supra note 35, at 222–26.

46. 83 U.S. (16 Wall.) 130, 141 (1872).

47. *Frontiero*, 411 U.S. at 684.

48. Id. at 686.

49. Schwartz, supra note 35, at 224.

50. Id. at 225 (quoting Chief Justice Burger).

51. 416 U.S. 351 (1974).

52. Id. at 353.

53. 419 U.S. 498 (1975).

54. 419 U.S. 522 (1975).

55. Id. at 537.

56. 420 U.S. 636 (1975).

57. Id. at 648.

58. 421 U.S. 7 (1975).

59. Id. at 10 (quoting 517 P.2d 1010, 1012 (1974)).

60. Id. at 17.

61. Id. at 15.

62. 429 U.S. 190 (1976).

63. Tribe, *American Constitutional Law* § 16–26, at 1564 (2d ed. 1988).

64. Craig v. Boren, 429 U.S. at 197.

65. Id. at 198–99.

66. Id. at 210 and n* (Powell, J., concurring).

67. Id. at 217 (Burger, J., dissenting).

68. 430 U.S. 199 (1977).

69. Id. at 207.

70. 430 U.S. 313 (1977) (per curiam).

71. Id. at 317.

72. Id. (quoting Weinberger v. Wiesenfeld, 420 U.S. 636, 648 (1975)).

73. Schwartz, supra note 35, at 229; see also Maltz, "Legislative Inputs and Gender-Based Discrimination in the Burger Court," 90 *Mich. L. Rev.* 1023 (1992).

74. See Cavanaugh, supra note 3, at 391–400.

75. 381 U.S. 479 (1965).
76. Id. at 486.
77. See, e.g., Eisenstadt v. Baird, 405 U.S. 438 (1972).
78. 410 U.S. 113 (1973).
79. 458 U.S. 719 (1982).
80. Id. at 724–25.
81. Id. at 725.
82. Id. at 726.
83. Id. at 728 (quoting Weinberger v. Wiensenfeld, 420 U.S. 636, 648 (1975)).
84. Id. at 729–30.
85. Id. at 729 n. 15.
86. 511 U.S. 127 (1994).
87. Id. at 132.
88. Id. at 135 (citations omitted).
89. Id. at 138 (citation omitted).
90. Id. at 138–39 (footnote omitted).
91. Id. at 140.
92. Id. at 141–42 (footnote and citation omitted).
93. 116 S. Ct. 2264 (1996).
94. Id. at 2275.
95. Id. at 2276 (footnote and citations omitted).
96. Id. at 2280.
97. Id.
98. Id. (footnotes and citations omitted).
99. Id. at 2281.
100. Id. at 2282.
101. 458 U.S. at 724 n. 9.
102. 511 U.S. at 137 n. 6.
103. *VMI*, 116 S. Ct. at 2274.
104. Id. at 2275 (quoting *J.E.B.*, 511 U.S. at 152 (Kennedy, J., concurring)).

· 6 ·

LIBERTY AND SEXUALITY

DAVID J. GARROW

My assigned topic is one with which most students of the Burger Court are already relatively familiar, but Judge Henry's essay, earlier in this volume, has eased my task even further. When Judge Henry first emphasized that "activism is here to stay," that sounded like a statement that might come back to haunt him at his next confirmation hearing. But when he chose to underscore that exact same point a second time, I began to appreciate more fully how he had very succinctly captured an essential truth that applies not only to the history of the Burger Court but also—particularly in light of *Planned Parenthood of Southeastern Pennsylvania v. Casey* [1] as well as other decidedly different rulings such as *Dolan v. City of Tigard* [2] and *United States v. Lopez* [3]—to the still-evolving record of the Rehnquist Court.

Judge Henry's observation—that "activism is here to stay"—underscores the fact that the two most important Burger Court decisions in my subject area are also undoubtedly the two most famous (or infamous) legacies of the entire Burger Court: first, *Roe v. Wade*,[4] which now quite surprisingly the Rehnquist Court has vindicated in *Casey* and second, *Bowers v. Hardwick*,[5] which now even more surprisingly the Rehnquist Court has sotto voce vitiated in *Romer v. Evans*.[6]

The evolutionary relationship between the Warren Court and the Burger Court is especially important for this essay because of the degree to which *Roe v. Wade* and its equally momentous partner case, *Doe v. Bolton*,[7] and indeed most everything pertaining to abortion rights jurisprudence in the early 1970s, was doctrinally so directly descended from the Warren Court's 1965 decision in *Griswold v. Connecticut*.[8] The historical record is undeniably clear that without *Griswold*, and without the vindication of a constitutional right to privacy that *Griswold* represented, anything like *Roe*'s holding would have been very difficult to imagine as a "privacy" or a substantive due process liberty holding.[9]

When one looks carefully at the development of abortion rights litigation and chronologically at the way in which the Burger Court responded to the appearance of abortion rights cases, *Griswold*'s significance becomes all the more critical. The interest in its doctrinal potentials that *Griswold* stimulated among constitutional litigators, and particularly at law schools during 1965–68, was *the* most influential underpinning for the flood of abortion rights cases that began to be filed in federal district courts all across the country—including New York, Texas, and Georgia—in 1969 and 1970 and continued onward right up through 1971 and 1972.[10] In fact, a very strong argument can be made that given *Griswold*'s privacy analysis, the abortion–liberty conclusion that the Court by a margin of 7–2 drew in *Roe v. Wade* and *Doe v. Bolton* was almost inevitable. Indeed, a few years ago in *Casey* Justice John Paul Stevens observed how *Roe*'s central holding "was a natural sequel to the protection of individual liberty established in *Griswold*."[11] In addition, *Roe* and *Doe*'s direct derivation from *Griswold* also merits emphasis because some commentators with a highly incomplete appreciation of the Court's history may see, and present, *Roe* and *Doe* as the beginning of the abortion story when they most decidedly were not.

Given *Griswold*'s doctrinal originality concerning reproductive privacy rights, it should not be seen as surprising in the least that so much abortion litigation activity, particularly on the part of young lawyers in their mid to late twenties, began spreading across the country in the immediately ensuing years. Indeed, by the time that the U.S. Supreme Court first accepted *Roe* and *Doe* for review, there were already more than a dozen other similar abortion cases pending in the lower federal courts.[12] Thus, when the Court, in May 1971, decided that it was going to address the substantive claim that abortion was a constitutionally protected right, it faced a situation in which the doctrinal underpinning was supplied by its own six-year-old ruling in *Griswold*—and then notably amplified by a strong endorsement from retired Justice Tom C. Clark[13]—and when an impressive number of abortion cases were moving forward in courts throughout the country.

The first time that the Burger Court—or indeed any prior "Court"—really confronted abortion as a subject matter came in early 1971 in *United States v. Vuitch*,[14] which started as a criminal prosecution of a doctor in the District of Columbia, a doctor who for many years was metropolitan Washington's best known abortion provider, Milan Vuitch, a Serbian immigrant. *Vuitch*, as it was argued and decided by the Burger Court in the early months of 1971, was essentially a case that ended up being primarily focused on a question of appellate jurisdiction—namely whether a case such as *Vuitch* could be appealed directly from the federal D.C. District Court to the Supreme Court without first passing through the U.S. Court of Appeals for the D.C. Circuit—and only secondarily concerned with whether the "health" language in the relevant statute was unconstitutionally vague. Only as tertiary issues were the constitutional rights claims that were spreading throughout the lower courts really brought before the high Court in *Vuitch*.[15]

The January 1971 Supreme Court oral arguments in *Vuitch* did, however, illuminate several important elements. One surprising one was that Justice Potter Stewart, who was one of the two dissenters in *Griswold* six years earlier,[16] now seemed potentially sympathetic to constitutional protection for abortion.[17] Second, Justice Hugo Black, who in many overly simplistic ways was then—and still is now—thought of as a predictable "liberal,"[18] came across instead as an instinctive right-to-life advocate concerned first and foremost with the status of the fetus. Indeed, during the oral argument, Justice Black questioned Washington attorney Joseph Nellis, who was speaking on behalf of Dr. Vuitch, about the status of "the child" who might be aborted. Politely but firmly, Nellis told the Justice that he was unwilling to accept Black's use of the word "child" as pertaining to a fetus.[19] This story from January 1971 underscores very memorably how the abortion arguments of these last twenty-five years since *Roe* and *Doe* have been a debate—including struggles over word usage—that did not in any way only first begin *with Roe* and *Doe* but very much, even in these modest details, *predated Roe* and *Doe*.

In May 1971, when the Burger Court accepted *Roe v. Wade* from Texas and *Doe v. Bolton* from Georgia for review, the political climate for abortion liberalization, which was so bright in 1969–70, was beginning to take a very decisive *downward* turn. When we look carefully at the political history of those years, that record again and again highlights how the issue with which the Burger Court was now starting to wrestle was already being debated—and litigated—so widely and fervently all across America that the Court was not "pushing the envelope" in any significant way, politically or legally, relative to what already was blossoming throughout American public life.

In 1970, abortion liberalization forces had won what in retrospect would be seen as their two greatest political victories. First came the passage of an abortion *repeal* statute in New York state. That new law took effect in July 1970 and essentially made abortion on request available to any woman with the wherewithal to afford the procedure and to travel to New York.[20] Indeed, people old enough to have been adults in 1970 may well remember how many women with unwanted pregnancies did in fact travel to New York during the early 1970s. Second, in November 1970, in a statewide referendum in the State of Washington, a similar abortion law repeal measure was adopted by popular vote.[21] At that time it appeared that this indeed represented the beginnings of a liberalizing wave that would spread further and further, from state to state.

However, by March and April 1971, when *Vuitch* was being decided and when the Justices were agreeing to review the proliberalization rulings that had been handed down by special three-judge federal district courts in both Texas and Georgia in *Roe* and *Doe*, the political climate was starting to change. Abortion rights forces were beginning to realize that all of a sudden *they* were on the defensive and were starting to lose ground. Both the New York and the Washington state victories were also battles that had witnessed the first popular emergence, and quick political growth, of the right-to-life organizations and campaign tactics that have been seen in much fuller flower in the years since 1973.[22] However, the years 1971 and 1972 were characterized by exactly those same political dynamics and featured exactly the same sort of photos that were utilized in much more recent times in the debate over President Clinton's 1996 veto of the Partial-Birth Abortion Ban Act.[23] All we have seen in the abortion debates of the 1980s and 1990s was also present in those 1971–72 days prior to *Roe* and *Doe*.

When the Burger Court first heard argument in *Roe v. Wade* and *Doe v. Bolton* in December 1971, it was a Court of seven rather than nine Justices, for at that point neither Justices Powell nor Rehnquist had yet taken their seats as the successors to Hugo Black and John Harlan.[24] Following those initial oral arguments, the Justices' private conference discussion of *Roe and Doe* would in time become perhaps the most infamous single event in the Court's unpleasant internal debates about Warren Burger's honesty and competence as Chief Justice of the United States. This issue need not be revisited here in its full particulars, but in *Roe* and *Doe* several Justices initially were concerned with whether Chief Justice Burger was seeking to assign both the *Roe* and *Doe* majority opinions to Justice Harry Blackmun despite the fact that he himself at conference had sounded more like a dissenter than a member of the nascent majority.[25]

The story of Justice William O. Douglas's anger at Burger over the assignments in *Roe* and *Doe*, and particularly with respect to the subsequent Court decision, initiated by Justice Blackmun and supported by Justices Powell and Rehnquist as well as the Chief Justice, to hold *Roe* and *Doe* over for reargument in the subsequent term that fall, is already well-known within the historiography of the Burger Court.[26] The ensuing situation, and the embarrassing upshot of how news of Douglas's complaint about Burger's behavior leaked to the *Washington Post* and resulted in an (unbylined) front-page story (*not* written by Bob Woodward!), a story that at that time was utterly unprecedented in the Court's history, has also been related more fully elsewhere.[27] But feelings about Burger's behavior were perhaps most strongly felt not by Justice Douglas but by Justice Potter Stewart, and it may be insufficiently appreciated that the tensions about Burger's handling of his job were both personal and professional rather than in any way ideological.

Throughout the six months following those initial oral arguments in *Roe* and *Doe*, the substantive situation within the Court was extremely unsettled and uncertain. Justice Blackmun, and what, in retrospect, looks like a decidedly firm majority of Justices, believed that the very old-fashioned, nineteenth-century Texas antiabortion statute that was struck down by the special three-judge panel that had first heard *Roe* was indeed at least constitutionally void for vagueness. Blackmun as well as several of his colleagues were considerably more uncertain, however, about what the Court should do with the more basic constitutional challenge that *Doe v. Bolton* posed to Georgia's decidedly more liberal therapeutic "reform" law that was enacted less than three years earlier in 1968.

In May and June 1972, Justice Blackmun took the lead, notwithstanding objections from Justices Douglas, Brennan, and Marshall, in recommending that both *Roe* and *Doe* should be held over for reargument in the fall, particularly so that the two newest members of the Court, Justices Powell and Rehnquist, could hear the rearguments and thereby allow for the abortion cases to be decided by a full Court of nine rather than by simply seven. That initiative provoked considerable outrage on the part of some of the expectant members of the supposed *Roe* majority, but when Chief Justice Burger and Justices White, Powell, and Rehnquist all joined with Blackmun in advocating reargument, the cases indeed were carried over.[28]

The situation within the Court shifted quietly but very significantly between June and October 1972. What at the conclusion of O.T. 1971 was a very uncertain situation for the two abortion cases was, by the beginning of O.T. 1972, no longer much in doubt. Nineteen years earlier, much the same thing had happened in the months preceding the reargument of the five cases that comprised *Brown v. Board of Education*.[29] In 1953, after setting down four questions for the reargument, the Court returned in October to find itself no longer much in doubt about what it soon would hold.[30] Much the same thing happened in the fall of 1972 with *Roe v. Wade* and *Doe v. Bolton*.

William O. Douglas's concerns to the contrary notwithstanding, Harry Blackmun was never really in much doubt about what he would do on the underlying constitutional question of abortion.[31] The numerical gap inside the Court widened even further when, to at least some people's surprise, Lewis F. Powell during September privately concluded that he too without question was going to vote in favor of a *Griswold*-type constitutional privacy holding.[32] Thus by the time that the cases were indeed reargued in October 1972, the fundamental constitutional outcome was no longer in any significant doubt.

However, what nonetheless *did* prove to be an important and surprising development was the manner in which the *Roe* and *Doe* majority opinions and holdings evolved following Justice Blackmun's first circulation of revised drafts in late November. In those drafts, Blackmun laid out an analysis under which constitutionally protected access to abortion would be available *only* up through the end of the first trimester of pregnancy. After that point, abortions would be subject to extremely far-reaching state regulation and prohibition.[33] Then, beginning in late November and reaching into mid-December, both the Brennan and Marshall chambers, in a crucially important and analytically impressive way, successfully lobbied Justice Blackmun toward an appreciation that viability, rather than the end of the first trimester, should be the fundamental cutoff point that was utilized in the *Roe* and *Doe* opinions. It was out of that process, and largely out of the impressive and well-honed input that the Brennan and Marshall chambers offered to Justice Blackmun, that *Roe* and *Doe*'s subsequently famous three-stage analysis of pregnancy arose.[34]

In retrospect, there are two primary points that ought to be emphasized about the final and official versions of the *Roe* and *Doe* opinions. Number one, as Justice Blackmun later said publicly, with his eye in part on how many earlier lower court opinions already had articulated much the same constitutional conclusion, in January 1973 *Roe* was "not such a revolutionary opinion at the time."[35] No one who has read all the decisions from that 1969–72 period preceding *Roe* and *Doe* could argue successfully against Justice Blackmun's observation.

Number two, surprising as it may seem to some people, was how relatively modest and indeed almost understated the two dissents in *Roe* and *Doe*—one by Justice White and the other by Justice Rehnquist—actually were. Both of those Justices, even in the weeks after the *Roe* and *Doe* rearguments in October 1972, said privately within the Court that they might well concur in at least some parts of the *Roe* and *Doe* holdings.[36] Indeed White's eventual dissent, if read very carefully, seems to acknowledge that perhaps the Constitution would indeed require states to allow at least those "therapeutic" abortions when an individual woman could demonstrate a particular "life" or "health" reason for terminating a pregnancy.[37] Somewhat similarly, Justice Rehnquist in his additional dissent went out of his way to acknowledge that Justice Blackmun's work on behalf of the seven-Justice majority "commands my respect."[38] These qualifying concessions or acknowledgements, it is fair to say, are a significant part of the Burger Court's experience with *Roe* and *Doe* but are also undeniably a part of the story that in subsequent years has been almost totally omitted from virtually all renditions or recapitulations of abortion law history. Highlighting the relative modesty of those two 1973 dissents also helps underscore how the internal divisions within the Burger Court over abortion grew much more intense in the years after 1973, and particularly in the years 1980–86, than was the case at any time during the 1970–73 period.

Part of that intensified divisiveness resulted from the intensely critical reactions of legal academia to *Roe* and *Doe*. Most students of abortion law will remember John Hart Ely's famous and influential article that in many ways stimulated and encouraged criticism of the Blackmun opinions.[39] Ely's essay represented a stance that a number of voices, particularly the *New Republic* magazine, continued to articulate all throughout the 1970s and 1980s in what became an unfailingly sustained drumbeat of criticism.[40] At least at the *New Republic*, that criticism intensified even further in the wake of the *Casey* decision in 1992.[41]

One need touch only briefly on what happened within the Burger Court during the late 1970s and early 1980s with respect to the abortion funding cases. First in *Maher v. Roe*[42] from Connecticut in 1977, and then more notably in *Harris v. McRae*[43] in 1980, the outcomes—particularly the 5–4 split in *Harris*—very much raise the question whether or to what extent we should speak of the 1970s and 1980s as having been the "Powell Court" rather than the "Burger Court," in much the same way that we at times wonder whether we should talk about the "Brennan Court" rather than the "Warren Court." Particularly when one looks at the period from 1980–86, when Justice Powell time and time again was the decisive vote in a host of areas, not just abortion and sexual privacy, the Court's track record requires us to acknowledge explicitly the extent to which Justice Powell represented the balance wheel of the Burger Court.

When one examines the post-*Roe* abortion cases such as *Danforth*[44] in 1976, *Colautti v. Franklin*[45] in 1979, *Akron Center*[46] in 1983, and *Thornburgh*[47] in 1986, two points most need to be underscored. One is the visibly increased intensity and emotional energy that both Justices White and Rehnquist brought to their dissents. When, for example, one looks at Justice White's opinion in *Thornburgh*,[48] it may come as something of a surprise to contrast that declaration with the much more calm and understated White dissent back in *Roe v. Wade*.[49] The increased intensity that both Justice White and Justice Rehnquist brought to the abortion divisions within the Burger Court during the 1980s was at least in part an intensity that was fueled by the criticisms and political arguments that were being voiced outside the Court itself.

Second, in addition to the intensification of White's and Rehnquist's dissents, the abortion stance that was taken by Justice O'Connor in her first two abortion cases—*Akron Center* and *Thornburgh*—and the 1986 change of heart by Chief Justice Burger in *Thornburgh* accounted for how, by 1986, what had been a 7–2 margin back in *Roe* and *Doe* in 1973 became instead a much narrower 5–4 margin in *Thornburgh*. By 1986, it again was Justice Powell who represented the fifth and determinative vote for upholding and reaffirming *Roe* and *Doe*.

But what was most notable about the final days of the Burger Court, preceding Chief Justice Burger's retirement in the summer of 1986, was not the narrow reaffirmation of *Roe* in *Thornburgh* but was instead the Burger Court's second "great"—or infamous—sexual privacy decision: its upholding of Georgia's criminal sodomy statute in *Bowers v. Hardwick*.[50] Any discussion of *Bowers* requires us to remember the particular circumstances that gave rise to the case: namely, how Michael Hardwick and his publicly unnamed sexual partner were arrested in Hardwick's own bedroom, for engaging in mutual oral sex, by a police officer who had entered Hardwick's home on other business.

Nowadays there is something of a consensus among most historians and commentators that in retrospect it was a huge error for Hardwick's attorneys to take the case forward. If interested litigators had been more painstaking and less naive in looking at what the Burger Court was doing with sexual privacy petitions prior to 1985, they could have had much more accurate—and pessimistic—expectations about what would probably come to pass in *Bowers*. Two very explicit earlier warning signs were among those that were fatally passed over. First, back in 1976, in an underappreciated case called *Doe v. Commonwealth's Attorney*,[51] from Richmond, Virginia, a declaratory judgment suit against Virginia's sodomy statute was rejected by a 2–1 margin in a three-judge federal court.[52] That defeat was appealed immediately to the Supreme Court, which, much to the amazement and consternation of the plaintiffs' attorneys, summarily affirmed the district court ruling by a 6–3 margin without even hearing arguments.[53]

Seven years after *Doe v. Commonwealth's Attorney*, an even more obscure sexual activity case, *Uplinger v. New York*,[54] was accepted for full Supreme Court review—as we in retrospect can tell from the docket sheets in the Thurgood Marshall Papers[55]—by a minimum vote of four Justices: Chief Justice Burger and Justices White, Rehnquist, and O'Connor. Argument was heard in early 1984, but four months later, *Uplinger*, by a 5–4 vote (with those four in dissent), was dismissed as improvidently granted because a prior New York state case, *People v. Onofre*,[56] on which *Uplinger* was premised, had already been denied High Court review.[57] If interested observers had paid far more careful attention at that time to what happened with *Uplinger*, they might well have realized and appreciated what would most probably come to pass in *Bowers*.

The inside-the-Court history of *Bowers* is about as fascinating a Burger Court story as there is. The latter part of that story, concerning Justice Powell's ambivalence, his switching of his vote from affirmance to reversal, and then his subsequent, postretirement acknowledgement that he believed he indeed had erred in making that switch, is already well-known among students of the Court.[58]

But the earlier part of the *Bowers* history is as good a single-case window as one can find concerning just how strategically calculating so much behavior within the Burger Court was in the mid-1980s. The initial four votes to grant were cast by Justices White, Rehnquist, Brennan, and Marshall—what we might call both ends against the middle. However, at least one Justice in that middle, Harry Blackmun, could, unlike the litigators, see what might well be coming, and Justice Blackmun went to Justice Brennan and persuaded him to withdraw his vote to grant. Nevertheless, when Brennan circulated a Memorandum to the Conference saying that he had taken a "second look" and was changing his vote to "deny," within twenty-four hours Chief Justice Burger circulated a similar memo saying that "I, too, have taken a second look" and that he would now vote to grant certiorari. Efforts to persuade Justice Marshall to shift his vote in the same way that Justice Brennan had were without avail, and hence *Bowers* in the end actually was taken by just four votes—those of Justices White, Rehnquist, Burger, and Marshall, the latter of whom certainly disagreed with the other three on the merits but who apparently did not want to so visibly follow Justice Brennan in making such a stark shift of votes.

Justice White's eventual majority opinion in *Bowers* is unquestionably the most widely and harshly criticized Supreme Court opinion of the last fifty years,[59] perhaps since *Korematsu*[60] back in 1944. However, as opposite as *Bowers* and *Roe* are, there nonetheless is no getting around the fact that within the entire substantive due process/fundamental liberty arena, those two decisions are for better and for worse the two great legacies of the Burger Court.

In conclusion, one must highlight how in the intervening ten or more years since the end of the Burger Court, the ensuing Rehnquist Court has—perhaps very surprisingly in *both* instances—vindicated one of those Burger Court legacies—*Roe*—while appearing to vitiate the other. In 1992, in *Planned Parenthood of Southeastern Pennsylvania v. Casey*,[61] and most particularly in the O'Connor-Kennedy-Souter joint opinion, a Rehnquist Court majority provided not only a fundamental reaffirmation of *Roe's* constitutional core but also what in many particulars, as any number of commentators have highlighted, was a *better* enunciation and defense of the fundamental rights at issue in *Roe* than had been offered by the majority back in 1973.

Finally, as is already clear to many observers and students of the Court, the 6–3 decision written by Justice Kennedy in May 1996 in *Romer v. Evans*,[62] the gay rights case from Colorado, started to pull the rug out from under *Bowers v. Hardwick* to at least a very significant extent. If the utter silence of the Kennedy majority opinion in *Romer* about *Bowers* was by itself not enough to point anyone toward that conclusion, then Justice Antonin Scalia's angry dissent more than completed the requirement. Scalia's *Romer* dissent—in which, in all-too-typical emotive language, he protested the majority's refusal to say anything at all about, or even cite, that ostensible precedent from only ten years earlier—actually left *Bowers* even more visibly abandoned than would have been the case if Scalia too had ignored rather than highlighted it.

Thus, it more than plausibly appears to be the case that not only is *Roe v. Wade* a *living* legacy of the Burger Court, but *Bowers v. Hardwick* now appears to be a dying legacy of the Burger Court. Indeed, both *Planned Parenthood v. Casey* and *Romer v. Evans* suggest that just as the Burger Court often extended as well as followed the work of the Warren Court, now very similarly too the Rehnquist Court has followed the Burger Court in illustrating and endorsing Judge Henry's observation that activism indeed is "here to stay."

Notes

1. 505 U.S. 833 (1992).
2. 114 S. Ct. 2309 (1994).
3. 115 S. Ct. 1624 (1995).
4. 410 U.S. 113 (1973).
5. 478 U.S. 186 (1986).
6. 116 S. Ct. 1620 (1996).
7. 410 U.S. 179 (1973).

8. 381 U.S. 479 (1965).

9. See generally Garrow, *Liberty and Sexuality: The Right to Privacy and the Making of* Roe v. Wade 335–472 (1994).

10. See id. at 335–39.

11. 505 U.S. at 912.

12. See generally Garrow, supra note 9, at 379–491.

13. See Clark, "Religion, Morality, and Abortion: A Constitutional Appraisal," 2 *Loy. U. L. Rev.* 1–11 (1969); see also Garrow, supra note 9, at 372, 416, 453, 471, 481.

14. 402 U.S. 62 (1971).

15. See Garrow, supra note 9, at 318, 350, 382–83, 417–18, 468–70.

16. See 381 U.S. at 527.

17. See Garrow, supra note 9, at 475.

18. But see Garrow, "Doing Justice," 260 *The Nation* 278–81 (Feb. 27, 1995) (reviewing Newman, *Hugo Black: A Biography*); Gerhardt, "A Tale of Two Textualists: A Critical Comparison of Justices Black and Scalia," 74 *B.U. L. Rev.* 25–66 (1994).

19. See Garrow, supra note 9, at 476.

20. See id. at 418–21, 456.

21. See id. at 466.

22. See id. at 483–84.

23. See, e.g., Garrow, "The Perils of Congress Imposing Its Medical Ideas," *Philadelphia Inquirer*, Sept. 25, 1996, at A23.

24. See Garrow, supra note 9 at 521–22.

25. See id. at 533–34.

26. See id. at 548, 552–55.

27. See id. at 555–58.

28. See id. at 552–56.

29. 347 U.S. 483 (1954).

30. See Tushnet, *Making Civil Rights Law: Thurgood Marshall and the Supreme Court, 1936–1961,* 203–04 (1994).

31. Garrow, supra note 9, at 558–59.

32. Id. at 575–76.

33. Id. at 580–81.

34. Id. at 581–86.

35. See id. at 599.

36. Id. at 581.

37. See 410 U.S. at 222–23.

38. 410 U.S. at 171.

39. See Ely, "The Wages of Crying Wolf: A Comment on *Roe v. Wade*," 82 *Yale L. J.* 920–49 (1973). See also Garrow, supra note 9, at 609–11.

40. See Garrow, supra note 9, at 606–07, 616, 692 (discussing *The New Republic*); see also Ginsburg, "Some Thoughts on Autonomy and Equality in Relation to *Roe v. Wade*," 63 *N.C. L. Rev.* 375–86 (1985), as discussed in Garrow, supra note 9, at 613, 616.

41. See Garrow, supra note 9, at 701 (discussing *The New Republic*, July 27, 1992, at 7).

42. 432 U.S. 464 (1977).

43. 448 U.S. 297 (1980).

44. Planned Parenthood of Cent. Mo. v. Danforth, 438 U.S. 52 (1976).

45. 439 U.S. 379 (1979).

46. City of Akron v. Akron Center for Reproductive Health, 462 U.S. 416 (1983).

47. Thornburgh v. American College of Obstetricians and Gynecologists, 476 U.S. 747 (1986).

48. Id. at 785.

49. 410 U.S. at 221.

50. 478 U.S. 186 (1986).

51. 425 U.S. 901 (1976).

52. 403 F. Supp. 1199 (E.D. Va. 1975).

53. See generally Garrow, supra note 9, at 621–22.

54. 467 U.S. 246 (1984).

55. See Garrow, supra note 9, at 644–46.

56. 415 N.E.2d 936, 434 N.Y.S.2d 947 (1980).

57. 451 U.S. 987 (1981).

58. See Garrow, supra note 9, at 659–61, 663–64, 666. See also Jeffries, *Justice Lewis F. Powell, Jr.* 514–30 (1994).

59. See Garrow, supra note 9, at 665–66.

60. Korematsu v. United States, 323 U.S. 214 (1944).

61. 505 U.S. 833 (1992).

62. 116 S. Ct. 1620 (1996).

· 7 ·

FREEDOM OF SPEECH

BERNARD SCHWARTZ

In August 1996, President Clinton announced new Food and Drug Administration regulations which limited cigarette advertising to which children are exposed.[1] In particular, the regulations restricted advertisements on billboards and in publications to black-and-white text-only messages and prohibited billboards with cigarette advertising within 1,000 feet of schools and playgrounds.[2] Tobacco companies responded by promising a long legal war on the restrictions, maintaining that the restrictions violated the industry's free speech rights under the First Amendment.[3] Even a *New York Times* editorial conceded that "[t]he most worrisome element of the new plan is a crackdown on advertising that may infringe the commercial free-speech rights of the tobacco industry."[4]

Commercial Speech

Before the Burger Court decisions on the subject, the term "commercial free-speech rights" was, at best, an oxymoron. That was true because, in earlier Courts, commercial speech was not protected by the First Amendment. Whatever restrictions may otherwise be imposed on governmental power over expression, affirmed *Valentine v. Chrestenson*,[5] the leading pre-Burger Court case, "the Constitution imposes no such restraint on government as respects purely commercial advertising."[6]

This was all changed when, in 1976, *Virginia State Board of Pharmacy v. Virginia Consumer Council*,[7] ruled squarely that commercial speech came within the protection of the First Amendment. A consumer group had brought an action challenging a state statute barring a pharmacist from advertising prescription drug prices. With only Justice Rehnquist dissenting, the Court struck down the law restricting prescription price advertising. Speech "which does 'no more than propose a commercial transaction'"[8] was ruled squarely within the protection of the First Amendment. Society has a strong interest in the free flow of commercial information, even advertisements.

But the Burger Court's protection of commercial speech did not stop with the prescription-price type of commercial advertising. The *Virginia State Board of*

Pharmacy opinion distinguished regulation of commercial advertising by pharmacists from regulation of other professions, noting that "[p]hysicians and lawyers, for example, do not dispense standardized products; they render professional *services* of almost infinite variety and nature."[9] A year later, in 1977, in *Bates v. State Bar*,[10] the Court dealt directly with the barring of attorney advertising. Two Arizona attorneys had opened a "legal clinic" and advertised "legal services at very reasonable fees," listing fees for certain services.

As Chief Justice Burger put it at the conference, here were "only a couple of guys soliciting clients." But he was troubled by the extension of *Virginia State Board of Pharmacy* to lawyer advertising. "Lawyers for me are a special breed of officers of the court whose First Amendment rights are inhibited. If we're ready to extend *Virginia Pharmacy* to professional services, I'm not." However, he passed on the decision.

On the First Amendment issue, five Justices (Brennan, White, Marshall, Blackmun, and Stevens) expressed the view that the Arizona rule invalidly restricted the free flow of commercial speech. As Justice Blackmun, who wrote the opinion, put it at the conference, "*Virginia Pharmacy* goes far to sustain the First Amendment attack here." However, Blackmun did say, "I'm not sure I'd go too far. Maybe we ought to stop with saying this ad is O.K."

The three dissenters at the conference (Justices Stewart, Powell, and Rehnquist) agreed with the view urged in the American Bar Association amicus brief—that all lawyer advertising was deceptive. Justice Rehnquist said, "I'd say, treat this as if it were [deceptive]. You allow the state to legislate against that danger. I'd let the State Bar assume that as to price advertising." Justice Powell, a former ABA president and the only member of the Court appointed directly from private practice, expressed the greatest concern at the proposed majority decision. "Anything beyond *Martindale* [—*Hubbell Law Directory*] is likely to be inherently deceptive and misleading. Once you let this genie out of the bottle, there will be hell to pay. A state is constitutionally free to decide that an ad like this is inherently deceptive."

The *Bates* decision, by a bare majority (the Chief Justice having joined the dissenters), struck down the Arizona rule. The state may not prohibit truthful advertisements concerning the availability and terms of routine legal services. Justice Powell continued to express concern at *Bates* and in the next case on lawyer advertising, *In re R.M.J.*[11] He told the conference that they all knew "my *Bates* views. . . . It destroyed the essential character of our profession." Despite this, Powell delivered the *R.M.J.* opinion, striking down a Missouri regulation that required lawyers to list areas of practice in the precise wording stated in the rule and prohibiting mailing of announcement cards to persons others than lawyers, friends, and relatives. At the *R.M.J.* conference, Powell had stated, "I'd reverse because everything the lawyer did was protected by *Bates*."

The lawyer advertising cases were, in many ways, the culmination of the Burger Court jurisprudence extending First Amendment protection to commercial speech. Speech proposing a commercial transaction is within the constitutional guarantee. That is as true of professional advertisements, which were considered unprofessional conduct before *Bates*, as of other advertisements proposing commercial transactions.

At the *Bates* conference, Justice Blackmun had noted that "states are entitled to time, place, and manner regulations," as far as the commercial speech at issue was concerned. But the Burger Court also held that although commercial speech is entitled to protection, the protection afforded it is "less extensive than that afforded 'noncommercial speech.'"[12] Thus, government remains free to prevent dissemination of commercial speech that is false, deceptive, or misleading or that proposes an illegal transaction. Although the state may not, as seen, prohibit truthful lawyer advertising of the type at issue in *Bates*, it may restrain or bar in-person solicitation of clients even though the solicitation is carried out by speech.[13]

Justice Powell was the primary author of the Burger Court jurisprudence covering commercial speech. The Powell approach was summarized in a Blackmun comment on the Powell draft in a case on lawyer solicitation of clients: "I read your opinion as centering between the more extreme views expressed at the conference of January 18. Although it does not express my precise position, any more than it does the positions of some of the others, it is a good middle-of-the-road opinion."[14]

The Powell approach lay between the pre-Burger extreme of no constitutional protection of commercial speech and the opposite extreme of treating commercial speech like other types of speech. While rejecting the pre-Burger holding, Justice Powell and his colleagues did not discard "the 'common-sense' distinction" between commercial speech and other varieties of speech.[15] Under the Burger Court jurisprudence, there is no parity of constitutional protection between commercial and non-commercial speech. Instead, as Justice Stevens put it in a May 16, 1980, letter to Powell, "[T]here is a lesser First Amendment interest in protecting proposals to engage in commercial transactions than there is in more pure forms of communication."[16] Hence, commercial speech is placed in a lower position in the scale of First Amendment values, making it subject to regulation that might not be permissible in the realm of noncommercial expression.[17]

Government may control commercial speech that is false, deceptive, or misleading or proposes an illegal transaction. Commercial speech that does not come within these categories is governed by the test stated by Justice Powell in *Central Hudson Gas & Electric Co. v. Public Service Commission*.[18] The Court struck down a regulation banning public utility advertising promoting electricity use, which the commission found contrary to the national policy of conserving energy. The Powell opinion—the culmination of his contribution to the Burger Court jurisprudence in this area—stated a four-part test for commercial-speech cases:

> At the outset, we must determine whether the expression is protected by the First Amendment. For commercial speech to come within that provision, it at least must concern lawful activity and not be misleading. Next, we ask whether the asserted governmental interest is substantial. If both inquiries yield positive answers, we must determine whether the regulation directly advances the governmental interest asserted, and whether it is not more extensive than is necessary to serve that interest.[19]

The first three parts were met in the *Central Hudson* case: The promotional ads were lawful commercial speech, governmental interest in conservation was substantial, and it was advanced by the regulation. But the complete ban on promotional advertising was more extensive than necessary to further energy conservation. Thus, the state's interest did not justify suppression of information about devices or services that would cause no net increase in energy use. Nor had the state shown that its interest in conservation could not be protected by more limited regulation.

Justice Powell defined commercial speech both as "speech proposing a commercial transaction" and as "expression related solely to the economic interests of the speaker and its audience."[20] In his concurring opinion, Justice Stevens asserted that the latter definition was "unquestionably too broad."[21] In a letter to Stevens, Powell stated that he believed it was entirely proper to rely on both formulations. The second definition was not at all intended to expand the scope of commercial speech. On the contrary, Powell wrote, "To me they [that is, both definitions] seem to have substantially the same reach."[22]

Justice Stevens also asserted that the challenged regulation involved "total censorship" of more than only commercial speech. "Perhaps I miss your thought," Justice Powell replied, "but I see no political content in the exhortation to purchase electricity. I have not thought there was any First Amendment distinction between the advertising of drugs by regulated pharmacists and the advertising of electricity by regulated power companies."

Political Speech

In a 1977 letter to Justice Stewart, Justice Powell referred to the view "that there can be no distinction in First Amendment analysis between, say, economic and political issues. In general theory, this may be true. But no First Amendment right is absolute, and in the balancing process that often must be applied I think we have weighted the scales more favorably where political speech is concerned."

Justice Stewart replied to Powell that "calling [expression] political rather than economic, philosophical, ethical, or social, does not lead to any difference under the First Amendment. . . . [T]he First Amendment protects the expression of *ideas*, not just those that can in one sense or another be characterized as 'political.'" The language in First Amendment cases "does not mean—and I know of no case holding—that the expression of ideas about art, literature, family life, religion, public morals, economic affairs, or other 'non-political' matters is not protected to exactly the same degree."

At the same time, there has never been any doubt that political speech is fully protected. Indeed, as Stewart put it to Powell, "[O]ur cases have on occasion suggested that speech about political matters could not be more central to the purposes of the First Amendment."[23]

In *First National Bank of Boston v. Bellotti*,[24] however, it was argued that although the state might not prohibit the commercial speech of corporations, it might ban their political speech—at least when the speech did not affect the corporation's own property or business. At issue was a statute prohibiting corporations from making contributions or expenditures to influence voting "on any question submitted to the voters, other than one materially affecting any of the property, business or assets of the corporation." Under a proviso in the law, no question "concerning the income, property or transactions of individuals" was to be deemed one affecting a corporation's property or business. The bank wanted to publicize its views on a proposed constitutional amendment authorizing a graduated personal income tax. The state attorney general decided that would violate the statute. The state court upheld the statute.

At the conference on the case, only Justice White thought that the statutory prohibition was clearly constitutional, though Justice Brennan said that he was inclined to agree with him. The other seven Justices disagreed. The Chief Justice asked, "Can the First Amendment be limited to corporations in respect of materially affecting their interests?" Burger thought not. "I can't distinguish *The New York Times* from other corporations. The state can't attach unconstitutional limitations." Justice Rehnquist asked, "Why should only *Time* and *The New York Times* have First Amendment protection?"

As Justice Stewart expressed it, they should "reverse on the ground Massachusetts can't tell the corporation it can't express its views on a proposal to have a personal income tax." But the conference decided to avoid the constitutionality of the general ban and focused on the proviso that no question concerning the taxation of individuals was to be deemed to affect a corporation's property or business. Justice Blackmun said that the proviso's "conclusive presumption is a content-related restriction" and, as such, violated the First Amendment. Justices Brennan, Powell, Rehnquist, and Stevens agreed with the Blackmun approach.

The result was an 8–1 (Justice White) vote at the conference to reverse, but only on the validity of the proviso. Justice Brennan summarized his position in a December 1, 1977, Memorandum to the Conference:

> My view at conference was that we should attempt to address only the statutory proviso and reverse on the ground of disagreement with the Supreme Judicial Court's view, implicit in its opinion, that the proviso may be constitutional. In such case, I would have reserved the question whether the First and Fourteenth Amendments invalidate the statute's provision that the only corporations that may advertise are those able to show that the referendum question is one "materially affecting any of the property, business or assets of the corporation."

Brennan was willing to go along with this approach even though at the conference he had agreed with Justice White that the statute's general prohibition was constitutional.

In a December 6 "Dear Bill" letter, Chief Justice Burger explained why he assigned the opinion to Justice Brennan. "I had assigned the case to you on the old English Judges' rule-of-thumb that when a case is to be narrowly written, it should be written by the judge 'least persuaded.'"

After considering the case, Justice Brennan wrote (again in the December 1 memo), "I am not the one who should write the Court opinion. . . . I am satisfied that the opinion cannot be limited to the constitutionality of the 'conclusive presumption' and that the constitutionality of the general ban must also be decided." The corporations "have on this record demonstrated that they have a constitutional right to spend money to oppose referenda questions concerning the adoption of graduated income taxation solely for individuals" and had attacked both the proviso and the general ban. "Since it's clear that the general prohibition would remain in effect if we struck down only the proviso, a failure to decide the constitutionality of the general prohibition would be to deny appellants relief on a constitutional claim—which is ripe for review and not moot—without deciding any issue against them."

Justice Brennan wrote that if he were to write an opinion on the general prohibition, "I presently feel that I would write to sustain its constitutionality." Hence, the opinion should be reassigned.

Justice Brennan also noted his principal concern with striking down the general Massachusetts prohibition: "Corporate spending as a corrupting influence in the political process has long been a national concern. . . . It seems to me that a decision invalidating the rather narrow Massachusetts general limitation must inevitably call into question the constitutionality of all corrupt practices acts."

This view was shared by other Justices. The Chief Justice stated in his December 6 letter, "Many of us at the Conference expressed concern about taking any step which would undermine state and federal Corrupt Practices Acts." And in a March 11, 1978, letter to Justice Powell he said, "I do not want corrupt practices statutes to be placed under a shadow."

Justice Powell himself had replied to Justice Brennan's anxiety over the corrupt practices laws in a December 6, 1977, Memorandum to the Conference:

> I share Bill Brennan's concern that we not undercut the Corrupt Practices Acts. But I do not think a holding in appellant's favor on this issue would "call into question" the constitutionality of those acts. In *Buckley v. Valeo*[25] we drew a distinction between contributions and expenditures. This case is a major step further removed even from expenditures. It involves only the expression of views on public issues; not views in support of or in opposition to a political candidate. (Even if the corporation made "contributions" in order to pool its resources with others of like mind, the dangers inherent in *political* contributions would be absent.) No problem of "corruption" is involved at all, using that term in the context of the Corrupt Practices Acts.

The Chief Justice now assigned the case to Justice Powell, whose opinion held that the states may not prohibit corporations from spending money to express their views even on issues not related to their business interests. First Amendment rights are not limited to corporations engaged in the communications business. On the contrary, "the press does not have a monopoly on either the First Amendment or the ability to enlighten."[26]

Justice Powell's view in this respect was succinctly stated in his December 6 memo: "I think it is too late to hold that persons who elect to do business in the corporate form may not express opinions through the corporation on issues of general public interest. It seems to me that circumscribing speech on the basis of its source, in the absence of a compelling interest that could not be attained otherwise, would be a most serious infringement of First Amendment rights."

The state had argued in *First National Bank* that political speech by corporations was entitled to less constitutional protection than commercial speech. The Court said that this argument would invert the First Amendment balance "by giving constitutional significance to a corporation's 'hawking of wares' while approving criminal sanctions for a bank's expression of [political] opinion."[27]

The *First National Bank* holding was applied in *Consolidated Edison Co. v. Public Service Commission*[28] to strike down a commission order that prohibited the inclusion with monthly bills of inserts discussing controversial issues. Justice Rehnquist had objected at the conference that, with the utilities' "complete monopoly, it's a too ready-made market for utility propaganda" and Justice Stevens had said that the "captive audience problem here is disturbing." The Court nevertheless ruled the prohibition invalid (with only Justice Blackmun and Rehnquist dissenting). The Powell opinion followed his conference statement "that this is regulation of speech content." As such it was subject to stricter scrutiny, but there was no compelling interest to support it. In Justice Stevens's pithy conference comment, "this is prior restraint and offensiveness to recipient [is] not a compelling interest."

The Burger Court decisions on political speech were not limited to these cases involving corporations. The Court also gave an entirely new dimension to political speech in *Buckley v. Valeo*.[29] At issue was the Federal Election Campaign Act of 1971, as amended in 1974. Under it, (1) Individual political contributions were limited to $1,000 to any single candidate, with an overall annual limitation of $25,000; independent expenditures by individuals and groups "relative to a clearly identified candidate" were limited to $1,000 a year; campaign spending by candidates for various federal offices and spending for national conventions by political parties were subject to prescribed limits; (2) contributions and expenditures above certain threshold levels must be reported and publicly disclosed; (3) a system for public funding of presidential campaign activities was established; and (4) a Federal Election Commission was established to administer and enforce the legislation.

The provisions dealing with political contributions and expenditures gave the Justices difficulty and the conference was divided. The presidential campaign funding provision and the power of Congress to require reporting and disclosure presented no problem. For Chief Justice Burger, the disclosure provisions are "the heart of the whole thing for me. I think they are constitutional and highly desirable." But he and Justices Brennan, Marshall, and Blackmun expressed doubts on the threshold limits of $10 and $100 that triggered the recordkeeping and disclosure requirements. Ultimately, however, all but the Chief Justice went along with the decision to uphold the limits, agreeing with Justice Stewart—it was "for Congress to fix the limits and not for us to second guess."

The strongest conference statement against the law was made by Justice Powell:

This statute is a revolutionary change in the system under which we've lived for 200 years. The entire Act, in purpose and effect, perpetrates the grossest infringement upon First Amendment rights. This Act, in effect, will advantage incumbents and disadvantage challengers. Instead of a system neutral on its face, where all scramble for all the money they can get, [they] rig the structure for the incumbent . . . only [to] guarantee greater concentrations of power to keep the "ins" in office.

The *Buckley* decision upheld the limitations on contributions, following the view stated by Justice Rehnquist, "It's an act, not speech." The decision was unanimous, although, at the conference, Justice Blackmun had stated, "I lean to reverse on contributions," and the Chief Justice and Justice Stewart had had doubts.

With regard to the expenditure provisions, the Chief Justice set the conference theme when he said, "This is pure speech." Justice Stewart, who was to write the portion of the opinion striking down the expenditure restrictions, stated that they were "wholly unconstitutional under the First Amendment." Justice Blackmun was of the opinion that "there's a serious First Amendment infringement, simply indefensible, in the expenditure provisions." And for Justice Powell the provisions were "the most drastic abridgements of political speech since the Alien and Sedition Acts." Justices Brennan, White, and Marshall dissented from the conference consensus on the expenditure provisions (though Brennan ultimately agreed).

At Justice Stewart's suggestion the Chief Justice gave up his assigning function and reluctantly agreed to have Justices Stewart, Brennan, and Powell work as a committee to draft the per curiam opinion. The portion dealing with expenditures was written by Stewart, who treated expenditures as a form of political speech. In effect, then, the statute infringed upon the First Amendment freedom to speak without legislative limits on candidacies for public office.

As restrictions on First Amendment rights of political expression, the challenged provisions had to satisfy the strict-scrutiny standard of review. They would be valid only if supported by a *compelling* state interest. The *Buckley* opinion rejected the argument, accepted by the court of appeals, that the governmental interest in equalizing the relative ability of individuals and groups to influence elections justified the limitations. In a November 10, 1977, Memorandum to the Conference in a later case, Justice Rehnquist stated his impression of the court of appeals acceptance of this argument in *Buckley*: "The Court of Appeals there, it seemed to me, appeared to say that in order to achieve the 'compelling state interest' of allowing everybody to be heard to some extent, Congress did not abridge the First Amendment by preventing some people from talking as much as they wanted. This seemed to me like something out of George Orwell, or like Rousseau's idea that people would be forced to be free."[30]

Symbolic Speech

The cases just discussed show that the right of free speech is not limited to mere expression of words. Thus, campaign expenditures were treated in *Buckley v. Valeo* as a form of political speech protected by the First Amendment. The notion of nonverbal speech had, however, been used to protect symbolic speech well before the Burger Court. Over half a century ago, the Court ruled that display of a red flag as a symbol of opposition to organized government is covered by First Amendment protection.[31]

In *Spence v. Washington*,[32] the Burger Court held that the same is true of a display of the flag upside down with a peace symbol affixed. The defendant in *Spence* had been convicted under a state law forbidding the exhibition of the U.S. flag with figures, symbols, or other extraneous material attached. The conference agreed (Justices White and Rehnquist dissenting) to reverse, but different views were expressed on the rationale for the decision.

On May 29, 1974, the Chief Justice circulated a three-and-a-half-page draft per curiam, which, he wrote in his covering memo, "does not fully satisfy me." Nor did it satisfy the other Justices. A new per curiam was circulated by Justice Powell essentially similar to the final plurality opinion. Although Justice Brennan had written to Justice Powell, "I . . . suggest you make it a signed opinion,"[33] the Powell draft was issued as a per curiam for a plurality of the Court.

The *Spence* per curiam held that in "the factual context and environment in which it was undertaken," the defendant's action was protected symbolic speech: "[T]here can be little doubt that appellant communicated through the use of symbols." Nor could the state justify its restriction of expression by any substantial state interest. On the contrary, there was "no interest the State may have in preserving the physical integrity of a privately owned flag [that] was significantly impaired on these facts."[34]

It should be stressed that *Spence* was not intended to indicate that flag desecration laws were, as such, violative of the First Amendment. On the contrary, as Justice Powell had stated at the *Spence* conference, although he was for reversal here, "I have a different feeling as to a desecration statute. The physical integrity of the flag may be protected"—so that the 1989 flag burning case[35] would probably have been decided differently had Powell not retired.

A few years later, in *Wooley v. Maynard*,[36] the symbolic speech concept was applied to the nonverbal expression at issue in the case. A New Hampshire law required motor vehicles to bear license plates embossed with the state motto, "Live Free or Die," and made it a misdemeanor to obscure the motto. Maynard and his wife, Jehovah's Witnesses, viewed the motto as repugnant to their moral, religious, and political beliefs and covered it up with tape. They were found guilty of violating the statute, but the district court granted an injunction against enforcement of the law.

The Burger opinion of the Court held that the New Hampshire law deprived the Maynards of their First Amendment right to refrain from speaking. The opinion asserted that the "statute in effect requires that appellees use their private property as a 'mobile billboard for the State's ideological message." Or, as a Brennan concurrence summarized the Court's holding, "Maynard cannot be compelled by the state to disseminate a message with which he disagrees."[37]

It should, however, be noted that neither *Spence* nor *Maynard* means that identifying nonverbal conduct as symbolic speech necessarily means the end of the First Amendment inquiry. As Justice Stewart put it in an April 14, 1977, letter to the Chief Justice on *Wooley v. Maynard*, "sometimes interests in free expression must be subordinated to strong societal policies." The countervailing governmental interest may be sufficiently compelling to justify the given restriction on the First Amendment right.

This may be seen from a case such as *Clark v. Community for Creative Non-Violence*,[38] decided in 1984. The National Park Service issued a permit to respondent for a demonstration to call attention to the homeless. The permit authorized erection of symbolic "tent cities" in Lafayette Park and on the Mall in Washington, D.C. Permission was, however, refused for the demonstrators to sleep in the tents. The Service relied on a regulation that allowed "camping" (defined as including sleeping) only in designated campgrounds. The lower court ruled that the regulation violated the demonstrators' right of free expression.

Opening the *Clark* conference, the Chief Justice conceded that the demonstrators' goal was "to make a 'statement' in this form." Despite this, the First Amendment claim was a "wholly frivolous claim, absolutely absurd." None of the others concurred in this characterization, but all except Justices Brennan and Marshall supported the Burger view that the decision below should be reversed. As Burger saw it, "*United States v. O'Brien*[39] supports this regulation." *O'Brien* was the case in which the Warren Court upheld a conviction for burning a draft card as an antiwar protest. The conference majority agreed that *O'Brien* required reversal. Their view was expressed by Justice Rehnquist. After stating that he agreed with the Chief Justice, Rehnquist said, "I'd treat it as symbolic speech and apply the *O'Brien* test to come out on the side of the Government. This is speech-plus, subject to regulation as plain speech is not."

The *Clark* decision followed the conference approach. The opinion recognized that sleeping in connection with the demonstration was expressive conduct. The regulation and its application to prohibit the sleeping was nevertheless ruled valid, because the *O'Brien* test was met. The regulation was upheld as a time, place, or manner restriction regulating symbolic conduct.

Speech and the Public Forum

Well before the Burger Court, the cases had developed the concept of the "public forum," giving a right of access to public places for First Amendment purposes. That concept was both applied and expanded during Chief Justice Burger's tenure. Whereas speech may not be prohibited in a public place that comes within the public forum concept, it may, nevertheless, be subjected to reasonable regulation; laws regulating the time, place, or manner of speech stand on a different footing from laws prohibiting speech altogether. Thus, the Court had held that reasonable time, place, and manner regulations, applicable to all speech irrespective of content, may be imposed.

The Burger Court applied the principle in the 1972 case of *Grayned v. Rockford*.[40] An ordinance prohibited a person from willfully making a noise or diversion that disturbed the peace or good order of a school in session. At the conference, only Justice Marshall voted to reverse the conviction. He subsequently changed his vote and was assigned the opinion upholding the ordinance as a constitutional regulation of activity around a school. The ordinance was aimed only at conduct disrupting normal school activities and, as such, was narrowly tailored to further the compelling interest in creating an atmosphere conducive to learning.

However, one thing is clear about the case law on the matter: Regulation of speech cannot be valid if it is not content neutral. A content-based restriction will be upheld only if the Court can find that the content fits within a category of speech that is itself unprotected by the First Amendment.

The principle barring content-based regulation was the basis of decision in *Southeastern Promotions v. Conrad*.[41] The petitioner had applied for use of a municipal theater for the showing of the controversial rock musical *Hair*. Although no other engagement for the theater was scheduled, the municipal board rejected the application. They determined that the production would not be "in the best interest of the community." The policy was to "allow those productions which are clean and healthful and culturally uplifting." The lower courts denied an injunction.

The *Southeastern Promotions* majority was disturbed by the board's action. A handwritten memorandum by one of the Justices asserts, "The holding below virtually annihilates much of modern theatre. The loss to culture and to First Amendment rights would be tragic."[42] The opinion of the Court compared the board's action to a censorship system. It was what Justice Douglas termed "content screening"[43] based on the board members' judgment of the musical's contents. Such a content-based prohibition was in categorical conflict with the First Amendment.

Southeastern holds that the city was not free to deny use of the public forum on the basis of a production's content. But that holding depends in turn on the holding that a municipal theater does come within the public forum concept. The *Southeastern Promotions* opinion declared categorically that municipal theaters "were public forums designed for and dedicated to expressive activities."[44] Under the decision, "a community-owned theater [is treated] as if it were the same as a city park or city street."[45] For First Amendment purposes, a public auditorium is equated with streets, parks, and other public places that come within the public forum concept.

The mere fact that a place is owned by the public does not mean that it comes within the public forum concept. Public facilities not performing speech-related functions may be treated differently. The Burger Court applied this principle to a military base in *Greer v. Spock*.[46] At issue were regulations that categorically banned partisan political speeches and demonstrations at Fort Dix. The lower courts ruled against the regulations on First Amendment grounds.

"This is the military," said Justice Stewart, who was to write the *Greer* opinion at the conference, "and our constitutional tradition to isolate the military from politics requires this." According to Justice White, the decision below "crosses the line against involving the military in politics unnecessarily. This is military property, and if we allow this, I don't know where to stop." The *Greer* opinion followed the conference consensus and upheld the challenged regulations. The Stewart opinion rejected "the principle that whenever members of the public are permitted freely to visit a place owned or operated by the Government, then that place becomes a 'public forum' for purposes of the First Amendment. Such a principle of constitutional law has never existed, and does not exist now."[47] The business of a military base like Fort Dix is to train soldiers, not to provide a public forum.

To be sure, even if a public forum is involved in the given case, it does not follow that all regulations of speech in it are invalid. Content-neutral reasonable time, place, and manner regulations will be upheld even though they regulate expression in a place coming within the public forum concept. In addition, not all public forums are alike for First Amendment purposes.

The Minnesota state fair, operated by a public corporation on state-owned land, prohibited sale or distribution of any merchandise except from a duly licensed and assigned location on the fairgrounds. Respondent, an organization espousing the Krishna religion, filed suit claiming that the rule violated their First Amendment rights. In 1981, in *Heffron v. International Society for Krishna Consciousness*,[48] the respondent asserted that the rule suppressed the practice of Sankirtan, which enjoins its members to go into public places to distribute or sell religious literature and to solicit donations. The highest state court held that the rule unconstitutionally restricted the Krishnas' religious practice.

The conference majority was for reversal, agreeing with the Chief Justice that the fair "can't allow roaming at will." Justice Stewart noted that it was "part of [Krishna] religious belief to pester people—give me money or give me back my flowers." But that did not mean the fair rule was invalid. On the contrary, said Stewart, "This is almost a paradigm of a time, place, and manner regulation and I'd reverse."

Justice Powell summed up the majority consensus by characterizing the rule as "a school book example of legitimacy." The decision upheld the challenged rule as a reasonable time, place, and manner regulation. The rule was content neutral and nondiscriminatory and served the significant state interest of order and crowd control at the state fair. Such a regulation might be too restrictive for a public street, but the state fair may be treated differently than a street, though both may come within the public forum concept. "The flow of the crowd and demands of safety are more pressing in the context of the Fair. As such, any comparisons to public streets are necessarily inexact."[49]

This essay concludes with the most criticized Burger Court decisions on the public forum concept—those dealing with privately owned shopping centers. In the 1946 case of *Marsh v. Alabama*,[50] the Court applied the public forum concept to a company-owned town, which was ruled subject to the First Amendment and might not prohibit literature distribution by a Jehovah's Witness. The Warren Court extended *Marsh* to a shopping center in the 1968 *Logan Valley* case,[51] which held that the center was the functional equivalent of the business district of the company town. The *Logan Valley* doctrine was, however, reconsidered by the Burger Court in *Lloyd Corp v. Tanner*.[52] The lower court there had ruled that a shopping center's policy of prohibiting distribution of handbills protesting the draft and the Vietnam War violated the First Amendment.

The conference voted five (Justices Douglas, Brennan, Stewart, Marshall, and Blackmun) to three for affirmance (with Chief Justice Burger passing).[53] At the conference, Justice Blackmun had declared, "This is a *Marsh* case, even if a close one." In his view, *Marsh* required affirmance, "even apart from *Logan Valley*." Blackmun, however, switched his vote and with the Chief Justice also joining the dissenters, the final decision was for reversal. The decision declined to apply *Logan Valley*, emphasizing instead factual differences between the two cases. Although *Lloyd* did not expressly overrule *Logan Valley*, it refused to treat the shopping center as a public forum for First Amendment purposes.

The refusal became established Burger Court doctrine in 1976 in *Hudgens v. National Labor Relations Board*.[54] The Court categorically ruled that the First Amendment does not apply to privately owned shopping centers. At issue was the right of strikers to enter an enclosed mall to picket their employer. The *Hudgens* decision followed the view expressed by the Chief Justice at the conference. "The mall or center is not public enough to allow this." As Burger saw it, there was "little left of *Logan Valley* and I'd expressly overrule it."

"For me," Justice Stewart, who wrote the *Hudgens* opinion, told the conference, "*Logan Valley* was a company town case. *Lloyd v. Tanner* repudiated that. Therefore, [there is] no constitutional right to picket." *Hudgens* expressly overruled *Logan Valley* and settled the law against the public forum status of shopping centers.

Conclusion

A dominant trend in the Warren Court was a shift in emphasis from property rights to personal rights. The preferred-position theory—that the Constitution gives a preferred status to personal, as opposed to property, rights—was confirmed as accepted doctrine. The result has been a double standard in the exercise by the Supreme Court of its review function. The tenet of judicial self-restraint does not rigidly bind the judge in cases involving civil liberties and other personal rights.[55] The presumption of validity gives way far more readily in cases in which life and liberty are restrained. In those cases, the legislative judgment must be scrutinized with much greater care.

Early in Chief Justice Burger's tenure, the Court stated "that the dichotomy between personal liberties and property rights is a false one. . . . In fact, a fundamental interdependence exists between the personal right to liberty and the personal right to property. Neither could have meaning without the other."[56] But the Burger Court did not abandon the preferred-position approach; on the contrary, like its predecessor, it recognized that each generation must necessarily have its own scale of values. Nineteenth-century America was concerned with the economic conquest of a continent, and property rights occupied the dominant place. A century later, individuality was dwarfed by concentrations of power and concern with personal rights had become more important. With the focus of concern on the need to preserve an area for the development of individuality, the Justices have been more ready to find legislative invasion when personal rights are involved than in the sphere of economics.[57]

The Burger Court was as willing as the Warren Court to recognize the rights guaranteed by the First Amendment as peculiarly suitable for inclusion in the preferred-position theory. The Burger Court jurisprudence definitely recognized the special constitutional function of the First Amendment—a function both explicit and indispensable.[58] The free society itself is inconceivable without what Justice Holmes called "free trade in ideas."[59] In the Burger Court, as in its predecessor, governmental power over First Amendment freedoms was narrower than that permitted over property rights.

Notes

Portions of this essay are based on conference notes and other documents made available on a confidential basis. They are identified in a manner consistent with that basis.

1. 61 Fed. Reg. 44,396 (1996).
2. *N.Y. Times*, Aug. 24, 1996, at 1.
3. Id. at 8.
4. Id. at 22.
5. 316 U.S. 52 (1942).
6. Id. at 55.
7. 425 U.S. 748 (1976).
8. Id. at 762.
9. Id. at 773 n. 25.

10. 433 U.S. 350 (1977).

11. 455 U.S. 191 (1982).

12. Zauderer v. Office of Disciplinary Counsel, 471 U.S. 626, 637 (1985).

13. Ohralik v. Ohio State Bar, 436 U.S. 447 (1978).

14. Blackmun-Powell, May 12, 1978.

15. Ohralik v. Ohio State Bar, 436 U.S. 447, 455–56 (1978).

16. Stevens-Powell, May 16, 1980.

17. Ohralik v. Ohio State Bar, 436 U.S. 447, 456 (1978).

18. 447 U.S. 557 (1980).

19. Id. at 566.

20. Id. at 562, 561.

21. Id. at 580.

22. Powell-Stevens, May 17, 1980.

23. The quotes are from Powell-Stevens, Jan. 18, 1977; Stevens-Powell, Jan. 14, 1977. Both letters are headed No. 75-1153 Abood v. Detroit Board.

24. 435 U.S. 765 (1978).

25. Infra note 29.

26. *First National Bank*, 435 U.S. at 782.

27. Id. at 784 n. 19.

28. 447 U.S. 530 (1980).

29. 424 U.S. 1 (1976).

30. See Schwartz, *Behind* Bakke: *The Supreme Court and Affirmative Action* 192 (1988).

31. Stromberg v. California, 283 U.S. 359 (1931).

32. 418 U.S. 405 (1974).

33. Brennan-Powell, June 12, 1974.

34. 418 U.S. at 410, 415.

35. Texas v. Johnson, 491 U.S. 397 (1989).

36. 430 U.S. 705 (1977).

37. Id. at 720.

38. 468 U.S. 288 (1984).

39. 391 U.S. 367 (1968).

40. 408 U.S. 104 (1972).

41. 420 U.S. 546 (1975).

42. A typed version is headed No. 73-1004 Southern [sic] Promotions v. Conrad. It was apparently not circulated.

43. *Southeastern Promotions*, 420 U.S. at 563 (Douglas, J., concurring).

44. Id. at 555.

45. Id. at 570 Rehnquist, J., dissenting.

46. 424 U.S. 828 (1976).

47. Id. at 836.

48. 452 U.S. 640 (1981).

49. Id. at 651.

50. 326 U.S. 501 (1946).

51. Amalgamated Food Employees Union v. Logan Valley Plaza, 391 U.S. 308 (1968).

52. 407 U.S. 551 (1972).

53. There is a different vote count in Woodward and Armstrong, *The Brethren: Inside the Supreme Court* 179 (1979), but it is erroneous according to the docket book I have used.

54. 424 U.S. 507 (1976).

55. Letter of Justice Stone, April 12, 1941, quoted in Mason, "The Core of Free Government, 1938–40: Mr. Justice Stone and 'Preferred Freedoms,'" 65 *Yale L. J.* 597, 626 (1956).

56. Lynch v. Household Finance Corp., 405 U.S. 538, 552 (1972).

57. Compare Kovacs v. Cooper, 336 U.S. 77, 95 (1949).

58. Greer v. Spock, 424 U.S. 828, 852 (1976) (Brennan, J., dissenting).

59. Abrams v. United States, 250 U.S. 616, 630 (1919) (Holmes, J., dissenting).

· 8 ·

FREEDOM OF THE PRESS

ANTHONY LEWIS

Issues of press freedom played a surprisingly large part in the work of the Burger Court. Hardly a term went by without a decision affecting the interests of the print or broadcast press: more than twenty significant cases in the seventeen years that Warren E. Burger was Chief Justice. More often than not, press claims prevailed. But one reads through those decisions without sensing a clear or compelling vision of the freedom at stake. There is no opinion of the Court with the air of a great occasion: no *Near v. Minnesota*,[1] calling up Tudor and Stuart history to interpret the First Amendment's command against "abridging the freedom of speech, or of the press"; no *New York Times v. Sullivan*,[2] reordering 173 years of defamation law. On some occasions, indeed, the Burger Court left us unclear on exactly what had been decided. That was so, for example, in a case treated as a great victory for freedom of the press, the Pentagon Papers case.[3] It was so in *Branzburg v. Hayes*,[4] which rejected press claims of a constitutional privilege not to testify about confidential sources. Altogether, one could say of the Burger Court's decisions on freedom of the press what Winston Churchill supposedly said of a dessert served to him at a dinner party: "a pudding without a theme."

The Pentagon Papers case, *New York Times Co. v. United States*,[5] raised the most agitated questions of the time on press freedom and public policy. On June 13, 1971, the *Times* began publishing a series based on a secret history of the Vietnam War prepared in the Pentagon at the direction of former Secretary of Defense Robert McNamara. With the news article there were pages of excerpts from highly classified documents showing how United States involvement in the war had begun, and been intensified, in ways designed to mislead the American public or keep it ignorant of the real policy. After three days, publication was halted when Federal District Judge Murray I. Gurfein issued a temporary restraining order at the government's request. After a further hearing Judge Gurfein decided to deny an injunction, saying in an opinion that those in authority must suffer "a cantankerous press, an obstinate press, a ubiquitous press" in order to preserve the "greater values of freedom of expression and the right of the people to know."[6] On June 23, the U.S. Court of Appeals for the Second Circuit reversed Judge Gurfein, ordering further hearings on how disclosure of particular secrets might damage national security.[7] *The Washington Post* had meanwhile begun a series of articles based on the Pentagon Papers. The Court of Appeals for the District of Columbia, disagreeing with the Second Circuit, denied the government's request for an injunction against the *Post*.[8]

The freighted conflict reached the Supreme Court at once. On Friday, June 25, the Court granted petitions for certiorari and set the cases for argument the next day.[9] Four members of the Court—Justices Black, Douglas, Brennan, and Marshall—noted that they would have vacated all restraints on the newspapers without oral argument.

On June 30, just two weeks after the first restraining order against the *Times*, the extraordinary pell-mell litigation ended. The Supreme Court removed all restraints on publication. It was a famous victory[10] for freedom of the press. But when the celebrations cooled, editors and their lawyers understood that it was not so clear what the Court had decided.

In a three-paragraph per curiam opinion, the Court said only that the government had not met the "heavy burden" of justifying any prior restraint. There were three dissenting opinions, by Chief Justice Burger (who suggested that the *Times*, in failing to return "purloined documents" to the government, had shown less responsibility than a taxi driver), Justice Harlan, and Justice Blackmun. And each of the six Justices in the majority wrote an opinion. Justice Marshall based his on the absence of any statute authorizing injunctive relief against disclosure of defense secrets, indeed the past rejection by Congress of such proposals. Justice Douglas emphasized the same point. Justice White indicated that he concurred reluctantly and only because of the "extraordinary protections against prior restraints"; he said he would have "no difficulty in sustaining" criminal convictions for disclosure of these materials and helpfully pointed out criminal statutes that might be used against the newspapers and their staffs. Justice Brennan wrote to caution that the series of restraints imposed on the newspapers in these cases should not be taken as a precedent for temporary prior restraints. Justice Stewart said, in what became a much-quoted test, that he voted as he did because he did not believe that disclosure of the secret documents at issue would "surely result in direct, immediate and irreparable damage to our Nation or its people."[11] Justice Black alone summoned up First Amendment passion in what was to be his last opinion before his retirement and death. "The press was protected" by the amendment, he wrote, "so that it could bare the secrets of government and inform the people. Only a free and unrestrained press can effectively expose deception in government. . . . In revealing the workings of government that led to the Vietnam War, the newspapers nobly did precisely that which the Founding Fathers hoped and trusted they would do."[12]

Professor Alexander M. Bickel, who argued the Pentagon Papers case for the *Times*, wrote afterward that until then there had never been an attempt by the federal government to impose prior restraints on a newspaper. "The *New York Times* won its case," he said, "but that spell was broken, and in a sense freedom was thus diminished."[13]

And Justice Brennan's warning against letting the pattern of this litigation open the way for future restraints was not heeded. After 1971, judges did from time to time forbid publication temporarily. A notable example came in 1979 when the *Progressive* magazine prepared to publish an article entitled "The H-Bomb Secret: How We Got It, Why We're Telling It." The Department of Justice, which in the Pentagon Papers case had argued that the secrets in those documents mortally threatened the country, now explained that decision as one that dealt with merely historical material. It persuaded a federal district judge to forbid publication of the H-bomb article. The injunction lasted for months, until the *Progressive* showed that the "secrets" in its article were on the open shelves of libraries and were otherwise publicly available.[14]

The Burger Court's other venture into the area of government secrets produced a disaster for First Amendment values. This was *Snepp v. United States*,[15] decided in 1980. Frank Snepp was a CIA official in Vietnam. At the end of the war he saw the United States abandon intelligence that would point the victorious North Vietnamese toward those who had helped the United States, ensuring their punishment. In distress, he wrote a book called *Decent Interval*—and, after he resigned, had it published without first submitting the manuscript to the agency for censorship, as he had promised to do. The Supreme Court, in a per curiam that bore the marks of authorship by Chief Justice Burger, imposed on Snepp what it called a "constructive trust" requiring him to turn over to the U.S. Treasury all his royalties from the book. Snepp was also put under a lifetime injunction requiring him to clear with the CIA any writing or speech touching on matters with which he had dealt as an official, such as the Vietnam War. Under this Draconian restraint, Snepp had to submit for clearance a book review commissioned from him by *The Los Angeles Times* and even the manuscript of a novel.

The press did not pay great attention to the *Snepp* case because no press entity was directly involved. But the doctrine of the case was a menacing weapon to silence those on whom the press necessarily relied as sources for material on what Justice Black had called "deception in government"—and where deception was most common, in defense and security matters. The decision opened the way for the government to impose on large numbers of its employees, not just those in intelligence, rules requiring them to clear writings even after they left official life. Moreover, the *Snepp* case ignored what seemed to be the two critical protective strains in the various Pentagon Papers opinions. The Court did not require any basis in statute or precedent for the "constructive trust" it imposed on Snepp. Nor did it require the government to meet a "heavy burden," or any burden, to show what Snepp's writings would, as Justice Stewart said, "surely result in direct, immediate and irreparable damage."

In the years after the Pentagon Papers case, prior restraints on the press proliferated in one area especially: where judges saw a risk to fair trial. Journalists, adept at using words to protect their interest, coined a damning phrase for such restraints: "gag orders." The Burger Court addressed them in 1976 in *Nebraska Press Association v. Stuart*.[16] The case arose from a gruesome multiple murder in a small town in Nebraska. After the arrest of a suspect, the trial judge enjoined local and national media from publishing anything about his alleged confession or other material "strongly implicative" of his guilt until after the jury had been empaneled, so jurors would not be prejudiced. The Supreme Court held the order unconstitutional.

But the opinion of the Court, by Chief Justice Burger, declined to adopt a categorical rule that gag orders in criminal cases violate the First Amendment. Instead, it examined such particulars as the facts in this case and the utility of other means to prevent prejudiced jurors. As the standard for weighing the factors, it used the test laid down by Judge Learned Hand in 1950 in the *Dennis* case,[17] the prosecution of Communist Party leaders that marked a dismal low point of protection for free expression. "The gravity of the evil," Hand said, "discounted by its improbability, justifies such invasion of free speech as is necessary to avoid the danger."[18] The choice of that notoriously unsuccessful test led Benno Schmidt to describe the *Nebraska* decision as "an expansion of freedom and contraction of theory."[19] Yet if the Supreme Court was not prepared to allow restraints on publication of such highly prejudicial matters as a confession in an inflammatory murder case in a small town, it was hard to see when restraining orders would be allowable. And in fact the *Nebraska* decision just about ended them, despite its unconvincing doctrinal foundation.

The tension between fair trial and free press produced a pair of decisions that must be accounted among the strangest episodes in the Burger years. In *Gannett v. DePasquale*[20] in 1979 the Court rejected press objections to an upstate New York trial judge's closing of his courtroom to both press and public during a pretrial hearing on a defense motion to suppress evidence in a sensational murder case. The judge acted, he said, to prevent prejudice to a future jury, and both defense and prosecution agreed to the closing. The Supreme Court's opinion, by Justice Stewart, focused on the Sixth Amendment's guarantee to an accused of a "public trial." That right ran only to the accused, Justice Stewart said: "Members of the public have no constitutional right under the Sixth and Fourteenth Amendments to attend criminal trials."[21] Justice Blackmun, writing in dissent for himself and three others, argued that a pretrial suppression hearing may give the public its only chance to assess police behavior; in Seneca County, New York, where this hearing took place, not one criminal case proceeded to trial that year. Only Justice Powell, concurring, mentioned the First Amendment; if it applied, he said, its demand for a weighing of the interest in openness had been met.

The *Gannett* decision was denounced by the press, and it led a number of trial judges around the country to close criminal trials. Those reactions were evidently embarrassing to some of the Justices, who made defensive public comments. Chief Justice Burger told a Gannett News Service reporter that judges had misread the decision, which he said "referred to pretrial proceedings only."[22]

Then came a quick opportunity for the Court to heal the self-inflicted wound: the case of *Richmond Newspapers v. Virginia*.[23] Defense counsel in a Virginia murder trial had moved to close the courtroom, and with the prosecutor's agreement the judge so ordered. The Supreme Court, considering the newspapers' objections in the term after *Gannett*, could hardly reopen the Sixth Amendment question it had just decided. If it was to reverse the closing of the Richmond courtroom and allay press outrage, it was thrown back on the First Amendment as a ground for decision. But that raised hard problems. Through its history, the First Amendment had been held to protect the press in publishing what it knew, without restraint or penalty. But the Supreme Court had never interpreted the Amendment squarely to give the press a right of access to news. Indeed, the Burger Court in a series of prison cases had rejected just such a press claim. In *Pell v. Procunier*[24] and *Saxbe v. Washington Post*[25] in 1974, and again in *Houchins v. KQED*[26] in 1978, the Court refused to overturn various prison rules that, among other things, barred the press from interviewing particular prisoners.

The Court, deciding *Richmond Newspapers* a year to the day after *Gannett*, held by a 7–1 vote that the closing of the Virginia courtroom had violated the First Amendment. There was no opinion of the Court, and six separate opinions of those in the majority made a strange melange. Chief Justice Burger struggled to find a ground of decision that would not invite press claims of a constitutional right of access to all kinds of official institutions—the Supreme Court's conference, for example. To that end he emphasized the Anglo-American tradition of open trials. With that theme he joined the First Amendment value of "freedom of communication on matters relating to the functioning of government." And free speech, he said, "carries with it some freedom to listen." In sum, the First Amendment prohibited the closing of "courtroom doors which had long been open to the public at the time that amendment was adopted." The Chief Justice began his opinion by saying that the case presented a "narrow question."[27]

Justice Stevens joined that opinion along with Justice White, yet he had an opinion of his own that began: "This is a watershed case." For the first time, he said, "the Court unequivocally holds that an arbitrary interference with access to important information is an abridgment of the freedoms of speech and of the press protected by the First Amendment."[28] Justice Stevens, who had dissented in the last prison case, *Houchins*, saw the occasion as vindication. But so far the Court has not applied the new right of access to news beyond the courtroom context.

One strongly asserted press claim that did not fare well in the Burger Court was for a journalists' testimonial privilege. In *Branzburg v. Hayes*,[29] decided in 1972, reporters in Kentucky, Massachusetts, and California refused to appear before grand juries to answer questions about possible criminal activity that they had witnessed—the making of narcotic drugs in one case; meetings of the Black Panthers in another. The reporters argued that going behind the closed doors of a grand jury, even if they then refused to testify about confidential sources, would arouse suspicions in the minds of the sources of these stories and destroy confidential relationships. By a 5–4 vote, the Supreme Court declined to find in the First Amendment either an absolute privilege for journalists or a qualified one that would require the government to show a compelling interest in getting from reporters information otherwise unobtainable.

Justice White, writing the opinion of the Court, conceded in a reluctant double negative that "news gathering is not without its First Amendment protections."[30] (Chief Justice Burger invoked that slim reed as one foundation for the right of access to trials established in *Richmond Newspapers v. Virginia*.) But Justice White said a constitutional privilege for journalists would involve the judiciary in daunting problems of definition and balancing. Who, for example, should qualify as a journalist? Would it be right to exclude "the lonely pamphleteer"?[31] Not everyone in the press would disagree with that point, as the profession in this country is firmly opposed to any idea of official licensing.

Some in the press also worry that a constitutional privilege would seem to put them on a higher plane, increasing an already evident public resentment. Justice White observed, in a passing footnote, that Chief Justice Marshall had said that a subpoena could issue to the President of the United States.[32] Not so long afterward a subpoena issued to President Nixon, and the Supreme Court upheld it.[33] Should the Constitution be read to afford greater protection to press relationships with sources than to a President's conversations in the oval office?

Branzburg has not, in fact, had much of an impact on the world of journalism. Its rejection of the privilege claim was blurred because Justice Powell, while joining the opinion of the Court, also wrote one of his own that called on trial courts to balance, case by case, the interests of "freedom of the press and the obligation of all citizens to give relevant testimony with respect to criminal conduct."[34] Justice Stewart, dissenting, called the Powell opinion "enigmatic,"[35] and judges in lower courts have often seen in it a reason to give journalists something of a qualified privilege. In any event, few judges are eager for conflicts with the press. So it is happily a rare event when someone presses a journalist to the point of jail for contempt of court for refusing to testify.

No testimonial privilege case has been decided by the Supreme Court since *Branzburg*, undoubtedly a good thing from the point of view of press lawyers. In other cases the Burger Court showed little sympathy for similar press claims. In *Zurcher v. Stanford Daily*,[36] in 1978, it rejected the argument that police looking for photographs of a violent demonstration should not have used a warrant to search the Stanford newspaper but should have proceeded instead by subpoena. (Congress, in response to the decision, passed a law restricting search or seizure not only of press material—the press was wary of special legislation for itself—but of any material designed to be disseminated in a newspaper, book, broadcast, "or similar form of public communication," perhaps including the lonely pamphleteer.) And in *Herbert v. Lando*[37] in 1979, the Court held that a broadcaster defendant in a libel action had no privilege to withhold "outtakes"—that is, film and other material not used in the disputed program—sought by the plaintiff in discovery.

On one subject the press prevailed in every one of a series of cases that came to the Burger Court, though without establishing a categorical principle. The question was whether the press could be penalized for publishing truthful information, lawfully obtained, that the state had for one reason or another declared confidential. The series began in 1975 with the case of *Cox Broadcasting Corporation v. Cohn*.[38] Georgia law made it a crime to broadcast the name of a rape victim. A television company nevertheless broadcast the name of a young woman who had been raped and murdered. The victim's father sued the broadcaster for damages, and the Georgia courts held that he had a claim under the state's law of privacy. When the case came to the Supreme Court, it was seen as a vehicle to decide a question that had been open for decades. One of the classic privacy torts, developed from the famous article on privacy by Warren and Brandeis[39] and now part of statutory or common law in most states, is the publication of private facts. The question was whether the First Amendment permitted the award of damages for that tort when the publication was truthful. To give a well-known example, was California right to let a former bordello madam maintain a privacy action for publication of her lurid past after she had won respectability under another name? But the Supreme Court avoided resolving the ultimate question in the *Cohn* case. The broadcaster had obtained the name of the rape victim from state indictments, and the Court held that a state may not impose penalties for accurate publication of information from a public record.

Cox v. Cohn was followed by *Oklahoma Publishing Co. v. District Court.*[40] An Oklahoma court forbade the press to publish the name of an eleven-year-old boy charged, in a juvenile proceeding, with firing a fatal shot. The name had previously been disclosed in an open hearing. The Supreme Court summarily reversed, saying that the First Amendment did not allow a state court to prohibit the publication of "widely disseminated information obtained at court proceedings . . . open to the public."[41]

Next came *Landmark Communications v. Virginia.*[42] Virginia law provided that proceedings of a commission to investigate complaints of judicial misconduct should be confidential. A newspaper that published the name of a judge under investigation was convicted of a misdemeanor. The newspaper urged the Supreme Court to hold that the press could never be penalized for truthful reporting on public officials' conduct of their official duties, but the Court did not go that far. It reversed on the ground that the Virginia courts should have considered whether the publication presented a clear and present danger of creating unfairness in the administration of justice: a test most unlikely to be passed. Once again the Court held back from a categorical holding that truthful publication could never be penalized. Nearly twenty years later the question is still open.

If a newspaper could not, in the decided cases, be forbidden to publish what it had lawfully learned, could it be required by law to print material in what the state found to be the interest of fairness? That was the question in *Miami Herald Publishing Co. v. Tornillo.*[43] A Florida law provided that any candidate for election attacked by a newspaper could demand that the paper print a reply of equal length and prominence. The right-of-reply law grew out of concern about the growing number of one-newspaper towns in the United States, and other countries have adopted similar laws. But the Burger Court had no difficulty in finding the concept a violation of the First Amendment. The opinion of the Court, by Chief Justice Burger, said: "The choice of material to go into a newspaper . . . and treatment of public issues and public officials—whether fair or unfair—constitute the exercise of editorial control and judgment."[44] In that process, the opinion indicated, government could not intervene.

Finally, in the press decisions of the Burger Court, there are those dealing with the romantic subject of defamation: romantic, for Court watchers, because it is in defamation that the Supreme Court has made some of its most transforming decisions of modern times. The Burger Court's task was to carry on the development of *New York Times v. Sullivan,*[45] the 1964 case that said public officials must show knowing or reckless falsehood in a publication to collect libel damages. The first question addressed was whether, and to what extent, constitutional standards applied when the libel plaintiff was not an official. In 1971, in *Rosenbloom v. Metromedia,*[46] a divided Court said the test should focus not on the status of the plaintiff but on the subject of the publication. Justice Brennan, in a plurality opinion joined only by Chief Justice Burger and Justice Blackmum, said that the *Sullivan* test must be met in any case "involving matters of public or general concern, without regard to whether the persons involved are famous or anonymous."[47]

Three years later, in *Gertz v. Robert Welch, Inc.*,[48] a 5–4 majority took the opposite tack. Justice Powell, writing for the Court, said the requirement of knowing or reckless falsity should apply whenever the plaintiff was a "public figure." Powell described two kinds of public figures: those who have "thrust themselves to the forefront of particular public controversies"[49] and those of general prominence. Typical examples of the latter are movie stars, whose inclusion in a constitutional doctrine designed originally to protect citizen criticism of government seems to me an anomaly injurious to the integrity of the doctrine. Justice Powell went further. He said for the Court that in defamation cases with purely private plaintiffs the states could not impose liability without fault. That is, a plaintiff would have to show at least that the person who published a damaging statement was negligent in doing so.

This new constitutional rule, bitterly assailed by Justice White in dissent, reversed one of the main principles of the common law of defamation: that no fault need be shown beyond the mere fact of publication. In Britain, for example, it does not matter whether a damaging mistake in a newspaper story was entirely innocent or even made despite the most careful checking; the newspaper loses. And Justice Powell addressed one more question: damages. At common law, defamation actions—unlike those in other torts—require no proof of damages. Damage is presumed. Now Justice Powell said that there could be no recovery of presumed or punitive damages unless the test of knowing or reckless falsehood was met. Moreover, he said, compensatory damages must be limited to those for "actual injury."

That last aspect of the *Gertz* decision seemed at the time to promise another revolution in defamation law, with a developing constitutional standard of what could constitute damage for "actual injury." But Justice Powell added that "actual injury is not limited to out-of-pocket loss"[50] and could include personal humiliation, mental anguish, and suffering. Those vague concepts vitiated the seeming promise of limits on mushrooming libel damages. Juries continued to bring in libel verdicts in the millions, most though not all of them reversed for one reason or another but not because of any damage limit in constitutional doctrine.

After *Gertz* the Supreme Court spent some time defining who qualified as a public figure. Among those who did not were a society figure involved in a much-publicized divorce case,[51] a scientist whose federal grants for research on the emotional responses of monkeys were ridiculed by Senator William Proxmire,[52] and a man who years before had pleaded guilty to contempt for failing to respond to a subpoena from a grand jury investigating alleged Soviet espionage.[53]

Then came a moment when the whole constitutional defamation structure seemed at risk. In *Dun & Bradstreet v. Greenmoss Builders*,[54] in 1985, the Court held that the rule on presumed or punitive damages laid down in *Gertz* applied only when the challenged statements involved "matters of public concern."[55] There was no opinion of the Court, and two concurring Justices used their opinions to attack *New York Times v. Sullivan*.

Justice White, who had joined Justice Brennan's opinion in *Sullivan* in 1964, now called it a mistake that left press lies uncorrected. Chief Justice Burger said he agreed with Justice White that *Times v. Sullivan* "should be reexamined." He ended his opinion with what he called "an aphorism of journalism"—it is really a journalists' joke—that "too much checking on the facts has ruined many a good news story."[56]

In the atmosphere of anger at the press, many in the profession feared that the great protections established in *Times v. Sullivan* and the cases that followed would be lost. Certainly Justice Brennan was concerned. But then, in the last term of Warren Burger's tenure as Chief Justice, in 1986, the Supreme Court made a decision that solidified and even enlarged the constitutional defamation doctrine. The case was *Philadelphia Newspapers v. Hepps*[57]; the question there was whether a plaintiff who was a private figure had the burden of proving that a challenged statement was false. Justice O'Connor, for a majority of five, answered yes. That reversed one more common-law defamation rule, that the defendant in a libel case has the burden of proving truth. In the actual world of libel litigation, that was an extremely important change, as any British editor who has tried to meet the burden of proving a story true in all material particulars could painfully testify.

In defamation, then, as in other areas of First Amendment law, the Burger Court's opinions trace a wavering line. The shift from *Rosenbloom* to *Gertz,* like the contrast between Pentagon Papers and *Snepp* and the 180-degree turn from *Gannett* to *Richmond Newspapers,* marked a Court with no clear institutional vision of what our society means by "freedom of speech, or of the press." As Vincent Blasi said of the Burger Court generally, its work had "none of the generative quality or moral force of the Warren Court's legacy."[58]

When the Supreme Court rejected a press claim in the Burger years, editors and publishers too often reacted hysterically. *The Los Angeles Times* called the *Herbert* decision, requiring the press to answer questions about its editorial process in libel cases, "Orwellian."[59] An editor of the *St. Louis Post-Dispatch* said the same decision had "the potential of totally inhibiting the press to a degree seldom seen outside a dictatorial or Fascist country."[60] Justice Brennan commented—and the press had no better friend—that attacks of that kind were unjustified. He urged the press to be more careful and more credible, adding: "This may involve a certain loss of innocence, a certain recognition that the press, like other institutions, must accommodate a variety of important social interests."[61]

The truth is that the American press emerged from the Burger years, whatever the philosophical or rhetorical failings of the Court's opinions, with its freedom intact. It is a more legalized freedom now, as it is a more legalized society. But in no other country can the press be as confident of its rights.

Notes

1. 283 U.S. 697 (1931).
2. 376 U.S. 254 (1964).
3. New York Times Co. v. United States, 403 U.S. 713 (1971).
4. 408 U.S. 665 (1972).
5. 403 U.S. 713 (1971).
6. 328 F. Supp. 324 (S.D.N.Y. 1971).
7. 444 F.2d 544 (2d Cir. 1971).

8. 446 F.2d 1327 (D.C. Cir. 1971).

9. 403 U.S. 942, 943 (1971).

10. "But what good came of it at last? . . . 'Why that I cannot tell,' said he, 'But 'twas a famous victory.'" Southey, *The Battle of Blenheim* in *A Choice of Southey's Verse* 39 (1970).

11. 403 U.S. at 730.

12. Id. at 717.

13. Bickel, *The Morality of Consent* 61 (1975).

14. The case is discussed in Schwartz, *Constitutional Issues: Freedom of the Press* 23 (1992).

15. 444 U.S. 507 (1980).

16. 427 U.S. 539 (1976).

17. United States v. Dennis, 183 F.2d 201 (2d Cir. 1950), aff'd, 341 U.S. 494 (1951).

18. 183 F.2d. at 212.

19. Schmidt, "Nebraska Press Association: An Expansion of Freedom and Contraction of Theory," 29 *Stan. L. Rev.* 431 (1977).

20. 443 U.S. 368 (1979).

21. Id. at 391.

22. See *N.Y. Times*, Aug. 11, 1979, col. 4, at 43.

23. 448 U.S. 555 (1980).

24. 417 U.S. 817 (1974).

25. 417 U.S. 843 (1974).

26. 438 U.S. 1 (1978).

27. 448 U.S. at 575, 576, 558.

28. Id. at 582, 583.

29. 408 U.S. 665 (1972).

30. Id. at 707.

31. Id. at 704.

32. Id. at 688, n. 26.

33. United States v. Nixon, 418 U.S. 683 (1974).

34. 408 U.S. at 710.

35. Id.

36. 436 U.S. 547 (1978).

37. 441 U.S. 153 (1979).

38. 420 U.S. 469 (1975).

39. Warren and Brandeis, "The Right to Privacy," 4 *Harv. L. Rev.* 193 (1890).

40. 430 U.S. 308 (1977).

41. Id. at 310.

42. 435 U.S. 829 (1978).

43. 418 U.S. 241 (1974).

44. Id. at 258.

45. 376 U.S. 254 (1964).

46. 403 U.S. 29 (1971).

47. Id. at 44.

48. 418 U.S. 323 (1974).

49. Id. at 345.

50. Id. at 350.

51. Time, Inc. v. Firestone, 424 U.S. 448 (1976).

52. Hutchinson v. Proxmire, 443 U.S. 111 (1979).

53. Wolston v. Reader's Digest, 443 U.S. 157 (1979).

54. 472 U.S. 749 (1985).

55. Id. at 761.
56. Id. at 764.
57. 475 U.S. 767 (1986).
58. *The Burger Court: The Counter-Revolution That Wasn't* 216 (Blasi ed., 1983).
59. See "Address by William J. Brennan Jr.," 32 *Rutgers L. Rev.* 173, 180 & n. 19 (1979).
60. Id. at 179 & n. 15.
61. Id. at 181.

9

CHURCH AND STATE

ROBERT F. DRINAN, S.J.

W hen Warren E. Burger was appointed Chief Justice of the United States by President Nixon in 1969 it was widely assumed that the fundamental framework of the Earl Warren Court on church and state would be radically changed. This assumption became more commonly accepted when President Nixon during his first term as President was able to place three more persons on the Court— Harry A. Blackmun, Lewis F. Powell, Jr., and William H. Rehnquist.

Nevertheless, during the tenure of Chief Justice Burger from 1969 to 1986, there were few radical changes in the Court's interpretation of the two clauses about religion in the First Amendment. The Burger Court ruled on church-state issues in some thirty cases; the guidelines set forth in cases such as *Everson*,[1] *McCollum*,[2] *Zorach*,[3] and *Schempp*[4] were not radically altered. And Supreme Court decisions about the Free Exercise Clause were sometimes but not always expanded.

Church-state separationists in general take kindly to Warren Burger's jurisprudence on the relationship of religion and government. That jurisprudence has become somewhat confused and even incoherent since 1986 when Burger left the Court. Indeed, it may be that history will record that the Supreme Court in the Burger years was the last to continue and develop the traditional church-state positions of the Supreme Court. The Supreme Court since 1986 has weakened its precedents against aid to denominational schools and has confused, if not repudiated, some of the essential teachings of its approach to the free exercise of religion.

As a result, complex questions arise when one attempts to assess the results and the reasoning of the decisions of the Burger Court. If that tribunal had made its opinions more cogent and convincing, would the Rehnquist Court have departed so sharply from the legacy of the Warren and Burger Courts? Or has the nature of the problem shifted due to the radical change in the way the nation looks on issues related to religion and the law? Or are the appointees of the Reagan and Bush years so committed to a different view of the Establishment and Free Exercise Clauses that they are determined to bring about a substantial alteration of the approach to these issues that characterize the Court from 1947 until Burger retired?

No one can clearly predict what the Rehnquist Court will do to church-state relations, but the intense, widespread, and even sometimes hysterical feelings that the government should do more to encourage and foster religion may have an unforeseen effect even on the unelected judges in the nation's highest tribunal.

Financial Aid

Warren Burger's first constitutional decision was *Walz v. Tax Commission*[5] in 1970. With only Justice Douglas in dissent, the Court rejected a challenge to tax exemption for churches. For Burger personally it was not difficult to turn back a request to invalidate a privilege granted to religious groups almost from time immemorial. Clearly tax exemption was originally designed to aid religion by giving it material and financial benefits which are almost beyond calculation. But Chief Justice Burger rested his opinion on the newly minted idea that the government in its dealings with religion must avoid "excessive entanglement." Such entanglement would surely be inevitable, the Court reasoned, if agencies of government had to decide on what church-state entities had to pay by way of taxes. On this relatively new and still disputed element of church-state jurisprudence, the Burger Court evaded a plausible challenge made to tax exemption by Mr. Walz and the American Civil Liberties Union. The Court's position was, however, supported in briefs by all the major Protestant, Catholic, and Jewish organizations in the nation, as well as by briefs by thirty-six state attorneys general. Even the group called Protestants and Others United for the Separation of Church and State (now known as Americans United) urged in its brief that the courts sustain the constitutionality of tax exemption for churches.

Although the Burger Court's decision in *Walz* does not appear to be overwhelmingly learned or especially persuasive, it has never been questioned since it was decided in 1970. The acceptance of *Walz* suggests that there might well be a consensus on church-state matters which belies the abiding controversies that continue on issues related to prayer in public schools and financial assistance to religiously affiliated schools.

For the Burger Court the *Walz* decision was a ray of bright sunshine before the Court entered into the thicket of resolving the demands at the state level for financial assistance to nonpublic and particularly to Catholic schools. The request for aid to the secular aspects of Catholic schools and colleges came in 1971 in two cases—*Lemon v. Kurtzman*[6] and *Tilton v. Richardson*.[7]

Chief Justice Burger wrote the majority view and evolved the now famous *Lemon* test. In *DiCenso*,[8] decided the same day, the Court struck down the Rhode Island Salary Supplementation Act, a measure that permitted the government to pay 15 percent of the salary of teachers of secular subjects in parochial schools provided that the average per-pupil expenditure was below the average in public schools. In *Lemon*, the Court invalidated a Pennsylvania scheme that authorized the state superintendent of schools to "purchase" specified secular educational services just as the government can purchase services from private groups for orphans, sick people, or the elderly.

In 1984, Leo Pfeffer speculated that Chief Justice Burger probably lived to regret his decision in *Lemon*, because in later cases he almost always dissented from rulings that forbade aid to religiously affiliated schools.[9] But the three-part *Lemon* test declared by Burger lives on and is deemed by many to be one of Burger's contributions to the clarification of the Establishment Clause. The test prohibits a law whose primary purpose is to aid or deter religion or whose primary effect helps or hurts religion or results in "excessive entanglement" between government and religion. Any law therefore has to clear all three hurdles. Although Justice Antonin Scalia has spoken harshly about the *Lemon* ruling,[10] it has been durable since its creation in 1971 by the Burger Court.

The *Lemon* decision was unanimous except for a partial dissent by Justice White. But in *Tilton v. Richardson*, decided the same day, a 5–4 majority sustained the constitutionality of federal grants for buildings on the campuses of four Catholic colleges in Connecticut. *Lemon* and *Tilton* were the first examples of the deep unresolved differences in the Burger Court over the meaning of the Establishment Clause. It is easy to argue that *Tilton* is not consistent with the three-part test in *Lemon*, but the author of *Lemon*, writing the majority opinion in *Tilton*, rejected as "simplistic" the argument that every form of financial aid to church-sponsored activities violates the establishment rule.[11] Citing *Everson*[12] and also *Board of Education v. Allen*,[13] Chief Justice Burger saw no constitutional difficulty in allowing millions of dollars to four Catholic colleges because these grants were one-time events for clearly secular purposes, triggering no need of governmental inspection or entanglement. Justices Douglas, Brennan, Blackmun, and Marshall in their dissent saw it quite differently. Justice Douglas harkened back to *Everson* where the Court emphatically stated: "No tax in any amount, large or small, can be levied to support any religious activities or institutions, whatever they may be called, or whatever form they may adopt to teach or practice religion."[14]

Tilton v. Richardson settled the issue of government grants to church-related colleges. Since that decision, all church-related colleges, including the 232 under Catholic auspices, have participated in all federal grants with no reference to the nature of the linking of that institution with organized religion.

But *Lemon* began a long series of cases involving governmental assistance to church-related schools of less than collegiate rank. In *Levitt v. Committee for Public Education*,[15] Chief Justice Burger and Justice Rehnquist stayed with the majority in *Lemon*, but, in *Committee for Public Education v. Nyquist*,[16] they changed their positions and joined Justice White to form a new minority which would persist during the Reagan years.

In *Nyquist*, the Court extended the *Lemon* principle and disallowed grants from New York State for the maintenance and repair of Catholic school buildings, partial tuition reimbursement, and modest tax benefits to parents. *Sloan v. Lemon*[17] reached the same result, again with Chief Justice Burger and Justices White and Rehnquist in dissent.

In 1975, two years after *Nyquist*, the Burger Court in *Meek v. Pittenger*[18] felt constrained because of the *Allen* decision to permit the loan of secular textbooks but struck down the lending of other instructional materials and equipment.

The Burger Court never brought itself to face the challenge of Justice Marshall that *Allen* should be overruled. Dissenting in *Wolman v. Walter*,[19] Marshall openly urged the overruling of *Allen*. Allowing the loan of such textbooks to students and parochial schools lowers "the wall between church and state erected by the first amendment."[20]

Justice Powell, concurring and dissenting in *Wolman*, does not draw the hard line suggested by Marshall. He has high praise for parochial schools and rejects the idea that the dangers that prompted the framers of the Constitution to include the Establishment Clause are still of grave concern. He concedes that the Supreme Court's decision regarding the Establishment Clause has been fashioned "without resort to blind absolutism." But he concludes that if "this endeavor means a loss of some analytical tidiness, then that too is entirely tolerable."[21]

If students of the Court's jurisprudence on church and state are willing to accept Powell's rejection of "blind absolutism," then the lack of complete consistency on the part of the Burger Court can be characterized as an accommodation which seeks to recognize a relationship analogized to symbiosis—a word from biology describing the mutual interdependence of two inseparable substances.

But the question of aid to church-related schools is not easily compromised out. Partisans on both sides waged war before and after the Burger Court issued uneasy guidelines in the years from 1971 to 1980.

In 1983, in *Mueller v. Allen*,[22] a 5–4 majority of the Supreme Court upheld an arrangement in Minnesota under which parents with children in schools could claim a tax deduction (not a credit) for expenses including tuition of the child up to $700 a year. This benefit was available to *all parents*, but it was clearly designed to help the parents who had children in private, Catholic, or Lutheran schools. The Burger Court managed to sustain this privilege despite *Lemon* and all the other decisions that had disallowed benefits of almost any kind that would assist the parents and the children in private schools. In a strong dissent, Justice Marshall repudiated the Minnesota scheme, stating that it violates *Nyquist* and *Lemon*.

There are arguments that can justify the scheme in Minnesota because it benefits parents and offers no direct assistance to sectarian schools. But it surely offers more assistance to non-public schools than was generally allowed in previous Supreme Court decisions.

But any new status given to church-related schools in *Mueller* was removed two years later in *Aguilar v. Felton*[23] and *School District of Grand Rapids v. Ball*.[24] Decided on the same day, these rulings struck down the federal Elementary and Secondary Education Act (ESEA), a law passed in 1965 which extended certain benefits to children in private schools who needed remedial or compensatory services. Under ESEA, teachers paid by the federal government could visit parochial schools to offer remedial training to those whose achievement was under the minimal level. For twenty years, Title I of ESEA won wide approval from educators and observers. Federal courts resisted challenges to its constitutionality on the basis of standing until the Supreme Court in *Flast v. Cohen*[25] (1968) granted standing to plaintiffs who challenged a law on the basis of the Establishment Clause. The persistence of opponents of allowing Title I funds going to parochial schools generally prevailed in *Aguilar*. Writing for a majority of five, Justice Brennan upheld the opinion of the Second Circuit[26] that ESEA violated the Constitution. Dissenting were Chief Justice Burger and Justices White, Rehnquist, and O'Connor.

The majority cited *Lemon* and *Meek* to demonstrate that aid to schools that are pervasively religious is not allowed. Justice Brennan stressed the alleged need for in-spection which he felt would lead to entanglement in order that the government might make certain that teachers are not assisting religious objectives.

Justice Powell, giving the majority the winning vote, also emphasized the risk of entanglement. Justice O'Connor, entering the church-state area for the first time, dissented. She emphasized that in the nineteen years of the program, "there has never been a single incident in which Title I instructors subtly or overtly attempted to indoctrinate the students in particular religious texts at public expense."[27]

Chief Justice Burger, in a tone almost of exasperation, repudiated the majority and denied even the possibility of any threat to religious liberty in the arrangement thrown out by the Court. One must speculate whether Chief Justice Burger in 1985 regretted the vigor with which he wrote the *Lemon* decision. In the companion case to *Aguilar* out of Grand Rapids, the factual pattern was easier. In a scheme for shared facilities, a public school interchanged teachers and facilities in which clear material benefits came to the parochial school. On the basis of several precedents the Court found it easy to declare the program constitutionally impermissible.

Was the law on the Establishment Clause and church-related schools substan-tially the same at the end of the Burger Court in 1986 as it was in 1969? The answer is yes, with some exceptions. Limited aid for clearly secular purposes to church-related colleges was sustained in *Tilton v. Richardson* and carefully circumscribed benefits to the parents of children in private schools were permitted in *Mueller*. But other benefits were almost universally disallowed, including the largest financial as-sistance ever given to church-related schools—the benefits available under the ESEA.

As a result, it can be flatly asserted that, for better or for worse, the Supreme Court has been remarkably consistent in its opposition to financial aid for church-related schools. From *Everson* in 1947 to *Aguilar* in 1985 almost every state and fed-eral law designed to encourage private schools was struck down. The only ex-ceptions were bus rides in *Everson*, secular textbooks in *Allen*, and limited tax deductions in *Mueller*.

That tradition of denying aid to church-related schools was thirty-eight years old when the Burger Court ended. The Court presided over by Warren Burger con-stituted almost half the span of that legacy.

Other Establishment Issues

The record of the Burger Court in establishment issues beyond that of aid to de-nominational schools is less clear than it is in its remarkably consistent record in denying almost all aid to religiously affiliated educational institutions.

On the place of religion in public life the Burger Court was not as certain. The Court was decisive in affirming that the Ten Commandments could not be posted in a public school.[28] It was also firm in disallowing a moment of silence even if the statute did not specifically authorize prayer.[29]

But the Burger Court, by a bare majority, allowed chaplains to receive com-pensation for prayers before a legislative body. In *Marsh v. Chambers*[30] in 1983, Chief Justice Burger permitted the unicameral Nebraska legislature to have a compensated Protestant chaplain recite prayers even though the prayers were sometimes Christological. The prevailing argument derived from the fact that the very first Congress, in the very session that it voted the First Amendment, also made arrangements for a chaplain in both the House and the Senate. The use of history in this way echoed the appeal to history in *Walz* to sustain tax exemptions for churches. The dissent in *Marsh v. Chambers* and scores of commentators since have pointed out that if history is to be the guide in resolving church-state disputes, the pervasive pan-Protestant orientation of many of America's social institutions would regularly trump many challenges to laws or practices which are challenged by nonbelievers or by members of minority religions.

One has to wonder whether the Supreme Court in *Marsh* demonstrated deference to Congress. Both Houses of Congress filed a brief justifying the employment of chaplains. If the Supreme Court had defied that brief and ruled that Nebraska and inferentially Congress could not hire chaplains, would the Congress have continued the practice anyway although possibly without compensation? Did the Court in other words act prudentially to prevent an open clash with Congress?

Nowhere in the controversy involved in *Marsh v. Chambers* was it mentioned (and this is a special peeve of mine) that from the first Congress to the present day every chaplain in both the House and the Senate has been a white, male Protestant minister. Nor was there any discussion of the question whether the ceremonial invocations of God in legislatures and other public places actually benefit religion or tend to make it marginal and irrelevant.

The reliance on history in *Marsh* reappeared to some extent in a dispute about a Christmas crèche in Pawtucket, Rhode Island. In *Lynch v. Donnelly*,[31] a bitterly divided Court reversed both courts below and permitted a crèche which featured replicas of the Holy Family along with Santa and reindeer. The blistering dissent pointed in vain to *Lemon* and other precedents of the Court which should be read to disallow the city's approval of a clearly Christian exhibit.

In *Lynch v. Donnelly*, Justice O'Connor advanced for the first time her theory that the test should be whether the government is extending its "endorsement" to the practice in question. It remains to be seen whether this proposal will survive analysis. It is not clear what precisely "endorsement" adds to the *Lemon* test. Justice O'Connor seeks to be sensitive to non-Christians who may feel left out by the city's cooperation with the erection of the crèche. But Justice O'Connor clearly seeks to retain the benign ways by which the government encourages religion. She invokes *McGowan v. Maryland*,[32] which sustained Sunday closing laws, and *Zorach v. Clausen*,[33] which allowed release time for religious education off the school premises. She recalls governmental declarations of Thanksgiving as a public holiday and the placing of "in God we trust" on our coins. From these she concludes that the government can and should acknowledge religion when the observance of a religious festival coincides and reinforces the solemnization of public occasions.

In a vigorous dissent, Justice Brennan, joined by Justices Marshall, Blackmun, and Stevens, rejects *Marsh v. Chambers* and *McGowan v. Maryland* as justifications for the majority's allowance of the Christmas crèche. Justice Brennan is almost saying that the Burger Court lost its way and was departing from the solid Establishment Clause jurisprudence which it had inherited and it had developed.

Chief Justice Burger, writing for the majority of Justices White, Powell, Rehnquist, and O'Connor, seemed to want to make it clear that the Court over which he had presided had not secularized America. One has to wonder whether the rhetoric of the Reagan years about the need for religion and family values entered into the mind of the Chief Justice as he wrote the decision in the crèche case announced on March 5, 1984. He insists that the concept of a "wall" of separation between church and state is not an accurate description. The Constitution, he urges, affirmatively mandates accommodation, not merely tolerance of all religion. Burger somewhat naively claims that the city has a secular purpose for including the crèche in its Christmas display.

The Burger Court's majority opinion in *Lynch* seems to collide in result and in tone with its previous rulings on the Establishment Clause. Even though it was clarified a little in *County of Allegheny v. Civil Liberties Union*,[34] the fact is that while the Burger Court set forth clear and workable guidelines on aid to church-related schools and religious practices in the schools, it did not leave a satisfactory body of rulings on the public use of religion in areas outside the schools. In fairness to the Burger Court, it should be said that it did not have firm precedents to rely on for a field less susceptible to specific rules than is the area of educational institutions, whether public or private.

Free Exercise

If the record of the Burger Court on establishment issues is wobbly and wavering, its record on the Free Exercise Clause is quite impressive. The Burger Court did, of course, have the precedent of *Sherbert v. Verner*.[35] There the Supreme Court boldly declared that Mrs. Sherbert, a Seventh Day Adventist, could not be denied unemployment compensation because as a result of her faith she could not work on Saturday in a mill in a southern state. The 6–3 ruling was probably inconsistent with *Braunfeld v. Brown*,[36] where an Orthodox Jewish tailor was not allowed to open his store on Sunday even though for reasons of his religion he was required to abstain from work from sundown Friday to sundown Saturday. But Justice Brennan in *Sherbert* made it clear that the government, even in a law of general application, could not force citizens to violate their conscience to receive the benefits available to all under the legislation.

The Burger Court relied on *Sherbert* when it excused Amish children from continuing in school after the eighth grade. In *Wisconsin v. Yoder*,[37] the Burger Court found it easy to rule that Wisconsin could not compel Amish parents to send their children to high school when their faith tells them that their children will be led astray by worldly knowledge and learning. Chief Justice Burger was eloquent in his opinion in praising the virtuous Amish way of life. Only Justice Douglas dissented, raising without much conviction the question whether the children had consented to the deprivation of schooling and whether the courts yielding to the religious scruples of their parents could hurt the children who could be severely disadvantaged because they would lack a high school degree.

The decisions giving relief to Seventh Day Adventists and to the Amish were in the great tradition of the Supreme Court, which ruled in 1925 that even a plebiscite in Oregon could not close all non–public or parochial schools.[38] The monumental rulings of the Burger Court on religious freedom also echoed a long line of rulings granting certain exemptions to Jehovah's Witnesses.

The Burger Court extended the privilege granted in *Sherbert* to a similarly situated person in *Thomas v. Review Board Indiana Employment Security Division*[39] but pulled back in *United States v. Lee*.[40] In the latter case, even Justice Brennan agreed that the U.S. government has a right to collect social security even though a small group of religious citizens were opposed to such a practice on the ground that they should rely on God to provide for them in their old age.[41]

Similarly, in *TransWorld Airlines v. Hardison*,[42] the Supreme Court stated that there are limits to the administrative burden that can be imposed on the state when it seeks to accommodate the religious convictions of Sabbatarians.

The Burger Court's generosity to religious dissidents seems to have become very crabbed in *Bowen v. Roy*.[43] The majority's approach to the claims of native Americans to certain property rights can only be described as insensitive to the unusual but profoundly personal and collective convictions of American Indians about the right to possess ancestral sacred lands without interference motivated in part by commercial interest.

A case that seems to clash with the Burger Court's approach to the Free Exercise Clause is *Goldman v. Weinberger*.[44] A Jewish Ph.D. and a psychologist, Air Force Captain Goldman desired to wear his yarmulke while on duty. An elaborate set of regulations by the military about headdress while in uniform appeared to bar the yarmulke. The Supreme Court, 5–4, did not take into account the fact that, for the devout Jew, the yarmulke is a sacramental reminder of the constant presence of God. The Court gave deference to the military and minimized the violation of the religious freedom of Dr. Goldman. Congress overruled the *Goldman* decision and made the use of religious symbols permissible in the military.

The Burger Court was also clear that it wanted to forbid Tennessee from excluding ordained ministers from being elected members of the state legislature.[45] Although seven of the original thirteen colonies barred clergy from public office, the Burger Court held that Tennessee could not keep Reverend McDaniel out of the legislature. The Justices fragmented on the reasoning. Justice Brennan might have had the best approach in his contention that the ban violated both the Establishment and Free Exercise Clauses.

Leo Pfeffer opined that the Burger Court changed around 1981 and became more accommodationist rather than separationist.[46] But a closer reading of the cases suggests that the matter is not that clear-cut. Warren Burger, always a conservative, may have reacted to the changing climate of the Reagan Administration, but he was also returning to his philosophical roots. On other issues such as civil rights and criminal procedure, he seems to have shifted to the more conservative side. Although Chief Justice Burger voted with the majority in *Roe v. Wade*[47] in 1973, his subsequent votes appear to have edged away from an expansive reading of *Roe*.

It is easy for a commentator reviewing the seventeen years of the Burger Court to say that the opinions do not add up to form a consistent body of teaching. The fact is that the whole country, not merely the Supreme Court, is groping for some way to produce a harmonious linking of the seemingly opposed demands of the two clauses of the First Amendment. If the Establishment Clause is construed too narrowly, it can limit the free exercise of religion. That is the heart of the claim to public money made by Catholic and other parents who feel obliged to send their children to a religiously affiliated primary or secondary school. If the ban on state aid to Catholic schools is very severe, a significant burden is imposed on Catholics. The government makes the observance of their religious convictions and makes it much more burdensome and expensive. On the other hand, if the Free Exercise Clause is construed in a literal way, the practices of certain religious groups will be allowed, with a burden on the taxpayers who are of a different religious persuasion.

Can there be a balancing, a harmonization of the potentially conflicting values preserved in the two parts of the First Amendment? That is the question that underlines almost every decision on church-state issues that comes before the Supreme Court. It is not clear that there will ever be the perfect harmonization of the two competing clauses of the First Amendment. Indeed, a happy blending of them will become more difficult as the religious composition of the nation becomes more diverse. The number of Muslims and Buddhists in the United States continues to grow—foreshadowing requests for accommodations to religion which are now almost unimaginable. The number of persons with no formal affiliation with a religious body will in all probability also continue to grow. It should be noted that nonbelievers or nonadherents may well want to relitigate the *Walz* decision,[48] in which the Burger Court did not reflect extensively on the right those not connected with the church have to prevent their being assessed with some of the cost of exempting the vast assets of religiously affiliated entities at the local, state, and federal levels. The continuation of very substantial subsidies to religious groups by way of taxation is arguably due to a clear preference for religion over nonreligion and is consequently one of the problems not yet really confronted or resolved by the Supreme Court.

It may be that the Burger Court was so imprecise and unclear in its decisions on the Free Exercise Clause that the Court laid the groundwork for the enactment in 1993 of the Religious Freedom Restoration Act. The emergence of this law, unique in the church–state history of the United States, is not a direct part of the story of the Burger Court on church and state, but it demonstrates that the unfolding of the Supreme Court's jurisprudence on the Free Exercise Clause touches on something profound and pervasive in the American psyche—the desire and determination of everyone across the ideological spectrum to broaden the horizons of religious freedom.

The Religious Freedom Restoration Act sought to reverse at least in part the result of the 5–4 decision in *Department of Human Resources v. Smith*.[49] In the majority opinion, Justice Scalia construed the previous jurisprudence of the Supreme Court on the Free Exercise Clause to permit the Court to invalidate provisions of statutory law in the name of free exercise only when unemployment compensation is involved. Justice Scalia consequently confined the thrust of the *Sherbert* decision and its progeny in ways that a majority of the Court had never before agreed to.

This constriction of religious freedom created an angry uproar among religious believers and civil libertarians. They came together to prepare and enact the Religious Freedom Restoration Act.[50] That measure, signed by President Clinton on

November 16, 1993, clarified and possibly expanded the legacy of the Burger Court on the Free Exercise Clause. The provisions of the Religious Freedom Restoration Act have been construed or utilized by litigants in dozens of cases. It remains to be seen whether a majority of the Supreme Court will eventually rule that Congress exceeded its jurisdiction in enacting the Religious Freedom Restoration Act.

History will identify the purpose-effect-entanglement test with the Burger Court. That test is still a good synthesis of what the Supreme Court has said about the Establishment Clause since the *Everson* decision in 1947.[51] There have been deviations from the *Lemon* test,[52] or rather failures to employ it. The result has been that neither the separationists nor the accommodationists are completely satisfied with the stance the Supreme Court has taken on the meaning and measure of the wall of separation. But the place of the Burger Court in history seems guaranteed because of its crafting of the purpose-effect-entanglement rule. That norm will have to be regularly reexamined and its relationship to the Free Exercise Clause continually reassessed.

There are strong, indeed vehement, forces in the country that want to restore prayer to the public schools and give financial aid to church-related educational institutions. Since 1947, the Supreme Court has exercised an antimajoritarian role in stopping both of these activities. The Earl Warren and Warren Burger Courts have generally agreed in the line of cases that began in *Everson* and *McCollum*.[53] Whether the Rehnquist Court in the end will eventually follow that tradition is not clear at this time.

Afterword

Although the invalidation of the Religious Freedom Restoration Act in *City of Boerne v. Flores*[54] is not directly relevant to the church-state jurisprudence of the Burger Court, it is so significant that a reference to it should be included in any essay on church–state law in the past generation.

The enactment of the Religious Freedom Restoration Act in 1993 was a direct result of the decision of the Supreme Court in *Employment Division v. Smith.*[55] In that 5–4 ruling, the Supreme Court held that a law of general applicability is not unconstitutional even though it impacts adversely on religion.

The implications of that ruling on minority or unpopular religions was such that the Congress felt obliged to restore the original rulings of the U.S. Supreme Court, which said that the free exercise clause gives protections to Seventh Day Adventists and others who request exemptions from neutral laws that impact on their religious exercises.

The Religious Freedom Restoration Act simply stated that when any individual asserts in court that a particular law infringes his religious freedom the burden of proof shifts to the defendant. The defendant then must prove that it has a compelling interest to restrict a citizen's religious freedom and that the law in question is the least restrictive of the ways available to the defendant.

The decision in *Boerne* is not as clear as one would wish. The House Judiciary Committee of the House of Representatives conducted a hearing on the decision on July 14, 1997. But there did not seem to be a consensus as to what the Congress should do. Several of the witnesses expressed surprise that the Supreme Court had in effect denied Congress the power to exercise its constitutional right under the Fourteenth Amendment to enact "appropriate" legislation to implement the amendment that now of course includes the right to the free exercise of religion guaranteed in the First Amendment.

The *Boerne* decision deprives the *Sherbert* decision[56] of some of its validity. The *Smith* ruling clearly modified the thrust of *Sherbert* even though technically *Smith* might not have overturned *Sherbert*.

The *Boerne* decision and the demise of the Religious Freedom Restoration Act demonstrate once again that the development of the First Amendment's clauses on religion is seemingly an endless process. The Burger Court contributed in significant ways to that development. Its contributions have been modified but have not been reversed or rejected.

Notes

1. Everson v. Board of Educ., 330 U.S. 1 (1947).
2. McCollum v. Board of Educ., 333 U.S. 203 (1948).
3. Zorach v. Clauson, 343 U.S. 306 (1952).
4. Abington School Dist. v. Schempp, 374 U.S. 203 (1963).
5. 397 U.S. 664 (1970).
6. 403 U.S. 602 (1971).
7. 403 U.S. 672 (1971).
8. Earley v. DiCenso 403 U.S. 602 (1971).
9. Pfeffer, *Religion, State and the Burger Court* 26 (1984).
10. Lamb's Chapel v. Center Moriches Union Free School Dist., 508 U.S. 384, 398 (1993).
11. 403 U.S. at 679.
12. Supra note 1.
13. 392 U.S. 236 (1968).
14. 330 U.S. at 16.
15. 413 U.S. 472 (1973).
16. 413 U.S. 756 (1973).
17. 413 U.S. 825 (1973).
18. 421 U.S. 349 (1975).
19. 433 U.S. 229 (1977).
20. Id. at 287.
21. Id. at 263.
22. 463 U.S. 388 (1983).
23. 473 U.S. 402 (1985).
24. 473 U.S. 373 (1985).
25. 392 U.S. 83 (1968).
26. Aguilar v. Felton, 473 U.S. 402 (1985).
27. Id. at 424. Aguilar was overruled in Agostini v. Felton, 1175. Ct. 1997 (1997).
28. Stone v. Graham, 449 U.S. 39 (1980).
29. Wallace v. Jaffree, 472 U.S. 38 (1985).
30. 463 U.S. 783 (1983).
31. 465 U.S. 668 (1984).
32. 366 U.S. 420 (1961).

33. Supra note 3.
34. 492 U.S. 573 (1989).
35. 474 U.S. 398 (1963).
36. 366 U.S. 599 (1961).
37. 406 U.S. 205 (1972).
38. Pierce v. Society of Sisters, 268 U.S. 510 (1925).
39. 450 U.S. 707 (1981).
40. 455 U.S. 228 (1982).
41. It is significant that Congress reacted to this ruling and made provisions for exceptions to the social security tax for those who are conscientiously opposed to being involved.
42. 432 U.S. 63 (1977).
43. 476 U.S. 693 (1986).
44. 473 U.S. 402 (1985).
45. McDaniel v. Paty, 435 U.S. 618 (1978).
46. Pfeffer, supra note 9, at 26.
47. 410 U.S. 113 (1973).
48. Supra note 5.
49. 494 U.S. 872 (1990).
50. 42 U.S.C. § 2000bb (1993).
51. Supra note 1.
52. Supra note 6.
53. Supra note 2.
54. 117 S. Ct. 2157 (1997).
55. Employment Division v. Smith, 495 U.S. 872 (1990).
56. Sherbert v. Verner, 374 U.S. 398 (1963).

10

THE BURGER COURT AND CRIMINAL JUSTICE
A Counter-Revolution in Expectations

MARTIN H. BELSKY

Let me indicate my perspective—or, to be more accurate, my bias. Although I have been teaching law for almost twenty-five years, and have been a full-time academic for fifteen,[1] I fall into that category former Dean Gordon Gee described as a "practitioner-scholar."[2] Therefore, it should not come as a surprise that my remarks on the Burger Court's impact on criminal justice will not be from a casebook perspective but, rather, from a practitioner's experience.

I started my legal career as a prosecutor[3] who taught criminal procedure and criminal justice on the side.[4] I also was—and am—someone who has been actively involved in organizations dedicated to protecting constitutional—or more often termed "civil"—rights.[5] My views therefore reflect both my ideology of classic liberalism and my pragmatism of community security.

My first prosecutorial experience was as a summer law student intern in 1967, the height of the Warren Court era. My employment as an assistant district attorney ended in 1974, when the Burger Court was just getting into full swing.[6] I was therefore able to observe the impact of Supreme Court decision making on the day-to-day work of criminal investigation and prosecution.[7]

Much has been written about the Burger Court and its impact on criminal justice. President Richard M. Nixon campaigned on a law-and-order platform and it was widely expected that his Supreme Court appointees would implement that platform. "Many feared that the Burger Court would soon relegate the criminal law landmarks of the Warren Court's constitutional law 'revolution' to legal limbo."[8]

These concerns (or, depending on your position, hopes) "did not materialize." In fact, the common wisdom now is that "the essentials of the Warren jurisprudential edifice were preserved."[9]

To quote a leading liberal criminal justice scholar, Professor Yale Kamisar:

> But in hindsight, with one notable exception (pretrial identification), the fears that the Burger Court would dismantle the work of the Warren Court (or the Bill of Rights itself), and the reports that such dismantling was well underway, seem to have been considerably exaggerated.[10]

Scholars agree that the Burger Court pragmatically contained the scope of the Warren Court criminal justice rulings and also challenged their theoretical premises.[11] It provided the nurturing soil for a more aggressive Rehnquist Court.[12]

The elevation of William H. Rehnquist to Chief Justice was an opportunity to overcome the vestigial power and influence of the liberals on the Burger Court, led by Justice Brennan.[13] Chief Justice Rehnquist was a more skillful, more congenial, and more ideological leader.

He would build on the precedents of the Burger Court that undercut some of the premises of the Warren Court. With the replacement of some liberal and moderate Justices with more conservative ones and the continuing public support for a more law-and-order approach, he would (and, in fact, did) implement a new conservative criminal justice agenda.[14]

This essay, however, does not focus on the Burger Court's transitional impact. Rather, I indicate how a cold review of the so-called pragmatic, moderate tone[15] of many of the decisions does not reflect the impact of the Court on the attitudes and day-to-day law enforcement activities of police officers and prosecutors.

An Overview

In the Warren Court era, police and prosecutors felt under attack and acted defensively. Civil libertarians and defense counsel felt encouraged and aggressively sought federal court mandates to control what they believed and urged were investigatory and trial improprieties, or at least excesses.[16]

With the arrival of a new Chief Justice and then the replacement of at least two "very liberal" Justices[17] later, there was an expectation that there was now a conservative majority, at least on criminal justice issues.[18]

Police and prosecutors hoped for a more sympathetic ear. No longer would police and prosecutor practices have to be justified in light of constitutional mandates. Rather, protections of rights would have to be justified as against protection of the national interest and personal security.[19]

This change in perspective was quickly adopted into the national popular and legal psyche. At both the local and national level, most political leaders sought to demonstrate that they were dealing with the "crime" problem.[20] The public did not seem concerned that changes in the scope of protections for an accused or a convicted offender would lead to a police state.[21]

This lack of opposition and, in fact, political and public support for fewer restrictions on police and prosecutorial powers paved the way for even more changes.[22] With the dynamic leadership of a truly conservative Chief Justice (Rehnquist)[23] and the departure of the last two "very liberal" Justices,[24] a new Court could, and, in fact, did, with very little opposition, minimize the interference by the federal courts in day-to-day law enforcement.[25]

I believe that this trend has now gone so far that it is irreversible. The Supreme Court will continue to be skeptical about the use of constitutional doctrines to restrict potential police and prosecutorial excesses.[26]

For at least the foreseeable future, there will be more recognition of the rights of the victim, of the need for security and protection, and less deference to the rights of the accused and the seemingly ephemeral need to protect constitutional rights in general.[27]

The Attitude and Perspective during the Warren Court Era

With the Warren Court "revolution," many law enforcement personnel, which includes police and experienced prosecutors,[28] felt that their power and, more important, their whole professional philosophy was being successfully challenged.[29]

Investigatory Techniques

A police officer saw the Warren Court forcing lawyers into his domain: the police station and even the police car. For example, the Court said that counsel had to be present at all lineups[30] and perhaps even photographic arrays.[31]

Even if counsel was not present or did not have to be, strict rules as to "fairness" meant at best delays and at worst, no identification.[32]

Escobedo v. Illinois[33] and *Miranda v. Arizona*[34] strongly hinted that a truly good investigator did not really need to get confessions and that confessions, as inquisitory techniques, were contrary to our adversary model. The initial fear of law enforcement was a prohibition of all interrogation.[35] At a minimum, counsel would be required for all stationhouse interrogations.[36]

Moreover, the requirements of warnings and explicit waiver, together with a broad definition of custody, would mean that statements could not be taken without warnings and counsel, on the street, in homes, or anywhere.[37] And, of course, if an accused did ask for an attorney, that attorney would insist that his or her client not talk and no statement would be possible.[38]

Police and prosecutors feared that acceptable uncounseled statements would be rare. Any waiver of counsel would have to be shown to be free, intelligent, and voluntary, and this could be difficult, if not impossible, to prove.[39] Even if earnest attempts were made to give the appropriate warnings, courts seemed willing to find more and more requirements for the warning ritual.[40]

Finally, even if there was a valid waiver, stricter rules as to length of interrogations, the need for documentation (writing and videotape), the nature of the questioning, and, for juveniles, the need for a parent or equivalent[41] meant at best more self-serving admissions and, at worse, no confessions at all.[42]

Police officers were also upset that their activities on the street were being hampered.[43] The courts would not recognize, let alone trust, the cop's sixth sense.[44] Prompt response would be thwarted as the police would have to stop and think and, more important, stop and document, before responding.

A search needed a warrant unless there was an arrest or other exigent circumstances.[45] Even then the arrest or search had to be based on articulated probable cause.[46] Moreover, a mere stop needed articulated, reasonable suspicion.[47]

If the police had confidential informants, technical requirements had to be followed before they could use that information[48] and even then, informants could be put at risk.[49]

The intrusion of lawyers into day-to-day police work was most evident with the increased role of prosecutors. Though supposedly on the same side, many police officers knew that these prosecutors would soon be on the other side.[50] Even now, these "counsel" had colleagues on the other side.[51] Yet, because of the new and technical rules of the game, police had to consult with prosecutors at almost all stages of any major investigation.[52]

Prosecutors and not police interpreted the standards and set the agenda. Prosecutors gave the lessons at the Police Academy, approved warrants and arrests, and even dismissed cases before trial when they felt the new procedures were not followed.[53]

Prosecutorial Strategy

Prosecutors felt under siege as well.[54] It was fun, of course, to instruct and work with police on the street.[55] It was not enjoyable to have to justify the inclusion of evidence in every case and with changing rules.[56] It was pure torture to attempt to uphold hard-won convictions on appeal or, years later, on postconviction state and federal challenge.[57]

The strategy to deal with the barrage of decisions from the Warren Court was straightforward: Avoid at all costs any federal court "liberal" second-guessing.[58] Try to make as many issues ones that could be determined by the more sympathetic state courts.[59]

For example, when there was a potentially post-*Wade* unconstitutional pretrial identification, prosecutors could avoid that issue by showing that this prior identification did not "taint" the in-court identification.[60] Lack of taint, of course, was hard to show. The fairness of the prior identification could affect the motions judge's perspective on taint[61] and certainly would be the basis for a vigorous cross-examination, based on constitutional principles, in front of the jury or judge fact finder.[62]

Similarly, the prosecutor had to make many hearings on the admissibility of confessions focus on factual findings that could be determined by the trial judge. In the not uncommon situation in which police took a statement on the street without warnings or waiver, the prosecutor sought to present detailed evidence showing a lack of custody—that the accused felt free to leave.[63]

In hearings concerning stationhouse confessions, the prosecutors similarly sought to make the issues factual and not legal. There were few situations in which police obtained a statement in a stationhouse and it was admitted that appropriate warnings were not given or waivers not obtained. Therefore, the determination by the hearing judge was based on a determination of the credibility of the police officer as against the suspect and then the nature of the waiver of rights. The validity of the waiver was also a factual issue and involved review of the chronological or maturalogical age of the victim, his or her intelligence and family history, and the nature of police questioning.[64]

For physical evidence, rapidly changing case law required prosecutors to articulate a police officer's justifications at the pretrial hearing[65] and thereby try to convince the judge that there was a valid reason for the police officer's conduct, even if the police officer could not precisely indicate what it was.[66]

Another common technique to avoid constitutional challenge to the seizure of evidence was to show that there was no search at all because the evidence was abandoned,[67] or to show that there was a free and willing consent by an appropriate person to the search and seizure.[68]

A prosecutor also sought to minimize the ability of a defendant to raise constitutional issues on appeal or postconviction review.[69]

If the prosecutor had done her job correctly in the state trial courts, she had made a factual record and had state court findings indicating that an in-court identification was not tainted, or that a statement was voluntary, or that a search was consensual or based on what the judge believed to be sufficient cause. The judge's rulings as to these factual issues or mixed questions of fact and law were given great deference.[70]

When constitutional issues could not be avoided, a prosecutor was to attempt to focus the issues on state procedural grounds, such as waiver.[71] Finally, if a constitutional error was obvious, on appellate or postconviction review, the prosecutor would try to build as strong a record as possible to show and seek findings from more sympathetic state judges that indicated that the error was harmless.[72]

Trial and Posttrial Challenges

Prosecutors felt they did not have many strategies available to deal with new restrictions placed on them in their management of cases and trials. The perceived one-sided nature of the new Warren Court rules, prosecutors lamented, was inconsistent with adversarial equality. Defense counsel had a free ride. They could do almost anything and if an acquittal was obtained, either because of the exclusion of evidence or lawyer forensics, there was no appeal.[73]

If a prosecutor made a technical or tactical mistake, such as not objecting to evidence introduced or trial improprieties by defense counsel, there was a waiver, and, of course, if there was an acquittal, there was no review. Even rank incompetence by a prosecutor was no basis for trial intervention or appellate review.[74]

If the prosecutor's misstep led to a mistrial, double-jeopardy rules could then prohibit retrial.[75] Even if no mistrial occurred, an appellate court, or a state or federal court, years later on habeas corpus or postconviction review, could find some error or some new constitutional rule that would mean reversal and retrial.[76]

In contrast, if a defense counsel made a mistake either pretrial, during trial, or even posttrial, a defendant could claim on appeal that the mistake was "plain error" and still should be considered and reviewed.[77]

Moreover, if the defendant did not agree with his or her counsel's tactical decision or believed that a mistake was made, he or she could then file a petition, even years later, challenging the conviction or sentence because the lawyer was "constitutionally ineffective."[78]

Prosecutors had responsibility for administration of large caseloads and thus had to balance individual case coverage with disposition of cases. They viewed the Warren Court as tying their hands even in this area. First, a major method of case disposition was waiver of jury trials and guilty pleas. New rules provided for extensive colloquies, which could convince defendants not to waive their rights.[79]

Moreover, even if a defendant did waive his or her rights and plead, the defendant could claim—sometimes years later—that the plea or waiver was involuntary or that a bargain was not kept. The defendant could also claim that his or her lawyer "should have" given different advice or better handled an evidentiary issue. These failures by counsel indicated that council was ineffective and the pleas or waivers invalid.[80]

If a defendant did not waive, he or she could rely on the multiple motions, courtroom conflicts, and hearings now allowed as to evidentiary issues to delay the trial date. This would, of course, discourage witnesses and victims who came back again and again because of trial continuances.[81] Moreover, if trial delays were caused by heavy court backlog or other problems within the control of the court or the prosecutor, defense counsel could urge that new speedy trial rules mandated discharge and dismissal.[82]

The Changed Perspective of the Burger Court

Piece by piece and issue by issue, the Burger Court gave police and prosecutors new expectations. The constitutional principles adopted could and should be adapted to the real world of crime fighting.[83] The federal courts, with judges to be appointed by a new law-and-order President (Nixon), were to be more sympathetic to the practical needs of law enforcement.

Although, perhaps, the decisions of the Burger Court did not go as far as Warren Court opponents might have liked, they still telegraphed a change in perspective. This change was first reflected in the stationhouse and the prosecutors' offices.

In the days before LEXIS and WESTLAW, information on new cases from the Supreme Court came first from press inquiries, stories on television and radio or in the local papers and then excerpts in *The New York Times*. Details were often not obtained for several days, when the next issue of *Law Week* finally arrived.

Decisions in the mid- and late 1960s were often handed down on a particular day. Prosecutors and their assistants often dreaded those days and hearing of a new decision. It meant developing a strategy to deal with it.

- How do we describe the opinion to trial judges and distinguish it for pending cases?
- How fast can we convey the application of the opinion to the police to avoid later problems and possible exclusion of evidence?
- Does the new decision apply to cases on posttrial motions, on appeal, or under state or federal postconviction challenge?
- What will be the next case that builds on this one?
- Should we encourage investigatory or trial strategy based on our prediction of the future next step?

Starting in the early 1970s with the arrival of the new Chief Justice and the development of the Burger Court, decision day was, at first, awaited with less tension, and then even with anticipation. The Court, at last, was recognizing practicalities. Police and prosecutors believed that the criminal justice revolution had, at last, turned the corner. Some cases here and there might be lost, but on balance the trend had been stopped, and may, in fact, have been reversed.

The basic lesson from the new Burger Court was one of flexibility. If law enforcers played by the rules fairly, or to use a phrase actually indicated by the Court, "in good faith," success was more probable.

Investigatory Techniques

Fears by police about interference by lawyers and courts in their day-to-day investigatory activities were first alleviated by a series of decisions dealing with identifications. Both *United States v. Wade* and *Stovall v. Denno* noted that on-scene one-on-one "showups" are highly suggestive and looked upon with strong disfavor.[84]

In addition, suggested *Wade*, the required lineup is to be with counsel.[85] Some courts interpreted these cases to mean that counsel was required for photographic arrays as well.[86]

In 1972, over vigorous dissents, the new Burger Court ruled in *Kirby v. Illinois*[87] that the counsel requirement for lineups was limited to only postindictment lineups. *Kirby* also involved a one-to-one showup and there was no suggestion that such procedures were invalid.[88]

A year later in *United States v. Ash*,[89] the Court held that pretrial photographic identifications, even after indictment, did not require counsel's presence.

Finally, the police fears about technical rules as to fairness in confrontations were reduced by the decision in *Manson v. Braithwaite*.[90] The Warren Court in *Stovall v. Denno* had laid down a "strict rule barring evidence of unnecessarily suggestive identifications."[91] The Burger Court in *Manson* indicated that a balancing or "totality of the circumstances" rule should apply. Even an unnecessarily suggestive out-of-court identification would be admissible if other "features of reliability"[92] were present.

Miranda also became less of a problem. The fears that confessions would be barred were ended once and for all by *Harris v. New York*[93] and *Michigan v. Tucker*.[94] Warnings and waivers detailed by *Miranda* were "not themselves rights protected by the Constitution" but only "prophylactic standards" designed to "provide practical reinforcement" as to prior rules "guaranteeing the privilege against self-incrimination."[95]

Thus, a statement taken without warnings could still be used to impeach a defendant's credibility (*Harris*), and a witness's testimony was still admissible despite the fact that the identification of the witness was obtained from the defendant's statement, which itself was inadmissible because of a defect in the warnings given (*Tucker*).

These cases became the basis for later decisions that reinforced the principle that confessions were acceptable pieces of evidence. Although involuntary confessions would, of course, be excluded, different standards would be applied to statements not actually coerced or compelled but rather "merely" obtained in violation of *Miranda*'s procedural or prophylactic requirements.[96]

The issue of custody became less significant. The Burger Court made it clear that because even some questioning in police stations might not be custodial,[97] on the street questioning was certainly not custodial.[98]

In fact, by the 1980s, if the police "accompanied" an individual to the stationhouse, and questioned him or her there, as long as the person was told that he or she was not under arrest, there was no custody.[99]

Even the need to prove a valid waiver seemed not to be much of a problem. The issue of voluntariness had always been an issue in the securing of a confession. As a practical matter, the issue remained the same under *Miranda*. The issue merely changed from whether the confession was given knowingly, voluntarily, and intelligently to whether the waiver of rights prior to the confession was given knowingly, voluntarily, and intelligently.[100] Even silence, in certain circumstances, could show a waiver of rights.[101]

Technical requirements as to the warnings were also eliminated.[102] Though the outline of *Miranda* was retained, requirements for documentation and special rules for juveniles were never mandated.[103] Moreover, said the Burger Court, "overriding considerations of public safety" can justify failure to even give warnings.[104]

The Warren Court's rules dealing with searches were similarly modified to provide police officers with a renewed confidence in their ability to gather admissible evidence. They would be left alone, absent egregious circumstances, in their day-to-day on the street activities.[105]

The Court indicated affirmatively that police officers should be trusted. If they operated "in good faith," searches with warrants would not be excluded.[106] Even searches incident to an arrest may have a good-faith standard.[107]

In fact, the Court was skeptical in general about the exclusionary rule and its application to searches and seizures.[108] The exclusionary rule would only be applied to those persons who had a "strong expectation of privacy" and not to those who could not show they were directly affected by a search and seizure or could not claim a sole property interest in the items seized.[109]

Finally, a more expansive rule allowed more searches by consent[110] and indicated that this Court or a future Court might be even more willing to find requirements for probable cause or reasonable suspicion to be easily waived by consent.[111]

Police soon had less concerns about prosecutorial interference. With decisions indicating the acceptance of the good faith and the needs of law enforcement, prosecutors' fears of lost convictions due to suppression diminished[112] and they were willing to give police more room to maneuver.

Prosecutors also became more professional and saw their careers in the prosecution function.[113] Police fears about "switching sides" were therefore reduced.[114]

Prosecutorial Strategy

Prosecutors also had less concern and more optimism. Fewer rules would be established by the Supreme Court and cases lost because of the new rules. They had successfully been able to develop appropriate factual records so that exclusion of evidence or reversals because of Warren Court rules had been minimized.[115]

They could now be more aggressive and, in appropriate cases, urge the Supreme Court to review decisions and have the "liberal" decisions of the 1960s limited or even overruled.[116]

There was one glitch, however. Some state supreme courts, with the active encouragement of at least one holdover Warren Court Justice,[117] were interpreting their state constitutions to provide more protection for defendants than the U.S. Supreme Court was providing.[118]

In addition, some trial judges were now using factual findings or state procedures to block attempts by the prosecution to seek changes in the Warren Court rulings.[119] When decisions were made in state courts based on such state issues, there was no federal remedy as there were "adequate and independent state grounds."[120]

Trial and Posttrial Challenges

Even under the Burger Court, prosecutors could do nothing directly about acquittals they felt were unfair.[121] However, the Burger Court was willing to provide much more leeway for the prosecutor who made a mistake or who sought a mistrial.[122]

Prosecutors also had less concern about appeals and postconviction reviews. First, the Burger Court was much more willing to make any new rule prospective only.[123] Next, it was totally willing to bar application of any constitutional rule to federal postconviction and postappeal review if there had been an opportunity for a full and fair hearing in the state courts.[124]

Finally, the Court applied a much broader doctrine of "harmless error" to allow it (and lower courts) to determine that, in the context of a whole trial, an error, even a constitutional error, did not justify reversal.[125]

Prosecutors also observed that the Burger Court was more willing to treat defense counsel the same as prosecutors when it came to their actions and tactics. For example, the "plain error" rule was not to be broadly applied.[126] Next the standard for review of a lawyer's actions was narrowed. A lawyer's failure to object even to an allegedly improperly secured incriminating statement was not to be an automatic basis for federal review.[127] On appeal, or on postconviction review, a reversal and new trial was to be granted only if it could be shown that the lawyer's errors were "so serious" that, in effect, the lawyer was not acting as a real counsel *and* the deficient performance specifically prejudiced the defendant.[128]

Prosecutors, operating during the Burger Court years, of course, still had to face many motions and delays by counsel or delay caused by backlog or other problems. The Burger Court, however, expressed its sympathy with the prosecutory view of these problems. In deciding whether a defendant was deprived of his or her right to a speedy trial, the Court would use a balancing test: weighing the length of the delay, the reasons for the delay, the defendants' assertion of his or her right to a speedy trial, and the prejudice, to the defendant.[129]

The Court also supported prosecutors attempts to resolve cases and dispose of motions by pleas. The Chief Justice, speaking for a majority of the Court, expressly endorsed plea bargaining as a means to expedite justice.[130] To promote pleas, in fact, a prosecutor can warn a defendant of his or her intent to seek a higher sentence or bring more charges if a defendant turns down a plea and then, in fact, do so.[131] A defendant may plead guilty, even if he or she simultaneously claims innocence.[132]

Although a colloquy should be given to ensure that a plea is voluntary, a mere mistake in the colloquy that is not shown to be prejudicial is not a basis for ousting the plea.[133] Moreover, a defendant was not able to easily argue—sometimes years later—that his or her lawyer should have challenged a confession[134] or made some other procedural motion.[135] As long as the attorney's advice was "within the range of competence required of attorneys representing defendants in criminal cases," the plea was valid.[136]

Conclusion

This essay sought to explain the perspective of the police and the prosecutor on the changes actually made to criminal procedure by the Burger Court and the expectations these changes raised for the future. From conversations with colleagues, and my experience in working on criminal justice issues as a prosecutor, defense counsel, legislative attorney, and then law professor, I can state that this perspective was shared by the defense bar and civil libertarians. Of course, for them these changes led to pessimistic and not optimistic views of the future.[137]

Notes

1. I started teaching as a part-time lecturer in law at Temple University College of Law in 1972. I also taught at Georgetown University School of Law and other law schools as an adjunct. In 1982, I began to teach full time as an associate professor at the University of Florida College of Law. AALS, *Directory of Law Teachers*—1995–96, 227 (1995).

2. See Gee and Jackson, "Bridging the Gap: Legal Education and Lawyer Competency," 1977 *B.Y.U. L. Rev.* 695, 933:

> Such professors have usually gained some professional expertise in practice, often in a highly specialized field, and then have moved to law school teaching rather early in their careers. Practitioner-scholars are more likely to identify with the practicing bar than are traditional legal scholars but they are also inclined to use traditional teaching methods and to identify substantive legal research as one of their primary goals. This professor sees less cleavage between law school and the practice of law than does the traditional legal scholar and is more likely to accept practical training as one of several goals of the law school.

3. In law school, I worked for Professor Herbert Wechsler, then the reporter for the Model Penal Code. I spent the summer between my second and third year working as a legal intern at the Philadelphia District Attorney's Office. I spent a year after law school in postgraduate studies at the Institute of Criminology at Cambridge University. Upon returning to Philadelphia and a large law firm, I was asked by the then district attorney to take a one-year leave of absence to work in his office. The one year stretched into five. I served as a motions, appellate, and trial assistant; then chief of the motions division, chief of adult prosecutions, and finally chief of all prosecution planning.

4. In 1972, I started my official teaching career co-teaching a clinic and a seminar in prosecution function. See Belsky, "Students as Prosecutors: The Philadelphia Experience," 45 *Pa. Bar Ass'n Q.* 423, 424 n. 6 (1974), *reprinted in* 10 *The Prosecutor* 13 (1974) [hereinafter 1974 Belsky article]. I also taught classes in criminal law, criminal procedure, and criminal practice. In 1977, I started teaching a seminar in the prosecution function at Georgetown University Law Center. See Belsky, "On Becoming and Being a Prosecutor," 78 Nw. U. L. Rev. 1485, 1495 n. 88 (1984), 18 *The Prosecutor* 22 (Summer 1984) [hereinafter 1984 Belsky article].

5. See Belsky, "Living with *Miranda*: A Reply to Professor Grano," 43 *Drake L. Rev.* 127, 130 (1994) [hereinafter "Living with *Miranda*"].

6. I left the district attorney's office at the end of what Professor Kamisar calls the "'first' Burger Court," which was much more police oriented than the later or second Burger Court. Yale Kamisar, "The Warren Court (Was It Really So Defense-Minded?), The Burger Court (Is It Really So Prosecution-Oriented?), and Police Investigatory Practices," in *The Burger Court: The Counter-Revolution That Wasn't* 62, 68 (Blasi ed., 1983).

7. For some earlier analyses based on these experiences, see Belsky, "Whither *Miranda*," 62 *Tex. L. Rev.* 1341 (1984) (book review) [hereinafter "Whither *Miranda*"]; Belsky, "The Retaliation Doctrine: Promoting Forensic Misconduct," 50 *Alb. L. Rev.* 763 (1986) [hereinafter "Forensic Misconduct"].

8. Schwartz, *The Ascent of Pragmatism: The Burger Court in Action* 320 (1990).

9. Id. at 320.

10. Kamisar, supra note 6, at 68.

11. Professor Alschuler calls the Burger Court decisions in the criminal justice area "a prolonged and rather bloody campaign of guerrilla warfare" against the Warren Court. Alschuler, "Failed Pragmatism: Reflections on the Burger Court," 100 *Harv. L. Rev.* 1436, 1442 (1987). See also Blasi, "The Rootless Activism of the Burger Court," in *The Burger Court: The Counter-Revolution That Wasn't*, supra note 6, at 198, 212–13, 214; Schwartz, supra note 8, at 320; Volling, infra note 12, at 43.

12. See, e.g., Volling, "Warren E. Burger: An Independent Pragmatist Remembered," 22 *Wm. Mitchell L. Rev.* 39, 43–5 (1996).

13. Savage, *Turning Right, The Making of the Rehnquist Supreme Court* 10 (1992).

14. See id. at 8, 10–11, 300, 305, 317–18.

15. See Schwartz, supra note 8 at 413 (Burger Court as "Court of Consolidation").

16. See "Whither *Miranda*", supra note 7, at 1350–52.

17. Justice Fortas was replaced by Nixon appointee Harry A. Blackmun; Justice Douglas was replaced by Nixon appointee John Paul Stevens.

18. See Schwartz, supra note 8, at 320.

19. See Richard M. Nixon, acceptance speech at the 1968 Republican Convention, *reprinted in* 24 *Cong. Q. Almanac*, 90th Cong., 2d Sess. 996 (1968) (Nixon promised that he would change the Warren Court, through new appointments, to favor the "peace forces" over the "criminal forces").

20. See National Advisory Commission on Criminal Justice Standards and Goals, *A National Strategy to Reduce Crime* 2 (1973).

21. See Rudovsky, "The Criminal Justice System and the Role of the Police," in *The Politics of Law: A Progressive Critique* 242 (Rudovsky ed., 1982) (public perception that criminal justice system is too lenient and unduly interferes with law enforcement"; procedures established to "secure fairness and equality" still "blamed" for crime and violence).

22. The Reagan Administration felt that the Burger Court could have been even more conservative than it was. Savage, supra note 13, at 8.

23. See Savage, supra note 13, at 8.

24. Justice Brennan was replaced by David Souter; Justice Marshall was replaced by Clarence Thomas.

25. See Savage, supra note 13, at 317–18:

> During the Earl Warren era, the liberal majority often agreed to hear appeals from convicted criminals and used their cases to rewrite the standards of criminal procedures. . . . In the Rehnquist Court, the process worked in reverse. The conservative majority rarely agreed to hear an appeal from a criminal whose conviction was upheld by a state or federal court. However, when prosecutors lost a case in the federal courts, the Rehnquist Court could be counted on to hear the appeal filed

by a state or the Justice Department. . . . Where the Warren Court gave a second chance to convicted criminals, the Rehnquist Court gave prosecutors a second chance to affirm convictions.

26. See Arizona v. Evans, 115 S. Ct. 1185 (1995) (7–2 majority, relying on United States v. Leon, 468 U.S. 897 (1984), found that exclusionary rule not appropriate to search incident to invalid arrest); Whren v. United States, 116 S. Ct. 1769 (1996) (unanimous Court holds that police entitled to temporarily detain motorist, even if traffic stop may be pretextual).

27. See, e.g., 1996 Republican Platform, *reprinted in* 54 *Cong. Q.* 2317, 2322–23, 2325–26 (Aug. 17, 1996).

28. The changes caused by the Warren Court "revolution" had less of an impact on those young prosecutors and new police officers who had only known criminal procedure post-*Mapp*, post-*Wade*, and post-*Miranda*. See "Living with *Miranda*," supra note 5, at 129–30.

29. See Nissman and Hagen, *The Prosecution Function* 77 (1982) ("one-sided rules" that have "nothing to do with convicting the guilty and acquitting the innocent").

30. United States v. Wade, 388 U.S. 218 (1967).

31. See, e.g., United States v. Coades, 468 F.2d 1061 (3d Cir. 1972); Commonwealth v. Whiting, 439 Pa. 205 (1970).

32. Stovall v. Denno, 388 U.S. 293 (1967); Simmons v. United States, 390 U.S. 377 (1968).

33. 378 U.S. 478 (1964).

34. 384 U.S. 436 (1966).

35. See "Whither *Miranda*," supra note 7, at 1349–50; Kamisar, "The Warren Court and Criminal Justice," in *The Warren Court: A Retrospective* 116, 119 (Schwartz ed., 1996).

36. See Commonwealth v. Thomas Banks, Nos. 1143–46 (Phila. Ct. P. April Sess. 1972) at 8 (memorandum opinion), *aff'd per curiam*, 266 Pa. Super. 703 (1973) (should be a lawyer present at all interrogations in stationhouse).

37. Miranda v. Arizona, 384 U.S. 436, 444–45 (1966) (requirements were to apply when a person was "taken into custody" or "otherwise deprived of his liberty in any significant way"). *Miranda* hinted that its requirements were also applied to whenever an individual was the "focus" of an investigation. Id. at 444 n. 4. See Commonwealth v. D'Nicuola, 448 Pa. 54 (1972) (Pennsylvania Supreme Court said *Miranda* intended to apply whenever anyone was in custody or is the focus of an investigation).

38. See "Whither *Miranda*," supra note 7, at 1355.

39. In Philadelphia, one judge ruled that it was not credible that any individual who would be warned of his or her rights could ever knowingly, voluntarily, and intelligently waive his or her rights. Commonwealth v. Thomas Banks, Nos. 1143–46 (Phila. Ct. C. P. April Sess. 1972) (memorandum opinion), *aff'd per curiam*, 266 Pa. Super. 703 (1973).

40. See Belsky, "Criminal Procedure in Pennsylvania: The Pre-Trial Issues in Four Parts," 78 *Dick. L. Rev.* 209, 218–20 (1974) [hereinafter "Pre-Trial Issues"] (examples of additional requirements for warnings include not being able to say that statement might be used "for or against" a defendant; must explicitly say counsel will be provided "free of charge" and not merely that counsel will be provided; must include nature of charges in any warning).

41. See id. at 223–28.

42. See George, "Interrogation of Criminal Defendants—Some Views on *Miranda v. Arizona*," 35 *Fordham L. Rev.* 190 (1966).

43. See President's Commission on Law Enforcement and the Administration of Justice, *The Challenge of Crime in a Free Society* 94 (1967).

44. See Quick, "Attitudinal Aspects of Police Compliance with Procedural Due

Process," 6 *Am. J. Crim. L.* 25, 26–7 (1978). See generally President's Commission on Law Enforcement and the Administration of Justice, supra note 43, at 92–94.

45. See Katz v. United States, 389 U.S. 347, 357 (1967).

46. See, e.g., Whitely v. Warden, 401 U.S. 560 (1971); Spinelli v. United States, 393 U.S. 410 (1969).

47. See Terry v. Ohio, 392 U.S. 1 (1968).

48. See, e.g., Whiteley v. Warden, 401 U.S. 560 (1971) (all information in warrant; police information known at same time not allowable); Coolidge v. New Hampshire, 403 U.S. 443 (1971) (warrant not extended to items that were or should have been anticipated by affiant).

49. See, e.g., Aguilar v. Texas, 378 U.S. 108(1964) (specific details must be provided to show present reliability of informant).

50. See Moldovsky and De Wolf, *The Best Defense* (1975). Moldovsky was a leading law-and-order homicide attorney. He then became a defense attorney. His book describes how he used his knowledge, particularly of particular police officers, gained as assistant district attorney in his new position.

51. Just as it was difficult for a defendant to see his or her lawyer meet the prosecutor at a social event or lunch, so was it difficult for some police to understand the same occurrence. See National District Attorneys Association, *National Prosecution Standards* 395–96 (1977) [hereinafter *NDAA 1977 Standards*].

52. See Specter, District Attorney, *The 1969 Report to the People of Philadelphia* 196–97 (1970) [hereinafter *1969 D.A.'s Report*].

53. See *NDAA 1977 Standards*, supra note 51, at 362–65.

54. See Nissman and Hagen, supra note 29, at 77.

55. See "Living with *Miranda*," supra note 5; at 131.

56. See *1969 D.A.'s Report*, supra note 52, at 196–200.

57. See Specter, *The 1970–71 Report to the People of Philadelphia* 178–235 (1972) [hereinafter *1970–71 D.A.'s Report*].

58. See *NDAA 1977 Standards*, supra note 51, at 300.

59. Under the doctrine of "adequate and independent state grounds," a decision based on state law would not be reviewed in the federal courts. See Herb v. Pitcairn, 324 U.S. 117, 125–26 (1945).

60. See United States v. Wade, 388 U.S. 218, 241 (1967).

61. See Gilbert v. United States, 388 U.S. 263 (1968).

62. See "Pre-Trial Issues," supra note 40, at 278–80.

63. See Rudovsky, supra note 21, at 247.

64. See "Pre-Trial Issues," supra note 40, at 211–30.

65. See Adams v. Williams, 407 U.S. 142 (1972) (protective search).

66. See Ker v. California, 374 U.S. 23 (1963).

67. This is part of the "plain view" doctrine, that evidence seen by police after an abandonment is in "plain view" and can be seized. See "Pre-Trial Issues," supra note 40, at 250–51. For a criticism of these "dropsy cases," see Rudovsky, supra note 21, at 247.

68. See "Pre-Trial Issues," supra note 40, at 247–49.

69. Clearly, the best way to have issues not appealed is to secure guilty pleas. See National District Attorneys Association, *National Prosecution Standards* 197 (2d ed. 1991) [hereinafter *NDAA 1991 Standards*] (guilty pleas allow prosecutor to "maximize the benefits of conviction without trial").

70. See "Pre-Trial Issues," supra note 40, at 223, 234–35.

71. Obviously, if the state can show a clear waiver of rights, that waiver will provide a means to avoid review of the issue or issues waived, including constitutional issues. Compare Fay v. Noia, 372 U.S. 391 (1963) with Wainwright v. Sykes, 433 U.S. 72 (1977).

72. See generally Saltzburg, "The Harm of Harmless Error," 59 *Va. L. Rev.* 988 (1973).

73. This, of course, is the essential component of the double-jeopardy prohibition. Benton v. Maryland, 395 U.S. 784 (1969). See "Pre-Trial Issues," supra note 40, at 288–90 (concept of *autrefois* acquit and *autrefois* convict).

74. As stated by one of my colleagues in arguing for aggressive trial tactics against defendants, "a not guilty is a not guilty is a not guilty." See "Forensic Misconduct," supra note 7, at 794–95.

75. See Downum v. United States, 372 U.S. 734 (1964).

76. See, e.g., Linkletter v. Walker, 381 U.S. 618 (1965) (applying *Mapp v. Ohio* to all cases still on appeal at time of decision). On state postconviction or federal habeas corpus review, the defendant could argue that failure to raise an issue was "ineffective assistance of counsel." McMann v. Richardson, 397 U.S. 759, 771 n. 14 (1970).

77. See LaFave and Israel, *Criminal Procedure* § 27.5(d), 1159–60 (2d ed. 1992). See, e.g., United States v. Young, 736 F.2d 565, 570 (10th Cir. 1983), *rev'd*, 470 U.S. 1 (1985).

78. See LaFave and Israel, supra note 77, §§ 11.6–.10, at 557–95. See generally Belsky, *Handbook for Trial Judges* XV-38–44 (1975) [hereinafter *Handbook*].

79. Boykin v. Alabama, 395 U.S. 238 (1969) (guilty pleas). The same rule of a need for a voluntary waiver of the right to jury is assumed. Patton v. United States, 281 U.S. 276 (1930) (waiver of jury trial must be pursuant to express and intelligent consent of defendant).

80. See *Handbook*, supra note 76, at II-1–33.

81. See *1970–71 D.A.'s Report*, supra note 57, at 97–101.

82. Klopfer v. Wingo, 386 U.S. 213 (1967); Barker v. Wingo, 407 U.S. 514 (1972). Many states adopted "speedy-trial rules" mandating trial within a certain period. In Pennsylvania, a trial was required [with limited exceptions] within 180 days. See *Pa. R. Crim. P.* 1100 (1972).

83. See Schwartz, supra note 8 at 401: "There is no doubt that Chief Justice Burger came to the Court with an agenda that included some dismantling of the jurisprudential structure erected under his predecessor, particularly in the field of criminal justice."

84. United States v. Wade, 388 U.S. 218, 234 (1967); Stovall v. Denno, 388 U.S. 293, 302 (1967).

85. "[P]olice conduct of such a lineup without notice to and in the absence of his counsel denies the accused his Sixth Amendment right to counsel. . . ." 388 U.S. at 272. The clear intent of *Wade* was to cover all lineups. See Schwartz, supra note 8, at 321. See, e.g., Commonwealth v. Spencer, 442 Pa. 328 (1971); Long v. United States, 424 F.2d 799 (D.C. Cir. 1969); Palmer v. State, 5 Md. App. 691, 249 A.2d 482 (1969); People v. Banks, 2 Cal. 3d 127, 465 P.2d 263 (1970). But see *Wade*, 388 US. at 236–37 ("post-indictment lineup was a critical stage . . .").

86. See, e.g., United States v. Coades, 468 F.2d 1061 (3d Cir. 1972); Commonwealth v. Whiting, 439 Pa. 205 (1970).

87. 406 U.S. 682 (1972).

88. See also Manson v. Braithwaite, 432 U.S. 98 (1977).

89. 413 U.S. 300 (1973).

90. 432 U.S. 98 (1977).

91. Neil v. Biggers, 409 U.S. 188, 199 (1972). See *Stovall*, 388 U.S. at 302 ("unnecessarily suggestive").

92. 432 U.S. at 110.

93. 401 U.S. 222 (1971).

94. 417 U.S. 433 (1974).

95. Id. at 444.

96. See New York v. Quarles, 467 U.S. 649 (1984); Oregon v. Elstad, 470 U.S. 298 (1985). See also Oregon v. Haas, 420 U.S. 712 (1975) (statements obtained after request for counsel could be used for impeachment).

97. Oregon v. Mathiason, 429 U.S. 492 (1977).

98. See Schneckloth v. Bustamonte, 412 U.S. 218 (1973) (warnings not required for normal consent searches). See also Kamisar, supra note 6, at 84. By 1984, even Justice Marshall agreed that roadside questioning of a motorist detained pursuant to a traffic stop was not custodial. Berkemer v. McCarty, 468 U.S. 420 (1984).

99. California v. Beheler, 463 U.S. 1121 (1983).

100. See "Whither *Miranda*," supra note 7, at 1356. See also Rudovsky, supra note 21, at 246–47.

101. North Carolina v. Butler, 441 U.S. 369 (1979).

102. California v. Prusock, 453 U.S. 355 (1981) (*Miranda* not to be rigidly applied; no "talismanic incantation was required to satisfy its strictures").

103. See Kamisar, LaFave, and Israel, *Modern Criminal Procedure* 541–42 (8th ed. 1994).

104. New York v. Quarles, 467 U.S. 649 (1984).

105. Another issue facing police had to do with civil suits against them for improper conduct. See Bivens v. Six Unknown Named Agents, 403 U.S. 388 (1971). However, the Burger Court, in a series of technical decisions, made it almost impossible to sue police for constitutional infringements, by doctrines of good faith, official immunity, standing, and ripeness. See, e.g., Rizzo v. Goode, 423 U.S. 362 (1976).

106. See, e.g., United States v. Leon, 468 U.S. 897 (1984).

107. See INS v. Lopez-Mendoza, 468 U.S. 1032, 1056 (1984) (White, J., dissenting).

108. Stone v. Powell, 428 U.S. 465 (1976) (exclusionary rule not a constitutional one; involves high costs and should be restricted to where necessary).

109. See Rakus v. Illinois, 439 U.S. 128 (1978); Rawlings v. Kentucky, 448 U.S. 98 (1980).

110. See, e.g., Schneckloth v. Bustamonte, 412 U.S. 218 (1973) (no requirements as to warnings before consent to search obtained).

111. See, e.g., Illinois v. Rodriguez, 497 U.S. 177 (reasonable belief that third party had right to consent); Florida v. Jimeno, 500 U.S. 248 (1991) ("objectively reasonable" that police officer would assume that consent was broad).

112. Prosecutors changed their focus from police practices to the facts of the crime and the impact on the victim. See Whitebread, "The Burger Court's Counterrevolution in Criminal Procedure: The Recent Criminal Decisions of the United States Supreme Court," 24 *Washburn L.J.* 471, 474 (1985).

113. See 1984 Belsky article, supra note 4, at 1518–20.

114. Rightly or wrongly, many prosecutors saw themselves as the allies of the police in their fight against the "criminal forces": the defendant and his attorney. See, e.g., Nissman and Hagen, supra note 29, at 5.

115. See "Living with *Miranda*," supra note 5, at 134–35. See also "Criminal Justice in Crisis," in ABA Section on Criminal Justice, *Special Committee on Criminal Justice in a Free Society* 28 (1988).

116. See *NDAA 1977 Standards*, supra note 51, at 298 (arguing for prosecutors' right to not merely wait for defendants claims and refute them but also to have expanded right to appeal).

117. Michigan v. Mosely, 423 U.S. 96, 111, 120–21 (1975) (Brennan, J., dissenting, joined by Marshall, J.). See Brennan, "The Bill of Rights and the States: The Revival of State Constitutions as Guardians of Individual Rights," 61 *N.Y. U. L. Rev.* 535 (1986).

118. See Abrahamson, *Criminal Law and State Constitutions: The Emergence of State Constitutional Law* 1141 (1985).

119. See Commonwealth v. Banks, Nos. 1143–46 (Phila. Ct. C.P. April Sess. 1972) (memorandum opinion), *aff'd per curiam*, 266 Pa. Super. 703 (1973).

120. Chief Justice Burger, himself, criticized these actions by state supreme courts in re-

quiring more protection for criminal defendants that did the United States Constitution as not leading to "rational law enforcement." Florida v. Casal, 462 U.S. 637 (1983) (Burger, C.J. concurring in denial of certiorari).

121. Of course, indirectly, they might be able to secure prosecutions, without violating the double-jeopardy clause, through another sovereign (i.e., by the federal prosecutor in the federal courts). Bartkus v. Illinois, 359 U.S. 121 (1959). Or there could be a second prosecution when an issue was not fully litigated in a prior verdict or resulted from a different standard of proof. Compare Ashe v. Swenson, 397 U.S. 436 (1970) with Dowling v. United States, 493 U.S. 342 (1990).

122. See Illinois v. Somerville, 410 U.S. 458 (1973); Arizona v. Washington, 434 U.S. 497 (1978).

123. See Solem v. Stumes, 465 U.S. 638 (1984). The Supreme Court, it would seem, has now adopted the rule that new rules are generally not applicable to "final convictions" and final convictions are defined as the date the direct appeal is final (i.e., when a petition for a writ of certiorari is denied). See Butler v. McKellar, 494 U.S. 407 (1990).

124. See Stone v. Powell, 428 U.S. 465 (1976) (as long as there was an opportunity for full and fair litigation of an issue in the state courts, no habeas corpus relief). See Withrow v. Williams, 113 S. Ct. 1745 (1993) (*Stone v. Powell* rule does not apply to confessions).

125. See, e.g., United States v. Hasting, 461 U.S. 499 (1983) (comment on defendant's failure to testify); Moore v. Illinois, 434 U.S. 220(1977) (witness identification made in violation of *United States v. Wade*); Milton v. Wainwright, 407 U.S. 371 (1972) (statement obtained in violation of *Miranda*).

126. See United States v. Young, 470 U.S. 1 (1970). For a criticism of this narrowing of the plain error doctrine, see "Forensic Misconduct," supra note 7.

127. Wainwright v. Sykes, 433 U.S. 72 (1977) (confession issue not raised at trial; failure to object is a waiver for purposes of federal habeas corpus).

128. Strickland v. Washington, 466 U.S. 668 (1984).

129. Barker v. Wingo, 407 U.S. 514 (1972).

130. Santobello v. New York, 404 U.S. 257 (1971).

131. Bordenkircher v. Hayes, 434 U.S. 357 (1978).

132. North Carolina v. Alford, 400 U.S. 25 (1970).

133. United States v. Timmreck, 441 U.S. 780 (1979).

134. McMann v. Richardson, 397 U.S. 759 (1970).

135. Tollett v. Henderson, 411 U.S. 258 (1973) (attorney not challenge unconstitutionally defective indicting grand jury).

136. Parker v. North Carolina, 397 U.S. 790 (1970).

137. See Rudovsky, supra note 21, at 247–50; Genego, "The Future of Effective Assistance of Counsel: Performance Standards and Competent Representation," 22 *Am. Crim. L. Rev.* 181 (1984); Whitebread, "The Burger Court's Counterrevolution in Criminal Procedure," 24 *Washburn L.J.* 471 (1985) (crime control philosophy of Burger Court assumes that police comply with "constitutional ideal"; Warren Court worried about police practices).

11

ECONOMIC RIGHTS

LINO A. GRAGLIA

One immediate effect of President Nixon's first appointment to the U.S. Supreme Court was to transpose the names of the Chief Justice from Earl Warren to Warren Earl. That there were other significant effects, at least in regard to constitutional law, is less clear. Warren Earl Burger served as Chief Justice of the United States from 1969 to 1986. The replacement of one Justice, even a Chief Justice, by another does not of course in itself necessarily produce a shift in Court policy. It was thought, however, that the appointment of Warren Burger signaled a change from the enthusiastic activism of the Warren era, although he joined a Court that still included Justices Brennan, Douglas, Marshall, and Black, the engines of that activism.

Burger was soon to be joined, in 1970, by his friend and fellow Minnesotan, Harry A. Blackmun—a man whose career has demonstrated, even more clearly than Burger's, that if it is conservatives you are looking for, Minnesota is not a good place to look. In 1972, Burger was joined by two more Nixon appointees, Justices Lewis F. Powell and William H. Rehnquist. As of then, at least, it might be meaningful, it seems, to speak of a Burger Court, but the Nixon appointees were of course still a minority, and they could do no more than dissent as a block in some important early cases.[1]

In 1975, Gerald Ford, our only nonelected President, appointed John Paul Stevens to replace William O. Douglas, who had finally come, after thirty-six years, as close as he could to dying in office. Gerald Ford's most memorable deed in his long service in the House of Representatives was his attempt to impeach Justice Douglas.[2] As a mischievous fate would have it, he found himself in a position to replace Douglas when the time came that even Douglas could hang on no longer. As if to ensure that his tenure in office would be of no real consequence, however, President Ford replaced Justice Douglas with John Paul Stevens, whose position on most issues proved to be not very different from that of Douglas.[3] The only other change in the Court's membership during Burger's tenure was the replacement of Potter Stewart with Sandra Day O'Connor in 1981. This was also of no great consequence except that it ended the historic practice of referring to Court members as "*Mister* Justice."

The most important thing, surely, to be said about the Burger Court is that it failed almost totally to bring about the change that was expected of it. If our purpose here is to appraise the accuracy of the statement of *The Burger Court: The Counter-Revolution That Wasn't*,[4] I can only conclude that it was all too accurate. Far from ending, or even curbing, the judicial imperialism established by its predecessor, the Burger Court brought rule by judges to new heights. It had taken President Franklin D. Roosevelt only a few appointments to ensure that the Constitution would never again give his New Deal the least bit of trouble. Federal laws were never again invalidated for lack of legislative authority,[5] and property[6] and contract rights[7] no longer presented an obstacle to state or federal economic regulation.

There was every reason to believe that a few appointments to the Court by President Nixon, who ran on a platform of curbing judicial power, would be sufficient to work a similar revolution. Many of the most dramatic Warren Court innovations, such as *Miranda v. Arizona*,[8] after all, were by a close vote and seemed expressions of a counterculture era that surely would quickly pass away. Such Justices as Black and Douglas, vestiges of the upheavals of the 1930s and 1940s, and Brennan and Marshall, vestiges of the moral euphoria of the 1960s and early 1970s, could not be expected to come along again. The Constitution, one could confidently predict, would soon cease to prohibit state laws providing for prayer in the schools or seeking to suppress pornography; defendant's guilt, not the manner in which evidence of guilt was obtained, would again become the central issue in criminal trials; the Court's wildly ambitious move in 1968 from prohibiting racial segregation to requiring racial integration[9] would certainly come to a halt.

Amazingly, none of this was to be. Not a single one of the controversial innovations of the Warren Court was reversed during the Burger era. On the contrary, additional innovations, as in the creation[10] of a constitutional right to an abortion[10] and the requirement of busing for school racial balance,[11] continued to issue forth. The Warren Court had apparently so solidly established the superiority of policymaking by judges on the basis of principle over policymaking by mere politicians subject to electoral constraints that the return of basic social policy issues to the ordinary political process could no longer be expected. The system of government by elected representatives, largely on a state-by-state basis, created by the Constitution had permanently evolved, it seemed, into something like its opposite: government by majority vote of a committee of nine lawyers, unelected and holding office for life, making policy for the nation as a whole from Washington, D.C.

The basic defect of the Constitution's scheme of government, as most academics and other liberal intellectuals see it, is that it leaves decision making on basic issues of social policy in the hands of the American people. The function of constitutional law, in their view, is to remedy this defect, and the constitutional law of the last four decades, at least, has performed this function. The first thing to understand about the constitutional law that resulted is that it has very little to do with the Constitution.[12] The notion that the Justices arrive at their rulings of unconstitutionality by interpreting the Constitution is almost purely fictional. This is evident enough from the fact that there is so little that the Justices even purport to interpret. The vast majority of rulings of unconstitutionality purport to be based on a single sentence in the Fourteenth Amendment and, indeed, on four words: "due process" and "equal protection." It does not require jurisprudential sophistication to realize that the Justices do not decide a vast array of difficult issues of social policy by studying those words. Without the Fourteenth Amendment, constitutional law would largely go away, and we would have to get by as best we can with representative self-government in a federalist system.

The next and final thing to understand about the constitutional law of the last several decades is that it has not been random in its political impact. Warren Court activism served almost without exception to move policy choices to the left. It would be only a small exaggeration to say that the American Civil Liberties Union, the paradigmatic constitutional litigator of our time, never lost in the Warren Court, even though it did not always win. It either obtained from the Court a policy choice rejected in the political process or it was left where it was to try again on another day. For conservatives or traditionalists, on the other hand, a "victory" in the Court meant only that they would be permitted to continue, for the present at least, to fight for their policy choice in the ordinary political process.

The left, almost by definition, is not interested in protecting—it is more interested in undermining—economic rights. The Warren Court's hyperactivism in creating and protecting what it saw as "civil rights" was, therefore, matched by its total lack of interest in protecting property and contract rights. In this, as in virtually all other aspects of constitutional law, the Burger Court made very little difference.

Constitutional Economic Rights

Economic Substantive Due Process

The Supreme Court once saw the protection of economic rights as its primary function. Indeed, beginning in the 1890s, it created the doctrine of "substantive due process" to authorize itself to invalidate as "unreasonable" restrictions on economic freedom of which it disapproved.[13] The economic substantive due process, or *Lochner*,[14] era came to a dramatic end, however, with the Court's 1937 decision in *West Coast Hotel Co. v. Parrish*,[15] upholding a state minimum wage law—and illustrating, incidentally, that good constitutional law can permit very bad social policy. The Warren Court certainly had no interest in reviving economic substantive due process, and the Burger Court's interest was no greater.

The Nixon Justices were no doubt more sympathetic, or at least less antagonistic, to private property interests than, say, Justices Black and Douglas, but they were no more willing to revive economic substantive due process. They purported to be generally committed to a policy of judicial restraint and found this restraint easiest to exercise—least likely to result in criticism from colleagues or academics—when business or property interests were involved. Far from seeking to revive economic substantive due process, they were willing to put further nails in its coffin. The Court very rarely reviewed a challenge to a business regulation, and then only, as in *New Orleans v. Dukes*,[16] to reverse a court of appeals decision that upheld the claim. In *Dukes*, the Court not only unanimously upheld the regulation but in the process overruled *Morey v. Doud*,[17] the one decision since 1937 that had invalidated a business regulation. In *Dukes* as in *Morey*, the "unreasonableness" claim was stated in equal protection rather than due process terms, but as the Court recognized by citing substantive due process cases, that is a distinction without a difference.[18]

Just Compensation

The two other major sources of economic rights in the Constitution are, of course, the Contracts Clause of Article I, Section 10[19] and the just compensation or Takings Clause of the Fifth Amendment,[20] said to be applicable to the states, strangely enough, by reason of "incorporation" in the Due Process Clause of the Fourteenth Amendment. The Takings Clause has become a matter of heightened interest in recent years by reason of the Supreme Court's upholding just compensation claims in no fewer than four cases.[21] The Burger Court upheld such claims, however, only in two cases, both of little significance.

In *Loretto v. Teleprompter Markets CATV Corp.*,[22] the Court held that a New York statute requiring landlords to permit local cable companies to attach cable equipment to their buildings constituted a taking of property that required compensation. A physical invasion was involved, even if one of no economic consequence.[23] On remand, the lower court found that a one-time payment of $1, which is the payment the New York statute required, would be adequate compensation.[24] In the second case, *Kaiser Aetna v. United States*,[25] the claimant dredged and deepened a large pond and built a channel connecting it to the sea.[26] The government could not require the grant of public access to the pond, the Court held, without exercising the power of eminent domain and paying just compensation.

The Burger Court's two most significant Takings Clause decisions continued the Warren Court's trend of giving the clause a very limited construction. In *Hawaii Housing Authority v. Midkiff*,[27] the Court upheld a statute that permitted the state to condemn private property by eminent domain to transfer it to other private owners, even though the Takings Clause permits property to be taken only "for public use." Reaffirming and perhaps extending an earlier decision,[28] the Court held that "[t]he 'public use' requirement is coterminous with the scope of a sovereign's police powers."[29] This amounts to saying, of course, that there is no "public use" limitation on the eminent domain power.

The other significant Burger Court decision on the Takings Clause is *Penn Central Transportation Co. v. New York City*.[30] When the Penn Central Railroad's predecessor built Grand Central terminal on Park Avenue in New York City in 1913, it made what later proved to be the serious mistake of making it architecturally significant and very attractive. The terminal was built with the expectation that a tower would later be placed above it. By the time it came to do that a half-century later, however, New York City had created a Landmarks Preservation Commission, which prohibited building over the terminal on the ground that it would mar the view of what had become a classic example of French beaux arts architecture.[31] The prohibition would cost the company millions of dollars in annual revenue for which New York City did not offer just compensation.[32] The Court denied the company's claim for compensation, however, on the ground that no taking had occurred. New York City had not, after all, occupied or claimed title to the terminal; it was able to appropriate the property to its own use without touching it, by merely prohibiting its owner from putting it to the owner's best use.

Perhaps the major value of a requirement of just compensation is that it serves to ensure a measure of fiscal responsibility by government.[33] The need to pay for a benefit induces government to seek it only when its value to the community exceeds its costs. This makes it possible, at least in theory, to pay the losers from a move with part of the gains of the winners, leaving the losers whole and the community better off. As New York City's Landmarks Preservation Commission did not operate under any such restraint, one may surmise that many if not most of the restrictions it imposed could not withstand a cost-benefit analysis and had the effect of making the city as a whole poorer.

The Commission's regulation of Penn Central was likely the paradigm of a confiscatory, welfare-reducing restriction. It would seem, therefore, an excellent candidate for a requirement of compensation, if there is to be any such general requirement. The Court denied compensation, however, without stating—indeed, acknowledging its inability to state—a general rule.[34] It explicitly denied that it was adopting the rule that a taking cannot occur without physical possession or occupation,[35] but it is difficult to explain the result in *Penn Central* on any other grounds.[36]

The Contracts Clause

The principal specific protection of economic rights in the original Constitution was the provision prohibiting the states from enacting any "Law impairing the Obligation of Contracts."[37] The central defect, if not an inherent contradiction, of democracy, as the framers saw it, was that debtors—mainly farmers in those days— would always be far more numerous than creditors. If the people could make the laws, they surely would quickly discover that they held it in their power to free themselves from debt by simply enacting any one of a variety of debtor-relief measures.[38] This had indeed been the experience in many states under the Articles of Confederation, and it provided an important impetus for the constitutional convention.[39] The framers therefore inserted the Contracts Clause in the Constitution, the only important limitation on state power, at least in terms of litigation, in the original Constitution. The framers saw little need for federal protection of civil rights as we understand them—the Constitution, after all, repeatedly recognized and protected slavery[40]—but they saw a clear need to protect the bankers.

The paucity of constitutional limitations on state power meant that Chief Justice John Marshall, the Court's first hyperactivist, the rightwing William Brennan of his day, had little to work with to substitute his policy preferences for those of the people of the states. One of his responses to this was his invention of the "dormant" or "negative" Commerce Clause, purporting to find in the grant of the commerce power to Congress a grant of power to judges to invalidate state commercial and financial regulation more or less at will.[41] In a pinch, all else failing, Marshall simply resorted to "natural law,"[42] which has the happy facility, of course, of meaning whatever its discoverer wants it to mean: All that is required is a willingness to assume that one has access to sources of authority unavailable to ordinary mortals. Insofar, however, as Marshall wished to appear to be enforcing something actually in the Constitution, it had to be the Contracts Clause, which he therefore proceeded to expand and distort beyond all recognition. He used it, for example, to prohibit

Georgia from canceling a massive corrupt land transaction[43] and to prevent New Hampshire from restructuring the governing board of a college.[44]

Marshall's successor, Chief Justice Taney, cut back on what Marshall had made of the Contracts Clause,[45] but it remained a major source of constitutional litigation, often in connection with municipal financing, through the nineteenth and early twentieth centuries. It met a sudden and dramatic demise, however, in 1934, in the depths of the Great Depression, in *Home Building & Loan Association v. Blaisdell*.[46] Farmers unable to make mortgage payments were being driven from their farms to wander homeless with their families and few possessions in a world without jobs. Some of them, insufficiently cognizant of the sanctity of contract rights, were proposing to shoot judges and sheriffs who ordered or executed mortgage foreclosures. Minnesota, deciding that something had to be done, enacted a mortgage moratorium law, precluding or delaying foreclosures despite defaults.[47] Bankers challenged the law, bringing to the Court at last exactly the sort of debtor-relief measure the Contracts Clause was meant to prohibit, perhaps the most clearly unconstitutional law to come to the Court in its history.

The *Blaisdell* case presents a clear illustration of the fundamental problem of constitutionalism, namely, that the attempt to govern the living by the dead hand of the past can be a very bad idea. It is simply not possible to improve on a political arrangement in which the policy issues of today are decided by the people of today in light of current knowledge and circumstances and not necessarily in accord with the views of people who are no longer with us. Perceiving the obvious wisdom of this, the Court in *Blaisdell* upheld the Minnesota law, although only by a 5–4 vote, thereby losing its best, if not its only, opportunity to hold unconstitutional a law that really was. This required the Court, however, to explicitly divorce constitutional law from the intent of the framers and, therefore, from the Constitution, leaving it simply a vehicle for enactment of the policy views of the Justices.

The Court denounced as patently invalid the view that "the great clauses of the Constitution must be confined to the interpretation which the framers, under the conditions and outlook of their time, would have placed upon them."[48] This, however, is not an argument for a method of interpretation not dependent on the framers' (and ratifiers') intent—there is no such method—but an argument against constitutionalism.[49] The argument can be justified as pro-democratic when used, as in *Blaisdell*, to escape or permit escape from a constitutional restriction and thereby return a policy issue to the political process. Unfortunately, *Blaisdell's* argument against original intent has since been used not to eliminate but to multiply constitutional restraints and thereby justify judicial activism, the invalidation as unconstitutional policy choices that the Constitution does not prohibit. The result of *Blaisdell's* explicit divorcing of constitutional law from the Constitution, therefore, has been not to enhance but to limit the right of self-government, not to free us from government by the dead but to subject us to rule by electorally unaccountable judges who are all too much alive.

The result of *Blaisdell* was to remove the Contracts Clause as a significant obstacle to state policymaking. Surely the most important, if not the only, contribution by the Burger Court to the protection of constitutional economic rights is that it partially revived the clause by using it to invalidate state laws in two decisions.

The first, *United States Trust Co. of New York v. New Jersey*,[50] involved the Port Authority of New York and New Jersey, an agency created by a compact between the two states to construct and operate interstate bridges, tunnels, and other transportation facilities.[51] The Authority raised funds for its projects by selling bonds backed by the revenues from its profit-making facilities.[52] To facilitate bond sales, the states covenanted with the Authority that it would not be required to use any part of its revenues to subsidize deficit-generating commuter rail facilities.[53]

Each state, however, thereafter passed a law explicitly abrogating the covenant, and a bondholder sued, claiming a violation of the Contracts Clause.[54] In a 4–3 decision, the Court for the first time in many decades upheld a Contracts Clause claim. The Court did not overrule *Blaisdell*, of course, or purport to restore the Contracts Clause to anything like its former full vigor. On the contrary, the Court was explicit that states *may* impair the obligation of contracts, despite the clause.[55] The impairment, however, the Court said, must be "reasonable and necessary to serve an important public purpose."[56] That is, an impairment will be impermissible only whenever a majority of the Justices decide, on a purely ad hoc basis, not to permit it. Getting the matter exactly backwards, the Court stated that the Contracts Clause is particularly restrictive when it is a state's own contracts that are involved.[57]

Justice Brennan, joined by Justices White and Marshall, issued a long and bitter dissent, outraged that the Court should deviate from its mission of advancing liberal causes to protect an economic right.[58] Under the functional judicial review he favored, one asks not whether a challenged policy choice is disallowed by the Constitution—it almost never is—but whether it involves an issue the judge feels should be taken from the political process to impose a resolution more to the left. Unsurprisingly, Brennan concluded that the "financial welfare" of bondholders was "being adequately policed by the political process" and therefore not in need of judicial protection.[59] The significance of *United States Trust* is not that the Court laid down a new rule of law—it did not lay down any rule—but simply that it relied on the Contracts Clause to invalidate a state law, apparently restoring it to some, even if an unpredictable, constitutional role.

The following year, in *Allied Structural Steel Co. v. Spannaus*,[60] lightning struck again. A second state law fell to a Contracts Clause challenge, this time by a 5–3 vote and in a case involving only a private contract.[61] Justice Blackmun, the author of the Court's opinion in *United States Trust*, did not participate. A Minnesota statute operated to increase the rights of employees under a private employer's pension plan, subjecting the employer to greater liability.[62] The Court again held that states may impair the obligation of contracts, despite the Constitution, but "the severity of the impairment measures the height of the hurdle the state legislation must clear,"[63] a formula for unlimited judicial discretion having no relation to a rule of law. Here, the law was found not to deal with a broad problem, or to operate in an area already subject to regulation, or to work only a temporary alteration in a contractual relationship, and it applied to only a few employers all factors that were found to operate against its validity. The impairment, therefore, was found not to be sufficiently justified.[64] Again in dissent, Justice Brennan, showing an attachment to the framers' original intent that is not evident in some of his other opinions, found that no Contracts Clause claim was even involved because the statute was not a debtor-relief measure.[65]

These two decisions mark the end, however, of the surprising Contracts Clause revival, at least as of now. In 1983, two more cases involving the clause came to the Court, and in each the claim was rejected. In *Energy Reserves Group, Inc. v. Kansas Power & Light Co.*,[66] Kansas passed a law prohibiting a natural gas company from taking advantage of a price increase that it was entitled to under the terms of its sales contracts.[67] Under *United States Trust* and *Spannaus*, the Court said, a Contracts Clause claim requires a plaintiff to show that a law has "operated as a substantial impairment of a contractual relationship."[68] Such a showing does not invalidate the law, however, but merely requires the state to show that the law serves "a significant and legitimate public purpose," imposes "reasonable conditions," and is "of a character appropriate to the public purpose."[69] When the state is not itself a contracting party, Justice Blackmun's opinion for a unanimous Court said, "[a]s is customary in reviewing economic and social regulation . . . courts properly defer to a legislative judgment as to the necessity and reasonableness of a particular measure."[70] This would seem to be very bad news for Contracts Clause claims based on private contracts, reducing them again to the status of claims based on economic substantive due process, that is, *de facto* unprotected.

The Court found that in the circumstances of a price-regulated industry, the impairment of contract obligations caused by the Kansas law was not "substantial."[71] The Court added gratuitously, over the protest of Justices Rehnquist and Powell, that in any event, the law served a legitimate purpose by reasonable means.[72] The decision may not necessarily be inconsistent with *United States Trust*—though it does seem inconsistent with *Spannaus*—but it undoubtedly restricts, if it does not terminate, the limited revival of the Contracts Clause that decision seemed to signal.

Finally, in 1983 in *Exxon Corp. v. Eagerton*,[73] a unanimous Court upheld against a Contracts Clause claim an Alabama law that prohibited oil and gas producers from passing on a tax increase to their customers, as they were permitted to do under their contracts.[74] The Court held, reasonably enough it seems, that the challenged law, unlike the laws in *United States Trust* and *Spannaus*, created a rule of general applicability; it was not specifically directed to altering contract obligations and affected them only incidentally.[75]

In a decision handed down one year later, the Court delivered the further discouraging news to Contracts Clause claimants that the Due Process Clause of the Fifth Amendment does not make the Contracts Clause, unlike the Equal Protection Clause,[76] applicable to the federal government.[77] Only the due process requirement applies to federal law, which, the Court said, imposes a less rigorous standard.[78] The Supreme Court has not made any later significant Contracts Clause decisions. It seems fair to conclude that the Burger Court's one innovation or deviation as to constitutional economic rights is unlikely to prove of continuing importance.

Antitrust

Although the Burger Court era was rather uneventful in terms of constitutional economic rights, it was little short of revolutionary in terms of economic rights under the antitrust laws. Although antitrust is supposedly a matter of statutory, not constitutional, law, the difference is not as great as might appear. The Supreme Court once noted that the Sherman Act, the basic antitrust statute, "has a generality and adaptability comparable to that found to be desirable in constitutional provisions."[79] That is, it too is essentially devoid of content. Both antitrust and constitutional law are essentially common-law subjects, created by the Supreme Court almost entirely out of whole cloth. Antitrust decisions are theoretically subject to congressional revision, but that rarely happens, and constitutional law, too, it seems, is sometimes subject to change by ordinary legislation. The 1965 Voting Rights Act,[80] for example, "overruled" a Supreme Court decision upholding literacy tests,[81] and more recently, the Religious Freedom Restoration Act[82] "overruled" the Court's decision that religious practices are not generally exempt from the application of ordinary law.[83]

The Warren Court

The Burger Court inherited from its predecessor a body of antitrust law that had been inflated almost to the bursting point. The Warren Court essentially took the position that it was not competent to determine the competitive consequences of challenged business arrangements.[84] One can hardly quarrel with that premise, but it should lead, one would think, to the conclusion that very few business arrangements can be held illegal because the Court is not able to find them to be anticompetitive. In the euphoria of an era encompassing the 1960s, however, that believed that more law, government, and coercion was a prescription for social progress, it led to the opposite conclusion, that nearly all challenged business arrangements, no matter how apparently reasonable, efficient, and productive, were illegal per se, that is, illegal without inquiry into either their anticompetitive effects or their procompetitive justifications.

By the time the Warren Court finished its work, the so-called per se offenses encompassed nearly all of antitrust. They included horizontal price-fixing agreements, whether setting minimum[85] or, more questionably, maximum prices[86]; resale price maintenance agreements, again whether setting minimum[87] or, more questionably still, maximum prices[88]; group boycotts or concerted refusals to deal[89]; tie-in arrangements[90] and, in effect, exclusive dealing[91]; and most surprisingly and questionably, all agreements between manufacturers and dealers restricting the dealers' freedom in the distribution of the manufacturer's goods.[92] If it is a desideratum of law that results be predictable, antitrust law approached the ideal; the rule could not have been more simple and clear: Plaintiff always wins. As Justice Potter Stewart put it, dissenting in a merger case, "the sole consistency that I can find is that under [merger law], the Government always wins."[93]

Local price cutting by large national companies to the injury of smaller competitors was likely to be condemned as illegal price discrimination under the Clayton Act, as amended by the Robinson-Patman Act,[94] and as an attempt to monopolize by predatory pricing under Section 2 of the Sherman Act.[95] An illegal conspiracy under Section 1 of the Sherman Act could be found on the basis of a company's dealing with a wholly owned corporate subsidiary (i.e., a company could be found guilty of conspiring with itself).[96] Summary judgment for defendants was virtually eliminated as a possibility,[97] giving antitrust law, with its mandatory treble damages and attorneys' fees, almost unlimited potential as a tool of extortion, a potential that was frequently realized. In sum, instead of protecting and encouraging competition, antitrust law often operated to make competition dangerous.

A New Era Begins

All of this was changed and changed drastically by the Burger Court.[98] After being expanded to the point of encompassing almost every business transaction, antitrust has now been shrunk to the point of almost disappearing. Like labor law, antitrust is in danger of becoming—and in both cases clearly to the common good—a subject largely of historical interest.

The dawning of a new antitrust day was indicated by the Court's 1974 decision in *United States v. General Dynamics Corp.*[99] in which the apparently firm rule that the government always wins in merger cases was broken. In the past, merger cases were decided almost entirely on the basis of market shares, with the definition of the relevant market typically being manipulated to maximize defendant's market share and, therefore, the merger's vulnerability. In *General Dynamics*, however, the Court looked behind the numbers to market and economic realities and found that the merger was not likely to have the anticompetitive consequences that the market shares alone might suggest.[100] It is possible to distinguish *General Dynamics* on its facts from earlier cases, but the vigorous dissent of Justice Douglas, joined by Justices Brennan, White, and Marshall, from the Court's rejection of market share as determinative corroborated that the law had changed direction.

With the Court's 1977 decision in *Continental TV, Inc. v. GTE Sylvania*,[101] the change in direction became undeniable and almost total. Perhaps the high point of the Warren Court's drive to expand antitrust liability was its literally incredible— neither the lower courts nor most commentators could bring themselves to believe it[102]—1967 decision in *United States v. Arnold, Schwinn & Co.*[103] In a 1911 decision, *Dr. Miles Medical Co. v. John D. Park & Sons Co.*,[104] the Court held, over the dissent of Justice Holmes, that the Sherman Act applied to vertical (i.e., buyer-seller) as well as horizontal (i.e., competitor) agreements and, specifically, that it prohibited manufacturer-dealer agreements setting a minimum dealer resale price.[105] The Court mistakenly believed that such agreements were the result of and equivalent to a price-fixing conspiracy among dealers. In *Schwinn*, the Court extended the *Dr. Miles* prohibition of vertical price agreements to every type of vertical restraint on a dealer's resale of goods.[106] All manufacturer-dealer agreements confining dealers as to location, territory, or class of customers were declared illegal per se.[107]

Although per se rules are supposed to make the law clear and certain, the effect of *Schwinn* was to make it impossible for manufacturers to protect their legitimate interests in the distribution of their goods without inviting treble-damage suits by disgruntled or simply litigious dealers. The Sherman Antitrust Act, enacted to combat the Standard Oil Trust and other national monopolies, had degenerated into a dealer protection act. Antitrust was reduced from a protector of competition in national markets to a species of tort law. The more and the worse the law, however, the better it is for lawyers, and few things were better for antitrust lawyers than *Schwinn*.

The Burger era coincided with an era of growing skepticism about the benefits of government regulation. Nobel laureate Milton Friedman and other economists at the University of Chicago preached the gospel of free markets.[108] George Stigler, another future Nobel laureate at Chicago, focused the analysis on microeconomics or price theory, concluding that the effects of government regulations of business are generally counterproductive.[109] Aaron Director, Edward Levi, and later Ronald Coase, also a Nobel laureate, brought the new learning into the Chicago Law School, beginning the modern era of the economic analysis of law.[110] Robert H. Bork,[111] who studied at the Chicago Law School, and Richard A. Posner,[112] who still teaches there, applied economic analysis to all aspects of antitrust, the most obviously economic area of law, and found much to criticize.

Bork and Posner argued that the purpose of antitrust was, or should be, protection of consumer interests, not the often anticonsumer interests of small business.[113] They convincingly demonstrated that many, if not most, antitrust doctrines were based on a misunderstanding of the economic and business purposes and effects of various commercial practices and arrangements.[114] As a result, the doctrines often served to hinder rather than advance efficiency and, therefore, to increase costs and harm consumers. They pointed out, for example, that manufacturers have an interest in the efficient distribution of their products. Their efforts to limit competition among their dealers are likely, therefore, to be for efficiency purposes. Such limits are rarely, if ever, a means of gaining monopoly power, the power to raise the market price of a product by restricting its supply. Vertical restrictions on distribution, therefore, Bork and Posner concluded, should not only not be illegal per se but should not be illegal at all,[115] not a matter of antitrust concern.

Bork and Posner are also extremely skeptical that it is possible to achieve monopoly power by so-called exclusionary or predatory practices or any form of single-firm (noncollusive) conduct except by obtaining government-imposed limitations on competition.[116] In their view, therefore, antitrust should prohibit little if anything more than pure and simple, or "naked" (i.e., not involving any integration of operations or facilities), horizontal price-fixing agreements and horizontal mergers that result in a very high (say, two-thirds) market share.[117]

In *Sylvania*, the Court with only Justices Brennan, White, and Marshall dissenting, explicitly overruled *Schwinn*'s rule of per se illegality for vertical nonprice restrictions.[118] The decision marked a decisive turning point in antitrust not only because of what it held but, even more important, because it represented an almost complete acceptance by the Court of the Chicago School approach to antitrust. The writings of Bork and Posner were cited and relied on throughout Justice Powell's opinion for the Court.[119] The Court agreed, most fundamentally, that antitrust cannot be "divorced from market considerations,"[120] that is, that it should be used to serve only economic protection of consumer welfare—not social or political ends.

No business practice or arrangement should be condemned, the Court said, unless shown to have an adverse economic effect. Per se rules of illegality are applicable, therefore, the Court concluded, only to practices known to have a "pernicious effect" on competition and to be without "redeeming virtue."[121] This is not typically the case, the Court found, with vertical nonprice restrictions. Although they limit or end intrabrand competition—competition among dealers in a particular brand of a product—they can increase interbrand competition—competition with other brands. They do this by permitting dealers to engage in costly promotions or provide needed services without having to fear that a competing dealer can "free ride" on their efforts by not making the expenditures and thus being able to sell the product at a lower price.

It happens that except for naked agreements not to compete, very few, if any, business practices or arrangements meet *Sylvania's* strict specifications for a per se rule. If followed consistently by the Court, the result would be very few per se rules. Plaintiffs would be required to show in every case that a challenged arrangement has a net anticompetitive effect, something they are rarely able to do. The result would be, and to a large extent has been, very much less antitrust liability and litigation.

The Court's statement on per se rules has not been consistently followed, however, not even in *Sylvania* itself. The Court accepted the Chicago view that as monopoly power is rarely achievable through restrictions on one's dealers, such restrictions should be assumed to be efficiency increasing. The Court nonetheless explicitly refused to overrule the *Dr. Miles* per se rule for vertical price restraints, even though, as Bork and Posner have shown, such restraints are quite similar in purpose and effect to vertical nonprice restraints.[122]

Nor did the Court hold that vertical nonprice restrictions were necessarily legal, but only that they were not illegal per se. They are therefore to be tested by the so-called rule of reason and prohibited only if shown to be net anticompetitive. Because of the difficulty of proving anticompetitive effects, however, the practical effect of a rule-of-reason approach is much the same as a rule of per se legality. Although *Sylvania* did not go quite all the way with the Chicago School, it left little doubt that the Chicago approach, highly skeptical of most of antitrust, would receive a sympathetic hearing in cases involving other antitrust areas.

PRICE-FIXING AGREEMENTS   The promise of *Sylvania* has largely been kept.[123] In *Broadcast Music, Inc. v. Columbia Broadcasting System, Inc.,*[124] the Court refused to apply a per se rule even to a combination of competitors—composers and other music copyright owners—that had the effect of eliminating almost all price competition in the sale of music performance rights.[125] An agreement among competitors is not necessarily illegal, the Court said, merely because it "literally" involves price fixing.[126] It is illegal only if it is shown to be "'plainly anticompetitive' and very likely without 'redeeming virtue.'"[127] This amounts to saying that there is no per se rule, that no arrangement or practice (other than a naked agreement not to compete) can be condemned as illegal without examining its actual competitive effects and justifications.

If applied consistently, the *Broadcast Music* approach would be a welcome development in antitrust. The supposed distinction between per se and rule-of-reason offenses has been a source of endless confusion.[128] It should be abandoned in favor of the simple rule that only naked agreements not to compete are necessarily illegal. Antitrust is based on the assumption, whether or not correct, that competition is a good thing; arrangements that have no purpose or effect other than to end competition are therefore necessarily prohibited. All other arrangements, however, those that involve some integration of operations or facilities and therefore have possible efficiency justifications, cannot be condemned without investigation of their competitive effects and justifications.

Consistency, however, is too much to ask of the Supreme Court.[129] In *Arizona v. Maricopa County Medical Society*[130] in 1982, the Court condemned as illegal per se a physician-created health care arrangement that clearly involved the creation of a new product or service and had possible efficiency justifications. The 4–3 decision may be seen as an aberration, however, the result of a temporary return to power of the antitrust enthusiasts—Justices Brennan, White, Marshall, and Stevens—made possible by the absence of a full Court. An illegal price-fixing agreement was also found the following year in *NCAA v. Board of Regents of the University of Oklahoma*,[131] involving the joint sale to television networks of rights to broadcast college football games. It was found, however, not on the basis of a per se rule but only after a thorough analysis of competitive harms and justifications.

TIE-INS   In any listing of the least defensible of Warren Court antitrust decisions, *Fortner Enterprises, Inc. v. U.S. Steel Corp.* [132] must rank high, carrying the supposed per se rule against tying arrangements to a new extreme. The rule was established by judges, at first in patent cases, on the mistaken notion that a monopolist of one product, say a patented motion picture projector, could obtain an additional monopoly, say of motion picture films, by requiring buyers of the first (the "tying") product to also buy from the monopolist all they need of the second (the "tied") product.[133] Economic analysis shows that although such an arrangement might facilitate price discrimination—charging more to users who have greater use for the tying product as measured by greater use of the tied—it will not multiply or expand monopoly power.[134] Indeed, price discrimination can reduce the evil of monopoly power by permitting the monopolist to increase output above the level that would be most profitable if he were required to charge all buyers a single price. This is because price discrimination allows a seller to charge a low (though still profitable) price to marginal users of a product without having to lower the price to high-demand users.

The notion that a tie-in is a device for increasing monopoly power is even more clearly mistaken when the two products are used in fixed proportions. A monopolist of bolts, for example, cannot gain additional monopoly profits by requiring each bolt purchaser also to purchase a nut. Bolts and nuts are merely components of a single product, a fastening device, and no additional monopoly profit can be made by becoming the sole supplier of more than one component of a single product.[135]

In *Fortner*, one division of U.S. Steel, the Homes Division, sold prefabricated houses, and another division facilitated these sales by providing low-cost financing for the houses and related development expenses. Fortner, a developer who negotiated a very favorable deal with U.S. Steel's struggling Homes Division, claimed that the homes were of inferior quality. Instead of bringing a mere breach-of-contract action for damages, his imaginative lawyer added an antitrust claim for treble damages and attorneys' fees, claiming that U.S. Steel had tied the sale of houses to the sale of credit.

The idea that U.S. Steel had monopoly power in credit (money) and was using it to monopolize prefabricated housing was absurd, but the beauty of per se rules is that they make reality irrelevant. Finding no tie, the district court granted,[136] and the court of appeals affirmed, summary judgment for U.S. Steel.[137] The Supreme Court, in an opinion by Justice Black, the paradigmatic southern populist, reversed and sent the case back for further investigation of U.S. Steel's alleged monopoly power over money.[138] After bouncing around in the baffled lower courts for eight years, the case returned to an embarrassed Supreme Court in 1977. In *Fortner II*, the Court quickly disposed of it by finding that no monopoly-expanding tying arrangement was involved because U.S. Steel did not have monopoly power in credit, the alleged tying product.[139] It is not illegal, the Court stated, to sell high-priced homes with the aid of low-priced credit, which is all that was involved.[140] This reasoning applies equally to most or all alleged fixed-proportion ties. It is difficult to see, in any event, how a buyer, such as Fortner—rather than a competitor of the seller—can claim to be injured by an arrangement he voluntarily entered into, presumably because it was the best available.

Fortner II appeared to mean that the requirement of monopoly power in the alleged tying product—without which, by definition, there could be no tie—was now to be taken seriously. As a result, the per se rule as to tie-ins was very much weakened. In the Burger Court's next and last tie-in case, *Jefferson Parish Hospital District No. 2 v. Hyde*[141] in 1984, four Justices voted to eliminate the per se rule entirely.[142] The majority purported to retain it but weakened it still further by holding that a 30 percent share of the relevant market did not indicate a sufficient degree of power to make the (supposed) per se rule applicable.

BOYCOTTS   Boycotts or concerted refusals to deal are the final practice that had traditionally been listed, along with price-fixing, horizontal market division, and tie-ins, as illegal per se.[143] In *Northwest Wholesale Stationers, Inc. v. Pacific Stationary & Printing Co.*,[144] however, the Court in effect eliminated the per se rule as to boycotts by holding, as it had regarding price fixing in *Broadcast Music*, that not every arrangement that could be described as a concerted refusal to deal was necessarily illegal.[145] It is not necessarily an antitrust violation, the Court held, for a group of retailers to exclude a competitor from an efficient joint wholesale buying arrangement. Such conduct is illegal only when "characteristically likely to result in predominantly anticompetitive effects."[146] The result, again, would seem to be to make an investigation of the effects of and justifications for a challenged arrangement relevant in all or nearly all cases.

MONOPOLIZATION   An apparent peculiarity of antitrust (i.e., antimonopoly) law is that it does not in fact prohibit monopolies. One reason is that some monopolies are the result of government grants such as patents, and the government cannot usefully prohibit with one hand what it bestows with the other. Another reason is that some markets cannot support more than one efficient company, making monopoly inevitable, the "natural monopoly" situation. Finally, some monopolies may result from exceptional competitive skill—good products sold at low prices—which antitrust seeks to encourage, not condemn. The law, therefore, prohibits not monopoly as such, but only monopolization, the obtaining or retaining of monopoly power by objectionable conduct,[147] for example, by some mergers.

Another peculiarity is that antitrust, at least since the breakup of the Standard Oil[148] and American Tobacco[149] companies in 1911, has involved few monopolization cases, which may indicate that the need for this body of law is easily overstated. Most peculiar, surely, is that the most important of these few cases have nearly all been lower court decisions.[150] The Supreme Court, it seems, has largely avoided, perhaps wisely, addressing the subject. The most famous and important of monopoly cases, virtually the bible of monopolization law for more than four decades, was *United States v. Aluminum Company of America*,[151] decided by the Second Circuit in an opinion by Judge Learned Hand, a judge who generally merited his impressive name, although not in this case. The Second Circuit heard the case pursuant to a special act of Congress[152] after Supreme Court review of the district court decision in defendant's favor was precluded by lack of a quorum.[153]

Although the *Alcoa* decision, as it is known, was made before the Warren Court era, it was very much in its spirit in that its effect was to make monopoly, or even a very large market share, at least in an important industry, illegal per se. Alcoa was condemned, incredibly, not for restraining output to increase market price, the basic objection to monopoly power, but for the "exclusionary practice"[154] of expanding output to meet an increasing demand, a demand it did much to stimulate. Apparently, it should have held output down to let prices rise and reap monopoly profits to give less efficient companies a better chance to enter the industry. If justice requires treatment according to preexisting law, not law made up for the occasion, few defendants have been treated more unjustly than Alcoa. The result of the decision was to make vigorous competition by large companies dangerous, ushering in an era of "soft competition." Antitrust thus became and remained until the time of the Burger Court a body of law that served less to protect than to deter competition.

The Burger era saw an unusual number of monopolization cases, most notably the government's suit against International Business Machines,[155] followed by a dozen private suits,[156] but with one peculiar exception, none was decided by the Supreme Court. Perhaps the most significant monopolization decision of the era was *Berkey Photo, Inc. v. Eastman Kodak Co.*, a 1980 decision by the Second Circuit.[157] Although decided by the court that decided *Alcoa*, the tenor of the two decisions could hardly be more different. The *Alcoa* decision was now described as "cryptic" and a "litigant's wishing well" and all but explicitly overruled.[158] The fact that Kodak dominated nearly all aspects of the photography industry—film, processing, cameras—did not require it, the court said, to refrain from vigorous competition or take steps to aid small competitors. Even monopolists, the court now made clear, may vigorously compete.

Plaintiff Berkey Photo filed a petition for certiorari, but the Supreme Court, inexplicably, declined to hear the case, permitting the Second Circuit's decision to stand. The only expression of a view from the Supreme Court was in an opinion by Justice Powell, joined by Justice Rehnquist, dissenting from the Court's denial of certiorari.[159] They apparently would have been even more emphatic than the Second Circuit in insisting that antitrust favors hard competition. They found it "little less than bizarre"[160] and "difficult to fathom"[161] that a claim could be based, as it was in part in this case, on a monopolist's failure to assist its competitors.

Having declined to take a real monopolization case, the Court, in its inscrutable wisdom, decided five years later to take a specious one, *Aspen Skiing Co. v. Aspen Highlands Skiing Corp.* (1985).[162] Defendant Ski Co. owned and operated skiing facilities on three mountains in Aspen, Colorado; plaintiff Highlands owned and operated a ski facility on a fourth mountain. In the 1950s, the parties entered an agreement to sell a multiday all-lifts ticket, whereby customers could with one ticket ski on any of the four mountains. This arrangement, obviously subject to objection on antitrust grounds as price fixing, was challenged by the attorney general of Colorado in a suit that was settled by a consent decree. The current case involved, however, not the creation of this questionable arrangement but its termination in 1977, when Highlands declined to continue the arrangement on the terms that Ski Co. offered.

Highlands then sued Ski Co. for illegal monopolization, and obtained a $2.5 million jury award, automatically trebled to $7.5 million plus attorneys' fees.[163] Reverting to its bad old habits, the Court apparently saw the case as a morality play involving a small company mistreated by a bully and unanimously affirmed the judgment.[164] A company, even a monopolist, the Court agreed, has no "general duty" to help a competitor.[165] The Court thought it highly significant, however, that the case involved not a refusal to help but a refusal to *continue* to help.[166] That the case was wrongly decided should be sufficiently clear from the fact that it almost surely would have been decided differently if Ski Co. had not entered into the arrangement with Highlands in the first place. One may be generally skeptical of the validity of a rule that makes it illegal to terminate what one is not legally required to begin. It did not appear that Highlands would have been better off if Ski Co. had never entered into the arrangement. It is clear, therefore, that its complaint was not that it was injured by Ski Co. but that it ceased to be benefited.

Highlands lacked a valid monopoly claim, in any event, because Aspen was not the relevant geographical market. Aspen is a "destination" ski resort, competing with many other such resorts on a national and international basis. The elimination of Highlands would not, therefore, have given Ski Co. monopoly power over the price of skiing. The district court escaped this obvious and dispositive conclusion by finding that Aspen constituted a "submarket,"[167] a finding with no basis in economic reality. The Supreme Court escaped it by finding that the market definition question was not presented, but that does not make the Court's finding of monopolization any less invalid. *Aspen* would appear to stand for the proposition that every refusal by a dominant company to help a competitor provides the basis for an antitrust suit unless it is justified as efficient to the satisfaction of a judge. That is not a workable rule, however, and probably not the rule of *Aspen*, which likely will be treated as *sui generis*, more an atavistic foray into tort or social welfare law than an application of antitrust law.[168]

Attempt to Monopolize: Predatory Pricing

Section 2 of the Sherman Act prohibits attempts to monopolize as well as monopolization. Because the attempt offense does not, like the completed offense, require a showing that the defendant is a monopolist, it has been a much more fertile source of litigation. The most common basis for the attempt offense is a charge of "predatory pricing," that is, the use of excessively low prices, however defined, to drive less wealthy competitors into bankruptcy and thereby gain monopoly power. Economic analysis indicates, however, that in general such a tactic is not economically rational and therefore unlikely to occur.[169]

A competitor can drive an equally efficient competitor (one with the same costs) into bankruptcy only by pricing below cost. This, however, involves incurring present losses, usually at a much greater rate than the competitor,[170] for future (and therefore to be discounted by the interest rate) gains. The strategy can succeed only if competitors are driven out and the losses involved can be recouped from future monopoly profits, all of which is highly speculative. Competitors may be able to stay in the market by obtaining funds from customers—who would be harmed by monopoly—or from capital markets.[171] Even if driven into bankruptcy, competitors often reenter the market after reorganization, and with reduced fixed costs. Most important, having achieved monopoly by bankrupting competitors, monopolists will be able to recoup their losses from monopoly profits only in the unlikely event that their monopoly prices do not encourage new entry or reentry.

The conclusion that predatory pricing is irrational in principle as a monopolizing technique is apparently corroborated by the fact that there are few, if any, examples of its successful use.[172] Further, because low prices are generally beneficial to consumers and an objective of antitrust, there is an obvious danger in making them the basis of an antitrust offense. If predatory pricing is not a serious problem, as appears to be the case, the best policy may be simply to ignore it. The loss to competition involved, if any, will likely be outweighed by the gain of removing a possible deterrent to competition. That, at least, was the conclusion of the Chicago School.

In 1975, Professors Phillip Areeda and Donald Turner of the Harvard Law School, authors of an extremely influential antitrust treatise,[173] published an article recommending an approach to predatory pricing claims less absolute than the Chicago approach, but which proved in practice to have very much the same effect.[174] They recommended, first, that questions of defendant's alleged intent to injure plaintiff should play no role in attempt to monopolize or monopolization cases. Showing a supposed evil intent to injure plaintiff was the traditional means by which failed small companies won jury sympathy awards against larger companies. Because competition necessarily injures rivals, however, an intent to injure cannot validly be the basis of an antitrust claim.

Predatory pricing claims should turn, instead, Areeda and Turner argued, simply on the relationship between the alleged predatory price and defendant's costs. A price should not be considered predatory unless it is below some measure of costs, and the proper measure is marginal cost, the additional cost of producing the last unit. A price is profitable—that is, makes a contribution to revenue—and economically rational, even if below full cost, as long as it exceeds marginal cost. Pricing at or above marginal cost, therefore, should not be considered predatory. Because marginal cost data are ordinarily not available, average variable cost should be used as a proxy.

Some variant of the Areeda-Turner approach has been adopted in every circuit.[175] In 1986, in *Matsushita Electric Industrial Co. v. Zenith Radio Corp.*,[176] the Supreme Court indicated its acceptance of the Areeda-Turner view that a predatory price is a price "below some appropriate measure of cost."[177] Citing and quoting Robert Bork and other Chicago analysts, the Court also expressly endorsed the view that predatory pricing claims should be greeted with great skepticism.[178] Predatory pricing, it said, is "by nature speculative,"[179] "rarely tried and even more rarely successful."[180] The effect of the Areeda-Turner approach to predatory pricing, at least partly endorsed in *Matsushita*, has been largely to eliminate attempts to monopolize suits based on predatory pricing claims. Such suits had been a major source of private antitrust litigation.

Summary Judgment Made Available to Defendants

The *Matsushita* decision is also important because the Court affirmed a district court grant of summary judgment to defendants. This illustrated and endorsed another major change in antitrust law, the availability of summary disposal of antitrust claims. Indeed, *Matsushita* shows not only that summary judgment is now available to antitrust defendants but that it may be granted even in the face of complicated and contested facts when economic analysis indicates that a claim is without merit.

Resale Price Maintenance

As already noted, antitrust long ago degenerated from a means of protecting a competitive national economy to a species of dealer-protection law. The demise of *Schwinn* in *Sylvania* left resale price maintenance or vertical price fixing as the only per se illegal vertical arrangement. Although the Court in *Sylvania* declined to overrule the *Dr. Miles* per se rule as to resale price maintenance, it has largely achieved the same effect by making claims of illegal resale price maintenance very hard to prove. In *United States v. Colgate & Co.* in 1919,[181] the Court effectively overruled *Dr. Miles* by holding that a manufacturer may control his dealers' resale price by simply telling the dealers what the price should be and that they will be cut off if they fail to comply. In that situation, the Court said, quite illogically, the "contract, combination, or conspiracy" (or "agreement") requirement of Section 1 of the Sherman Act is not met.[182] The manufacturer was said to have acted "unilaterally" even though he explicitly sought and successfully obtained the cooperation of his dealers.

Though *Colgate* in effect overruled *Dr. Miles*, it was in turn also effectively overruled, though never explicitly, by later decisions that found the agreement requirement met by manufacturer conduct—the identification and termination of noncomplying dealers—that *Colgate* supposedly allowed.[183] In *Monsanto Co. v. Spray Rite Service Corp.*,[184] however, the Burger Court apparently restored the so-called *Colgate* doctrine to full vigor.[185] The fact that a manufacturer has demonstrated "a strongly felt concern about resale prices" does not prove, the Court said, that he had obtained illegal "agreements" from dealers as to resale prices.[186] And, as *Colgate* held, absent proof of an agreement, there is no liability under *Dr.*

Miles.[187] Minimum care by manufacturers to avoid obtaining express statements of agreement on resale prices from dealers should be enough, it seems, to permit them to effectively control resale prices without antitrust liability.[188]

No Single-Firm "Conspiracy"

The Burger Court eliminated another basis of antitrust liability in *Copperweld Corp. v. Independence Tube Corp.*,[189] by holding, contrary to indications in prior decisions, that a business firm cannot be found guilty of conspiring with itself.[190] Specifically, no illegal contract, combination, or conspiracy can be found under Section 1 of the Sherman Act on the basis of a corporation's dealings with its incorporated wholly owned subsidiaries.[191]

Robinson-Patman Act

The Robinson-Patman Act was enacted in 1936,[192] in the depths of the Great Depression, when competition, like capitalism itself, was held in low esteem. It prohibits certain price discriminations or differences that have or may have anticompetitive effects. Although purportedly an antitrust statute, in practice it has had less to do with protecting competition than with protecting small businesses from the competition of larger ones. It has therefore long been a favorite target of antitrust skeptics.[193] Wide recognition of its anticompetitive effects led to its being very little enforced by the government during the Burger Court era, and in the few cases brought by private parties, the Court generally limited the reach of the act. In *Gulf Oil Corp. v. Copp Paving Co., Inc.*,[194] the Court held that the act did not apply to a company with wholly intrastate operations because it extended only to activities "in" interstate commerce and not, like the Sherman Act, also to activities that merely "affect" interstate commerce.[195]

In *J. Truett Payne Co. v. Chrysler Motors Corp.*,[196] the Court made clear that a plaintiff does not establish a Robinson-Patman claim by merely showing that his supplier made sales at lower prices to his competitors. Plaintiff must also show that defendant's conduct violated the act (i.e., was anticompetitive) and that plaintiff was injured as a result of its anticompetitive effects. Finally, in *Falls City Industries, Inc. v. Vanco Beverage, Inc.*,[197] the Court read the act's "meeting competition" defense very broadly and further indicated that the requirement of showing an injury to competition, not just to the plaintiff, a showing difficult to make, must be taken seriously.[198]

Conclusion

The Burger Court had little impact on economic rights as a matter of constitutional law. The most interesting development was its use of the Contracts Clause to invalidate state laws in two cases in successive years. The limited significance of this partial revival of the clause is indicated by the fact that no claim based on it has prevailed in the nearly two decades since.

In regard to economic freedom under the antitrust laws, however, the work of the Burger Court has been little less than revolutionary. The Court rendered major decisions in almost every antitrust area, and the result almost always was to increase business freedom and reduce antitrust liability. The Court took an area of law that had become a cancerous growth on the body of American commerce and business, restricting competition and spawning expensive and extensive litigation, and returned it to something like its original purpose, which was to remove, not impose, restraints on commerce and trade.

The Burger Court so thoroughly revised almost every aspect of antitrust law as to leave relatively little for its successor to do. There have been only a few major antitrust decisions in the past ten years, and they have mostly confirmed and continued the work of the Burger Court.[199]

Notes

1. See, e.g., Wright v. Council of City of Emporia, 407 U.S. 451 (1972).

2. See 116 *Cong. Rec.* 11913 (1970) (statement of former Rep. Gerald Ford) ("impeachable offense is whatever a majority of the House of Representatives considers [it] to be"); Peterson, "The Role of the Executive Branch in the Discipline and Removal of Federal Judges," 1993 *U. Ill. L. Rev.* 809, 849 (Gerald Ford's attempt to impeach Justice Douglas is the most "overt threat to judicial independence").

3. The nomination of Robert Bork, which might have been of some consequence, was urged on Ford by conservatives, but an election was coming in which he feared for his chances, rightly as it turned out. When a Republican politician is concerned about an election, it means a move to the left, but in this instance, as almost always, it did Ford, and certainly the rest of us, no good.

4. *The Burger Court: The Counter-Revolution That Wasn't* (Blasi ed., 1983).

5. Until United States v. Lopez, 115 S. Ct. 1624 (1995); see Graglia, "*United States v. Lopez*: Judicial Review under the Commerce Clause," 74 *Tex. L. Rev.* 719 (1996).

6. But see text accompanying infra note 21.

7. But see the section "The Contracts Clause," infra, pp. 151–54.

8. 384 U.S. 436 (1966).

9. Green v. County School Bd. of New Kent County, 391 U.S. 430 (1968).

10. Roe v. Wade, 410 U.S. 113 (1973).

11. Swann v. Charlotte-Mecklenburg Bd. of Educ., 402 U.S. 1 (1971).

12. See Graglia, "Interpreting the Constitution: Posner on Bork," 44 *Stan. L. Rev.* 1019, 1047 (1992).

13. See, e.g., Allgeyer v. Louisiana, 165 U.S. 578, 589–93 (1897).

14. Lochner v. New York, 198 U.S. 45 (1905).

15. 300 U.S. 379 (1937).

16. 427 U.S. 297 (1976).

17. 354 U.S. 457 (1957).

18. *Dukes*, 427 U.S. at 304.

19. U.S. Const. art. I, § 10, cl.1: "No State shall . . . pass any . . . Law impairing the Obligation of Contracts. . . ."

20. U.S. Const. amend. V: "[N]or shall private property be taken for public use without just compensation."

21. See Dolan v. Tigard, 512 U.S. 374 (1994); Lucas v. South Carolina Coastal Council, 505 U.S. 1003 (1992); Nollan v. California Coastal Comm'n, 483 U.S. 825 (1987); First English Evangelical Lutheran Church of Glendale v. Los Angeles, 482 U.S. 304 (1987).

22. 458 U.S. 419 (1982).

23. Id. at 420.

24. See Loretto v. Teleprompter Manhattan CATV Corp., 446 N.E.2d 428, 429 (N.Y. 1983). In PruneYard Shopping Center v. Robbins, 447 U.S. 74 (1980), however, it is interesting to note, the Court found that a California statute requiring shopping mall owners to permit distribution of leaflets on their property did not constitute a taking even though physical invasion was no less involved than in Loretto. See Jones, "Confiscation: A Rationale of the Law of Takings," 24 *Hofstra L. Rev.* 1, 17 (1995).

25. 444 U.S. 164 (1979).

26. Id. at 165.

27. 467 U.S. 229 (1984).

28. Berman v. Parker, 344 U.S. 26 (1954).

29. Id. at 240.

30. 438 U.S. 104 (1978).

31. Id. at 115.

32. Id. at 104.

33. See Jones, supra note 24, at 10.

34. See *Penn Central*, 438 U.S. at 105.

35. Id. at 122 n. 25.

36. That the Court had in effect adopted a physical possession requirement for a taking to be found was further indicated by its decision in Keystone Bituminous Coal Ass'n. v. DeBenedictis, 480 U.S. 470 (1987), decided one year after Burger left the Court. *Keystone* seems indistinguishable from, and therefore virtually to overrule, Pennsylvania v. Mahon, 260 U.S. 393 (1922), the only case in which the Supreme Court upheld a takings claim in the absence of some form of physical invasion or assertion of ownership. In a sharp reversal of direction, however, such claims have been upheld in several recent cases. See supra note 21.

37. U.S. Const. art. I, § 10.

38. See, e.g., Act of July 13, 1933, 1933 Ill. Laws 682 (lengthening the debt repayment time); Act of Dec, 7, 1861, ch. 7, 1861 Tex. Gen. Laws 5, as amended by Act of Dec. 14, 1863, ch. 40, 1863 Tex. Gen. Laws 26 (extending debt repayment until after the war); Act of Dec. 20, 1784, ch. 167, Pa. 9th Gen. Ass. Laws 233 (allowing debtors more time to repay their debts).

39. See Lawless, "The American Response to Farm Crises: Procedural Debtor Relief," 1988 *U. Ill. L. Rev.* 1037, 1039 (1988) ("early attempts at procedural relief worsened the post-revolutionary war financial crisis and prompted the framers of the Constitution to include the contract clause").

40. See, e.g., U.S. Const. art. IV, § 2; art. I, § 1; art. I, § 9.

41. See, e.g., Gibbons v. Ogden, 22 U.S. 1 (1824); Wilson v. Black-bird Creek Marsh Co., 27 U.S. 245 (1829).

42. See Fletcher v. Peck, 10 U.S. 87, 139 (1810) (holding a Georgia law in violation of "general principles which are common to our free institutions"); see also Grey, "Do We Have an Unwritten Constitution?," 27 *Stan. L. Rev.* 703, 708 (1975) (asserting that in *Fletcher*, "[c]onspicuously absent is a dissent arguing that this [general] principle is nowhere stated in the constitutional text").

43. *Fletcher*, 10 U.S. at 87.

44. Dartmouth College v. Woodward, 17 U.S. 518 (1819).

45. See, e.g., Charles River Bridge v. Warren Bridge, 36 U.S. 420 (1837); West River Bridge Co. v. Dix, 47 U.S. 507 (1848).

46. 290 U.S. 398 (1934).

47. 1933 Minn. Laws 339.

48. 290 U.S. at 443.

49. See Graglia, supra note 12, at 1020–26.
50. 431 U.S. 1 (1977).
51. Id. at 4.
52. Id. at 4–5.
53. Id.
54. Id. at 3.
55. Id. at 16.
56. Id. at 2.
57. Id. at 16.
58. Id. at 32.
59. Id. at 61.
60. 438 U.S. 234 (1978).
61. Id. at 244.
62. Minn. Stat. §§ 181B.01 et seq. (1974).
63. *Allied*, 438 U.S. at 243.
64. Id. at 234.
65. Id. at 257.
66. 459 U.S. 400 (1983).
67. Id.
68. *Allied*, 438 U.S. at 244.
69. United States Trust Co. v. New Jersey, 431 U.S. 1, 22 (1977).
70. Id. at 22–3.
71. *Energy Reserves Group, Inc.*, 459 U.S. at 402.
72. Id. at 416.
73. 462 U.S. 176 (1983).
74. Id.
75. Id. at 191.
76. See Bolling v. Sharpe, 347 U.S. 497 (1954).
77. See Pension Benefit Guar. Co. v. R.A. Gray, 467 U.S. 717 (1984).
78. Id. at 719.
79. Appalachian Coals, Inc. v. United States, 288 U.S. 344, 359 (1933).
80. Pub. L. No. 89-110, 79 Stat. 445 (codified as amended at 42 U.S.C. § 1971 (1994)), *upheld in* Katzenbach v. Morgan, 384 U.S. 641 (1966).
81. Lassiter v. Northampton County Bd. of Elections, 360 U.S. 45 (1963).
82. 42 U.S.C. § 2000bb (Supp. V 1993).
83. Employment Div., Dep't of Human Resources of Or. v. Smith, 494 U.S. 872 (1990).
84. See United States v. Topco Assoc., 405 U.S. 596, 609 (1972): "[C]ourts are of limited utility in examining difficult economic problems" (post-Warren, but reflecting Warren Court attitudes).
85. See United States v. Socony-Vacuum Oil Co., 310 U.S. 150 (1940).
86. See Kiefer-Stewart Co. v. Joseph E. Seagram & Sons, Inc., 340 U.S. 211 (1951).
87. See Dr. Miles Med. Co. v. John D. Park & Sons Co., 220 U.S. 373 (1911).
88. See Albrecht v. Herald Co., 390 U.S. 145 (1968).
89. See Klor's, Inc. v. Broadway-Hale Stores, Inc., 359 U.S. 207 (1959).
90. See International Salt Co. v. United States, 332 U.S. 392 (1947).
91. See Standard Oil Co. v. United States, 337 U.S. 293 (1949).
92. See United States v. Arnold, Schwinn & Co., 388 U.S. 365 (1967).
93. United States v. Von's Grocery Co., 384 U.S. 270, 301 (1966) (Stewart, J., dissenting).
94. Clayton Act § 2(a), 38 Stat. 730 (1914), *as amended by* Robinson-Patman Act, 49 Stat. 1526 (1936) (codified as amended at 15 U.S.C. § 13(a) (1994)).

95. See Utah Pie Co. v. Continental Banking Co., 386 U.S. 685 (1967).

96. See United States v. Yellow Cab Co., 332 U.S. 218 (1947).

97. See Poller v. Columbia Broadcasting Sys., Inc., 368 U.S. 464 (1962).

98. But see Posner, "The Antitrust Decisions of the Burger Court," 47 *Antitrust L.J.* 819, 819 (1978) ("the Burger Court's impact . . . has been relatively small").

99. 415 U.S. 486 (1974).

100. Id.

101. 433 U.S. 36 (1977).

102. See id. at 48 n. 13.

103. 388 U.S. 365 (1967).

104. 220 U.S. 373 (1911).

105. Id.

106. *Schwinn*, 388 U.S. at 367.

107. Id. at 367–68.

108. See, e.g., Friedman and Friedman, *Free to Choose: A Personal Statement* (1980); Friedman, *Capitalism and Freedom* (1962).

109. See, e.g., Stigler, *The Theory of Price* (4th ed. 1987); Stigler, *Perfect Competition, Historically Contemplated, in Microeconomics: Selected Readings* 183 (Mansfield ed., 1971).

110. See, e.g., Posner, "The Chicago School of Antitrust Analysis," 127 *U. Pa. L. Rev.* 925 (1979).

111. See, e.g., Bork, *The Antitrust Paradox: A Policy at War with Itself* (1978).

112. See, e.g., Posner, *Antitrust Law: An Economic Perspective* (1976).

113. See, e.g., supra note 111, at 407 (asserting "that competition must be understood as the maximization of consumer welfare"); supra note 112 at 19 (stating that "antitrust enforcement is an inappropriate method of trying to promote the interests of small business"); Bork, "Legislative Intent and the Policy of the Sherman Act," 9 *J.L. & Econ.* 7–14 (1966) (stating that Congress's motivation in enacting antitrust regulation was to promote consumer welfare).

114. See, e.g., Bork, "Vertical Integration and the Sherman Act: The Legal History of an Economic Misconception," 22 *U. Chi. L. Rev.* 157 (1954); Posner, "Antitrust Policy and the Supreme Court: An Analysis of the Restricted Distribution, Horizontal Merger and Potential Competition Decisions," 75 *Colum. L. Rev.* 282 (1975).

115. See Posner, "The Next Step in the Antitrust Treatment of Restricted Distribution: Per Se Legality," 48 *U. Chi. L. Rev.* 6 (1981) (arguing for a rule of per se legality); Posner, "The Rule of Reason and the Economic Approach: Reflections on the *Sylvania* Decision," 45 *U. Chi. L. Rev.* 1, 19 (1977) (arguing against the "inappropriate per se rule of illegality"); Bork, "Vertical Restraints: *Schwinn* Overruled," 1977 *Sup. Ct. Rev.* 171 (1977).

116. See Bork, supra note 111, at 407 (arguing for "intervention in [government] . . . regulatory processes to extend the competitive ethic as broadly as possible").

117. See Bork, supra note 111, at 405–6 ("the law should be reformed so that it strikes at . . . a) The suppression of competition by horizontal agreement . . . b) Horizontal mergers creating very large market shares. . . .").

118. Continental T.V., Inc. v. GTE Sylvania, Inc., 433 U.S. 36, 36 (1977).

119. See, e.g., Bork, supra note 113; Bork, "The Rule of Reason and the Per Se Concept: Price Fixing and Market Division," 75 *Yale L.J.* 373 (1966); Posner, supra note 112; Posner and Easterbrook, *Antitrust Cases, Economic Notes and Other Materials* (1974).

120. *Continental T.V.*, 433 U.S. at 54.

121. Id. at 36.

122. See *Continental T.V.*, 433 U.S. at 69 (White, J., concurring).

123. The Court did extend antitrust liability in one respect, however, by making clear,

quite appropriately, that there is no general exemption for the so-called learned professions. Antitrust applies to lawyers and engineers as well as to industrialists. See Goldfarb v. Virginia State Bar, 421 U.S. 773 (1975); National Soc'y of Professional Eng'rs v. United States, 435 U.S. 679 (1978).

124. 441 U.S. 1 (1979).

125. Id.

126. Id. at 9.

127. Id.

128. See Areeda, *The "Rule of Reason" in Antitrust Analysis: General Issues* (Federal Judicial Center, June 1981).

129. Indeed, consistency is impossible, Judge Frank Easterbrook, another leading Chicago School analyst of antitrust, has shown, according to the basic premises of public-choice theory. Easterbrook, "Foreword: The Court and the Economic System," 98 *Harv. L. Rev.* 4 (1984).

130. 457 U.S. 332 (1982).

131. 468 U.S. 85 (1984).

132. 394 U.S. 495 (1969).

133. See Motion Picture Patents Co. v. Universal Film Mfg. Co., 243 U.S. 502 (1917).

134. See Bowman, "Tying Arrangements and the Leverage Problem," 67 *Yale L.J.* 19, 20–1 (1957).

135. See id.

136. Fortner Enters., Inc. v. United States Steel Corp., 293 F. Supp. 762 (W.D. Ky. 1966).

137. Fortner Enters., Inc. v. United States Steel Corp., 404 F.2d 936 (6th Cir. 1968).

138. *Fortner Enters.*, 394 U.S. at 495.

139. United States Steel Corp. v. Fortner Enters., Inc., 429 U.S. 610 (1977).

140. Id. at 610–11.

141. 466 U.S. 2 (1984).

142. Id. at 35.

143. See, e.g., Silver v. New York Stock Exch., 373 U.S. 341 (1963); Radiant Burners v. Peoples Gas Light & Coke Co., 364 U.S. 656 (1961); Northern Pac. Ry. Co. v. United States, 356 U.S. 1 (1958); Associated Press v. United States, 326 U.S. 1 (1945); Fashion Originator's Guild of Am. v. FTC, 312 U.S. 457 (1941).

144. 472 U.S. 284 (1985).

145. Id. at 285.

146. Id. at 296.

147. See United States v. Grinnell Corp., 384 U.S. 563, 570–71 ("The offense of monopoly . . . has two elements: (1) the possession of monopoly power in the relevant market and (2) the willful acquisition or maintenance of that power as distinguished from growth or development as a consequence of a superior product, business acumen, or historic accident. . . .").

148. Standard Oil Co. of N.J. v. United States, 221 U.S. 1 (1911).

149. American Tobacco Co. v. United States, 221 U.S. 106 (1911).

150. See, e.g., United States v. Aluminum Co. of Am., 148 F.2d 416 (2d Cir. 1945); United States v. United Shoe Mach. Corp., 110 F. Supp. 295 (D. Mass. 1953), *aff'd per curiam*, 347 U.S. 521 (1954).

151. 148 F.2d 416 (2d Cir. 1945); see also United States v. United Shoe Mach. Corp., 110 F. Supp. 295, 295 (D. Mass. 1953).

152. 15 U.S.C.A. § 29 (1944).

153. *Aluminum Co. of Am.*, 148 F.2d at 421 (the Supreme Court "declared that a quorum

of six justices qualified to hear the case was wanting"); United States v. Aluminum Co. of Am., 44 F. Supp. 97 (S.D.N.Y. 1941).

154. *Aluminum Co. of Am.*, 148 F.2d at 423.

155. International Bus. Machs. v. United States, 480 F.2d 293 (2d Cir. 1973).

156. See, e.g., Transamerica Computer Co. v. International Bus. Machs., 698 F.2d 1377 (9th Cir. 1983); Memorex Corp. v. International Bus. Machs., 636 F.2d 1188 (9th Cir. 1980); California Computer Prods., Inc. v. International Bus. Machs., 613 F.2d 727 (9th Cir. 1979); ILC Peripherals Leasing Corp. v. International Bus. Machs., 458 F. Supp. 423 (N.D. Cal. 1978); Greyhound Computer Corp. v. International Bus. Machs., 559 F.2d 488 (9th Cir. 1977); Telex Corp. v. International Bus. Machs., 423 U.S. 802 (1975) (cert. dismissed).

157. 603 F.2d 263 (2d Cir. 1979).

158. Id. at 273.

159. See Berkey Photo v. Eastman Kodak, 444 U.S. 1093, 1094 (1980).

160. Id. at 1093.

161. Id. at 1094.

162. 472 U.S. 585 (1985).

163. Id. at 644.

164. Id. at 648.

165. Id. at 586.

166. Id. at 610.

167. See Aspen Highlands Skiing Corp. v. Aspen Skiing Co., 738 F.2d 1509, 1513 (10th Cir. 1984) (discussing the district court's use of the submarket classification).

168. See Olympia Equip. Leasing Co. v. Western Union Telegraph Co., 797 F.2d 370 (7th Cir. 1986) (stating that *Aspen* does not impose on a lawful monopolist a "general duty to help its competitors").

169. See Easterbrook, "Predatory Strategies and Counterstrategies," 48 *U. Chi. L. Rev.* 263, 281 (1981) (asserting "that any approach to predation emphasizing below-cost pricing as a device to drive out rivals is unproductive"); McGee, "Predatory Pricing Revisited," 23 *J.L. & Econ.* 289, 292 (1980); McGee, "Predatory Price Cutting: The *Standard Oil* (N.J.) Case," 1 *J.L.& Econ.* 137, 141 (1958).

170. A company with a 75 percent share of the market, for example, will lose money three times as fast as a company with a 25 percent share.

171. See, e.g., Easterbrook, supra note 169, at 269–70 ("Investors should be willing to back the intended victim, because it would be the more profitable survivor. . . .").

172. See Koller II, "The Myth of Predatory Pricing: An Empirical Study," 4 *Antitrust L. & Econ. Rev.* 105, 112 (Summer 1971) (finding only four successful predation cases: three "to precipitate a merger or collusion" and one "to eliminate a rival").

173. See Areeda and Turner, *Antitrust Law* (1978).

174. See Areeda and Turner, "Predatory Pricing and Related Practices under Section 2 of the Sherman Act," 88 *Harv. L. Rev.* 697 (1975).

175. See, e.g., Barry Wright Corp. v. ITT Grinnell Corp., 724 F.2d 227 (1st Cir. 1983); William Inglis & Sons Baking Co. v. ITT Continental Baking Co., 526 F.2d 86 (9th Cir. 1975).

176. 475 U.S. 574 (1985).

177. Id. at 585.

178. Id. at 589.

179. Id. at 575.

180. Id. at 589.

181. 250 U.S. 300 (1919).

182. Id. at 307.

183. See, e.g., United States v. Parke, Davis & Co., 362 U.S. 29 (1960).

184. 465 U.S. 752 (1984).

185. Id. at 763.

186. Id. at 762.

187. Id. at 753.

188. See also Business Elec. Corp. v. Sharp Elec. Corp., 485 U.S. 717 (1988).

189. 467 U.S. 752 (1984).

190. Id.

191. Id. at 767.

192. Robinson-Patman Act, 49 Stat. 1526 (1936) (codified as amended at 15 U.S.C. § 13 (1994).

193. See, e.g., Bowman, "Restraint of Trade by the Supreme Court: The *Utah Pie Case*," 77 *Yale L.J.* 70 (1967).

194. 419 U.S. 186 (1974).

195. Id. at 206.

196. 451 U.S. 557 (1981).

197. 460 U.S. 428 (1983).

198. Id. at 451.

199. See, e.g., Brooke Group Ltd. v. Brown & Willliamson Tobacco Corp., 509 U.S. 209 (1993); Spectrum Sports, Inc. v. McQuillan, 506 U.S. 447 (1993). But see Eastman Kodak Co. v. Image Technical Serv., Inc., 504 U.S. 451 (1992).

• 12 •

FEDERALISM

SHIRLEY S. ABRAHAMSON

THOMAS N. HILBINK

There is good news and bad news about federalism. The good news is that federalism was not among the topics a group of legal scholars recently labeled stupid.[1] The bad news is that the topic has a reputation for being dull. United States Senator Charles Robb once joked that the quickest way to empty a room is to shout "federalism."[2] Not only does federalism have a reputation for being dull, but it is a notoriously slippery concept as well.

At the adoption of the Constitution, those who favored a strong central government were dubbed the Federalists. Today federalism—and the phrase "New Federalism"—connote criticism of central government and imply restoration of power to the states. As Justice Scalia has sagely observed, federalism is a stick that can be used to beat either dog—state power or federal power.[3] The word "federalism" is used here in a neutral sense to mean the distribution of power between the central authority and the states.

I

Whatever Senator Robb's opinion about federalism, the issue has stirred passionate debate in every era of American history.

New Federalism envisioning a shift of power to the states traces its origins to the great expansion of national power to fight the Depression, World War II, and then the Cold War; to the birth of the New Right in Barry Goldwater's failed 1964 presidential campaign; and to the New Left's disillusion with and distrust of the national government during the Vietnam era.

The renaissance of state government in the years after World War II also contributed to the New Federalism movement. The Warren Court's one-man, one-vote decision in *Baker v. Carr*[4] forced state governments to become more representative. After 1950, most of the states updated their constitutions and reorganized their court systems. The executive and legislative branches added professional staff. The increased competence of state governments spawned a desire for increased authority.

New Federalism was also a major, although marginally successful, initiative of the Nixon administration. In 1969, three months after nominating Warren Burger to the Supreme Court, Richard Nixon delivered a televised address, written by

Patrick Buchanan and calling for a "New Federalism," in which "power, funds, and responsibility" would flow to the states and to the people.[5] The New Federalism blossomed in President Reagan's 1982 State of the Union address. Promising to make the New Federalism the "intellectual center" of his administration, Reagan proposed a sweeping program of block grants which would return $47 billion in federal programs—most notably welfare—to the states.[6]

Hence the rise of the New Federalism in American politics coincided with the tenure of the Burger Court. Or perhaps more accurately, the Burger Court years coincided with a transformation in America's vision of our federalism. The Burger Court cases were part of a larger debate and ideological shift taking place in American political life during this period.

The thread of federalism winds through a wide range of American legal issues, including defamation,[7] criminal procedure,[8] state constitutional law,[9] and federal jurisdiction.[10] To comprehensively cover the many facets of American federalism reflected in the Burger court, even if I were capable of this feat, would be impossible in an essay such as this. Therefore, I have selected two topics and attempted to cull from them a view of federalism in the Burger Court. My topics are, first, what limitations, if any, are imposed by the Tenth Amendment on congressional powers under the Commerce Clause? Second, what limitations, if any, are imposed on federal judicial power by the Eleventh Amendment? In concluding, I describe what is to me Chief Justice Burger's greatest contribution to federalism: his influence in promoting the improvement of state courts.

II

We begin with the Tenth Amendment. It provides: "The powers not delegated to the United States by the Constitution, nor prohibited by it to the States, are reserved to the States respectively, or to the people."

The Tenth Amendment was very popular in 1996. Presidential candidate Bob Dole reportedly carried a tattered copy in his pocket at all times. California Governor Pete Wilson argued that unfunded congressional mandates requiring states to provide education to the children of illegal immigrants violate the Tenth Amendment.[11]

To understand the Burger Court's reliance on the Tenth Amendment, we need some historical background. From about 1870 to the mid-1930s, congressional enactments were successfully challenged on two grounds: (1) that they were outside Congress's constitutional grants of power or (2) that they infringed on essential elements of state sovereignty.[12]

The late 1930s and early 1940s saw both the broadening of Congress's powers and the demise of the Tenth Amendment as a limitation on that power. The 1936 *Carter Coal Co.* case[13] was, prior to the Burger Court, the last case invalidating legislation enacted under the Commerce Clause. Thus, for a forty-year period beginning in 1936, the Court upheld Congress's expanding power.

As an example, the Warren Court, in *Maryland v. Wirtz*,[14] upheld federally established minimum wage and maximum hour requirements for state employees under the Fair Labor Standards Act. The Court ruled that the Tenth Amendment could not limit the central government when it acted within its granted powers.

Justice Douglas's dissent in *Wirtz* warned that, should the constitutional principles of federalism not limit the central government's regulation of state activities, the central government could "devour the essentials of state sovereignty, though that sovereignty is attested by the Tenth Amendment."[15]

The Burger Court offered its first interpretation of the Tenth Amendment in 1975, when it upheld President Nixon's Economic Stabilization Act of 1970.[16] In an effort to stem inflation, the Act authorized the President to issue orders and regulations controlling the wages and salaries of workers, including state and local government employees. Yet, though the Court upheld the Act, it seemed to be nudging awake the long-sleeping Tenth Amendment. Congress may not, wrote the Court, exercise power to impair the states' "integrity or their ability to function effectively in a federal system."[17] Then-Justice Rehnquist, alone in dissent, called for the overruling of *Wirtz*.[18]

The following year, 1976, brought a sea change. Joined by four colleagues, Justice Rehnquist overruled *Wirtz* in *National League of Cities v. Usery*.[19]

As in *Wirtz*, amendments to the Fair Labor Standards Act were at issue in *National League of Cities*. The challengers argued that the states, unlike private employers, were immune from minimum-wage/maximum-hour requirements. Writing for the majority invalidating the Act, Justice Rehnquist did not question Congress's commerce power; it was "beyond peradventure," he wrote, that Congress's power in the area is "plenary."[20]

But having acknowledged Congressional power on the one hand, Rehnquist decreased Congressional power with the other, basing his *National League of Cities* decision on attributes of state sovereignty which may not be impaired by Congress. Mentioning the Tenth Amendment only once, Rehnquist invoked the full body of the Constitution and its "tacit postulates"[21] to limit the power the Constitution grants Congress. Congress, he wrote, could not, "directly displace the States' freedom to structure integral operations in areas of traditional governmental functions"[22] or otherwise undermine the states' separate and independent existence. The Fair Labor Standards Act infringed on state sovereignty through increased costs borne by the states, a forced reallocation of resources, and a displacement of state policies.

National League of Cities offered a return to pre-1936 thinking about federalism. According to *The Brethren*, when *National League of Cities* came before the Court, "Rehnquist felt that if he could win this case, it would once and for all break the forty-year chain of decisions that allowed Congress to do virtually anything in the name of regulating interstate commerce."[23]

Justice Rehnquist's opinion "met with almost universal criticism."[24] None was more severe than Justice Brennan's scathing dissent, which called the opinion a "catastrophic judicial body blow at Congress' power under the Commerce Clause."[25] Brennan accused the majority of overturning precedent as old as *Gibbons v. Ogden*,[26] decided in 1824. Brennan also criticized the attribute of state sovereignty standard, the states qua states standard, as an "abstraction without substance,"[27] allowing the Court to conclude that any federal regulation violated a state's prerogatives.[28]

Justice Brennan's dire predictions about impairment of congressional power did not come true. The Burger Court never again struck down a federal statute on Tenth Amendment state sovereignty grounds. From 1976 to 1985, the Court heard only four cases in which *National League of Cities* was central.[29]

These cases did little to clarify the state sovereignty standard. Two unanimous opinions were marked by ambiguity, doing little more than rewording the *National League of Cities* standard.[30] Two split decisions were marked by vehement and divergent statements on the nature of the federal system, portending future developments and aiding in the demise of *National League of Cities*.[31]

The proponents of state sovereignty under the Tenth Amendment suffered a temporary defeat with *Garcia v. San Antonio Metropolitan Transit Authority*.[32] In *Garcia*, the Brennan bloc's vision of federalism prevailed and returned the Burger Court's Tenth Amendment jurisprudence almost to square one.

Garcia raised the question whether San Antonio's operation of the transit system constituted an area of "traditional governmental function" that was free from congressional wage and hour regulation under the Fair Labor Standards Act. At the Court conference, a five-Justice majority voted to invalidate the law. Chief Justice Burger assigned the opinion to Justice Blackmun, the shaky fifth vote in *National League of Cities*. As any judge knows, writing an opinion often solidifies one's vote. But sometimes it does not. Attempting to write *Garcia* persuaded Blackmun that his conference vote was wrong. He reported to the Court that "our customary reliance on the 'historical' and the 'traditional' is misplaced and that something more fundamental is required to eliminate widespread confusion in the area."[33] The case was reargued. After reargument, the Court overruled *National League of Cities* in a 5–4 decision.

Justice Blackmun explained that the *National League of Cities* method of identifying areas of state immunity from congressional regulation in terms of traditional state functions was unworkable. The *Garcia* majority nevertheless acknowledged that the existence of states and the structure of the Constitution imposed limitations on congressional power. The opinion failed, however, to define those limitations.

More important, under *Garcia*, the sole remedy for congressional attempts to invade the state's position in our constitutional system was apparently political, not judicial. The state's representation in Congress and the state's role in selection of the President shield the state's interests. It seems that under *Garcia* the Tenth Amendment may not present a judicial question.

Justices Powell, O'Connor, and Rehnquist issued separate dissents in *Garcia*. At the end of their respective opinions, both Rehnquist and O'Connor vowed that the Court had not written its last word on the Tenth Amendment. Like Arnold Schwartzenegger as "The Terminator," each seemed to be saying "I'll be back." Rehnquist ended his one-paragraph dissent somewhat ominously. "I do not," he wrote, "think it incumbent on those of us in dissent to spell out further the fine points of a principle that will, I am confident, in time again command the support of a majority of this Court."[34]

Scholarly commentary following the *Garcia* decision was voluminous. Not surprisingly, the Tenth Amendment was pronounced "dead" once again.[35]

But reports of the death of the Tenth Amendment were greatly exaggerated. The Amendment was resurrected in 1992 with *New York v. United States*.[36] The Rehnquist Court, relying on the Tenth Amendment, held that Congress infringed on state sovereignty when it compelled the states to adopt low-level radioactive waste disposal plans meeting national standards. Furthermore, the Rehnquist Court was successful in curtailing the power of the central government not only through the Tenth Amendment but by reconsidering the sweeping interpretations of congressional power under Article I. In the 1995 *Lopez* decision,[37] the Rehnquist Court struck down the Federal Gun Free School Zones Act as exceeding the congressional commerce power.

Further analysis of the vitality of the Tenth Amendment will have to wait for future decisions. That the debate about the Tenth Amendment continues at all during the Rehnquist years, however, reveals that the Burger Court did more to define what the federalism debate is about than to resolve it.

III

Interpretation of the Tenth Amendment was but "one battle in a war [about federalism] being fought on several fronts."[38] Another key battleground was the Eleventh Amendment. It was here that the Burger Court, led by Justice Rehnquist, staged a minor counterrevolution, expanding state sovereign immunity under the Eleventh Amendment. This expansion of state immunity was part of a broader theme of curtailing access to federal courts. The Eleventh Amendment which provides: "The judicial power of the United States shall not be construed to extend to any suit in law or equity, commenced or prosecuted against one of the United States by Citizens of another State or by Citizens or Subjects of any Foreign State."

The Eleventh Amendment is at the heart of the tension between the desire to create federal remedies for state violations of federal rights and the desire to protect the states from suit in federal court. Two of the many facets of Eleventh Amendment jurisprudence are discussed here. First, the Burger Court required that if Congress wanted the states to be subject to suit in federal court on a federal cause of action, it must expressly state this intention. Second, the Burger Court restricted the types of relief available to plaintiffs who bring suit against state officials in federal court.

A

The Eleventh Amendment was the first amendment passed expressly to overturn a decision of the Supreme Court, namely, *Chisholm v. Georgia*,[39] in which a state was a defendant. In *Chisholm*, the Court approved a suit by a South Carolina resident against the State of Georgia to recover payment on revolutionary war debts. The states were to have none of that in 1798.

In 1890, in *Hans v. Louisiana*,[40] the Court interpreted the Eleventh Amendment far beyond its literal language. The Court read the amendment as embodying broad constitutional immunity of states from federal judicial power regardless of the citizenship of the plaintiff or the source of law underlying the claim. The Court's decisions and the scholarly commentators tended to view the Eleventh Amendment as constitutionalizing the common-law doctrine of sovereign immunity. Meanwhile, sovereign immunity was falling into disrepute, giving way to the idea that government-caused injuries demand a remedy.

The Burger Court's first Eleventh Amendment case involved—once again—

the Fair Labor Standards Act. In *Employees v. Missouri Public Health Depart-ment*,[41] the Court held that neither the text nor the legislative history of the Act dis-closed a congressional intent to deprive the states of their immunity from suit. Ac-cordingly, wrote Justice Douglas, adopting a clear statement rule, the Court was "reluctant to believe that Congress in pursuit of a harmonious federalism desired to treat the states so harshly [as to make them subject to double damages in a suit in federal court]."[42]

Justice Brennan, in a lone dissent more lengthy than the majority and concur-ring opinions combined, took a stance he would hold for the remainder of his time on the Court. Brennan argued that the Eleventh Amendment was not a general grant of state immunity from suit in federal court. According to Brennan, the Eleventh Amendment means what it says: Only federal court suits against states by citizens of other states are barred.[43]

Throughout the Burger years, the Court continued its expansion of the clear statement rule. Justice White, who joined the Brennan bloc in *Garcia*, aligned with the Rehnquist bloc in finding an expansive Eleventh Amendment limitation on federal power. In 1985 the Court, by a 5–4 vote in *Atascadero State Hospital v. Scan-lon*,[44] held that a state's Eleventh Amendment immunity from suit could be abro-gated only if congressional intent was "unmistakably clear in the language of the statute."[45] Recourse to legislative history would not suffice.

Commentators generally view *Atascadero* as irreconcilable with *Garcia*. As one commentator quipped, "The tenth amendment is dead! Long live the eleventh!"[46] The basic premise of *Garcia* is that the states are protected by the legislative processes of Congress, not by the federal courts. Under *Atascadero*, the states must be protected *from* Congress, with the federal courts enforcing Eleventh Amend-ment limits.

Justice White saw no inconsistency in joining both *Garcia* and *Atascadero*. Each holding can be said to protect state interests through the political processes of federal lawmaking. The Burger court's Eleventh Amendment cases support this re-liance on the political process by requiring that Congress do its job openly, by pro-viding a clear statement that it is abrogating states' immunity from suit in federal court. The Eleventh Amendment cases, like *Garcia*, can be read as "process feder-alism." In contrast, *National League of Cities* was judicially enforced "substantive federalism."

The impact of *Atascadero* should not be underestimated. The heightened clear statement rule ensured consideration of the states' interests at the congressional level. *Atascadero* imposed a retroactive check on congressional power. To subject a state to federal suit, an existing statute which did not explicitly express a legislative intent to abrogate state immunity would have to be rewritten and reenacted by the House and Senate. Otherwise, litigants would be forced to seek vindication of fed-eral rights in state court.

In 1989, during the Rehnquist Court, Justice Brennan won a temporary victory over the *Atascadero* line of cases. In *Pennsylvania v. Union Gas*,[47] a five-member majority (including Justice White) held that Congress could abrogate state sover-eign immmunity pursuant to its Commerce Clause powers.

However, in 1996 the Court overturned *Union Gas*. In *Seminole Tribe v.*

Florida,[48] Chief Justice Rehnquist wrote that "[t]he Eleventh Amendment restricts the judicial power under Article III, and Article I cannot be used to circumvent the constitutional limitations placed upon federal jurisdiction."[49] Congress can, however, as the Burger Court held, abrogate state sovereignty when acting under section 5 of the Fourteenth Amendment.[50]

B

This essay turns now to the types of relief available to plaintiffs who sue the states in federal court. Despite the doctrine of sovereign immunity, states can be sued if litigants follow the appropriate ritual. The 1908 decision in *Ex Parte Young*[51] allowed a suit in federal court against the Minnesota Attorney General to enjoin him from enforcing an allegedly unconstitutional law. This was not, according to *Young*, a suit against the State of Minnesota. Accordingly, the Eleventh Amendment did not apply.

The *Ex Parte Young* fiction has its roots in common-law sovereign immunity. If the King can do no wrong, he can authorize no wrong. Thus, enforcement of an unconstitutional law by an individual state official cannot be deemed to be authorized by the state.

This fiction was necessary to ensure federal supremacy against recalcitrant states unwilling to comply with the Fourteenth Amendment. To keep the *Ex Parte Young* fiction of ultra vires acts from undermining the Eleventh Amendment's protective value, the Burger Court developed rules limiting the relief available in such suits. As in *National League of Cities*, several Justices were concerned about federal court interference with a state's sovereign power to make fiscal decisions.

In *Edelman v. Jordan*,[52] the plaintiffs sought relief against Illinois officials for violations of a federal program. Justice Rehnquist, writing for the Court, viewed the Eleventh Amendment as barring payment of retroactive benefits. This "equitable restitution" was deemed to be too much like the payment of damages from the state treasury, and the plaintiffs were limited to prospective injunctive relief mandating compliance.

As cases continued to apply the prospective-retroactive distinction, the distinction blurred. Attorneys reformulated their complaints to request only prospective relief, with the resulting relief not very different from retroactive money damages. The decisions demonstrated the significant effect that even prospective relief could have on state treasuries.[53]

It was in this atmosphere that the Supreme Court decided the *Pennhurst* case.[54] In *Pennhurst*, a state institution for the mentally retarded was sued for violations of federal and state statutory rights. Relying in part on state law, the lower federal courts ordered Pennsylvania to close the institution and open smaller community-based facilities around the state. The Supreme Court reversed.

In *Pennhurst*, the Court limited the relief federal courts could grant. A federal judge could no longer issue an injunction against a state officer based on a state law claim. The Court concluded in *Pennhurst* that it was "difficult to think of a greater intrusion on state sovereignty than when a federal court instructs state officials on how to conform their conduct to state law."[55] Plaintiffs' federal claims would have to be either brought in state courts (with the federal claim heard by a state judge) or have to be brought as a separate federal suit.

Commentators, echoing Justice Stevens's dissent in *Pennhurst*,[56] asserted that the Burger Court's concern for federalism had apparently curtailed litigants' access to federal courts.

IV

What lesson can we take away from the Burger Court's Tenth and Eleventh Amendment cases?

The Constitution does not set forth with precision the relationship between the central government and the states. Nor could it. Neither the Tenth nor the Eleventh Amendment, nor any other constitutional provision, provides a blueprint for the division of powers.

Reflecting the period in which they deliberated, some members of the Burger Court would increasingly emphasize the states' importance in our system of government. Nevertheless, the Burger Court's Tenth and Eleventh Amendment cases illuminate "the counterrevolution that wasn't." The Burger Court largely deflected the ultimate questions concerning whether and when Congress might invade the states' sphere in the name of national interests.

The Brennan bloc prevailed in Tenth Amendment cases, preserving Congress's expansive powers from intrusion by either the judiciary or the states. But the Brennan bloc was impeded in the Eleventh Amendment cases from granting citizens the broad means of enforcing federal rights in the federal courts. The Rehnquist bloc dominated Eleventh Amendment cases, but largely failed, during the Burger years, in the important task of curtailing Congress's Article I powers.

The Burger Court Justices nevertheless explored and articulated their individual views on the appropriate relationship between the central government and the states. Their decisions and opinions were harbingers of what was to come in the Rehnquist Court.

Justice Rehnquist took a penumbral approach to issues of federalism. He wrote:

> [W]hen the Constitution is ambiguous or silent on a particular issue [as it is on federalism], this Court has often relied on notions of a constitutional plan—the implicit ordering of relationships within the federal system necessary to make the Constitution a workable governing charter and to give each provision within that document the full effect intended by the Framers. The tacit postulates yielded by that ordering are as much ingrained in the fabric of the document as its express provisions, because without them the Constitution is denied force and often meaning.[57]

Justices O'Connor, Powell, and Stevens examined historical evidence, drawing different conclusions about federalism from the same facts. Justices Brennan and Blackmun relied on scholarly analysis for their views that the state role in federal lawmaking precludes judicial protection of the states from congressional action.

The Burger Court opinions make clear that federalism, although a "cardinal question" of our constitutional system, is essentially a philosophical issue. There is little, if any, empirical data on the advantages of centralization or decentralization.

James Madison wrote in *The Federalist* that the Constitution created neither a national nor a federal Constitution but rather a composition of both.[58] de Tocqueville observed that America does not have a federal government but an incomplete national government, for which no descriptive word exists.[59] The Burger court proved both Madison and de Tocqueville correct, offering neither a formula for deciding how a federal and national system of government can be combined nor a definitive description for our form of government.

Whether one accepts the view of the commentators that Tenth and Eleventh Amendment cases cannot be reconciled or endorses Justice White's view that they can be, two things are clear: (1) by endorsing the view that the meaning of federalism would have to be worked out through the political process rather than in the courts, the Burger Court chose to reflect rather than resolve the ideological disagreements about how our federalism should work, and (2) by closing the doors of the federal courts, the Burger Court was forcing litigants to seek relief in state courts.

To some, state courts are not equivalent to federal courts. Correctly or not, too many attorneys and scholars perceive the state judges as less qualified and less attuned to federal constitutional arguments than the federal courts.

V

Writing as a state court judge, I conclude, however, that the Burger Court did make a significant and lasting contribution to federalism—to judicial federalism, and to the issue of the parity of federal and state courts. This contribution came not from the Court's decisions or from Warren Burger's position as Chief Justice of the Supreme Court but from Warren Burger's position as Chief Justice of the United States. Chief Justice Burger made the distinction significant.

A Chief Justice may define his role as chief executive of the judicial branch as he chooses. Chief Justice Burger used the office as a bully pulpit to persuade judges, lawyers, legislators, and the public to his viewpoint and to seek government and private support for his initiatives.[60] In his extrajudicial writings and speeches, unencumbered by precedent or the facts of any particular case, the Chief Justice freely expounded his views of federalism.[61]

Burger's vision of state courts was firmly planted in Justice Brandeis's conception of the states as laboratories. In Burger's view, states were better able than a central government to determine what worked best for them.

Burger's jurisprudence of limited federal judicial power intersected with his administrative agenda. It stemmed not only from a philosophical devotion to his vision of the framers' intent but also from pragmatic considerations relating to his responsibilities as chief administrator of the federal courts.

As the scope of congressional legislation expanded, the workload of the federal courts increased, threatening the efficiency of the federal judicial system. Delays became a matter of concern. To ease pressure on the federal courts, Burger urged that judicial business be allocated between state and federal courts according to basic principles of federalism.

Chief Justice Burger realized that expansion of federal jurisdiction was fueled in part by concern about the quality of state courts. He also foresaw that with increased federal jurisdiction, the state courts might atrophy and might possibly be subsumed within the federal court system. Burger challenged those in the Bar who were "prepared to sacrifice our concepts of federalism based on an assumption that state courts [were] either incapable, inadequate, or unwilling to enforce claims and rights which we would all agree [are] proper."[62] Expressly rejecting this view of state courts, Burger repeatedly argued that state court judges were as competent and committed to interpreting the federal Constitution as were federal judges.[63] He stressed the Bar's obligation to work for the improvement of state courts. Thus, by forcefully and effectively advocating for the improvement of independent state courts, Burger was able to promote his federalist principles while attending to his administrative mandate.

Burger's administrative mission, then, was twofold: (1) reduce federal jurisdiction and (2) improve state courts. (In writing about federalism, everything is twofold.)

To reduce federal jurisdiction, Burger urged the elimination of the Supreme Court's mandatory appellate jurisdiction. This has been achieved. He also called for the elimination of diversity jurisdiction. This idea is still being promoted.

To improve state courts, Burger initiated several programs. He repeatedly called for improved judicial education for all judges, state and federal. His support was influential in the New York University Institute for Judicial Administration, where he served on the faculty teaching state and federal judges; the National Judicial College, which now trains a significant number of state judges each year; and the Institute for Court Management, which trains managers for the courts.

Appearing before the National Governors' Association in 1983, Burger urged the governors to lobby for the creation of a State Justice Institute, a federally funded entity to help state courts conduct studies and experimental programs they could not afford to do themselves. The State Justice Institute was created and is an important source of funding for state court projects.

In 1970, in his first annual State of the Judiciary address before the American Bar Association, Burger called for the creation of state-federal judicial councils to ease friction between the two systems, thereby aiding the smooth functioning of federalism.[64] Within one year, more than half the states had created such councils. Although the councils fell into disuse in the 1980s, they have been reformed in the 1990s and have been credited with such advances as intercourt cooperation in airline crash litigation and other major tort claims, coordinated calendaring, continuing education for judges, and certification of state law questions in federal court.

In 1971, in what is probably his most important administrative achievement at the state court level, Burger called for the creation of a "national clearinghouse" which would "accumulate and make available all information necessary for comprehensive examination of the problems of justice in the fifty states."[65] This national clearinghouse, modeled on the Federal Judicial Center founded a few years earlier under Chief Justice Warren, became the National Center for State Courts.

According to a history of the National Center, Chief Justice Burger played a guiding role in the Center's formation and early years. Burger called the National

Center the "most important development in judicial reform since the turn of the century."[66] His characterization may not be too far off the mark. Vincent McKusick, the retired Chief Justice of Maine, wrote that "it is impossible to exaggerate Chief Justice Burger's contributions to improving the courts, state quite as much as federal, [and he] has done more than any other person in history to improve the operation of all our nation's courts."[67]

VI

Chief Justice Burger supported a central government with an effective federal judiciary yet at the same time supported a division of power that reserved important, traditional functions for the states and their judiciaries. Burger's message as Chief Justice of the United States was one of cooperative judicial federalism. Our two judiciaries—state and federal—are complementary parts of a single system and must collaborate with and cross-fertilize one another.

Chief Justice Warren E. Burger supported strong, independent state courts. With that message, Chief Justice Abrahamson, concurs.

Notes

1. Levinson and Eskridge, "Introduction, Constitutional Stupidities: A Symposium," 12 *Const. Commentary* 139 (1995). But see Nagel, "The Last Centrifugal Force," 12 *Const. Commentary* 187 (1995).

2. Kincaid, "Foreword: The New Federalism Context of the New Judicial Federalism," 26 *Rutgers L.J.* 913, 913 (1995).

3. Scalia, "The Two Faces of Federalism," 6 *Harv. J.L. & Pub. Pol'y* 19, 19 (1982).

4. 369 U.S. 186 (1962).

5. Richard Nixon, Address to the Nation on Domestic Programs, Aug. 8, 1969, *1969 Public Papers of the Presidents* No. 324 (1971).

6. Transcript of State of the Union Message, N.Y. *Times*, Jan. 27, 1982, § A, col. 1 (late city final ed.), at 16.

7. Supra p. 93.

8. Supra p. 131.

9. Infra p. 244.

10. Infra p. 286.

11. Wilson, "Piety, But No Help on Illegal Aliens," N.Y. *Times* July 11, 1996, § A, col. 1, at 23.

12. Tribe, *American Constitutional Law* 381 n. 16 (1988).

13. Carter v. Carter Coal Co., 298 U.S. 238 (1936).

14. 392 U.S. 183 (1968).

15. Id. at 205 (Douglas, J., dissenting).

16. Fry v. United States, 421 U.S. 542 (1975).

17. Id. at 547 n. 7 ("While the Tenth Amendment has been characterized as a 'truism,' . . . it is not without significance").

18. Id. at 559 (Rehnquist, J., dissenting).

19. 426 U.S. 833 (1976).

20. Id. at 840.

21. Nevada v. Hall, 440 U.S. 410, 433 (1979) (Rehnquist, J., dissenting).

22. National League of Cities v. Usery, 426 U.S. at 852.

23. Woodward and Armstrong, *The Brethren* 406 (1979).

24. Myers, "The Burger Court and the Commerce Clause: An Evaluation of the Role of State Sovereignty," 60 *Notre Dame L. Rev.* 1056, 1062 (1985). For additional critical comments, see Cantrell, "Judicial Review in American Federalism: An Uncertain Future," 4 *Det. C.L. Rev.* 955, 958 n. 18 (1986).

25. National League of Cities v. Usery, 426 U.S. at 880 (Brennan, J., dissenting).

26. 9 Wheat. 1 (U.S. 1824).

27. *National League of Cities v. Usery,* 426 U.S. at 860 (Brennan, J., dissenting).

28. In Justice Brennan's view the political branches are structured to protect the interests of the states, as well as the nation, and the states can protect their own interests through the legislators elected from the states. Id. at 876 (Brennan, J., dissenting).

See also Garcia v. San Antonio Metro. Transit Auth., 469 U.S. 528, 554 (1985) ("the fundamental limitation that the constitutional scheme imposes on the Commerce Clause to protect the 'States as States' is one of process rather than one of result. Any substantive restraint on the exercise of Commerce Clause powers must find its justification in the procedural nature of this basic limitation, and it must be tailored to compensate for possible failings in the national political process rather than to dictate a 'sacred province of state autonomy.'").

This process approach was set forth by Wechsler, "The Political Safeguards of Federalism: The Role of the States in the Composition and Selection of the National Government," 54 *Colum. L. Rev.* 543 (1954).

29. See EEOC v. Wyoming, 460 U.S. 226 (1983); FERC v. Mississippi, 456 U.S. 742 (1982); United Transp. Union v. Long Island R.R., 455 U.S. 678 (1982); Hodel v. Virginia Mining & Reclamation Ass'n, 452 U.S. 264 (1981).

30. FERC v. Mississippi, 456 U.S. 742 (1982); United Transp. Union v. Long Island R.R., 455 U.S. 678 (1982).

31. EEOC v. Wyoming, 460 U.S. 226 (1983); Hodel v. Virginia Mining & Reclamation Ass'n, 452 U.S. 264 (1981).

Justice Rehnquist's concurrence in *Hodel* attacked the Commerce Clause cases which he had left untouched in his *National League of Cities* opinion. His position on the Commerce Clause would ripen into United States v. Lopez, 115 S. Ct. 1624 (1995), striking down a federal act regulating guns near schools as being outside the commerce power.

32. 469 U.S. 528 (1985).

33. See Schwartz, *The Ascent of Pragmatism: The Burger Court in Action* 106 (1990).

34. *Garcia* 469 U.S. at 580 (Rehnquist, J., dissenting). See also id. at 589 (O'Connor, J., dissenting).

35. Van Alstyne, "The Second Death of Federalism," 83 *Mich. L. Rev.* 1709 (1985).

36. 505 U.S. 144 (1992).

37. United States v. Lopez, 115 S. Ct. 1624 (1995).

38. Field, "*Garcia v. San Antonio Metropolitan Transit Authority*: The Demise of a Misguided Doctrine," 99 *Harv. L. Rev.* 84, 115 (1985). See also Reuben, "The New Federalism," 76 A.B.A. J. 76 (April 1995).

39. 2 Dall. 419 (U.S. 1793).

40. 134 U.S. 1 (1890).

41. 411 U.S. 279 (1973).

42. Id. at 286.

43. Id. at 298–324.

44. 473 U.S. 234 (1985).

45. Id. at 242.

46. Brown, "State Sovereignty under the Burger Court—How the Eleventh Amend-

ment Survived the Death of the Tenth: Some Broader Implications of *Atascadero State Hospital v. Scanlon*," 74 *Geo. L.J.* 363, 363 (1985).

47. 491 U.S. 1 (1989).

48. 116 S. Ct. 1114 (1996), 64 U.S.L.W. 4167 (1996).

49. Id. at 1131–32.

50. Fitzpatrick v. Bitzer, 427 U.S. 445 (1976).

51. 209 U.S. 123 (1908).

52. 415 U.S. 651 (1974).

53. See, e.g., Hutto v. Finney, 437 U.S. 678 (1978) (attorneys' fees awarded to be paid out of state Department of Correction funds).

54. Pennhurst State School & Hosp. v. Halderman, 465 U.S. 89 (1984).

55. Id. at 106.

56. Id. at 126 (Stevens, J., dissenting).

57. Nevada v. Hall, 440 U.S. 410, 433 (1979) (Rehnquist, J., dissenting).

58. *The Federalist* No. 39, at 246 (Clinton Rossiter ed. 1961).

59. de Tocqueville, *Democracy in America* 143 (J. Mayer and M. Lerner eds., 1966).

60. Burger, *Delivery of Justice: Proposals for Changes to Improve the Administration of Justice* 118 (1990); Tamm and Reardon, "Warren E. Burger and the Administration of Justice," 1981 *B.Y.U. L. Rev.* 447 (1981).

61. See Greene and Smith, "Chief Justice Burger's Administrative Agenda: A Chronology of His Speeches Made Available through Legal Publications and the Media, with Noteworthy Responses: 1969–1986," 80 *Law Libr. J.* 665 (1988); Kurland, "Mr. Chief Justice Burger on the State of the Judiciary–1981," 15 *Suffolk U.L. Rev.* 1105 (1981); Burger, "State–Federal Jurisdiction, a De Facto Merger?," 4 *Am. J. Trial Advoc.* 333 (1980).

62. Burger, *Delivery of Justice: Proposals for Changes to Improve the Administration of Justice* 118 (1990).

63. Id. at 56, 118.

64. Id. at 44, 55.

65. Id. at 60.

66. Low, *The National Center for State Courts: A Commemorative History of its Structure and Organization in Honor of 20 Years of Service to the State Courts* 32 (1991).

67. Burger, supra note 62, at III (1990).

· II ·

A
BROADER
PERSPECTIVE

CHIEF JUSTICE WARREN E. BURGER
AND THE LEGAL PROFESSION

JEROME J. SHESTACK

Whether one lauds, reproves, or is ambivalent about the Burger Court's constitutional imprint, no one can doubt that during the Burger era, more attention was paid to the legal profession and the organized Bar than during any Court era before or since.[1]

The attention, for the most part, was not by the Burger Court as a whole, for the Court rendered only a few Bar-impacting decisions.[2] Nor was the attention by individual Justices of the Court, who except for occasional uplifting speeches at Bar occasions, did not often swerve from cases before them to problems of the profession. Rather, the attention was paid directly by Warren Burger, the Chief Justice himself, for nearly a quarter of a century. And so, this essay focuses on the Chief Justice.

How does one describe the relationship of the Chief Justice with the Bar?

Paternal? Yes, as with a child—praising the profession and spurring it to higher ground; chastising it for its faults and bemoaning its shortcomings; also demanding, sensitive to slights, and unrealistically eager for affection.

Statesman-leader? Surely, in ways both minute and grand, yet sadly temporal, without the intellectual depth and passion that secured eternity for a Cardozo, a Holmes, or a Hand, who labored less for the profession but are remembered better.

Whatever the complex, emotional, compulsive forces that drove Warren Burger's relationship with the Bar, it remains that he materially advanced the administration of justice and the initiatives of the organized Bar as innovator and catalyst. He defended the legal profession against unjust carping and cavil, even as he scolded it for its defects. He addressed causes of dissatisfaction with the justice system and immersed the Bar in his reform efforts. He held out a standard of professionalism to which lawyers should aspire and commit. And if he was sometimes heavy-handed and oft times unrealistic, still, unlike so many of his colleagues, he never recused himself from our profession but, rather, affirmed the obligation of the nation's High Court Justices to address and help redress the frailties of our calling.

Surely, these endeavors alone on behalf of the administration of justice and the legal profession merit a respected niche in judicial history, one that bears recall even in an age when many who advanced our profession are given little homage or remembrance. Let us now relate some of that history.

Background

It was almost immediately after Warren Burger became Chief Justice in 1969, that William T. Gossett, then president of the American Bar Association, and Bernard G. Segal, then president-elect, urged the new Chief Justice to attend the ABA meeting in Dallas and discuss his thoughts. Years later, the Chief Justice recalled: "At the 1969 meeting, I said that I did not expect we would always agree, but I gave you my assurance that I would never 'walk out.' Rather, I said I would insist upon equal time."[3]

And equal time he received. At the suggestion of Bernard Segal, by then ABA president, the Chief Justice delivered his first State of the Judiciary message at the ABA annual meeting, in August 1970. And he continued to deliver these addresses at annual or midyear meetings of the ABA until he retired in 1986.

His faith in the American Bar Association leadership was remarkable, particularly during his early years as Chief Justice. He often referred to the ABA as "our association." On more than one occasion, he referred to the ABA as "a force for enormous, almost unlimited, good with respect to every problem in the administration of justice." His attendance at ABA meetings was constant. At such meetings, after his address, any one present could approach his leonine presence and find his ear, except for television journalists, whom he abhorred. He appeared on the pages of the *American Bar Association Journal* more than any other Justice. His responses to letters from the bar were prompt and thoughtful. His relationships with many ABA leaders was warm and collegial and with some close and sharing. As a young lawyer in Segal's firm, I would often walk into his office deep into the evening and he and the Chief Justice would be immersed in intense and lengthy telephone conversation. The bar was a large part of Warren Burger's life, the Court notwithstanding.

Such a relationship with the Bar was not merely a rotarian indulgence. The Chief Justice understood well the symbiotic relationship between the Court and the Bar. It is not just the Court's opinions which, of course, can mold the operation of our practice and the rights and culture of our society, but the special feeling the profession has for the Court. For any lawyer emerging from our system of legal education, the Court's place in our profession is unparalleled in any other secular or professional assembly. The Justices are the subject of our reverence, our anecdotes, our mealtime parlance. We may cheer or deplore particular opinions, but the Justices represent the pinnacle of our profession. They have the capacity to inspire and the power to enlist the Bar full force in their initiatives and endeavors, particularly on behalf of the administration of justice. And Chief Justice Burger surely used that power.

The "Wheels" of Justice

The Chief Justice believed his office vested him with responsibility not only to lead the Court but to address the needs of the nation's entire judicial system.[4] Early in his judicial career, Burger came to appreciate that inefficient and deferred administration of justice impaired the quality of justice and eroded confidence in the courts. The best train of justice, he often said, could not move without efficient wheels.

The Warren Court was valiant and successful in making the Bill of Rights a vital force in American democracy. But that Court paid scant attention to the wheels of administration, which desperately needed repair. By the time Burger became Chief Justice, the administration of justice in the federal courts had suffered years of neglect. Methods, training, technology, and court administration procedures were antiquated and inadequate. At the same time, the caseload in the federal courts was expanding dramatically. New areas of law, such as environmental protection, health law, and disability law, were the subject of massive regulation and increasing litigation. New causes of action — civil rights cases, mass tort cases, class actions, poverty law, and an avalanche of drug cases — geometrically multiplied the federal dockets. The number of judges nearly doubled in the decade of the 1960s and court staff expanded even more. Burger appreciated that judges were not qualified administrators and that mushrooming administrative demands on judges and inefficient machinery would result in neglect, undue waste, and inappropriate judicial delegation, undermining the quality of judicial work at both trial and appellate levels.

With pragmatic astuteness, he gave his reforms a neutral flavor — eschewing debate over philosophic concepts of justice and concentrating on administrative programs that would receive consensus approval. But consensus also needs marshaling and marshall he did. He knew that with the judiciary's limited budget and sparse resources, he needed the strength of the organized bar to facilitate realization of the reforms and repairs he advocated. He rightly believed that it is the obligation of the Bar to deal with justice and he did not hesitate in placing an obligation on the ABA to support his myriad administrative reforms. As he put it in an early State of the Judiciary Address to the ABA,[5] "[T]oday I place this burden [of administrative reform] squarely on you, the leaders of the legal profession in common with all judges. If the 144,000 lawyers you represent in 1700 state and local bar associations will act promptly, you will prevent a grave deterioration in the work of the federal courts."

Indeed, he did receive the enthusiastic help of the ABA in a variety of reforms. Thus, with the support of the organized Bar, he initiated an Institute for Court Management to train multitudes of court administrators and within a decade increased their number by fiftyfold. He obtained legislation for the Office of Circuit Executives to free up chief judges of the circuits to perform their judicial functions. He openly lobbied for more federal judges to deal with the increasing caseload. He helped sponsor a Commission on Judicial Administration to help speed the work of the courts. He advanced the Federal Judicial Center with programs of research and continuing education for judges and court personnel. And more.

No aspect of the federal system escaped his gaze — expanding jurisdiction of magistrates, curtailing wasteful three-judge courts, establishing a court of international trade, encouraging nonbinding mandatory pretrial arbitration, increasing the compensation of judges, even an attempt to divide the large and unwieldy Fifth and Ninth Circuits.[6]

He also concerned himself with needs of state courts, stating that the basic system of justice is the state courts, and if "they are not strong and effective," then all the work of the federal judges will not provide "a meaningful system of justice."[7] After some prolonged advocacy, he succeeded in 1971 in bringing about the National Center for State Judges, and later he helped found the National Judicial College. The result was that a substantial percentage of state judges began receiving needed judicial training. Of course, the defects in state court systems far exceeded the remedy of judicial training and were beyond his reach. Still, at least, he paid attention.

Some of Burger's initiatives never saw fruition. He fought hard to curtail federal cases based on diversity in an effort to reduce the federal caseload. The motive was good but the consequences unacceptable. The original rationale for diversity jurisdiction was to provide a level playing field for the out-of-state litigants. But that rationale had become largely irrelevant in cosmopolitan jurisdictions and arguably could be overcome by use of local lawyers in noncosmopolitan arenas. The real reason why the Bar and particularly, the corporate Bar, wanted to retain diversity jurisdiction was because of the excellent quality of federal judges and the poor quality of so many state judges chosen by an elective system with retained loyalty to politicians. So the Bar never endorsed that initiative, and it failed. It would have been more productive for the Chief Justice to have expended less effort on crusading against diversity jurisdiction and more on promoting merit selection.

Bettering the administration of justice is a tedious block-building process and as Chief Justice Arthur T. Vanderbilt once said, it is no sport for the short-winded. Burger was not short-winded. Through patience and persistence, he added many solid blocks to the betterment of the judicial administrative structure. In these many improvements, the American Bar Association almost always championed the Chief Justice's initiatives and brought its influence to bear on achieving them. And the Chief Justice never hesitated in giving the ABA full credit for these accomplishments.

Taken one by one, and viewed in retrospect, Burger's administrative achievements may now seem mundane, even trivial. But, progress to substantive justice is often along paths paved by process and administration, and a path full of potholes impedes that progress. Burger saw his reforms as a response to the "great fervor for court improvement which he saw gaining momentum slowly over a period of time."[8] His reforms were innovative at the time and brought the federal judicial system into modernity, to a point where it could be administered efficiently and be sparing of judicial time, best spent elsewhere. These were far from trivial achievements.

Causes of Dissatisfaction

The Chief Justice's reforms were not focused on administration alone but embraced a much larger compass. As a lawyer and judge in Minnesota, he had become absorbed by a speech given in 1906 by a young man from Nebraska, Roscoe Pound. Pound, as we know, was later to become dean of Harvard Law School and the law's foremost exponent of sociological jurisprudence. But in 1906, he had not yet achieved prominence.

Pound's speech, later to become famous, was entitled, "The Causes of Popular

Dissatisfaction With the Administration of Justice," and he delivered it at an ABA meeting in 1906. As Chief Justice Burger recalled in one of his addresses, the ABA at the time had 2,600 members and "was an establishment oriented organization quite satisfied with the status quo. The leaders of the Association rejected Pound's criticisms to the point that the Association initially refused to publish his speech."[9] By the time he became Chief Justice, Burger was much absorbed with Pound's causes of dissatisfaction and he referred to Pound's call in his First State of Judiciary address.[10] Burger was delighted when the ABA, in 1976, some seventy years after Pound's address, undertook to address the causes of dissatisfaction then existing in the American justice system. Many of them were ones pointed to by Pound in 1906 but still not redressed in 1976.

One of the most troubling and abiding causes for dissatisfaction was the operation of the criminal justice system. Early in his stewardship, Burger addressed the defects in the criminal justice correction system. Writing in the ABA Journal in 1970, he referred to 200,000 inmates of federal and state prisons. (How low that number now appears.) He called for changes in the prison system to gladden the heart of any prison reform idealist: modern institutions, less crowding, psychological and psychiatric services, recreation programs, vocational training, work release programs, transitional facilities, better pay scales for prison attendants, and more. And with atypical eloquence he wrote: "We take on a burden when we put a man behind a wall and that burden is to give him a chance to change. If we deny him that, we deny his status as a human being and to deny that is to diminish our own humanity and plant the seeds of future anguish for ourselves."[11]

It is perhaps an insight into the relationship between out-of-court commitment and in-court decision that the Burger Court was enormously receptive to prisoners' rights, a receptivity that dwindled toward the end of his term and came to a rather abrupt halt after he retired.[12]

In this area as well, he formed a partnership with the Bar. In 1970, the ABA created a Commission on Correction and Correctional Facilities first chaired by former New Jersey Governor Richard Hughes. The Chief Justice frequently and enthusiastically endorsed the Commission's projects and even invited the Commission to hold its meetings at the Supreme Court. One such program was to provide qualified volunteer caseworkers to assist hard-pressed parole officers. Another was to bring extension school education into penal institutions and still another was to provide employment opportunities for released prisoners. As Burger said in his 1971 State of the Judiciary Address: "This is the largest undertaking in the corrections area ever taken by the organized bar and it deserves continued support. It is a measure of the new horizon of public service of the American Bar Association."[13]

But corrections then and now have defied successful achievement. And although Burger never entirely gave up on the value of prisoner rehabilitation and other correctional reforms, as the years progressed, he focused more on other aspects of the criminal justice system. He inveighed against the short tenure of lawyers in the offices of United States Attorneys and on public defender staffs, pointing out that "no private firm could function effectively and perhaps could not even survive with that kind of rapid turnover of personnel."[14] He deplored the high number of crimes committed by persons on bail and called for bail laws to address future dangerousness of repeat offenders. He warned of dire results from the Speedy Trial Act when judges were not given the resources to cope with speedy trials. He railed against the length of criminal appeals and their lack of finality. Although his complaints had groundings in fact, here solutions did not come readily and his speeches often sounded like jeremiads without the prospect of redemption.

A particular emphasis of the Chief Justice was the institution of standards. In 1965, the ABA started a project to develop a comprehensive set of minimum standards for the administration of criminal justice. While serving on the D.C. Court of Appeals, Burger himself had chaired the ABA Special Committee charged with that project.[15] When the first edition of the standards came out in 1974, he said it was probably the most monumental undertaking in the field of criminal justice ever attempted by the American legal profession in our entire national history.[16] His encouragement no doubt helped advance that project which ultimately developed standards of criminal justice endorsed by most states.

He dealt as well with other causes of dissatisfaction with the justice system. A particular concern of Burger was the High Court's inefficiency and delays in litigation. Burger's approach to redressing this issue was to stimulate judges and Bar leaders to address the problems and their solutions through conferences and commissions.

Thus, he lent his support to an ABA Commission to reduce court costs; he promoted a Federal Judicial Center study identifying steps to reduce costs in class actions; he reactivated a Judicial Conference Committee to study the problem of appeal costs in printing large records of trials; he encouraged an ABA Action Commission to deal with unnecessary discovery; he sought to reduce the judicial role in rulemaking; he appointed a special Judicial Conference Subcommittee to address the problems of protracted cases and multi-district litigation; he appointed a pioneer Special Committee on Experimentation (of which I was a member) to examine the potential of justice system experimentation and its ethical ramifications.[17] He was also an early supporter of federally fueled legal services to the poor, even when some segments of the organized Bar showed ambivalence toward such services. In all these endeavors, he encouraged and received participation of the American Bar Association and other segments of the organized Bar.

Some of the problems he addressed were solved; some were ameliorated; for the most part, they are with us still. It is hard to say why. High-powered conferences and mind-boggling reports are not enough; well-meaning resolutions are not enough. Even the will to reform is not enough. Systemic and institutional change do not easily root in an adversary system. Leadership tires or changes. There are dozens of reasons why the causes for dissatisfaction with the justice system persist and recur like an unassailable virus. As Burger recognized, even as progress on current problems is made, "new problems tend to outrun solutions."[18] To the Chief Justice's credit, his zeal in addressing the administrative causes of dissatisfaction with the justice system did not flag. Sadly, however, the results never matched the efforts.

Quest for Professionalism

I cannot think of a Supreme Court Chief Justice more concerned with professional qualifications of lawyers than Warren Burger. To be sure, Justices have written occasional essays about trial advocacy, professional ethics, legal education, skills, and values. But none gave as much attention to professional qualifications as did Burger.

Burger saw the legal profession as a noble and learned profession nourished by a tradition of exemplary service. He saw the lawyers' obligation to be "a healer of conflicts." He yearned for the civility he found in the English bar. He had no tolerance for slipshod practice or checker-play with ethics. Professionalism to him was not just a casual cloak but a sacred vestment of honor worn for life.

Burger's view of the lawyer's professional obligation was an idealistic one, and he believed that too many lawyers failed to meet his standard. And this frustrated and angered Burger.

In address after address he called on the Bar to be leaders in enforcing strict professional standards, to eschew conflict, play down the adversary system, and embrace alternate resolutions of disputes. He called on the Bar to impose strict professional discipline, to condemn advertising,[19] and to look askance on the emphasis on billable hours. He called on law schools to teach ethics and professionalism meaningfully long before such teaching turned into a trend.[20] He called for civility in practice years before that call became a popular motif.[21] Most of his aspirations were laudatory and many have been and still are being addressed by the organized Bar. In these respects, he did well to raise a standard.

But, perhaps because the pace of achievement did not meet his expectations or for whatever reasons still unknown, he became increasingly shrill about the Bar's shortcomings, and in his later appearances before the Bar, he was regarded more as a scolder than an inspirer. The profession, as a whole, does not take well to criticism, perhaps because there has been so much of it that is unjust (including much by Burger) that even just criticism brings denial or excuse. Still, Burger deserved greater heed; most of the time, though not always, his points were solid and his impatience justified. But in some instances, as I turn to next, he was far from the mark.

Early in his term he gave the John F. Sonnett Memorial Lecture at Fordham University Law School on the special skills of advocacy.[22] The lecture was a thorough, historical survey of advocacy with heavy reliance on English practice. He elaborated gently on the inadequacies of American advocates and, as a remedy, he proposed comprehensive training and a specialty certification in trial advocacy. The address was soft in tone and modest in its suggestion of "cautious progress."

In 1995, his last major address was again the John F. Sonnett Lecture at Fordham. This time, his topic was the decline of professionalism.[23] Between his first lecture at Fordham and his last, his optimism about the profession had waned, and his relationship with the organized Bar had become adversarial. How different was his last speech from his first.

Now, he began without amenities:

> The bedrock of our profession [he said] in his opening paragraph, "from Blackstone's day has been the professional ideal, the lawyer as an officer of the court, compelled as such to maintain a standard of conduct that rises above the standard we would expect from a tradesman engaged in what many now call the business of law. The law is not and never had been a business. But we are well on the way to making it less than a profession."

> I see decisive evidence that there has been a broad decline in professionalism over the past twenty to twenty-five years not only in these so-called "learned professions"—the clergy, medicine and the law—but in many other important activities. . . . The decline of professionalism, especially in the law, has taken on epidemic proportions.

As a general proposition, his perception was wrong. In the years since Burger became Chief Justice, the American Bar Association, as leader of the nation's organized Bar, had developed ethical codes, vigorously promoted legal services for the poor, endorsed civil rights legislation, opposed racial and gender discrimination, endorsed human rights treaties, advanced competence and standards for specialization, built coalitions to help repair the justice system, and made pro bono service an ethical requirement and otherwise raised the standards of professionalism.

Burger argued his case on decline on three specific propositions. First, he castigated lawyers who "try cases on the courthouse steps to newspapers and television reporters." No prosecutor he said and "especially that new creature of the law, the 'Special Prosecutor'—should, except in the most remarkable circumstances, ever make out-of-court statements about a pending investigation or a pending case." Parenthetically, his admonition has been cavalierly disregarded by special prosecutors in our time. But Burger's call on the organized Bar to act on this phenomena was largely misplaced. The remedy lay in court control, and that was limited given the strictures of the First Amendment.

Next in his "bill of particulars," as he called it, was the so-called Rambo lawyer, the lawyer who fails to practice civility, "who disrespects his opponent, disrespects the Court, and the legal process as well. If we are a profession that tolerates that attitude among some of our practitioners, we cannot expect more from the public." Here, his point was solid: Incivility is an ongoing plague, but he was unrealistic in believing that its eradication could be brought about by simple Bar Association edict.

And then he angrily hurled his final condemnation against "the outrageous breach of professional conduct we see in the huckster advertising of some attorneys." He did not stop there: For some years Burger had become fixated by lawyer advertising, but in this last speech he was particularly vitriolic: "Perhaps huckster is not strong enough of a word: shyster is more appropriate, but I find on consulting the dictionary that even 'shyster' is not strong enough. I will settle for 'hucksode-shyster' advertising."

The condemnation continued in belligerent tones against the organized Bar. He acknowledged that "Bar Association bashing would be a more accurate description of what I have engaged in," and he castigated the Bar for the advertising explosion, severely charging the Bar with failure to maintain high standards of ethics and professionalism.

Burger's emotional obsession with this subject is strange—and sad. It colored the Chief Justice's long and felicitous relationship with the Bar, substantially souring it in his declining years. The subject deserves the following excursus to this essay.

The Sad Story of Lawyer Advertising

The Chief Justice's stormiest and most antagonistic relationship with the Bar was over lawyer advertising. And this is exceedingly odd, for it was the Burger Court that created the condition that he found so irksome and unprofessional and which embittered so many of his addresses in later years.

The sperm that spawned the advertising creature was *Bates v. Arizona*.[24] In the late 1970s, two attorneys in Phoenix, Arizona, opened a "legal clinic" to provide legal services at modest fees to persons of moderate income who did not qualify for governmental legal aid. They placed an ad in the Arizona Republic stating that they offered "legal services at very reasonable fees" and listed their fees for certain services.

The advertisement was a violation of an Arizona Supreme Court disciplinary rule that barred legal advertising. A disciplinary hearing was held under the Arizona rules and a short suspension was recommended. The lawyers challenged the rule on antitrust grounds and as a violation of the First Amendment, and both claims were rejected by the Arizona Supreme Court. On appeal, the U.S. Supreme Court easily affirmed the Arizona court's determination that the restraint on attorney advertising was not subject to attack under the antitrust laws.

The real issue before the Court was whether the advertisement was protected speech under the First Amendment and the heart of that dispute, Justice Blackmun said, was whether lawyers might advertise prices at which certain services will be performed.[25]

A major argument against the lawyer advertising was its adverse effect on professionalism. Justice Blackmun's succinct summary of that argument is gem-like:

> Appellee places particular emphasis on the adverse effects that it feels price advertising will have on the legal profession. The key to professionalism, it is argued, is the sense of pride that involvement in the discipline generates. It is claimed that price advertising will bring about commercialization, which will undermine the attorney's sense of dignity and self-worth. The hustle of the marketplace will adversely affect the profession's service orientation, and irreparably damage the delicate balance between the lawyer's need to earn and his obligation selflessly to serve. Advertising is also said to erode the client's trust in his attorney: Once the client perceives that the lawyer is motivated by profit, his confidence that the attorney is acting out of a commitment to the client's welfare is jeopardized. And advertising is said to tarnish the dignified public image of the profession.

Despite the eloquence with which Justice Blackmun presented the case for appellees, he rejected the argument. Justice Blackmun's reasoning was not his loftiest. He said that there would be reason to pause "if the spirit of public service with which the profession of law is practiced and to which it is dedicated" was undercut by the Court's decision. But he found the connection between advertising and the erosion of true professionalism "to be severely strained." Essentially, he saw the ban as "a rule of etiquette and not as a rule of ethics." More startling was his statement that the belief that lawyers are "above" trade has become an "anachronism" and therefore, the "foundation for the advertising restraint has crumbled."[26] The rationale was a black commentary on the majority's view of the profession, in which most of the Justices had practiced little.

One argument for the restriction was that because the public lacks sophistication in legal matters, it may be particularly susceptible to misleading or deceptive advertising by lawyers. Justice Blackmun's reply was as follows:

[W]e suspect that, with advertising, most lawyers will behave as they always have: They will abide by their solemn oaths to uphold the integrity and honor of their profession and of the legal system. For every attorney who overreaches through advertising, there will be thousands of others who will be candid and honest and straightforward. And, of course, it will be in the latter's interest, as in other cases of misconduct at the bar, to assist in weeding out those few who abuse their trust.[27]

Justice Blackmun's naïveté was extraordinary, reflecting his disassociation with the world of practice.

To be sure, Blackmun did insert the caveat that false, deceptive, or misleading advertising is subject to restraint, and he did try to limit his opinion to the routine, nonmisleading services of the lawyers in the Arizona case. But, of course, as we now know, the dike was pierced and for the remainder of the Burger era, there was never the five fingers that might have stopped the advertising flood.

Chief Justice Burger dissented, but it was a remarkably weak and disappointing dissent, considering the vehemence with which he later attacked lawyer advertising. Burger did not take on Justice Blackmun's arguments. He did not even mention the First Amendment. He set no standard of lawyer professionalism as a compelling interest. Rather, he took issue only with the majority's statement that the Bar and courts will be able to protect the public from those practitioners who abuse their trust, arguing that this called for unmanageable regulatory burdens on the courts.

It was left to Justice Powell, a former President of the ABA, to point out the effects of the majority opinion. Mincing no words, he said, "[I]t is clear that within undefined limits today's decision will effect profound changes in the practice of law, viewed for centuries as a learned profession. The supervisory power of the courts over members of the bar, as officers of the courts, and the authority of the respective States to oversee the regulation of the profession have been weakened."[28] And he went on:

I am apprehensive, despite the Court's expressed intent to proceed cautiously, that today's holding will be viewed by tens of thousands of lawyers as an invitation—by the public-spirited and the selfish lawyers alike—to engage in competitive advertising on an escalating basis. Some lawyers may gain temporary advantages; others will suffer from the economic power of stronger lawyers, or by the subtle deceit of less scrupulous lawyers. Some members of the public may benefit marginally, but the risk is that many others will be victimized by simplistic price advertising of professional services almost infinite [in] variety and nature. . . . Until today, in the long history of the legal profession, it was not thought that this risk of public deception was not required by the marginal First Amendment interests asserted by the Court.[29]

Powell's dissent was clairvoyant. After *Bates*, there was no stopping the advertising tide. And subsequent opinions reinforced the worst of *Bates*, discarding Blackmun's cautionary language and giving legal advertising free reign.[30] Only Justices Rehnquist and O'Connor pleaded for greater regulation of professional conduct than for others engaged in commerce, but to slight avail.[31]

We all know and many of us deplore the cheapening of the profession that the flood of advertising—often vulgar, often cunning, often misleading—has caused in the wake of *Bates* and its progeny. That flood became an obsession with the Chief Justice. In speech after speech, he condemned advertising and condemned the Bar for not containing it. What particularly irked lawyers was Burger's assumption that the organized Bar had a broad power to restrain advertising when his own Court had taken away that power and opened the advertising floodgates.

In his final speech on the decline of professionalism, which I referred to earlier, he made excuses for *Bates*. He said that the "shyster lawyers" relied on *Bates* for their advertising. Yet, he said, "If the idea of a profession means anything, it means that a profession must have standards that are above the minimum commands of law."

He proceeded to vilify "the shyster conduct" in solicitation and advertising. He dismissed the point "that lawyer advertising furthered effective access to the judicial system, as nonsense, saying that access can be accomplished through a "greater emphasis on pro bono work and through lawyer referral services provided by the bar associations themselves."

Then he took off on his longtime ally, the American Bar Association, which he now said had "compromised professional integrity" by not restraining legal advertising. He attacked the standards on advertising in the ABA Model Rules of Professional Conduct as irresponsible. Still not satisfied, he went on to ridicule the ABA for not setting higher standards and focusing on a public relations campaign, which he thought would not have been necessary if the public were not already bombarded with huskster-shyster advertising. His advice on what the ABA should tell the public about lawyer advertising was: "Never, never, never engage the services of a lawyer *who finds it necessary to advertise in order to get clients.*" He concluded by saying there was "a failure of leadership of the organized bar to set high standards and then of local bar associations to enforce those standards."

One wonders what led the Chief Justice to this diatribe. Did he not appreciate that once *Bates* and its offspring validated legal advertising, the prospect of meaningful restraint was submerged by the First Amendment standards that the Court had endorsed for commercial advertising? Did he not realize, as Justice Powell pointed out, that *Bates* had effected profound changes in the practice of law?

Why the unabashed bashing of a bar organization that had, in fact, embraced high standards of professionalism and for years had worked with the Chief Justice in reforming elements of judicial administration. Was it a guilty conscience because he had been so passive in *Bates* and had not led the Court to find the compelling interest in lawyer regulation that he now wanted the Bar to enforce without it having the power to do so? His fixation remains a mystery without a satisfactory ending.

Conclusion

The complexities of Burger's jurisprudence—its shifting currents, contradictions, ambivalences, and tensions have been chronicled by others in this volume and elsewhere. This essay has focused on his leadership, not of Court jurisprudence but of the administration of the judicial system and the practice of the legal profession. He pioneered and fought hard to give the justice system what he called the tools it needed.

His endeavors in this area produced many successes and were praiseworthy, providing rooting for more efficient delivery of justice, without which justice must falter.

His standards of professionalism for the Bar were high, reflecting the noble and learned profession for which most of us aspire and led us to law's calling in the first instance. But he allowed his high moral stance to be diminished by heavy-handedness and shrillness and by unreasonably blaming the Bar for a dragon his own Court had created.

In the final weighing, what should be remembered most is that Warren Burger as Chief Justice accepted the mantle of leadership in addressing the needs of the judicial system and the passions of our profession. Unlike so many of his brethren, he rejected recusal from those obligations. At times he exercised leadership exceptionally well; at times he faltered and was prey to his weaknesses. Still, the lesson he taught well is that the High Court has a responsibility to address the needs of the justice system and to advance the profession through its organized Bar. It is a lesson that needs remembering. For his initiative, his achievements, his courage and his caring, we have reason to be grateful.

Notes

1. Professor Schwartz has noted that Burger played a more active role in Court administration than any Court head since Chief Justice Taft. Schwartz, *The Ascent of Pragmatism, The Burger Court in Action*, 1–8 (1990).

2. These dealt with advertising by lawyers, discussed infra. at pp. 196–99.

3. Burger, Address to the midyear meeting of the American Bar Association, February 12, 1984.

4. In his first State of the Judiciary speech in 1970, he expressed a sterling creed:

A sense of confidence in the courts is essential to maintain the fabric of ordered liberty for a free people, and three things could destroy that confidence and do incalculable damage to society:

That people come to believe that inefficiency and delay will drain even a just judgment of its value;

That people who have long been exploited in the small transactions of daily life come to believe that courts cannot vindicate their legal rights from fraud and overreaching;

That people come to believe the law—in the larger sense—cannot fulfill its primary function to protect them and their families in their homes, at their work and on the public streets.

I have great confidence in our basic system and its foundations, in the dedicated judges and others in the judicial system, and in the lawyers of America. Continuity with change is the genius of the American system, and both are essential to fulfill the promise of equal justice under law.

If we want to maintain these crucial values, we must make some changes in our methods, our procedure and our machinery, and I ask your help to make sure this is done.

56 A.B.A. J. 929, 934 (1970).

5. Address to ABA, July 5, 1971.

6. He succeeded as to the Fifth Circuit (despite formidable opposition from some of the circuit court judges) and created the Eleventh Circuit. But he was unsuccessful with the Ninth Circuit, and it remains unwieldy notwithstanding dedicated service by the prior and the current Chief Judge of that enormous circuit.

7. Burger, remarks to Conference on National Institute of Justice, Dec. 6, 1972.

8. See e.g., *The Court That Was, The Burger Years: Rights and Wrongs in the Supreme Court, 1969–86*, ed. H. Schwartz and E. Sifton (New York: Viking Press).

9. Burger, Address to the midyear meeting of the American Bar Association, February 12, 1984.

10. See supra note 4.

11. Burger, *No Man Is an Island*, 56 A.B.A. J. 325, 328 (1970). In his February 12, 1978, annual report at the midyear meeting, he put it this way: "The goal should be to develop positive educational programs so that prisoners will have a better chance to leave correctional institutions somewhat better human beings than when they entered and traveled in a marketable skill. Then we must encourage employers to hire them. . . . Society must provide not just walls and bars but meaningful training for their return to society."

12. See Schwartz, "The Burger Court and the Prisoner," in *The Burger Years*, ch. 11 (H. Schwartz ed., 1987).

13. Burger, State of the Federal Judiciary 1971, Address delivered at the ABA annual meeting, July 5, 1971.

14. Burger, State of the Judiciary 1975, Address delivered at the ABA midyear meeting, Feb. 23, 1975.

15. Among those on the committee were Chief Judge William H. Hastie of the Third Circuit and Louis F. Powell, then a practicing lawyer.

16. Burger, Introduction, *The ABA Standards for Criminal Justice*, 12 A. Criml. Rev. 251, 1974.

17. Experimentation in the Law, report of the Federal Judicial Center Advisory Committee on Experimentation in the Law (1978). Judge Edward D. Re chaired the committee, whose members included Judges Wilfred Feinberg, Joseph T. Sneed, and Abraham P. Sofaer and Professors Paul Freund, Gerald Gunther, Alasdair MacIntyre, and Norman Redlich.

18. Burger, Agenda for 2000 A.D.—Need for Systematic Anticipation, 62 ABA J 727, 1976.

19. See a fuller discussion of the advertising issue, infra. pp. 196–99

20. Burger, The Future of Legal Education, remarks at ABA prayer breakfast, Aug. 10, 1969.

21. See supra note 9, P. M. Brown, *A Profession Losing Its Soul*, 72 ABA J 38, 1986.

22. "The Special Skills of Advocacy," lecture at Fordham University Law School, Nov. 26, 1978.

23. "The Decline of Professionalism," lecture at Fordham University School of Law, delivered January 23, 1995. 63 *Fordham L. Rev.* (1995).

24. 433 U.S. 350 (1977).

25. To a large extent, the issue had already been determined a year earlier in Virginia Pharmacy Bd. v. Virginia Citizens Counsel, Inc., 425 US 784 (1976), which overrode earlier precedent and gave First Amendment protection to commercial advertising by pharmacists. Although *Bates* indicated that a distinction could be drawn between ordinary commercial advertising and advertising of professional services by lawyers, *Virginia Pharmacy* laid down a constitutional standard difficult to distinguish for anyone genuinely respectful of precedent.

26. *Bates*, 433 U.S. at 368–71. The one salient point in the majority's reasoning was that advertising might enlarge access to legal services for the "not-quite-poor" and the unknowledgeable.

27. Id. at 379.

28. Id. at 389.

29. Id. at 404.

30. See, e.g., *Zauderer v. Office of Disciplinary Counsel of the Supreme Ct. of Ohio,* 471 U.S. 626 (1985); In re R.M.J., 455 U.S. 191 (1982); In re Primus, 436 U.S. 412 (1978); Ohralik v. Ohio State Bar Ass'n., 436 U.S. 447 (1978).

31. There is some recent indication that control of some of the excesses produced by *Bates* may pass Supreme Court review. See *Florida Var. v. Went For It, Inc.,* 515 U.S. 618 (1995) (opinion by O'Connor, Jr., with four Justices dissenting).

· 14 ·

THE BURGER COURT IN HISTORICAL PERSPECTIVE
The Triumph of Country-Club Republicanism

MARK TUSHNET

There are several standard and related characterizations of the Burger Court. The first is the subtitle of a relatively early assessment of the Burger Court: *The Counter-Revolution That Wasn't.*[1] A second is that the period was one in which the Court drifted in a more conservative direction. And a third, the title of the essay by the collection's editor, is that the period was characterized by a rootless activism.[2] The first and second characterizations can be reconciled by noting that a drift is not a revolution or a stampede. The third characterization, however, is in some tension with the second, which suggests that the Burger Court's activism did indeed have some roots in some version of conservatism. All three interpretations are to some degree inconsistent with the Burger Court's actual performance.

Consider first the sense in which the Burger Court "drifted" in a conservative direction. How could that be so if, as is true, no one could be executed in 1986 who could not have been executed in 1969,[3] the police could not engage in searches in 1986 that the Court had barred them from conducting by 1969,[4] and no woman or her doctor could be prosecuted in 1986 for obtaining or performing an abortion that she could have obtained in 1969?

These observations suggest that the Court's results were not demonstrably more conservative than the Warren Court's. Instead, the idea appears to be that the Court did not follow through on the implications necessarily drawn from the Warren Court's precedents. Probably the earliest criticism of the Burger Court along these lines was the charge by John Hart Ely and Alan Dershowitz[5] that the Burger Court's decision in *Harris v. New York*[6] rested on premises inconsistent with those that justified *Miranda v. Arizona*[7] even though the Court's opinion did not expressly repudiate those premises. And probably the last criticism of the Burger Court of this sort was the general academic reaction to *Bowers v. Hardwick*,[8] which chastised the Court for refusing to draw conclusions compelled by *Griswold v. Connecticut*[9] and *Stanley v. Georgia.*[10]

These criticisms rely on the view that there *are* principles necessarily underlying particular decisions that a court must fairly apply; they rely, in short, on Herbert Wechsler's account of neutral principles,[11] an account that the Warren Court's defenders and the Burger Court's critics often rejected. That approach is a lawyer's way of criticizing the Court. A historian must try to understand the Burger Court in rather different terms. A historian would focus in the first instance not on the logic of the Court's precedents but on the historical context in which the Court was located, the economic, social, and political events that provided the structure within which the Court operated. The intellectual environment, including the degree to which the legal academy and lawyers more generally were committed to a "neutral principles" understanding of the Court, is part of that context as well, but a historian would not automatically give it the priority that the "drift to the right" interpretation of the Burger Court must give it for that interpretation to be coherent.

Of course, there is no strong reason to believe that the economic, political, social, and intellectual events that provide the best understanding of the Supreme Court coincide with the tenure of Chief Justices. Indeed, to understand the modern Supreme Court we must see it as extending from the late New Deal to some time close to the present: The Supreme Court responded to the construction and gradual disintegration of the New Deal coalition. Historians generally agree that 1968 was a turning point in the history of the post–New Deal era. Chief Justice Burger's appointment in 1969 thus coincides with a historically relevant event, although his retirement in 1986 does not.

I begin with the economic context.[12] The Warren Court's decisions responded to the interests of the New Deal and Great Society coalitions: organized labor, African Americans, and liberal intellectuals. Those coalitions gradually disintegrated during the 1970s. As historian William Berman puts it, they had been held together by the Democratic party's ability "to serve as the champion of both corporate America and social decency." Stable and sustained economic growth made it possible for the Democratic coalition to satisfy the demands of working-class Americans and African Americans through a social welfare system financed by progressive taxes. Changes in the position of the United States in the world economy destroyed this "growth coalition." The "new politics of austerity all but precluded legislative deals that included benefits for the rich, the middle class, and the poor alike." Two other commentators observed, "In the context of slow and erratic growth . . . a gigantic squeeze began to develop on social spending. This . . . constrained [the Democrats'] ability to deliver the social benefits that had long secured them a real mass base."[13]

By the early 1970s the Democratic coalition began to fracture into interest groups competing with each other for their shares of a no-longer-expanding economic pie. The Warren Court's agenda of expanding rights exacerbated the Democrats' difficulties. Paying for the rights articulated by the Court meant increasing taxes. In journalist Thomas Edsall's words:

> Insofar as the granting of rights to some groups required others to sacrifice tax dollars and authority, to compromise longstanding values, to jeopardize status, power, or the habitual patterns of daily life, this new liberalism became, to a degree, a disruptive force in American life, and particularly so within the Democratic party.[14]

The party's leaders were unable to develop a program that would unite the declining labor movement, African Americans, environmentalists, and feminists, in part, political scientists Thomas Ferguson and Joel Rogers argue, because the party's leaders also needed to satisfy the requirements of its supporters in the business community.[15] Racial antagonisms that had been suppressed in the coalition's programs of general social welfare resurfaced. Republican leaders saw their opportunity to exploit these emerging divisions within the Democratic coalition. The political outcome was a shift in the presidency from Democratic to Republican control.

The Republican challenge to Democratic political control was partly intellectual. Conservatives began to articulate policy alternatives to the Democratic agenda that had dominated political discourse. One of their intellectual arenas was constitutional law. Conservative scholars developed critiques of the culture of rights they associated with the Warren Court. The rights the Warren Court protected, conservatives argued, were not grounded in the nation's constitutional traditions and contributed to the social fragmentation that so troubled many voters.

The Warren Court's Justices turned out to have few resources to turn back these challenges. The Warren Court's vision had important egalitarian elements in it, yet the Court's place in the American political system made it impossible for the Court to deliver consistently on its egalitarian promises. Occasional decisions embracing egalitarian views were accompanied by decisions incompatible with those views. As a result, the Warren Court could easily be tarred with the charge of being "unprincipled" or "political."

The Warren Court could not supply any alternative ideology, however. Its constitutional theory was founded on the New Deal experience, when the Supreme Court obstructed Congress and state legislatures seeking to address pressing economic issues through social welfare legislation such as minimum wage laws. President Franklin D. Roosevelt transformed the Court after 1937. The new Supreme Court aggressively protected individual rights, but the Justices no longer thought they had any basis in the Constitution for telling legislators that their economic and social programs were unconstitutional.

The Democratic coalition could have been held together by a unifying economic vision. Occasionally liberal Justices provided glimpses of such a vision. In 1972, for example, Justice Thurgood Marshall wrote a dissent resting on the proposition that everyone had a right to a government job unless the government had a good reason not to give the applicant a job.[16] Marshall also developed a way of understanding the Constitution's guarantee that governments may not deny people "the equal protection of the laws" that suggested how the courts might insist that governments pursue economic and social programs that benefited workers and the less-well-to-do. But these were only mild hints, usually in dissent and always in tension with the more openly stated lesson the Court learned after the New Deal, that social and economic matters were for legislatures to work out.

The Warren Court's academic supporters provided less assistance than conservative theorists provided their side. Their occasional suggestions that the Constitution required an expanded Welfare State and redistribution of wealth either failed to provide enough detail, and so seemed Utopian, or were overly programmatic and so seemed vulnerable to skepticism about the efficacy of social engineering. As the Warren Court faded, liberal academics became entirely defensive, criticizing the Court for changing course without providing much in the way of an argument for the Warren Court's path.

The Court could not provide the glue needed to hold the Democratic coalition together. Indeed, the Court exacerbated the divisions that were tearing the Democratic coalition apart when it handed out occasional victories to one or another of the interest groups struggling within the coalition. As Edsall put it:

> Instead of being seen as advancing the economic well-being of all voters, including white mainstream working and middle-class voters, liberalism and the Democratic party came to be perceived, in key sectors of the electorate, as promoting the establishment of new rights and government guarantees for previously marginalized, stigmatized, or historically disenfranchised groups, often at the expense of traditional constituencies.[17]

The Democratic coalition was further fractured by the issue of race. As economic conditions changed, working people came to see themselves as competing for shares of a fixed pie rather than attempting to secure a larger share of an expanding pie. Race provided a convenient focus for this competition. According to sociologist Jonathan Reider, for example, "Opposition to [affirmative action programs] sprang from the self-interest of vulnerable whites, whose hold on middle-class status was precarious. Integration threatened white ethnic monopolies on labor markets, the civil service, unions, and municipal power."[18] Whatever liberal Justices did in the 1970s and 1980s would compound the political difficulties of the coalition that provided essential support to them.[19]

By the early 1970s, Republicans dominated the presidential arena and provided an articulate alternative to the Warren Court's jurisprudence. Given the chance, Republican Presidents appointed relatively conservative Justices to the Supreme Court. With nearly every new appointment, liberals believed that the achievements of the Warren Court were in grave danger. Yet, although the Court gradually drifted to the right, the shift was less dramatic than some had feared and others had hoped.

The reasons were partly political and partly personal. Political scientist Martin Shapiro has forcefully argued that we must think of courts as, among other things, political institutions acting as other political institutions do. Among other things, they seek to develop constituencies that support them. The disintegration of the New Deal coalition freed up political space, but during Chief Justice Burger's tenure—and perhaps to the present—no alternative coalition replaced the New Deal coalition. That gave the Court an opportunity to act relatively freely to develop its own constituency of support. This accounts for the most dramatic nonconservative development during the Burger years—the Court's endorsement of a particular version of women's rights, including the right to choose—in its abortion decisions.

That women became such a constituency resulted again from a combination of social and political factors. The social welfare basis of the New Deal coalition disappeared, replaced by a pluralist interest group coalition. For Democrats, the emergence of women as an interest group, with claims made by an aggressive political leadership, did not pose a dramatic problem. They simply had to accommodate women's interests in the general pluralist bargaining that characterized the Great Society.

During the Burger tenure, Republicans as a party were divided over the claims asserted by the organized women's movement. The Republicans on the Supreme Court, however, were not—or at least there were enough Republicans on the Supreme Court responsive to those claims to make it relatively easy for the Court as a whole to develop women as a constituency of support.

The Court's conservatives represented a class of Republicans that has nearly faded from memory. They were country-club Republicans.[20] They accepted the basic contours of the New Deal and the Welfare State, were concerned about the fiscal consequences of New Deal policies, and, notably, could identify the claims made by the organized women's movement with their own class interests. Justice Harry A. Blackmun, for example, came to his views on abortion partly through his experience as general counsel to the Mayo Clinic and partly through the messages his daughters—representative of modern professional women—sent him. Justice Lewis F. Powell too was affected by his daughters' views, although he stated that an early experience in his professional career, when an employee of his law firm had to deal with the effects of a botched illegal abortion, also influenced his position.[21]

Country-club Republicanism accounts for the pattern of the Court's results in abortion cases. The Court's decisions made it possible for middle-class women accustomed to navigating their way through complex regulatory schemes to obtain abortions when they wished. They also made it possible for states to make it more difficult for less-well-off women to do so, most dramatically by allowing states to refrain from providing public assistance for abortions.[22] I want to be clear that neither here nor elsewhere in my analysis am I suggesting that the Justices at the Court's center consciously understood themselves to be acting in this way. Rather, the Justices' social backgrounds provided a context in which they found it easy to understand why the results they reached made sense.

The jurisprudence of country-club Republicanism also accounts for the Burger Court's qualified approval of affirmative action. Again, the basic political context is clear. The Republican party's efforts to construct an alternative to the New Deal and Great Society's coalitions turned importantly on identifying the Democratic Party with a particular position on race relations, and offering an alternative position, primarily to southern and working-class whites.

Translated into constitutional terms, that alternative called for a strong position of race neutrality. Conservative constitutional theory opposed race-conscious legislation in part because of its construction of constitutional history and in part because of its claim that constitutional rights were necessarily individual rather than the group rights that conservatives saw the Democratic Party pursuing.

The Burger Court's relatively conservative Justices could hardly ignore this political and intellectual background. At the same time, they came from a class that would itself bear few of the burdens of affirmative action, as Reider's description of the class impact of affirmative action suggests.[23] In addition, large businesses—the Fortune 500 companies—rather quickly adapted to the new affirmative regime. As one article put it, "Businessmen Like to Hire by Numbers."[24] Large businesses understood the benefits that flowed to them from having a reputation as "progressive" businesses with good race relations. They found it easy—far easier than small businesses—to create or restructure their human resource departments. They could use those departments to promote harmonious workplace relations.[25] In this area, one

Justice, Lewis F. Powell, played a decisive role. As one law clerk put it shortly after Powell's retirement, the Court's decisions depended so heavily on Powell's reactions to particular arrays of facts that "nobody knows what [a critical affirmative action] opinion stands for now that Justice Powell has retired."[26] The Burger Court's tepid endorsement of affirmative action was the result.[27]

In a similar vein, one dimension of some versions of country-club Republicanism affected the Burger Court's religion clause jurisprudence. The Nixon administration saw urban Catholic voters—and, again, southern whites—as prime targets for inclusion in a new governing coalition, and endorsed programs of aid to religious schools to attract those voters. However, the administration did not assert itself strongly on behalf of such programs. And support on the Court was even weaker. Country-club Republicans were, at their core, WASPs, and the "P" meant something. Chief Justice Burger and Justice Powell in particular emerged from social backgrounds in which aid to church-related schools was widely seen as support for Catholic schools that educated children of a different class, and importantly a different religion, from country-club Republicans. They could not enthusiastically endorse public aid to church-related schools. It is striking, then, that Burger's strongest statements rejecting strict separation came in *Lynch v. Donnelly*,[28] involving a generically Christian display with which mainline Protestants could be comfortable.

But if the Burger Court was a Court in which standard liberal Democrats sat with country-club Republicans, where did the drift to the right come from, and why was it not more substantial on such issues as criminal justice, on which the jurisprudence of country-club Republicanism was conventionally conservative?

Part of the answer is that the drift-to-the-right interpretation is indeed best supported by the Burger Court's criminal justice decisions.[29] True, the Burger Court invalidated, then revalidated capital punishment.[30] And equally true, it did not directly repudiate what the Warren Court had done. But its refusal to follow through on the Warren Court's promises, as that Court's admirers saw it, was certainly more dramatic in the criminal justice area than elsewhere. From the point of view of the Warren Court's admirers, in other areas the rate of progressive change had declined, and they feared that a further decline would mean that no advances would occur. In the criminal justice area, however, they believed that the Court would do nothing beyond what the Warren Court had done, and any additional changes in a conservative direction would mean a real cutback.

That did not happen during Chief Justice Burger's tenure. Interpersonal dynamics on the Court explain why. Here there were four crucial actors. Justices Powell, William J. Brennan, and William H. Rehnquist formed one group. In some sense, Powell had to choose between articulate representatives of other social classes. Neither Brennan nor Rehnquist was part of Powell's social "club," so to speak. Powell made his choice on the basis of his colleagues' views about law. Powell saw himself as the quintessentially reasonable person, and as he interacted with his colleagues he came to believe that the liberal Brennan simply was more reasonable than the conservative Rehnquist.[31]

Justice Brennan persuaded Justice Powell that the Warren Court's values of nationalism, equality, and individual dignity were closer to the nation's constitutional commitments, more centrist, than the values Rehnquist stood for.[32] Powell described Brennan as "a great advocate,"[33] but Brennan's skills went beyond advocacy. He was particularly effective in cobbling together the five votes needed to make constitutional law. Brennan made constant gentle efforts to induce Powell to take his side. They "frequently" "exchange[d] views privately," working out their difficulties without exposing them to the rest of the Court. Each gave the other "precirculation look[s]" at drafts. When Brennan added a footnote quoting Powell in an opinion, Powell responded with a personal note, "You are a scholar and a gentleman—and a generous one!" Early in Powell's tenure, Brennan drafted a separate opinion supporting Powell's decision restricting a college's ability to regulate student political organizations but sent it to Powell before circulating it because "the last thing I want to do is upset your applecart." Later Powell did "major surgery" on a criminal procedure opinion "to meet [Brennan's] views." Powell got along so well with Brennan because he saw Brennan as another "gentleman" who was entirely reasonable in his approach to constitutional law. Brennan got along so well with Powell because he understood how to persuade Powell to move away from Powell's instinctive conservatism to what Brennan and ultimately Powell regarded as a more reasonable and moderate position. By 1987 Powell felt comfortable in noting to Brennan, in a relatively minor case, that "we are on the side of righteousness."[34]

Justice Brennan's persuasive skills would not have retarded the Court's drift to the right had not Justice Powell been open to persuasion. Powell understood himself to be a centrist. His former law clerk, himself appointed to the federal bench by President Reagan, J. Harvie Wilkinson summarized Powell's self-understanding by describing Powell as offering "a perspective grounded in realism and leavened by decency, conscientious in detail and magnanimous in spirit, solicitous of personal dignity and protective of the public trust."[35] He saw himself as attempting to steer the Court down a middle path between the liberalism of Justices Marshall and Brennan, and the conservatism of Justice Rehnquist and Chief Justice Burger.[36]

The final actor was Chief Justice Burger himself. It is now clear that Burger was a failure as a leader inside the Court. Burger's leadership was a continual irritant that impeded the formation of a coherent conservative bloc. His colleagues at the Court repeatedly had to ask themselves whether Burger was merely a bumbling administrator or rather a Machiavellian manipulator. On reflection they generally concluded that he was the former, but the mere fact that the issue never went away kept tension high throughout Burger's tenure.

News stories about the new "Nixon-Burger Court" suggest one source of tension in Burger's early years. Nixon had campaigned in favor of changing the Court's direction dramatically. Insiders wondered "what effect the Court's new composition will have" on the law. Justices John Marshall Harlan, Byron R. White, and Potter Stewart, who disagreed with some of the Warren Court's major decisions, nonetheless were concerned that large doctrinal changes in a short period would fuel the public belief that the Court was a mere captive of political forces. In 1972, White opposed a Burger suggestion that some recent double-jeopardy cases be overruled even though White himself had dissented in those cases:

> I doubt that we should lightly overrule or put aside a rule of constitutional law fashioned in accordance with those institutional procedures contemplated by the Con-

stitution and Congress. A judgment reached in this fashion is entitled to at least some period for clinical observation before it is interred. It may be that experience will prove it as wise as its authors expected. On the other hand, it may prove improvident, in which event it will receive a timely enough burial.[37]

The question of how fast change would occur became particularly pressing after Justices Black and Harlan retired. A significant number of important cases were argued before Justices Powell and Rehnquist took their seats. The Justices decided that, as a rule of thumb, they would request reargument in cases in which the "bobtailed Court" of seven Justices divided 4–3. The Court's liberals remained suspicious, however. Late in the term, Justice Stewart "expressed his outrage at the high handed way things are going, particular the assumption that a single Justice if CJ can . . . hold up for nine months anything he chooses, even if the rest of us are ready to bring down 4–3s." In one case, written by Stewart, when the Justices voted to hand down a 4–3 decision, Justice Douglas became concerned that Chief Justice Burger was withholding his vote as part of a "strategy to have [the case] reargued." Burger replied, "If there is any 'strategy' to reargue this case, I have not heard of it. Perhaps it is only 'in the eye of the beholder'!" After Douglas expressed his concern about Burger's delay, Burger tried again: "I assume you read my brief note as an effort to relieve our pressures with a bit of flippancy. (Vera [Burger's wife] tells me I'm not very good at being flippant and that sometimes it is taken otherwise.)"[38]

Chief Justice Burger could not defuse suspicions about his motives so easily. Sometimes he suggested a strained reading of a case's facts to allow the Court to produce a conservative result, which Marshall and others derided as "reaching out." After years of working with Burger, Justice Powell found Burger "heavy-handed and insensitive." He was incredulous when Burger simply appropriated a couple of footnotes from a Powell draft dissent, without even asking Powell's permission, and then responded to Powell's complaint with a "cheery note telling Powell to 'Relax!'" Burger's presentations at the Justices' conferences were long-winded and vague, and he was "too self-important . . . and too self-engaged." Justice Blackmun resented being "taken for granted" as a "Minnesota Twin" of his old friend Burger and was annoyed that Burger assigned few important opinions to him. Eventually Blackmun found some of Burger's reactions to suggestions "petulant," and he disliked Burger's imperiousness. Justice Rehnquist once was "amazed" when Burger allowed an opinion to come down before Rehnquist had made "last-minute changes" in his dissent: "I realize there can be slipups and misunderstandings," Rehnquist wrote, "but it does seem to me that this opinion was put out with too much haste and without any adequate notification to those who presumably had a right to be notified." Burger sometimes got under Justice John Paul Stevens's skin as well. In one case Burger inserted a footnote in a dissent criticizing the majority's "haste" and its "strain[ing] to reach out" to decide a constitutional issue. Stevens was outraged and pointed out that the only ones who had voted to hear the case in the first place were the dissenters; it hardly made sense for them to criticize the majority for "reaching out."[39]

Although Chief Justice Burger tried to be sensitive to his colleagues' personal needs, even here he could fail. Burger scheduled a special conference to deal with administrative matters in April 1972. After the conference was set up, a favorite aunt of Justice Marshall died, and he asked Burger to reschedule the conference. Burger agreed. Then, when former Supreme Court Justice and South Carolina Governor James F. Byrnes died, Burger rescheduled the conference again so he could attend Byrnes's funeral. He set the conference for the time Marshall was attending his aunt's funeral. Marshall was furious; as he saw it Burger had thought the funeral of a leading segregationist more important than the funeral of a member of Marshall's family.[40]

The Chief Justice's actions in the abortion cases are well-known, and I will not describe them here in detail. In short form, Burger's successful assignment of the opinions to Justice Blackmun struck a number of his colleagues as a Machiavellian effort to manipulate the assignment process to produce opinions less supportive of the right to choose than, as they saw it, a majority on the Court believed appropriate. Burger's actions did indeed turn out to be part of a pattern, but not one of manipulation to achieve conservative results. The pattern, rather, was of ineptitude. He listed one case for reargument because there was a 4–3 vote; Justice Brennan corrected him that the vote was 5–3, and Burger apologized for basing his conclusion "on recollection." Burger misinterpreted a conference consensus for a "narrow" resolution of a voting rights case, thinking the majority wanted to vacate a broad decision rather than, as the votes were, to affirm the decision with a narrower theory. Once Burger erroneously listed a case for further discussion after four Justices had already voted to grant review. After a while Burger plaintively sought his colleagues' understanding: "Sometimes a change [in votes] is made directly to Bill Rehnquist [acting as secretary] either sotto voce or while the conversations going on impede communications."[41]

The Chief Justice opens the Court's discussions of its cases by summarizing the issues and indicating his views. Burger's case statements were rambling. He spent too much time on preliminary details, often said too little about the central issues, and frequently failed to say what he thought. He would "pass" on voting, later circulating a memorandum indicating where he eventually settled. Sometimes Burger's haziness occurred in cases with few ideological overtones. In one minor case, Brennan's clerk summarized the votes: "[N]ow you have: HLB, JMH[,] BW & Whatever on WEB." Brennan scribbled, "Since TM is out, that gives us four, so to h--- with it (him)."[42]

Burger kept the liberals' suspicions alive when he "passed" in cases that divided liberals from conservatives. When the Court took up the issue of the First Amendment rights of protestors at shopping malls, Justice Douglas initially assigned the opinion to Justice Marshall, relying on the "very tentative" Blackmun vote to affirm the protestors' claims. Burger immediately replied, "The vote was not 5–4 as I had reserved and not voted at all. . . . I will assign the case in due course if I vote to affirm." Douglas sent Brennan a note, "The CJ would rather die than affirm." Two weeks later Blackmun decided to reverse, as did Burger, who said he "continue[d] to find the case a very difficult one."[43]

Chief Justice Burger's practices in assigning opinions were also a persistent source of irritation. In 1985, Justice Brennan assigned two cases to himself, telling Burger in a note that none too subtly criticized Burger for giving Brennan too few cases, "Together with the two I assigned myself last week, this brings my total assignments to six, which at least approximates the total assignments to some of my other colleagues." When Burger assigned an opinion to Justice Blackmun as the "least persuaded" and "the need periodically for the 'good of the soul' and what Judge Hutcheson called 'intellectual discipline,'" Blackmun responded irritably that he was not the least persuaded and would write an opinion consistent both with the majority's views and with Blackmun's earlier dissents in related cases. But, Blackmun said, "All this has nothing whatsoever to do with your references to the 'good of the soul.'" He would keep the opinion, he said, to avoid a repetition of earlier experiences, when he received no opinion assignments.[44]

Burger believed as well that his role as Chief Justice gave him the obligation to write the Court's opinions in what he regarded as its most important cases. The results were often not happy. Burger thought, perhaps correctly, that the Court's opinion should be written by the Chief Justice when the Court voted to require President Nixon to comply with a court order in the Watergate affair that he turn over tapes made in his office. Burger believed that the President ought to have a somewhat broader executive privilege than most of his colleagues did. In addition, the case was decided under great time pressure. Different Justices prepared pieces of a final opinion. Burger had to stitch those pieces together and in the process gave his views about executive privilege more prominence than a majority thought proper. The Justices managed to get the opinion into a form they all could agree with after extensive negotiations. But, once again, Burger mishandled his colleagues.[45]

Part of Burger's difficulties occurred because he was sometimes obtuse about legal analysis and was unwilling to leave things in his clerks' hands.[46] His difficulties occurred in the small and the large cases. Once he proposed to reverse a state supreme court's interpretation of its own state's statute, a legally impossible result. Frequently his first drafts rambled, failing to distinguish between quite different approaches to the legal problems at hand. He wrote "sloppy" opinions, according to one Brennan law clerk, and his colleagues were accustomed to seeing in his opinions what Justice Powell called "dicta that no doubt you intend to condense or discard."[47]

Often, too, Burger simply did not understand what was at stake. He was sometimes "not on the same 'wave length'" after discussions with his colleagues. Upholding a search after a controlled delivery of drugs in which the police had lost control briefly, Burger did not see why his colleagues cared so much about changing his initial formulation, that the loss of control was irrelevant unless it was "more probable than not" that the drugs were removed during the period when the police lacked control, to the more stringent requirement that there be "no substantial likelihood that the contents have been changed." He overreached in saying that a sexually suggestive speech by a candidate for high school office "has no claim to First Amendment protection" and got Justice O'Connor to join his opinion only after he omitted the statement. His first draft in *Bowsher v. Synar*,[48] which struck down the Gramm–Rudman budget limitation program in 1986, concerned his colleagues because it "cast doubt on the constitutionality of independent agencies." Saying that the draft was "a 'rush job',", Burger replied to a flurry of memos that he did not disagree with any of them: "[T]he essence of the problem is whether we skin the tiger from the neck to the tail or vice versa. Either way suits me."[49]

Burger himself may have offered the most cogent comment on his leadership. *Vorchheimer v. School District*[50] was an attack on Philadelphia's use of separate academic high schools for young men and young women. Justice Rehnquist was absent from the hearing because of illness, and the Court's initial vote was 4–4. Burger tried to persuade his colleagues to have the case reargued after Rehnquist recovered, saying that the Court should not "evade[]" the constitutional question, and certainly anticipating that Rehnquist would vote to allow the "separate but equal" schools. His efforts failed, and Burger wrote Justice Blackmun, "I find it difficult to cope with four unregenerate, unreconstructed 'rebels'! In which case I conduct as orderly a retreat as possible."[51]

The context in which the Burger Court operated meant that a continuation of the Warren Court was simply impossible. Economic and political changes deprived the remaining liberal Justices of the support a court needs in the society. The New Deal–Great Society political coalition did not collapse in an instant, however, and as it disintegrated nothing arose in its place, at least during the Burger tenure. The political space that opened could have been occupied by any of a rather large range of possible alternatives to Warren Court liberalism. It was occupied by country-club Republicans in part because that was where the Court's center was, in part because Justice Brennan skillfully consolidated that center, and in part because Burger's performance as Chief Justice made it unlikely that the more conservative Justice Rehnquist could effectively put together an alternative conservative bloc.

Notes

1. *The Burger Court: The Counter-Revolution That Wasn't* (Blasi ed., 1983) [hereinafter *The Burger Court*].

2. Blasi, "The Rootless Activism of the Burger Court," in id. at 198.

3. I mean by this that the stated legal standards for capital punishment were more stringent in 1986 than they were in 1969. Of course, there was an effective moratorium on capital punishment in 1969 as the nation awaited the Court's resolution of the abolitionist challenge. I should add that although it is a conceptual possibility that the post-1976 standards for execution might encompass someone not eligible for capital punishment before 1969, I do not believe that it was a real possibility.

4. Indeed, I am aware of no significant police practice that was unconstitutional in 1969 but was legally permissible in 1986.

5. Dershowitz and Ely, "*Harris v. New York*: Some Anxious Observations on the Candor and Logic of the Emerging Nixon Majority," 80 *Yale L.J.* 1198 (1971).

6. 401 U.S. 222 (1970).

7. 384 U.S. 436 (1966).

8. 478 U.S. 186 (1986).

9. 381 U.S. 479 (1965).

10. 394 U.S. 557 (1969). Justice Blackmun's dissent invoked those two cases centrally, as well as the Burger Court's abortion decisions.

11. Wechsler, "Toward Neutral Principles of Constitutional Law," 73 *Harv. L. Rev.* 1 (1961).

12. The following eleven paragraphs are drawn from Tushnet, *Making Constitutional Law: Thurgood Marshall and the Supreme Court, 1961–1991*, 28–31 (1997).

13. Berman, *America's Right Turn: From Nixon to Bush* 40, 43, 58–9 (1994); Ferguson

and Rogers, *Right Turn: The Decline of the Democrats and the Future of American Politics* 103 (1986).

14. Thomas Byrne Edsall, with Mary D. Edsall, *Chain Reaction: The Impact of Race, Rights, and Taxes on American Politics* 9 (1991).

15. Ferguson and Rogers, supra note 13.

16. Board of Regents v. Roth, 408 U.S. 564 (1972).

17. Edsall, supra note 14, at 8.

18. Reider, "The Rise of the 'Silent Majority,'" in *The Rise and Fall of the New Deal Order, 1930–1980*, 254–55 (Fraser and Gerstle eds., 1989).

19. Edsall, supra note 14, at 8.

20. Tushnet, "Themes in Warren Court Biographies," 70 *N.Y.U. L. Rev.* 748 (1995).

21. Jeffries, *Justice Lewis F. Powell, Jr.: A Biography* 347 (1994).

22. Harris v. McRae, 448 U.S. 448 (1976). The pattern is even clearer after the Court's decision in Webster v. Reprod. Health Serv., 492 U.S. 490 (1989), and Casey v. Planned Parenthood of Southeastern Pa., 505 U.S. 833 (1992).

23. Reider, supra note 18.

24. Fisher, "Businessmen Like to Hire by Numbers," *Fortune*, Sept. 16, 1985, at 26.

25. See Edelman, Erlanger, and Lande, "Internal Dispute Resolution: The Transformation of Civil Rights in the Workplace," 27 *L. & Soc'y. Rev.* 497 (1993.)

26. CS [Carol Steiker], bench memo, 87-998, box 429, file 4, Thurgood Marshall Papers, Manuscript Division, Library of Congress.

27. Regents of the University of California v. Bakke, 438 U.S. 265 (1978).

28. 465 U.S. 668 (1984).

29. Notably, the essay on criminal procedure in *The Counter-Revolution that Wasn't*, supra note 1, raised questions about the subtitle's implication. Kamisar, "The Warren Court (Was It Really So Defense-Minded?), the Burger Court (Is It Really So Prosecution-Oriented?), and Police Practices," in *The Burger Court*, supra note 1, at 62.

30. Furman v. Georgia, 408 U.S. 238 (1972); Gregg v. Georgia, 428 U.S. 153 (1976).

31. Tushnet, "Lewis F. Powell and the Jurisprudence of Centrism," 93 *Mich. L. Rev.* 1854 (1995).

32. The following fifteen text paragraphs are drawn from Tushnet, supra note 12.

33. Powell to conference, June 3, 1987, box 420, file 1 (*Welch v. Texas Department of Highways*), Marshall Papers. For an analysis of Brennan's contributions, stressing the merits of his views rather than his personality, see Post, "William J. Brennan and the Warren Court," in *The Warren Court in Historical and Political Perspective* 123 (Tushnet ed., 1993).

34. Powell to Brennan, June 14, 1984, box 661, file 4 (*Roberts v. United States Jaycees*), William J. Brennan Papers, Manuscript Division, Library of Congress; Powell to Brennan, June 4, 1982, box 589, file 3 (*Youngberg v. Romeo*), id.; Powell to Brennan, undated, Box 535, File 5 (*Richmond Newspapers v. Virginia*), id.; Brennan to Powell, June 21, 1972, box 268, file 7 (*Healy v. James*), id.; Powell to Brennan, June 8, 1976, box 401, file 4 (*Doyle v. Ohio*), id.; Powell to Brennan, Jan. 20, 1987, Marshall Papers, box 417, file 8 (*Lukhard v. Reed*).

35. Wilkinson, quoted in Jeffries, supra note 21, at 562.

36. Jeffries, supra note 21, at 562.

37. SAS [Stephen Saltzburg], cert. memo, *Tillmon v. Wheaton-Haven*, Marshall Papers, box 75, file 4; White to Burger, Dec. 21, 1972, Brennan Papers, box 197, file 3 (*Illinois v. Somerville*).

38. Douglas to Brennan, White, and Thurgood Marshall, Feb. 4, 1973, Marshall Papers, box 104, file 10 (*Otter Tail Power Co. v. United States*) (where two Justices were disqualified); Garrow, *Liberty and Sexuality: The Right to Privacy and the Making of* Roe v. Wade 556 (1994); Douglas to Stewart, May 31, 1972, box 92, file 5 (*Fuentes v. Shevin*), id.; Burger to

Douglas, May 31, 1972, id.; Douglas to Burger, May 31, 1971, id.; Burger to Douglas, May 31, 1972 (second note), id.

39. Thurgood Marshall note on Burger to White, Dec. 27, 1977 (*Procunier v. Navarette*), Marshall Papers, box 201, file 4; Jeffries, supra note 21, at 248, 249, 432; Wasby, "Justice Harry A. Blackmun: Transformation from 'Minnesota Twin' to Independent Voice," in *The Burger Court: Political and Judicial Profiles* 70 (Lamb and Halpern eds., 1991), Blackmun to Brennan, undated, Brennan Papers, box 498, file 8 (*Michigan v. Doran*); Rehnquist to Burger, box 398, file 7 (*Connor v. Coleman*), id.; Stevens draft concurrence, June 1, 1982, box 594, file 2 (*School Board of Island Trees v. Pico*), id.

40. Thurgood Marshall to Burger, April 7, 1972, Marshall Papers, box 78, file 6; Burger to conference, April 10, 1972, id.; Woodward and Armstrong, *The Brethren* 178 (1979).

41. Burger to conference, Jan. 17, 1972, Brennan Papers, box 256, file 1 (*Gooding v. Wilson*); Brennan to Burger, Jan. 17, 1972, id.; Burger to Brennan, Jan. 17, 1972, id.; Brennan to Burger, March 6, 1973, box 297, file 1 (*Brown v. Chote*), id.; Stevens to Burger, Oct. 11, 1984, box 354, file 7, id.; Burger to conference, Oct. 3, 1975, box 155, file 8, id.

42. Note attached to Black to Brennan, Feb. 25, 1970, Brennan Papers, box 216, file 3 (*United States v. Seckinger*).

43. Burger to Douglas, April 24, 1972, Brennan Papers, box 268, file 8 (*Lloyd Corp. v. Tanner*); Douglas to Brennan, April 24, 1972, id.; Blackmun to Marshall, April 24, 1972, Marshall Papers, box 89, file 7; Blackmun to Burger, May 8, 1972, id.; Burger to conference, May 8, 1972, id.

44. Brennan to Burger, Dec. 13, 1985, Marshall Papers, box 397, file 2 (*Lee v. Illinois*); Burger to Blackmun, Oct. 17, 1983 (*Migra v. Warren County School Dist.*), id.; Blackmun to Burger, Oct. 18, 1983, id.

45. The most detailed account of the opinion-drafting process in the Watergate tapes case is Woodward and Armstrong, supra note 40, at 308–47. Other accounts, less overdramatized, are Ball, *"We Have a Duty": The Supreme Court and the Watergate Tapes Litigation* 112–30 (1990); Jeffries, supra note 21, at 382–97. Jeffries states that Woodward and Armstrong's account "is largely confirmed by the records." Id. at 395. The draft opinions in the case are reprinted in Schwartz, *The Unpublished Opinions of the Burger Court* 163–275 (1988).

46. Sometimes Burger's difficulties with legal analysis served him well. For an example, see the discussion of Thornton v. Caldor, 472 U.S. 703 (1985), in Tushnet, supra note 12.

47. Draft opinions, Brennan Papers, box 716, file 3 (*Arcara v. Cloud Books*); draft opinions, box 649, file 8 (*Hishon v. King & Spalding*), id.; Brennan to Burger, May 29, 1985, box 686, file 4 (*In re Snyder*), id.; Jim Feldman to Brennan, Dec. 6, 1984, box 606, file 4, id.; Powell to Burger, March 10, 1979, box 492, file 8 (*Parham v. J.L.*), id.

48. 478 U.S. 784 (1986).

49. Burger to O'Connor, Jan. 29, 1985, Marshall Papers, box 365, file 9 (*Marrese v. American Academy of Orthopedic Surgeons*); draft opinions, Brennan Papers, box 626, file 2 (*Illinois v. Andreas*); draft opinions, May 23 and June 12, 1986, Marshall Papers, box 390, file 3 (*Bethel School District v. Fraser*); O'Connor to Burger, June 2, 1986, box 396, file 2 (*Bowsher v. Synar*), id.; Burger to conference, June 3, 1986, id.; Burger to conference, June 4, 1986, id.

50. 441 U.S. 786 (1977).

51. Burger to conference, March 9, 1977, Marshall Papers, box 190, file 3; Burger to Blackmun, April 18, 1977, id.

· 15 ·

A JOURNALIST'S PERSPECTIVE

TONY MAURO

Just as it is often said that the Supreme Court has no army to enforce its rulings, it is also true that the court has no newspaper—and certainly no television station—to disseminate its decisions to the public. It is through the press that the public learns about the Court, probably to a greater degree than any other branch of government. Both Congress and the President have other ways to communicate directly with the public, but the Supreme Court does not—partly by its own choice. Thus, if we are to look back on the Burger Court more than ten years later in a well-rounded way, it is fitting to take into account how the Burger Court was perceived journalistically.

I begin, though, with a story not about Warren Burger but about the current Chief Justice, William Rehnquist. A few years ago at a social gathering at the Court, a group of reporters was surrounding Chief Justice Rehnquist when, as sometimes happens at such occasions, an awkward silence descended on the crowd. To keep the conversation going, the Chief Justice said, *a propos* of nothing, "You know, the difference between us and the other branches of government is that we don't need you people of the press."

It was quite an ice-breaker and I recall valiantly and courteously suggesting to the Chief Justice that he was wrong—that in fact the Court did need the press to build a public consensus behind its decisions and behind the rule of law.

I recall citing a particular case in my defense—the court's 1979 decision in *Gannett v. DePasquale.*[1] It was a Burger Court decision on press access to court proceedings. The Court itself made a mess of the decision and we in the press correspondingly made a mess of reporting it. The consequence was that judges were shutting down trials left and right to the press and public, even though that was not what the Court said needed to happen. But my point to Chief Justice Rehnquist was that we in the press had a role in setting things straight as well. Several Justices in speeches that summer engaged in off-the-bench reinterpretation of the decision, we reported that, and the court closings died down. The Court itself eventually clarified itself in *Richmond Newspapers v. Virginia*[2] and other decisions.

In any event, Chief Justice Rehnquist smiled at me for making a valiant effort, but it was clear I had not persuaded him of the importance of the press in the functioning of the Supreme Court, and I have not been able to since. I am not sure I would have had any better luck with Warren Burger, though in a sense Burger, through his active dislike of much of what the press wrote about his tenure, may have accorded us more importance than his more indifferent successor did.

As we begin to discuss the Burger Court, one more personal aside. I wrote part of this essay on Warren Burger's own typewriter. How do I happen to have his typewriter? I purchased it at the estate sale at his home in Arlington, Virginia, following his death. It is an old Royal typewriter, and of course as soon as I got it home my teen-age daughter asked me, "Dad, how do you turn it on?"

But that aside, I mention the estate sale because it was such a jarring, uncharacteristic event when you consider who Warren Burger was and what he stood for. To have members of the public picking through his silver and bidding on his commemorative photos and the like seemed like such an odd ending for a man who seemed to stand for dignity and decorum and professionalism. There were family considerations which no one outside can second-guess, I am sure, but this event did not correspond to the man I remembered.

Dignity and decorum defined his life and it certainly defined his aspirations for the press corps that covered him and the Court. I will never forget how the Chief would scan the press corps sitting in the Court to see whether we were dressed properly and behaving properly. Once, I recall, I did not make the grade. I was wearing a tie beneath a crew-neck sweater but no jacket, and I was banished to the area behind the curtains where reporters can hear but not see what is going on. I did not challenge the edict; it was just how things were when Warren Burger was in charge. He wanted so much for the press to be dignified, and if you know anything about the press corps, you know that that is a lot to ask.

But he kept trying. In the Pentagon papers case,[3] you recall, Burger dissented and said that in this instance, the press should have done what any taxi driver or Supreme Court Justice would do—return the stolen material to its proper owner or report it to the proper authorities. It was probably wishful thinking with respect to taxi drivers even then, but it certainly was about reporters.

The Thurgood Marshall papers are full of memoranda from Chief Justice Burger to other Justices warning them that *The Washington Post* was nosing around or that columnist Jack Anderson was snooping about, and that neither Justices nor law clerks should be lulled into thinking they can talk to reporters under any circumstances and stay out of trouble.

In one 1971 memo, Burger warned what would happen if anyone at the court made the mistake of speaking to a nosy *Wall Street Journal* reporter: "The reporter will inevitably extract information on the internal mechanisms of the court, one way or another, to our embarrassment." Of course, there is also the apocryphal ninety-second rule laid down by Warren Burger; any clerk seen talking to a reporter for more than ninety seconds would be dismissed.

In early 1973, the Chief Justice sent around a copy of a *Time* article that accurately forecast the outcome of *Roe v. Wade*,[4] clearly based on a leak from inside the court. Burger urged an investigation into the source of the leak, worrying that "if we sit placidly by, the impression may get around that we are tolerant of this kind of professional misconduct."

Burger was talking about the leaker, but I think he also was speaking of the journalist who received the leak as well. As you know, on occasion an employee of the printing office or some other suspected leaker was fired under Warren Burger.

And then there was the issue of cameras in the Court—what Fred Graham, who elevated the art of covering the Supreme Court along with Anthony Lewis, once called the court's deep-seated fear of electrons. Fred Graham, who covered the court for the *New York Times* and CBS News, once asked Burger what would advance the cause of cameras in the Court. Burger's answer was, "My funeral."

Regrettably, even that unfortunate event has not helped. In fact, it appears that as we approach the twenty-first century, the Supreme Court seems to be further and further away from embracing the premier news medium of the twentieth century. Justice David Souter recently borrowed a line from Burger when he told a congressional budget committee that cameras would come into the Supreme Court "over my dead body."

It is true that the Court has a variety of reasons for opposing the introduction of cameras into the courtroom, and it was not only Warren Burger who opposed them. Justice Byron White used to tell journalists that he felt no obligation to help make the television networks rich, a fairly dubious premise but one that White apparently believed. More recently, though, White confessed that the real reason he opposed cameras in the Court was that he coveted his privacy and anonymity—the ability to walk around Washington unrecognized and unmolested. That is clearly Chief Justice Rehnquist's view as well.

But it is almost certainly true that the Court would have moved further down the road toward allowing cameras inside—as have forty-seven state courts—if it had not been for Warren Burger's adamant opposition. And Warren Burger's reasons were not always rational.

Burger had written the Court's opinion in *Chandler v. Florida*,[5] which encouraged states to experiment with cameras in their courts, but he would have none of it in the Supreme Court itself.

When broadcasters petitioned the Court for one-time, experimental access for microphones during arguments in the case testing the constitutionality of the Gramm–Rudman budget law in 1986,[6] Burger replied with a formal denial. At the bottom, he penned in this postscript: "When you get Cabinet meetings on the air, call me!" The analogy between private Cabinet meetings and public oral arguments was hopelessly flawed, but Burger made the comparison without apparent embarrassment.

Soon after he retired in 1986, I had the opportunity to interview Burger, and could not resist asking him why he was so adamant in opposing the admission of cameras into the Supreme Court. "Television in a short snippet is simply incapable to making a proper report unless you put the whole thing on," was Burger's reply.

Anticipating an answer like that, I asked Burger how a television snippet differed from the kind of excerpting or summarizing done by newspapers. No newspaper prints complete transcripts of oral arguments, I noted. Burger's reply was that in newspapers, "The words aren't coming right out of the mouth of the judge or the attorney. On television, you see the person and it's coming right out of his mouth."

I wondered about Burger's response. At first I thought he was saying that television was in a way too accurate, that by showing a Justice actually saying the words, it gave the Justice less wiggle room, less ability to challenge the accuracy of the quote. But I have since come to the conclusion that Burger was making a very different point. I believe he was arguing that by having their images captured on television, Justices and lawyers would be aiding and abetting in something Burger viewed as utterly distasteful—an improper and undignified broadcast report on the Court's proceeding. Report on the Court if you must, Burger seemed to be telling broadcasters, but just do not get us involved.

So we return to decorum, to dignity. Warren Burger knew that we in the media had a job to do—a job that in his opinions he usually recognized was an important one in the constitutional scheme of things. But he wanted no part in becoming actors in our unseemly production. He wanted the Court and himself to be seen as above all that, above the fray—standing above and off to one side of the political and journalistic hurly burly.

Why do I dwell on this theme of Warren Burger's obsession with dignity when it came to his relations with the media? It is because it is the only way, I think, to explain the essential contradiction of Warren Burger and his Court—how Warren Burger could have such personal disdain for journalists and yet still write such ringing decisions in favor of the news media. It explains how he could despise the idea of allowing cameras into his court yet write *Chandler v. Florida*,[7] and how he could be dismissive of Supreme Court reporters yet give them a place in other courtrooms in *Richmond Newspapers*.[8] When you look at these opinions and others—*Miami Herald Publishing Co. v. Tornillo*,[9] for example—you realize that as a body of work, they constitute a fairly strong wall of protection for freedom of the press, for the work that we do.

And yet I think that came as something of a surprise to many of us in the news media when we looked back after his death. I think this is because, for better or worse, the personal antagonism of Warren Burger toward the media colored our entire outlook on the Court, not just on its free press jurisprudence but everything it did.

If you look back at some of what was written about the Burger Court at the time, much of it was tinged with antagonism toward him because of his disdain for us and for the cult of secrecy that he fostered at the court. When *Time* offered a rare cover story on the Court on October 8, 1984, it dwelled on the Court's secrecy and talked about its "antipress" reputation. An earlier *Time* story on November 5, 1979, also spoke of Burger's obsession with leaks and included a photograph of one of the Court's brass gates, intended to "seal off the justices' chambers."

What I think ended up happening is that we in the press translated Burger's personal animosity toward the press into a general opposition to the First Amendment. We overlooked our victories, and some of them indeed were written in a grudging, stingy tone. And there were enough antipress decisions emanating from the Burger Court to fuel our misperception. Many of us in the media then took the next step and concluded that if the Burger Court hates the First Amendment, it must be very conservative, especially in comparison to the Warren Court.

It is true that because of the business we are in, we tend to have tunnel vision when it comes to the First Amendment. We are not the only ones, by the way. Justice William Brennan was once asked what the most important part of the Constitution is and he said, without missing a beat, "The First Amendment. All the rest is window dressing." We in the media tend to choose up sides according to who is on the side of the First Amendment, or at least whom we perceive to be on the side of the First Amendment. Especially when we feel that we are under attack, we feel that we have to fight back, because no one else will fight for us. Walter Cronkite, who is revered for his objectivity among other things, once said the only bias he allowed himself was in favor of the First Amendment and that has certainly guided others in my profession as well. Warren Burger may have fallen victim to that bias.

Ironically, in part because the Burger Court settled so many areas of press law years ago, the same siege mentality barely afflicts the press today. The current Supreme Court has not taken up a major freedom of the press case in five terms or more, and in general the climate has eased in terms of libel and access.

Arguably the Rehnquist Court does not like the press any more than the Burger Court did, but we are perhaps more complacent, so we do not view the Rehnquist Court as quite so hostile or even as conservative generally as perhaps we ought to. There is at least a lot of debate on this point, witness the controversy over James Simon's book on the Court, *The Center Holds*.[10]

In any event, there is a fair amount of evidence that Warren Burger was upset with the way the press viewed him as an enemy. Fred Graham wrote that Burger's grudge against the news media "had the angry edge of a suitor scorned." Indeed, Burger did try to court the press from time to time and usually was rebuffed, which he ascribed partly to the liberal bias of the media but also to its opposition to his view on cameras in the Court.

In a variety of ways, Warren Burger made life easier for the media covering the Court. He was responsible for adding the syllabus to opinions, which helps us make at least an initial reading of the opinion on deadline. And Burger was responsible for smoothing out the June crush, by adding more days on which the Court sat and handed out opinions, instead of dropping all of them on a Monday.

But still the image lingered of a Chief Justice hostile to the press. After he retired from the bench, he engaged in what I call obituary adjustment. He did not want his obituary to read, "Warren Burger, enemy of the First Amendment, died. . . ." So in his waning years, he told any journalist within earshot—and I was in earshot a number of times—that he had gotten a clerk to do some research for him, and the clerk found that Warren Burger had written more pro-press opinions than any other Justice in history.

True or not, that more generous view of Warren Burger has begun to sink in, and I believe the journalistic "take" on the Burger Court has already begun to change. We are beginning to lump the Burger Court in with the Warren Court as a sort of liberal-to-moderate counterweight to the Rehnquist Court, which is seen as considerably more conservative. Conservative, but not that threatening to civil liberties or to freedom of the press.

But the revisionism is coming slowly, and that is in large part, I think, because of Warren Burger's pursuit of decorum and his disdain for the press that to many of us smacked of secrecy. Burger, it seems, failed to learn the lesson encapsulated in these words: "People in an open society do not demand infallibility from their institutions, but it is difficult for them to accept what they are prohibited from observing." Those words, of course, are from the majority opinion in *Richmond Newspapers*. They were written by Warren Burger.

Notes

1. 443 U.S. 368 (1979).
2. 448 U.S. 555 (1980).
3. New York Times v. United States, 403 U.S. 713 (1971).
4. 410 U.S. 113 (1973).
5. 449 U.S. 560 (1981).
6. Bowsher v. Synar, 478 U.S. 714 (1986).
7. 449 U.S. 560 (1981).
8. Richmond Newspapers v. Virginia, 448 U.S. 555 (1980).
9. 418 U.S. 241 (1974).
10. Simon, *The Center Holds: The Power Struggle inside the Rehnquist Court* (1995).

16

A PUBLIC INTEREST LAWYER'S PERSPECTIVE

ALAN B. MORRISON

When Professor Bernard Schwartz asked me to speak at this conference, he assigned me the topic "A Public Interest Lawyer's Perspective on the Burger Court." After thinking about the topic for a while, I asked Professor Schwartz what he had in mind, and he kindly, I suppose, told me that the choice was up to me. This was, of course, the proverbial good news and bad news, as there were no established criteria by which to judge even the framework for this essay, let alone an established law school course, a topic heading in the *Harvard Law Review*'s annual Supreme Court survey, or even a comparable symposium in the *Supreme Court Review*. Indeed, the topic is not generally thought of as a topic, let alone a topic for reviewing a tenure of a Chief Justice of the U.S. Supreme Court. On the other hand, I recognized that it would be difficult for anyone to criticize my choice of themes or cases as not being within some established norm.

The easiest part was to decide what not to include. First, I looked at the agenda for this conference and vowed to do my best not to duplicate any of the other topics, although there may be a few places where I talk about cases referred to by others. It was much harder to determine what I should include and why. Inevitably, it seemed that this essay had to be somewhat personal, because I had spent nearly twenty-five years as a public interest lawyer. My hope is that I have not been too personal because our office was involved in one way or the other in many of the cases I discuss.

If there is a common thread for public interest lawyers, it is their use of the courts to assist the disadvantaged. Most of us view our work as enforcing the law, although some would characterize it as law reform, whereas still others would say that we are attempting to change the law through the courts rather than the legislatures. But in attempting to use the courts for these purposes, a number of barriers must be surmounted to get to the merits. Perhaps the word that best seems to epitomize the public interest lawyer's, and ultimately the client's greatest need, and hence what this essay discusses, is "access": the ability (broadly defined) to present the merits of a claim and have the court decide it. Within that framework, this essay is organized around four separate topics.

First, it looks at the general issue of the Burger Court's response to substantive claims designed to improve the availability and affordability of legal services, as well as claims seeking to reduce other barriers, principally financial, to access to the courts. Although most of the remaining topics deal with cases involving claims against a governmental entity, the principles established in this area apply to all forms of litigation, as well as nonlitigation matters.

Next, part II.A considers issues of standing and other similar barriers that prevent a court from reaching the merits, with most of, but not all, the cases focusing on review of actions by federal officials. Subpart B then explores the ways in which nonstatutory claims and claims under section 1983 became more or less difficult to maintain during the seventeen years in which Warren Burger was Chief Justice of the United States.

The next part contains three units that look at procedural questions that arise in federal court litigation: class actions, attorneys' fees, and other procedural issues. Each of these has a real impact on the ability of public interest lawyers to obtain redress in the federal courts.

The final section focuses on three sets of substantive rules of law that have a transcending effect on the ability of individuals to assert their rights: separation of powers, preemption, and access to information under the Freedom of Information Act[1] and to court records.

There is one cautionary note. The Burger Court is not really one court but at least two Courts. From the summer of 1969, when Warren Burger became Chief Justice, until January 7, 1972, when Justices Lewis F. Powell and William H. Rehnquist were sworn in, the Court was still largely the same as during the Earl Warren tenure. Thereafter, for the remaining fourteen and one-half years of the Burger Court, there were only two changes: In 1975, John Paul Stevens replaced William O. Douglas, and in 1981 Sandra Day O'Connor replaced Potter Stewart. Although they may have been viewed differently at the time, at least today, those two changes would seem rather modest in scope and not partaking of the kind of sea change that took place in the late 1980s when Presidents Ronald Reagan and George Bush were able to replace the most liberal remaining members of the Warren Court.

In addition, Justices are not robots who decide cases according to some preplanned program; rather, they are responsive to many factors, including their different approaches to different kinds of issues and their evolving views of their roles as Justices. Among the Justices who sat during the Burger Court, Harry A. Blackmun, Lewis Powell, and John Paul Stevens were generally thought to have moved further to the left, whereas Byron R. White has been thought to have either shifted slightly to the right or remained in place as the Court moved somewhat away from him. Thus, despite the fact that five Associate Justices plus the Chief Justice were replaced during the term of Warren Burger, the Court was never really a Burger Court, in part because of the substantial influence of Justices William J. Brennan and Thurgood Marshall. Nonetheless, particularly over a seventeen-year period, there are discernible patterns from a public interest lawyer's perspective, and this essay attempts to set them forth in some coherent fashion.

I. Access to Justice: Availability and Affordability
of Lawyers and Removing Other Financial Barriers

No law or court rule requires that those who wish to go to court have a lawyer unless the person is a corporation. However, as a practical matter, to obtain justice in the courtroom or in many other situations, it is essential to be represented by counsel. There are no laws denying anyone counsel, but the problem of obtaining counsel is a practical one, often revolving around financial considerations.

A major barrier to individuals obtaining legal services when Warren Burger became Chief Justice in 1969 was the lack of availability of information about lawyers, including what they charge and in what areas of law they specialize. One of the real achievements in this area of the law under the Burger Court was that advertising by lawyers and other forms of commercial speech, were, for the first time, given substantial, but not full First Amendment protection.

The evolution began with a case apparently having little to do with lawyer advertising, *Bigelow v. Virginia*.[2] Bigelow had run an alternative newspaper in Virginia which accepted an ad for abortion services in New York, at a time when abortions were forbidden in Virginia but lawful in New York. Not only were abortions unlawful in Virginia, but the state contended that Bigelow's conduct violated its statute forbidding the procurement of abortions. The case went twice to the Supreme Court, once before *Roe v. Wade* was decided, and once following a remand in which the Virginia Supreme Court left unchanged its prior decision, notwithstanding *Roe*. What made *Bigelow* a seminal case was that Justice Blackmun's opinion focused on the importance of the availability of the information on abortion services to the reader which he found protected by the First Amendment. This shift in attention away from the speaker had been presaged to some extent by the decision three years earlier in *Kleindienst v. Mandell*,[3] in which the Court analyzed the claims under the First Amendment from the perspective of the rights of the potential audience rather than of the speaker's right to travel from Belgium to the United States to make his views known.

The following year, the Court made explicit what it had left implicit in *Bigelow*: that commercial speech was entitled to First Amendment protections, striking down another Virginia statute, this one prohibiting the advertising of the price of prescription drugs.[4] *Virginia State Board of Pharmacy v. Virginia Citizens Consumer Council*, 425 U.S. 748 (1976). And the next year, the Court leapt into the thicket of lawyer advertising, holding that the nearly universal rule prohibiting all advertising of legal services was unconstitutional as it applied to price advertising for routine legal services.[5] Then the following term the Court took on two cases, *In re Primus*[6] and *Ohralik v. Ohio State Bar Association*,[7] in which it accorded strikingly different treatment to oral solicitations by the attorneys in the two cases. Thus, Primus's activity was held protected because her solicitation was on behalf of a nonprofit institution (the American Civil Liberties Union), which was seeking to advance its ideological goals, whereas the Court sustained the discipline imposed on Ohralik for his solicitation, which, in addition to being in a hospital room where the would-be client was in some considerable physical and mental distress from her recent accident, was for a personal injury lawsuit in which Ohralik stood to earn a substantial fee.

The issue of lawyer advertising and its impact on the ability of the Bar to provide information and for consumers to learn about the availability of legal services, continued to be affected both by direct lawyer advertising cases, such as *Zauderer v. Office of Disciplinary Counsel of the Supreme Court of Ohio*,[8] and *Central Hudson Co. v. Public Service Commission*,[9] in which the Court set forth the general framework for analyzing commercial speech cases, including lawyer advertising. Most of these decisions made it easier for lawyers to advertise and easier for consumers to obtain necessary valuable information, although often the rulings were carefully circumscribed, reflecting in part the Court's obvious unease with the whole subject of professional advertising and solicitation.

Perhaps the most negative decision in the commercial speech area occurred on the final day of Chief Justice Burger's tenure, when the Court, by a 5–4 vote, ruled in *Posadas de Puerto Rico Association v. Tourism Co.*,[10] that laws forbidding the advertising of gambling casinos directly to Puerto Ricans were constitutional, even though identical ads could be run to non-Puerto Ricans who might be coming to the island for gambling and other recreational purposes. In the course of his majority opinion, Justice Rehnquist observed that it would be "a strange constitutional doctrine which would commit to the legislature the authority to totally ban a product, but to deny the legislature the authority to forbid the stimulation of demand for the product through advertising on behalf of those who would profit from such increased demand."[11] That ruling would have had no impact on rules on lawyer advertising but might well have been the green light to prohibit the advertising of tobacco, liquor, and other so-called vices. But at least that aspect of *Posadas* is no longer valid in light of the Court's most recent commercial speech case, *44 Liquormart v. Rhode Island*,[12] in which the Court declined to follow such a broad rationale in assessing the constitutionality of limitations on bans on liquor price advertising.

Outside the advertising area, the Burger Court issued three rulings that substantially aided the cause of increasing the availability and affordability of legal services. First, in *Goldfarb v. Virginia State Bar*,[13] the Court ruled that lawyers were not exempt from the Sherman Antitrust Act by reason of their professional status, that certain agreements in restraint of trade (in that case minimum fee schedules and related ethics opinions) could give rise to burdens on interstate commerce that satisfy the requirements of the Sherman Act, and that state bars and local bar associations were not exempt from liability under the Sherman Act on the theory that they were somehow arms of the state, at least where the state did not actively supervise the conduct being challenged. Because ethical rules are issued by state courts rather than by state bars, this final qualification restricted the number of potential situations in which bars could be liable under the Sherman Act. Indeed, in *Bates*, the Court rejected an antitrust claim against the state bar precisely because the advertising rules were issued by the state court which was immune from liability under the antitrust laws. The result was that although escaping antitrust liability, the actions of the state courts in promulgating rules became subject to any and all limitations imposed under the Constitution.

Second, the Court completed a series of cases begun with *NAACP v. Button*,[14] including *United Mine Workers v. Illinois State Bar Association*,[15] and ending with

United Transportation Union v. State Bar of Michigan,[16] in which it struck down a variety of rules restricting the ability of organizations, both ideological groups, such as the NAACP, and labor unions, such as the United Mine Workers and *United Transportation Union*, to band together and provide legal services for their members in ways that the states treated as barratry or other types of improper practices by lawyers. The elimination of these restrictions helped pave the way for the development of other forms of group legal services programs and other means designed to cut the cost of legal services to middle-income Americans. And, although upholding the right of a defendant in a criminal case to represent himself as a matter of constitutional law, in *Faretta v. California*,[17] the Court never went so far as to hold that individuals had a constitutional right to have someone who is not a lawyer represent them in court even if the state or federal law was to the contrary.

The final area in which state court restrictions limiting choice of counsel were set aside was the requirement that applicants for admission to a state bar had to reside in the state. In *Supreme Court of New Hampshire v. Piper*,[18] the Court ruled, 8–1, that such restrictions violated the Privileges and Immunities Clause in Article IV of the Constitution, at least in those situations in which the individual seeking admission was willing to take the bar exam. The case was undoubtedly helped to some degree by the fact that the plaintiff lived in Vermont, just a few miles from the New Hampshire border, and wanted to practice in New Hampshire because her husband had his practice in Vermont where they both lived. And, although based on a different part of the Constitution, the fact that in 1973 the Burger Court held in *In re Griffiths*,[19] that lawful aliens could not be denied membership in a state bar because they were not citizens, surely made it easier to sustain the challenge in *Piper*. Like the lawyer advertising cases, *Piper* (and to a lesser extent *Griffiths*) resulted in benefits both to lawyers, who now have greater flexibility in their practices, and to clients, who now have a wider range of choice because the residence requirement previously precluded most lawyers from practicing in more than one jurisdiction.

Another area in which the Court was quite active was in assessing the validity of state-created financial barriers to access. The early Burger Court decisions were quite favorable, as the Court set aside the requirement for an appeal bond equal to twice the amount at issue in *Lindsey v. Normet*,[20] and in *Boddie v. Connecticut*,[21] the Court held that it was a violation of due process for a state to insist on the payment of a $50 filing fee for an indigent seeking a divorce when the state courts maintained a monopoly over the ability to obtain a divorce, which the Court considered a fundamental right. However, in *United States v. Kras*,[22] by a vote of 5–4, the Court upheld the $50 filing fee for bankruptcy as applied to indigents on the ground that bankruptcy was not a fundamental right and the courts did not maintain a monopoly over the right to discharge one's debts.

Two other cases stand out. In *Bounds v. Smith*,[23] the Court ruled that a state prison system either had to provide a law library or had to establish some other form of assistance so that prisoners would not be prevented from exercising their right to seek relief through the courts. However, the Court took a decidedly different view on the question of access in *Walter v. National Association of Radiation Survivors*,[24] where it held that the statutory limit of $10 on payments to attorneys for assisting claimants before the Veterans Administration was constitutional because the proceeding was nonadversary and there was no demonstrated need for a lawyer to be able to assert one's rights. Thus, the potentially broad promise of breaking down barriers suggested by *Boddie* came to stand for much less in the end as the Court became, in this area as in others, less protective of the rights of individuals, or at least less willing to extend those rights in the latter years of the Burger Court than it was initially.

II. Barriers to Reaching the Merits

Public interest attorneys routinely encounter a variety of rules and doctrines that prevent them from reaching the merits of claims brought in federal court. To many plaintiffs' lawyers, these doctrines are seen as procedural roadblocks, whereas others would characterize them as ensuring that the courts maintain their historic role and decide only those matters that are truly cases or controversies within the meaning of Article III. However characterized, there can be no question that they control the flow of litigation, making it either easier or harder for courts to decide the merits of federal court cases. Among the most formidable of these doctrines is that of standing.

As described more fully below, the Burger Court applied the law of standing and other similar doctrines in challenges to determinations of federal agencies in a manner that generally, but not always, afforded access to those seeking judicial review. On the other hand, standing barriers were increased outside the field of federal administrative law and under certain specific civil rights statutes. Those parallel developments are traced in subpart A. In subpart B, I discuss similar issues regarding claims outside the administrative law area, including cases against state and local governments under 42 U.S.C. § 1983, implied causes of action, and issues of immunity under the Eleventh Amendment and elsewhere.

A. Standing and Other Barriers to Judicial Review

With regard to claims brought under the Administrative Procedure Act (the APA),[25] the Burger Court was quite generous to those who sought court intervention to overturn agency decisions. Somewhat ironically, the two cases that started this trend of allowing others, beyond those directly regulated, to seek judicial review of agency determinations[26] were both brought by a business entity challenging a decision that aided its competitors. The Court, in establishing the standards for standing, including a generous zone-of-interest test, indirectly benefited public interest lawyers and their clients, and those decisions became the basis for cases upholding standing in a variety of contexts including rights to sue under environmental laws and other similar statutes for which broad segments of the public are the intended beneficiaries. Indeed, the zenith of standing in APA cases, *United States v. SCRAP*,[27] rejected a standing challenge at the pleading stage to a claim that a decision of the Interstate Commerce Commission with regard to railroad rates would have an adverse impact on the environment because it would discourage conservation activities. The 5–3 ruling was seen as the green light for a wide range of environmental and other complaints, although developments during the Rehnquist Court have cut back on that hope significantly.[28]

The one anti-standing blip involving APA claims in the Burger Court era, *Sierra Club v. Morton*,[29] proved to be of little significance because the ruling only prevented an environmental group from suing on its own behalf to protect its interest in the environment but did not preclude it from suing on behalf of its members who might be directly injured as a result of the action being challenged. Coupled with the Court's subsequent decisions in *Hunt v. Washington State Apple Advertising Commission*,[30] and *UAW v. Brock*,[31] both of which made it relatively easy for organizations to sue on behalf of their members in most cases, the Burger Court created relatively few barriers under the standing doctrine to judicial review of administrative decisions. Similarly, the Court also upheld a broad view of standing in statutory cases challenging discrimination.[32]

But where there was no statutory cause of action for discrimination, plaintiffs were generally less successful in upholding their standing. The most significant barriers were created in *Warth v. Seldin*,[33] a 5–4 decision that has been repeatedly cited outside the discrimination area as a basis for not allowing standing. On the other hand, in *Village of Arlington Heights v. Metropolitan Housing Development Corp.*,[34] the Court upheld the standing of the challengers in circumstances similar to those in *Warth* but then ruled against them on the merits.

Outside APA challenges, the result was much different. The Warren Court decision in *Flast v. Cohen*,[35] in which the Court upheld the standing of taxpayers to challenge federal payments on the grounds that they violated the Establishment Clause of the First Amendment, was seen to be the dawning of a new era for challenges to unlawful federal conduct in which it was the statute, rather than the implementation of it, that was being protested. However, the Court made it clear in two 1974 opinions by Chief Justice Burger that there was no general citizen or taxpayer standing under federal law when attempts to contest the secrecy of the CIA budget and to challenge the practice under which members of Congress held commissions in the Military Reserve, allegedly in violation of the Incompatibility Clause of the Constitution, were derailed on standing grounds in *United States v. Richardson*,[36] and *Schlesinger v. Reservists Committee to Stop the War*.[37] Then in *Valley Forge Christian College v. Americans United for Separation of Church and State*,[38] the Court ruled that *Flast* applied only to statutes that authorized spending alleged to violate the Establishment Clause but not to administrative action taken by federal officials under statutes that were neutral on their face but allegedly unconstitutional as implemented.

With regard to challenges to favorable treatment given to nonprofit hospitals that were allegedly not entitled to it because they were not serving the poor as the law required, the Court had earlier ruled, in *Simon v. Eastern Kentucky Welfare Rights Organization*,[39] that such challenges could not be maintained, and in *Allen v. Wright*,[40] the Court refused to allow private persons to challenge the tax-exempt status of educational institutions that were allegedly discriminating in their admissions policy against the plaintiffs and other minorities.

When the question did not involve expenditures of federal funds or the functional equivalent of a failure to collect them, the results were nonetheless also against the challengers. Thus, in a series of cases the Court imposed a high standard of injury and required that those seeking to enjoin practices that had harmed them in the past establish with considerable certainty that they would be subject to such practices in the future. Thus, in *Laird v. Tatum*,[41] in one of the first cases in which the votes of Justices Rehnquist and Powell made a difference, the Court refused to allow challenges to surveillance practices of the military on the grounds that the plaintiffs had not established a sufficient continuing chill on their exercise of their First Amendment rights to warrant the continuation of the litigation. And in both *O'Shea v. Littleton*,[42] and *City of Los Angeles v. Lyons*[43] the Court relied on doctrines of standing and ripeness as a basis for dismissing claims of police misconduct brought by individuals who could not establish the likelihood that they personally would be adversely affected by such conduct in the future. And in *Bender v. Williamsport Area School District*,[44] individual school board members were found to lack standing to appeal an adverse court decision when the defendant school board voted not to appeal.

Among the claims not based on a statute in which standing was an issue, only *Duke Power Co. v. Carolina Environmental Study Group*[45] produced a victory for the challengers, but the affirmance of the district court's ruling on standing and ripeness principally allowed the Court to reverse the determination on the merits that the Price–Anderson Act was unconstitutional, a result that would not have been possible if the Supreme Court had reversed on justiciability grounds. In theory, in many of these cases seeking injunctive relief, the plaintiffs could have sued for money damages but, as we shall see later, that possibility became significantly less attractive as the law of immunity expanded.

Standing has not been the only arrow in the government's quiver in defending against APA cases. However, in most instances the Burger Court rejected the government's broad claims and allowed the courts to reach the merits. Thus, in *Barlow v. Collins*,[46] the Court established the general rule that administrative statutes allowing a particular form of judicial review should not be read to preclude others, although in *Block v. Community Nutrition Institute*,[47] the Court did preclude consumers from seeking judicial review of marketing orders when others in the food-supply chain with similar interests were specifically allowed to make similar challenges. The Court also rejected claims that the agency's determination was committed to its discretion, thereby precluding judicial review.[48] However, when it came to judicial review of decisions not to take law enforcement action, the Court put down its foot in *Heckler v. Chaney*.[49] The broad implications of *Chaney* remain to this day somewhat uncertain in part because of its unusual facts—the plaintiffs asked the Court to review the Food and Drug Administration's refusal to seize drugs used for executions by injection, on the ground that they were not "safe and effective" within the meaning of the Food, Drug and Cosmetic Act.

Finally, there is one decision that might have caused those challenging agency actions some difficulty, but did not.[50] There the Court ruled that the Administrative Procedure Act did not provide a basis for subject matter jurisdiction in federal court, but that had virtually no impact because the principal area in which such jurisdiction was needed was in cases in which the amount in controversy was not readily ascertainable. However, because Congress had abolished the $10,000 requirement for federal question cases under 28 U.S.C. § 1331 the previous year, the "loss" in *Califano* had no practical adverse effects.

Three other administrative law cases had implications which, taken as a whole, somewhat diminished the ability of public interest challengers to prevail in their case, although they are not uniformly harmful in the same way as are the other procedural barriers. For example, in *Vermont Yankee Nuclear Power Corp. v. NRDC*,[51] the Court put an abrupt halt to the trend in lower courts, principally in the District of Columbia Circuit, to create procedural rights outside those explicitly set forth in the APA. Decisions imposing additional procedural burdens on agencies, particularly in notice and comment rulemaking under 5 U.S.C. § 553, proved to be formidable weapons in the hands of public interest (and industry) challengers, but they were taken away in *Vermont Yankee*. Then, in *Motor Vehicles Manufacturers Association v. State Farm Mutual Auto Insurance Co.*,[52] the Court ruled first that agencies could change their minds and adopt positions previously rejected, but in doing so they had to articulate a reason and provide support for their change of position, a result that, by and large, favored public interest challenges, particularly during the Reagan era when the Administration sought to revoke many substantive rules simply because it did not like them.

Finally, in one of the most important cases of the Burger Court era, *Chevron USA v. NRDC*,[53] the Court ruled, without dissent, that agencies should be given substantial deference on questions of law, as well as on other kinds of determinations, and that the courts should not overturn an agency's interpretation of the statute unless Congress plainly spoke to the precise issue, or the agency's position was unreasonable. Although in theory the result applies to both public interest and business challenges, the primary impact seems to have fallen on the former, perhaps because those claims often depend on a reading of the statute different from that put forth by the agency.

If it is possible to balance all the different doctrines and the various outcomes, the overall result would probably be one that is moderately favorable to public interest challengers who seek to overturn administrative agency determinations. At the very least, no new barriers were erected, something that cannot be said in all areas discussed in this essay.

B. Claims Under 42 U.S.C. § 1983 and Other Federal Causes of Action

For many litigants, the right to use federal law as a basis for a claim is an extremely important one. Not only is federal law often more favorable than comparable provisions of state law, but if a federal cause of action exists, there is federal question jurisdiction which provides a number of advantages, at least to many plaintiffs.

For many years, the Supreme Court regularly implied private federal rights of action based on federal statutes when Congress had not specifically provided for them. The Court in *Mills v. Electric Auto-Lite Co.*,[54] continued that trend by upholding an implied cause of action for a violation of the proxy provisions in section 14(a) of the Securities Exchange Act of 1934. That trend came to an abrupt and unexpected end in 1975 in a unanimous opinion by Justice Brennan in *Cort v. Ash*.[55] The question presented was whether there was a federal cause of action for stockholders who alleged that their company had made corporate contributions in violation of the federal election laws, and the Court held that there was none. In doing so, the Court did not simply reject a federal claim under the circumstances of that case but set forth a wholly new approach in which the burden was essentially reversed from what it had been in the past: The proponent had a significant hurdle to overcome if he or she sought to establish a federal cause of action that Congress had not explicitly created. Although the Court did not eliminate all implied federal causes of action,[56] the impact was to substantially reduce the areas in which federal court jurisdiction could be obtained.

Nonetheless, when the Court was faced with whether it would imply a cause of action for violations of the Constitution, as opposed to a statute, the Court permitted such claims in *Bivens v. Six Unknown Named Agents of the Federal Bureau of Narcotics*,[57] and affirmed that decision in a post-*Cort* ruling in *Butz v. Economou*.[58] However, when Congress provided for statutory remedies for, in one case, conduct that also allegedly violated the Constitution, the Court refused to permit an implied constitutional claim.[59]

When there was a specific right of action in a federal statute, as there was in 42 U.S.C. § 1983, the Court's rulings generally favored plaintiffs. Thus, in *Monell v. Department of Social Services of New York*,[60] the Court overruled its 1961 decision in *Monroe v. Pape*[61] and held that governmental units below the level of the state were persons within the meaning of section 1983 and hence liable for violations of federal rights. And in *Maine v. Thiboutot*,[62] the Court construed section 1983 to apply to claims for violations of federal statutes, as well as the Constitution, thereby allowing a wide range of claims, such as actions brought to enforce the welfare and food stamp laws, to be maintained in federal court under section 1983. Finally, in *Wilson v. Garcia*,[63] the Court held that all claims under section 1983 were governed by the state statute of limitations for personal injury claims, thereby simplifying the matter for plaintiffs and generally producing a reasonable period within which to bring such an action.

Although the Court was generally favorable on the merits of section 1983 actions, it created a number of procedural barriers, the most significant of which was that of *Younger v. Harris*.[64] The Court there held that with very limited exceptions, section 1983 was not available to obtain injunctive relief for persons who were already subjects of state enforcement proceedings. That rule was extended in *Steffel v. Thompson*[65] to preclude actions for declaratory judgment as well as injunctions. The Court did rule, however, in *Wooley v. Maynard*,[66] that as long as an action by the state was not then pending, even though there had been a prior proceeding between the parties and there was a real possibility of a future one, the plaintiff could bring suit under Section 1983 in federal court. However, if the federal issue were actually decided in state court, the decision in *District of Columbia Court of Appeals v. Feldman*[67] would preclude the litigation of that federal claim in federal court (other than through a certiorari petition), although the Court left open the possibility that some general claims would not have to go through the state system.

In at least two areas, the Court did make procedural rulings favorable to Section 1983 plaintiffs. In *Mitchum v. Foster*,[68] the Court held that section 1983 was an exception to the Anti-Injunction Act,[69] thereby allowing federal courts to prevent state interference with a variety of cases under section 1983. And, of great practical significance, the Court ruled in *Patsy v. Board of Regents*,[70] that exhaustion of state remedies was not a prerequisite for filing section 1983 claims in federal court.

At the same time, the Court extended existing rulings on the law of immunity in ways that significantly impeded enforcement of federal rights. For example, in *Edelman v. Jordan*,[71] the Court held that retroactive payments to plaintiffs, for admitted violations of federal law, were barred by the Eleventh Amendment, and in *Pennhurst State School and Hospital v. Halderman*,[72] it ruled that the Eleventh Amendment precluded the federal courts from enforcing state laws in claims brought under section 1983.

The Court was also active, generally favoring defendants, in implied immunity cases. In *Butz v. Economou*,[73] the Court found absolute immunity from claims for damages based on certain constitutional violations but only qualified immunity for most others. Then in two cases decided together in 1982, *Harlow v. Fitzgerald*[74] and *Nixon v. Fitzgerald*,[75] the Court ruled both that the President had absolute immunity for all official acts undertaken while in office and that all government officials enjoy at least qualified immunity and some may enjoy more than that when acting at the direction of the President.

The ruling in *Harlow* was even more important for the new test that it established for qualified immunity: A defendant may escape liability for money damages if his conduct was objectively reasonable and the conduct did not violate any clearly established federal right. Thus, the prior element of subjective intent, which would usually entitle plaintiffs to take discovery, was eliminated, thereby substantially improving the impact of the defense and making damage recoveries much more difficult. And to ensure that such defenses were not erroneously rejected by district judges, the Court gave those claiming qualified immunity an absolute right to an interlocutory appeal in *Mitchell v. Forsyth*,[76] even though two days earlier the Court in *Richardson-Merrell, Inc. v. Koller*[77] had ruled that the disqualification of the plaintiff's lawyer was not immediately appealable but had to wait until a final judgment occurred. On the other hand, when the defendant was a governmental entity suable under section 1983, the Court in *Owen v. City of Independence*[78] rejected the defense of qualified immunity available to individuals, although the circumstances in which a unit of government can be held liable for money damages are quite limited.

Although it is difficult to draw an overall conclusion, on balance the Burger Court restricted the availability of remedies for claimed violations of federal law in many, but not all instances.

III. Other Procedural Rulings

A. Class Actions

The Burger Court rulings on class actions were, like most of its other rulings, a mixed bag, but in general they favored the maintaining of class actions and, in a somewhat ironic twist, may come to the subsequent aid of those putative class members who are opposing class actions in mass tort cases.

In two rulings, *Sosna v. Iowa*[79] and *U.S. Parole Commission v. Geraghty*,[80] the Court allowed class actions seeking injunctive relief to continue even after the individual claim of the named plaintiff had been mooted. In *Sosna* the class had already been certified, and in *Geraghty* the district court had denied certification, but in both cases the Court declined to require dismissal and recommencement of the action with a new plaintiff when the claims were by nature of temporary duration. And to make those rulings of even greater benefit, the Court ruled in *American Pipe and Construction Co. v. Utah*[81] that the statute of limitations was extended throughout the duration of a case brought as a class action until the ruling on the class status had been finally determined on appeal. Then, in a decision that plainly helped class plaintiffs, the Court declared in *Gulf Oil Co. v. Bernard*[82] that it was an abuse of discretion for the district court to limit all communications between plaintiffs' counsel and members of the class.

There were two other rulings that will permit a greater use of classes in both federal and state court cases. In *Califano v. Yamasaki*,[83] the Court upheld the certification of a nationwide class of social security claimants under rule 23(b)(2), and in *Phillips Petroleum Co. v. Shutts*,[84] the Court allowed a state court to adjudicate a nationwide damage class provided that there was notice, adequate representation, and an opportunity for class members to opt out.

Other rulings of the Burger Court in the area of class actions, that appeared to be decidedly pro-defendant when issued, may ultimately redound to many class members, although not to those who seek to employ the class action device in certain circumstances, particularly mass torts. Thus, in *Zahn v. International Paper Co.*,[85] the Court ruled that in diversity of citizenship cases, each member of the class must have the requisite amount in controversy and that it was not enough for the named plaintiffs to satisfy that requirement. And in *Eisen v. Carlisle & Jacquelin*,[86] the Court held that claims for damages under rule 23(b)(3) of the Federal Rules of Civil Procedure required the best practical individual notice, which in many cases makes it impossible to satisfy the rule and economically maintain the class action. Then, in *General Telephone Co. of the Southwest v. Falcon*,[87] the Court refused to allow a black worker, who claimed he had been discriminated against in promotion, also to represent a class of blacks whose discrimination claim was based on failure to hire them. Finally, in *United Airlines, Inc. v. McDonald*,[88] the court allowed an objecting class member to intervene after judgment when the need to do so arose only at that time.

All these rulings were seen as damaging to plaintiffs in class actions at the time they were issued, and they may well have been. But now, with the efforts to maintain nationwide classes in mass tort cases, including both claimants already injured and those who have been exposed to a product but have not yet developed symptoms, these cases loom large as defenses against such damage classes and may provide shields to absent class members even in the face of agreements by defendants to certify a class and waive any objection that they would have to class certification based on these rulings that were favorable to it. Similarly, the Court's statements in *Phillips Petroleum*,[89] that the right to opt out in all cases involving claims for money damages was required by due process, may also act as a break in preventing excessive reliance on the class action device in those situations.

One ruling stands out as unequivocally favorable to defendants and harmful to plaintiffs: the decision in *Evans v. Jeff D.*,[90] in which the Court held that a defendant in a civil rights case had the absolute right to condition settlement on the waiver by class counsel of all fees. Although the ruling enables defendants to place counsel for the plaintiffs in an intolerable position of having to either abandon their fees or abandon the class and urge rejection of a settlement that might be in the best interest of the class, but plainly not in the best interest of class counsel, the Court found nothing in the civil rights laws, rule 23, or the cannons of ethics that prevented defense counsel from placing their adversaries in that position.

B. Attorneys' Fees

The Burger Court's record on attorneys' fees, as in many other areas, was decidedly mixed. A number of cases were quite favorable to plaintiffs. Thus, in *Mills v. Electric Auto-Lite Co.*,[91] the Court ruled that the plaintiffs were entitled to attorneys' fees from the company for proving violations of the proxy rules even though there was no fund created as a result of their litigation, which did lead to improvements in the manner in which the company handled its proxies. Similarly, in *Hall v. Cole*,[92] the Court allowed union members to collect attorneys' fees from their union on a common benefit theory in cases brought under the Landrum-Griffin Act, despite the absence of any attorneys' fees provision for this particular violation and the existence of specific attorneys' fees provisions for other violations.

Other favorable rulings related to attorneys' fees for claims under section 1983. In *Hutto v. Finney*,[93] the Court ruled that attorneys' fees against state entities were not barred by the Eleventh Amendment, and in *Maher v. Gagne*,[94] the Court held that a plaintiff who prevailed through settlement would nonetheless be entitled to fees if there were benefits conferred on those whom they sought to represent, even without a judgment on the merits. And in *Supreme Court of Virginia v. Consumers Union*,[95] the Court held that the Virginia Supreme Court could be sued for enforcing the rules governing the bar, but not for promulgating them, thereby making it available as a source of funds for attorneys' fees in at least some cases. Finally, in a procedural ruling benefiting everyone seeking fees, the Court concluded in *White v. New Hampshire Department of Employment Services*[96] that the ten days in which to file a motion to amend judgment under rule 59(e) did not apply to claims for attorneys' fees which were not part of the basic claim but were available as a result of having prevailed on the merits.

Two attorneys' fees rulings were generally viewed as mixed for the plaintiffs. In *Hensley v. Eckerhart*,[97] the Court attempted to simplify the attorneys' fees process by, among other things, forbidding the defendant from challenging each particular step along the way in assessing whether the plaintiff had prevailed on the matter and had actually produced a benefit but instead required claims as a whole to be analyzed. It also insisted that attorneys' fee proceedings be simplified so that they do not turn into a second major litigation but at the same time made clear that plaintiffs would have to show concrete benefits from their actions, that the courts should insist on substantial documentation before awarding statutory attorneys' fees, and that the reasonableness of the fees would be determined by looking to the case as a whole.

Another divided ruling occurred in *Blum v. Stenson*,[98] in which the Court first ruled that lawyers employed by nonprofit organizations were entitled to the market rate for commercial law firms in determining their attorneys' fees but that they were not entitled to a multiplier of 50 percent in that case, strongly suggesting that such multipliers would generally not be available based on quality of representation. The possibility that risk-based multipliers could be used in statutory fee cases was also rejected in *Pennsylvania v. Delaware Valley Citizens' Council for Clean Air*,[99] in which, although allowing fees for the administrative phase, the Court explicitly ruled that there would be no adjustment for risks of not prevailing, nor for quality of representation. And in *Library of Congress v. Shaw*,[100] the Court held that there would be no prejudgment interest, or other comparable adjustments, based on delay in payment for claims of attorneys' fees against the federal government.

The attorneys' fees case that was seen to have the most negative impact on plaintiffs when it was issued was *Alyeska Pipeline Service Co. v. Wilderness Society*.[101] There the Court ruled that the federal courts had no authority to order fee shifting under a private attorney general theory in the absence of a federal statute. In the years preceding *Alyeska*, the federal courts were increasingly relying on such a rationale to award fees to plaintiffs, principally those represented by public interest organizations. The decision in *Alyeska* brought that trend to a screeching halt, but Congress stepped in and passed a number of statutes explicitly covering many of the cases that had sought to use a private attorney general rationale, the most significant of which was 42 U.S.C. § 1988, which augments the substantive rights granted in section 1983. Although the Congress of 1996 would not have been anywhere near as favorable as was Congress in 1976, the timing of *Alyeska* at least allowed the public interest bar to recoup in Congress what it lost in the Supreme Court.

C. Other Procedural Rulings

The decisions in this group can be divided between those interpreting the Federal Rules of Civil Procedure and those relating to federal jurisdiction. In the latter category, the Court in two cases, *Aldinger v. Howard*[102] and *Owen Equipment v. Kroger*,[103] construed the federal jurisdictional statute narrowly in *Aldinger* to preclude the attempt to bring in additional parties when the basic claim, but not the new claim, was based on federal question jurisdiction, and in Owen to preclude the continuation of an action against a third-party defendant as to whom there was no federal jurisdiction after the primary defendant had been dismissed from the case. Although, under the facts of those cases, the primary loser seemed to be the plaintiff, the result in other cases may be to burden defendants who have already made substantial investments in federal litigation, as well as the state court systems which must absorb these cases.

With regard to its rulings concerning the Federal Rules of Civil Procedure, the Court did no serious damage to the causes that public interest lawyers support, and some of its rulings were favorable to them. For example, in *Adickes v. Kress Co.*,[104] the Court's ruling with respect to motions to dismiss and summary judgment were quite favorable and made it clear that the courts should not lightly enter judgments against plaintiffs who had not had an opportunity to establish their case. Sixteen years later, the Court revisited the issue of summary judgment in two cases thought at the time to be Supreme Court encouragement for district judges to be more willing to grant summary judgment.[105] Although language in the opinions can fairly be read to make summary judgment easier, and the opinions do remove certain barriers in some categories of cases, there has been little discernible shift in summary judgment practice since that time, in part because the two decisions did not involve typical summary judgment situations, nor, of course, could they deal with the myriad circumstances in which factual disputes arise or in which the legal issues are far from clear.

In two cases involving rule 68, the Court had the potential, but did not do serious harm to the public interest community. In *Delta Airlines, Inc. v. August*,[106] the Court ruled that the offer in judgment sanctions under rule 68 could be invoked only if the plaintiff recovered less than the offer, but not if the plaintiff recovered nothing at all. And in *Marek v. Chesney*,[107] the Court held that rule 68 offers in judgments had to include attorneys' fees, when statutes provided them, but that rule 68 could coexist consistent with those statutes by permitting the denial of fees only after the offer in judgment was made, and only then if the recovery was less than the offer. The one decision involving a federal rule in which the result was clearly adverse to plaintiffs was *Schiavone v. Fortune, AKA Time, Inc.*[108] There the Court barred the use of the relation-back provision of rule 15(c) to avoid statute-of-limitations difficulties, when the plaintiff had named the wrong legal entity but the defendant had received timely notice by service of the complaint. The ruling was rather narrow at the time but in any event was quickly erased by an amendment to the rule itself, clarifying that innocent mistakes should not be the basis for denial of rule 15(c) benefits.

IV. The Substantive Areas Affecting the Public Interest Community

In part I of this essay, I described the substantive developments in the law of access to justice, focusing on the impact of Burger Court decisions on the organized Bar and on statutes that operated to deny indigents access to the court system at one level or another. In parts II and III, I discussed principally what could be termed "procedural issues," broadly defined, as they impact on the ability of public interest lawyers to serve their clients. In this part, I return to substantive law rulings of the Burger Court in three areas: separation of powers, preemption, and access to records of the executive branch and the courts. Before doing so, it may be helpful to explain why I view these as areas of public interest concern.

One dominant theme in public interest litigation is the need to control sources of power and see that they do not go unchecked. Among the most significant checks and balances in our system are those created by the provisions dealing with separation of powers which limit the role of each branch of the government. Because they are structural protections that cannot be "waived" by the respective branches, decisions construing the separation of powers have potentially great ramifications for controlling the government.

The Court's rulings on preemption implicate another important check in our system: that of federalism. In many of the cases raising preemption, the defendant, usually a large business enterprise, asserts that federal law precludes states from enforcing certain of their laws, either those that involve direct regulation or those that provide for damages remedies for victims of the defendant's misconduct. Although there can be no doubt of the power of the Federal Government to preempt contrary state laws, the question in most of these cases is whether Congress, or, in some cases, an administrative agency, has actually sought to do so or whether the doctrine of preemption is being used as a shield against liability. Seen from this perspective, court rulings narrowing the scope of preemption ensure that the check of state power is not diminished, except when the federal entity clearly intends that to be the result.

As for open government and access to agency and court records, in many cases in which the substantive law does not entitle a litigant to relief, relief may ultimately be available in the court of public opinion, but only if the information about the practices at issue is made public. Thus, open government is sometimes the only substitute for judicial or other control over governmental and in some cases private entities. For that reason, it is one of the most important tools of the public interest lawyer.

A. *Separation of Powers*

Separation-of-powers cases during the term of the Burger Court involved two separate areas: control of the executive branch and control of Congress, in the latter case both when Congress sought to aggrandize itself and when it sought to create new structural devices to solve real or perceived problems. Overall, the result was a series of decisions that maintained the relative balances between the branches of government.

The first major separation of powers case was *United States v. Nixon*,[109] in which the Court rejected a broad claim of executive privilege as a basis of the President's refusal to comply with a grand jury subpoena. The unanimous opinion made clear that the President was not above the law, while still recognizing a substantial place for executive privilege as part of our constitutional scheme. Although the President was found not to be above the law here, he was granted absolute immunity from civil damages actions for all presidential activities in *Nixon v. Fitzgerald*.[110]

In two other cases, the Court also rejected claims of executive power by President Nixon. In *Train v. City of New York*[111] and *Train v. Campaign Clean Water*,[112] the Court rejected a claim that the statute at issue gave the President discretion not to spend money that Congress had appropriated. Of perhaps even more interest is what the Administration did not argue: that, apart from Congressional statutes, the President had the inherent authority to refuse to spend money that Congress had appropriated. Then, in *Nixon v. General Services Administration*,[113] the Court again rejected the absolute claim of executive privilege as applied to a statute that took possession and control of the tapes and papers that the Nixon administration had generated and made them the property of the U.S. Government. While again recognizing the need for the privilege and for protecting the President from undue interference with his decisional processes as part of separation of powers, the Court created a balancing test under which considerable deference was given to Congress's judgment as long as reasonable protections were built in to ensure that the President could function in office in the manner envisioned in the Constitution.

Another important decision relating to executive power technically involved the interpretation of a statute under which President Carter claimed the right to transform claims against the Iranian Government and its assets in the United States into an alternative channel that, in all likelihood, would reduce recoveries for a number of persons suffering losses at the hands of the Iranian Government.[114] What is most significant about the case from a separation-of-powers perspective is that it gave the President broad authority to achieve an important political national security objective by utilizing statutes almost certainly not intended for that purpose, thereby increasing presidential power.

The final case involving presidential power during the Burger era is the one that did not involve a decision on the merits. When Senator Goldwater and others sought to challenge the decision of President Carter to withdraw from our existing treaty with Taiwan, the Court, on a highly expedited basis, dismissed the case without reaching the merits.[115] Based on the variety of grounds offered in the several opinions issued, the net effect was to insulate the President's decision from judicial review, thereby increasing his power, at least in this limited area.

The second set of decisions relate to control over Congress's powers. The first case, and the one that revived and increased the significance of the Appointments Clause, is *Buckley v. Valeo*.[116] Most people think of *Buckley* as a First Amendment case, but to separation-of-powers aficionados, it is important because it strictly construed the Appointments Clause to forbid additional methods of appointment beyond those authorized by that provision, here setting aside a scheme under which four members of the Federal Election Commission were appointed by Congress and the two presidential appointees had to be approved by both Houses and not just the Senate. It is also seen by some as the beginning of a more formal, less functional approach to separation of powers analysis.

Two of the most significant separation-of-powers cases involve situations in which Congress sought by statute to increase its own power over the administration of the laws. In *Immigration and Naturalization Service v. Chadha*,[117] in an opinion written by Chief Justice Burger, the Court found that the legislative veto, which existed in over 200 statutes, violated the separation of powers because it gave to Congress authority to make law by means other than that prescribed in the Constitution. Then in Chief Justice Burger's final opinion,[118] the Court set aside the portion of the Gramm-Rudman Act that authorized the Comptroller General to make certain determinations that resulted in the sequestration of appropriated funds. The Court concluded that because of the authority of Congress to fire the Comptroller General and other indicia of Congressional control over him, the Constitution did not permit the Controller General to make decisions to carry out the law.

In contrast to *Chadha* and *Bowsher*, which involved congressional aggrandizements, the Court looked somewhat more charitably to Congress's other attempts to create new structures for governmental decision-making. Thus, in *Thomas v. Union Carbide Co.*,[119] the Court approved an administrative mechanism for resolving claims that federal law had improperly taken the property of a pesticide company by requiring public disclosure of certain information, over a challenge that the determination had to be made by an Article III court. Similarly, in *Commodity Futures Trading Commission v. Schor*,[120] the Court held that Congress properly authorized the Commodity Futures Training Commission to entertain state law-based counterclaims in administrative proceedings when the counterclaim arose out of the same transaction as the principal claim before the agency. Once again the argument was made that such claims could only be adjudicated by the federal courts, and the Court rejected that contention. On the other side, however, in *Northern Pipeline Construction Co. v. Marathon Pipe Line Co.*,[121] the Court concluded that the attempt to allow bankruptcy judges who are not appointed in accordance with Article III of the Constitution to decide state law claims was inconsistent with Article III which required that all such claims be decided by lifetime federal judges.

The net effect of these decisions is to ensure that neither the executive branch nor the Congress significantly increased its powers, at the same time allowing for some degree of flexibility in creating new institutions, as long as they did not offend some specific provision in the Constitution.

B. Preemption

In response to civil actions for damages or regulatory proceedings brought by state or local entities, defendants increasingly began to claim during the era of the Burger Court that existing federal regulatory schemes preempted either some or all aspects of damage actions and state and local regulation. The Burger Court's response was decidedly mixed. For instance, it rejected a claim of preemption over charges of intentional overbooking in *Nader v. Allegheny Airlines*,[122] allowed the plaintiff in *Silkwood v. Kerr-McGee Corp.*,[123] to recover punitive damages against the operator of the nuclear power facility, which was heavily regulated by the Nuclear Regulatory Commission, and upheld efforts by California to require would-be nuclear power licensees to provide assurances that economic problems relating to waste disposal would be solved before the plant began operations, despite the NRC's responsibilities for waste disposal safety issues.[124] And in *Franchise Tax Board v. Construction Laborers Vacation Trust*,[125] the Court refused to allow removal to federal court of a state-based claim solely on the ground that the state claim was preempted by federal law.

On the other side, on the same day that it decided *Franchise Tax Board*, the Court gave an extremely broad construction to the Employee Retirement Income Security Act preemption provision's "relating to" language.[126] The Court had previously upheld a quite broad claim of implied preemption in *Jones v. Rath Packing Co.*,[127] and in *Southland Corp. v. Keating*,[128] the Court ruled that the preemption provisions of the Federal Arbitration Act applied to cases brought in state as well as federal court.

In the end, the number of preemption cases and the range of issues faced were relatively small. Thus, with *Shaw* on the one hand, and *Silkwood* on the other, it was not possible at the end of 1986 to say whether the Burger Court had broadened or restricted the doctrine of preemption.

C. Access to Records

I have previously written about the dismal record of the Burger Court in dealing with suits seeking records under the Freedom of Information Act (FOIA).[129] In virtually every case, the Court ruled in favor of the government, twice provoking Congress to overturn its decisions in very short order, as well as prompting legislative rejections of other lower court rulings which took their guidance from High Court decisions. Not only was the Burger Court unsympathetic to requesters on the merits, but when they lost below, the Court declined to hear their cases nearly 100 percent of the time, while granting nearly 90 percent of the petitions filed by the Solicitor General. Nothing changed of any significance in the last two years that Warren Burger was Chief Justice.

In addition, in two non-FOIA cases, involving access to court records, the Burger Court took a decidedly antidisclosure position. In one case involving the Nixon tapes, which had been played in open court during the Watergate trials, the Court refused to allow broadcasters to make copies of them, finding no First Amendment right to that kind of access, and relying on the alternative procedures for processing all of the Nixon tapes created by federal statute, which were moving very slowly.[130] And in *Seattle Times Co., v. Rhinehart*,[131] the Court concluded that a pretrial protective order that prevented the dissemination of information obtained in discovery did not violate the First Amendment or the common-law right of access to court records as long as there was good cause for entering the order.

Conclusion

If you had asked public interest lawyers in 1969 how they thought they would fare under the Burger Court, explaining to them that every one of the five post-Burger appointees would be chosen by a Republican President, the likely response would have been, "Not very well." In retrospect, the answer would more likely be, "Pretty well in some areas, not very well in others, but overall, much better than we could have expected."

Notes

1. 5 U.S.C. § 552

2. 421 U.S. 809 (1975).

3. 408 U.S. 753 (1972).

4. Virginia State Bd. of Pharmacy v. Virginia Citizens Consumer Council, 425 U.S. 748 (1976).

5. Bates v. State Bar of Ariz., 433 U.S. 350 (1977).

6. 436 U.S. 412 (1978).

7. 436 U.S. 447 (1978).

8. 471 U.S. 626 (1985).

9. 447 U.S. 557 (1980).

10. 478 U.S. 328 (1986).

11. Id. at 346.

12. 116 S. Ct. 1495 (1996).

13. 421 U.S. 773 (1975).

14. 371 U.S. 415 (1963).

15. 389 U.S. 217 (1967).

16. 401 U.S. 576 (1971).

17. Faretta v. California, 422 U.S. 806 (1975).

18. 470 U.S. 274 (1985).

19. 413 U.S. 717 (1973).

20. 405 U.S. 56 (1972).

21. 401 U.S. 371 (1971).

22. 409 U.S. 434 (1973).

23. 430 U.S. 817 (1977).

24. 473 U.S. 305 (1985).

25. 5 U.S.C. § 701.

26. Association of Data Procesors v. Camp, 397 U.S. 150 (1970); Arnold Tours v. Camp, 400 U.S. 45 (1970).

27. 412 U.S. 669 (1973).

28. Lujan v. Defenders of Wildlife, 504 U.S. 555 (1992); Lujan V. National Wildlife Fed'n, 497 U.S. 871 (1990).

29. 405 U.S. 727 (1972).

30. 432 U.S. 333 (1977).

31. 477 U.S. 274 (1986).

32. See, e.g., Trafficante v. Metropolitan Life Ins. Co., 409 U.S. 205 (1972) (aggrieved whites may sue to challenge housing discrimination); Gladstone Realtors v. Village of Belwood, 441 U.S. 91 (1979) (white living in neighborhood may sue over loss of integrated housing); Haven Reality Corp. v. Coleman, 455 U.S. 363 (1982) (testers who were victims of misreprentations were allowed to sue over claims of racial discrimination in housing rentals).

33. 422 U.S. 490 (1975).

34. 429 U.S. 252 (1977).

35. 392 U.S. 83 (1968).

36. 418 U.S. 166 (1974).

37. 418 U.S. 208 (1974).

38. 454 U.S. 464 (1982).

39. 426 U.S. (1976).

40. 468 U.S. 737 (1984).

41. 408 U.S. 1 (1972).

42. 414 U.S. 488 (1974).

43. 461 U.S. 95 (1983).

44. 475 U.S. 534 (1986).

45. 438 U.S. 59 (1978).

46. 397 U.S. 159 (1970).

47. 467 U.S. 340 (1984).

48. Citizens to Preserve Overton Park v. Volpe, 401 U.S. 402 (1971); Dunlop v. Bachowski, 421 U.S. 560 (1975).

49. 470 U.S. 821 (1985). Arguably, *Simon v. Eastern Kentucky Welfare Rights Organization* and *Allen v. Wright* can be seen as cases in which the basic claim was that

the government was not properly enforcing the law, which was the thrust of the *Chaney* action.

50. Califano v. Sanders, 430 U.S. 99 (1977).
51. 435 U.S. 519 (1978).
52. 463 U.S. 29 (1983).
53. 467 U.S. 837 (1984).
54. 396 U.S. 375 (1970).
55. 422 U.S. 66 (1975).
56. See Cannon v. University of Chicago, 441 U.S. 677 (1979).
57. 403 U.S. 388 (1971).
58. 438 U.S. 478 (1978).
59. Bush v. Lucas, 462 U.S. 367 (1983).
60. 436 U.S. 658 (1978).
61. 365 U.S. 167 (1961).
62. 448 U.S. 1 (1980).
63. 471 U.S. 261 (1985).
64. 401 U.S. 37 (1971).
65. 415 U.S. 452 (1974).
66. 430 U.S. 705 (1977).
67. 460 U.S. 462 (1983).
68. 407 U.S. 225 (1972).
69. U.S.C. § 2283.
70. 457 U.S. 496 (1982).
71. 415 U.S. 651 (1974).
72. 465 U.S. 89 (1984).
73. Supra note 58.
74. 457 U.S. 800 (1982).
75. 457 U.S. 731 (1982).
76. 472 U.S. 511 (1985).
77. 472 U.S. 424 (1985).
78. 445 U.S. 622 (1980).
79. 419 U.S. 393 (1975).
80. 445 U.S. 388 (1980).
81. 414 U.S. 538 (1974).
82. 452 U.S. 89 (1981).
83. 442 U.S. 682 (1979).
84. 472 U.S. 797 (1985).
85. 414 U.S. 291 (1973).
86. 417 U.S. 156 (1974).
87. 457 U.S. 147 (1982).
88. 432 U.S. 385 (1977).
89. Supra note 84.
90. 475 U.S. 717 (1986).
91. 396 U.S. 375 (1970).
92. 412 U.S. 1 (1973).
93. 437 U.S. 678 (1978).
94. 448 U.S. 122 (1980).
95. 446 U.S. 719 (1980).
96. 455 U.S. 445 (1982).
97. 461 U.S. 424 (1983).

98. 465 U.S. 886 (1984).

99. 478 U.S. 546 (1986).

100. 478 U.S. 310 (1986).

101. 421 U.S. 240 (1975).

102. 427 U.S. 1 (1976).

103. 437 U.S. 365 (1978).

104. 398 U.S. 144 (1970).

105. Anderson v. Liberty Lobby, Inc., 477 U.S. 242 (1986); Celotex Corp. v. Catrett, 477 U.S. 317 (1986).

106. 450 U.S. 346 (1981).

107. 473 U.S. 1 (1985).

108. 477 U.S. 21 (1986).

109. 418 U.S. 683 (1974).

110. 457 U.S. 741 (1982).

111. 420 U.S. 35 (1975).

112. 420 U.S. 136 (1975).

113. 433 U.S. 425 (1977).

114. Dames & Moore v. Regan, 453 U.S. 654 (1981).

115. Goldwater v. Carter, 444 U.S. 996 (1979).

116. 424 U.S. 1 (1976).

117. 462 U.S. 919 (1983).

118. Bowsher v. Synar, 478 U.S. 714 (1986).

119. 473 U.S. 568 (1985).

120. 478 U.S. 833 (1986).

121. 458 U.S. 50 (1982).

122. 426 U.S. 290 (1976).

123. 464 U.S. 238 (1984).

124. Pacific Gas & Elec. Co. v. State Energy Resources, Conservation & Dev. Comm'n, 461 U.S. 190 (1983).

125. 463 U.S. 1 (1983).

126. Shaw v. Delta Airlines Co., 463 U.S. 85 (1983).

127. 430 U.S. 519 (1977).

128. 465 U.S. 1 (1984).

129. See "Fifteen Years of the Burger Court," *The Nation*, Sept. 29, 1984, at 287.

130. Nixon v. Warner Communications, Inc., 435 U.S. 589 (1978).

131. 467 U.S. 20 (1984).

17

THE COURT AND STATE CONSTITUTIONAL LAW

STEWART G. POLLOCK

I

Sometimes, when you try to do one thing, even if you do not achieve your in-tended objective, something different, even better, happens. For example, Wil-helm Roentgen was experimenting with cathode rays in 1895. While working in a darkened closet, he unknowingly photographed a key inside a closed book. As a re-sult, he discovered the X ray.

Similarly, the Burger Court may have had other objectives in mind when it de-cided *Michigan v. Long*[1] and *United States v. Leon*.[2] The effect of those decisions, nevertheless, has been to stimulate a renaissance in state constitutional law.

The renaissance, it is true, has its detractors. Not everyone thinks that state con-stitutional law is a good thing. Indeed, if we were to judge state constitutional law by the number of law schools that list it in their course curriculum, we probably would conclude that it lacks academic respectability. That conclusion, however, would be both unfortunate and wrong.

Reasonable people can differ over the value and success of state constitutional law, but we should not ignore it. In a sense, moreover, state constitutional law has received the ultimate seal of academic approval. Respected scholars now debate with each other in law reviews about the importance and legitimacy of state constitutional law.[3]

The Burger Court invited state courts, sometimes considered country cousins in the federalist system, into the parlor. My undertaking is to discuss how the Burger Court affected state constitutional law. To illustrate that effect, I refer to the plain-statement requirement of *Michigan v. Long* and the good-faith exception to the ex-clusionary rule enunciated in *United States v. Leon*. I then discuss the state-court re-action to the good-faith exception and the counterreaction to that reaction. Finally, I hope to demonstrate that the state-constitutional-law movement is here to stay.

II

Let us start with some basic principles. The first principle concerns deference by the U.S. Supreme Court to state-court decisions based on adequate and independent state grounds. Since 1875, the Supreme Court has not reviewed state-court decisions based on such a ground.[4] But, what if a state court relied on both federal and state law in reaching its decision?

Until 1983, the Court used three approaches to determine whether a state court's holding that cited both federal and state law rested on an adequate and independent state ground. If the state court's decision cited both federal and state law, the U.S. Supreme Court would presume that the state court's decision rested on such a ground,[5] remand the case to the state court for clarification,[6] or undertake its own inquiry to determine whether the state court had used federal law as the basis for its decision or merely as a guide to interpreting state law.[7] These approaches deferred to state-court decisions either by presuming that the state court had based its decision on an adequate and independent state ground or by trying to ascertain whether the state court had used federal law as a guide.

In 1983, in *Michigan v. Long*, the Burger Court transformed that approach by requiring a state-court decision to include a "plain statement"[8] that the state court based its decision on such a ground. Justice O'Connor explained:

> We believe that [requiring state courts to make a plain statement] will provide state judges with a clearer opportunity to develop state jurisprudence unimpeded by federal interference, and yet will preserve the integrity of federal law.[9]

The Court held:

> [W]hen, as in this case, a state court decision fairly appears to rest primarily on federal law, or to be interwoven with federal law, and when the adequacy and independence of any possible state law ground is not clear from the face of the opinion, we will accept as the most reasonable explanation that the state court decided the case the way it did because it believed that federal law required it to do so.[10]

Now, unless the state-court decision includes a plain statement that the court has rested its decision on an adequate and independent state ground, the U.S. Supreme Court will assume no such ground exists when it fairly appears that the state-court decision rested primarily on federal law.[11]

The Burger Court intended its holding in *Michigan v. Long* to foster doctrinal consistency and to encourage the principles of federalism. Previously, the Court had acknowledged the power of state courts to interpret state law to afford their citizens greater protection than that required under the U.S. Constitution.[12] The Burger Court, however, wanted to ensure the accountability of state courts that granted criminal defendants greater constitutional protection than the Constitution required.

Some critics view the plain-statement requirement as an attempt to prevent state courts from exceeding federal courts in the protection of fundamental rights.[13] Others think it merely holds state courts directly accountable for their decisions, thereby preventing them from hiding beneath the robes of the Supreme Court.[14]

One consequence of the decision has been to wean state courts from relying on decisions of the Supreme Court and to encourage them to rely on state law. Thus, *Michigan v. Long* created an opening for state courts to strengthen their position in the federalist system. As in a chess game, however, lurking beneath an apparent opportunity to improve one's position may be hidden dangers.

This essay cannot analyze in detail the total impact of the Burger Court on state constitutional law. Consequently, it makes only passing reference to opinions such as *Pruneyard Shopping Center v. Robins*.[15] In that case, the Burger Court recognized that the California Supreme Court, relying on that state's constitution, could authorize pamphleteers to distribute literature and solicit signatures in shopping centers, although those activities contravened U.S. Supreme Court precedent interpreting the federal Constitution.[16] Similarly, state courts from New Jersey[17] to California[18] have ordered the continuation of medical assistance for indigent pregnant women, notwithstanding the decision of the Supreme Court in *Harris v. McRae*.[19] In that decision, the Court upheld the constitutionality of the Hyde Amendment, which prohibited the use of Medicaid funds for abortion except when carrying the fetus to term would endanger the mother's life or when the pregnancy resulted from rape or incest.[20] Instead, this essay focuses on the effect of the Burger Court on state-court criminal procedure. To illustrate the effect, it limits itself to one example, the good-faith exception to the exclusionary rule.

III

To appreciate the impact of the Burger Court on state constitutional law, including the effect of the good-faith exception, it may help to consider the conflicting views of Chief Justice Warren E. Burger and Justice William J. Brennan. Both Chief Justice Burger and Justice Brennan appreciated the importance of state courts in the development of constitutional law. Their perspectives, however, were quite different.

This may be oversimplifying, but we can consider Chief Justice Burger an advocate for law and order and Justice Brennan a champion of fundamental rights. In suggesting those roles for two such distinguished jurists, no disrespect is intended to either. In his own way, each honored both values. Understanding the difference in their viewpoints concerning the tension between fundamental rights and vigorous law enforcement, however, is critical to understanding the effect of the Burger Court on criminal procedure.

To help to describe that effect, envision a chess game between two contending factions on the Court, each represented by its champion. Chief Justice Burger sits at one side of the table. On the opposite side is Justice Brennan. Each brings a different judicial history and perspective to the game.

After serving in the U.S. Department of Justice, the Chief Justice joined the U.S. Court of Appeals for the District of Columbia. Justice Brennan's judicial career was in the state-court system. Following his initial appointment as a trial judge in the New Jersey Superior Court, he moved rapidly to the Appellate Division, the New Jersey Supreme Court, and finally to the Supreme Court of the United States.

The chessboard differs from the ones with which we are familiar. Instead of the normal sixty-four squares, it contains fifty squares—one for each state. At first glance, the pieces look like others, but once the game begins, the pieces sometimes move under their own power, without help from either player.

Surrounding the players are a circle of highly informed and articulate spectators, but even they differ from ordinary observers. They maintain a dialogue with the players, commenting on their moves, telling them where they went wrong, and what to do. In other circumstances, we might call them kibitzers. Here, we call them law professors.

The independent and unpredictable chess pieces—as you probably have discerned—are state courts.

To complete the setting and the metaphor, the players are seated in front of a rich tapestry, depicting the history of fundamental rights in the United States. At the far left of the tapestry is a scene depicting Peter Zenger, whose trial in 1735 gave rise to the freedom of the press under the law of the colony of New York. In the middle, the tapestry depicts heros and heroines in the movement to protect fundamental rights, such as Rosa Parks and Oliver Brown.[21] It also depicts such less admirable, but notable figures as Clarence Earl Gideon,[22] Ernesto Miranda,[23] and Dollree Mapp.[24] To their right are other litigants in significant cases, such as David Long[25] and even Alberto Leon.[26] To the far right is a blank screen waiting to be woven. Only imagination limits the richness and detail of the tapestry.

As the tapestry depicts, even before the adoption of the U.S. Constitution, states relied on their own law to protect their citizens' fundamental rights. Indeed, state constitutions provided the model for the federal Bill of Rights. Initially, the incorporation of much of the federal Bill of Rights through the Due Process Clause of the Fourteenth Amendment diminished the importance of state constitutional protections. Before the incorporation of federal constitutional rights, the Bill of Rights did not protect against state action. Thus, citizens frequently relied on state constitutional law to protect their individual rights.[27]

In the 1960s, under the Warren Court, the federal Constitution replaced state constitutions as the primary source of protection of individual rights.[28] Federal constitutional law dominated the protection of fundamental rights, and state constitutions faded into the background of the tapestry.[29]

Shortly after Warren Burger replaced Earl Warren as the Chief Justice of the United States, the Supreme Court began to retreat from the more liberal holdings of the Warren Court. Justice Brennan expressed his opposition to the Burger Court's opinions in dissents, speeches, and law review articles. Justice Brennan's article in the *Harvard Law Review,* advocating state constitutions as separate sources of individual liberties, created a significant opening in the chess game.[30]

At the urging of Justice Brennan, many state courts expanded state constitutional law to provide their citizens with greater protection than the U.S. Supreme Court provided under the federal Constitution. Some call it the "New Federalism."[31] The game took on a new dimension. This essay returns to the metaphor in explaining the effect of the Burger Court on state constitutional law, particularly the protection of the rights of criminal defendants.

IV

One of the best examples of the New Federalism is the rejection by some state courts of the good-faith exception to the exclusionary rule. In pointing out that many states have rejected *Leon*,[32] I do not overlook the fact that many other states, after due consideration, have accepted it.[33] Simply stated, the exclusionary rule prohibits a prosecutor from introducing evidence seized in violation of the Fourth Amendment in its case-in-chief against a criminal defendant.

The Supreme Court first adopted the exclusionary rule in *Weeks v. United States*,[34] in which it characterized the rule as a constitutional right.[35] Initially, the federal rule applied to criminal trials only in federal courts. In *Mapp v. Ohio*,[36] the Warren Court required state courts to apply the exclusionary rule in state prosecutions. The Court held that "all evidence obtained by searches and seizures in violation of the Constitution is, by that same authority, inadmissible in a state court."[37]

During the 1970s and early 1980s, scholars discussed whether the Supreme Court should adopt a good-faith exception to the exclusionary rule.[38] Chief Justice Burger believed that rigid adherence to the rule under all circumstances was irrational.[39] In 1984 that belief became law in *United States v. Leon*.[40]

In *Leon*, the District Court for the Central District of California granted a motion to suppress the seizure of drugs from Leon's residence.[41] Burbank police officers had seized the drugs pursuant to a facially valid search warrant issued by a California Superior Court judge.[42] The affidavits supporting the warrant, however, did not establish probable cause.[43] The Ninth Circuit affirmed.[44]

In reversing the judgment of the Ninth Circuit, the Burger Court held that the exclusionary rule should not bar the use in the prosecution's case-in-chief of evidence obtained by officers acting in reasonable reliance on a search warrant ultimately found to be invalid.[45] The Court reached this conclusion after balancing the "substantial social costs"[46] of the exclusionary rule against its "marginal to nonexistent"[47] deterrent effect on police officers who reasonably and in good faith rely on a subsequently invalidated search warrant.[48] The Court noted that the exclusionary rule was a judicially created remedy, not a constitutional right.[49] Even on the U.S. Supreme Court, *Leon* was a controversial decision.

In a strongly worded dissent, Justice Brennan referred to "the Court's gradual but determined strangulation of the [exclusionary] rule."[50] He continued, "[I]t now appears that the Court's victory over the Fourth Amendment is complete."[51] Justice Brennan disagreed with the Court's characterization of the exclusionary rule as a remedy, not a right.[52] He also disagreed that the sole purpose of the rule was to discourage individual police misconduct.[53] According to Justice Brennan, the majority overstated the societal cost of the rule and understated its benefits.[54] Finally, he warned of a "host of grave consequences," including judicial inattention resulting from the insulation of magistrates from the consequences of their decisions and the encouragement of police to provide only the bare minimum information to support the issuance of search warrants.[55] Many of the kibitzers agreed with Justice Brennan's criticism of the majority opinion.[56]

V

After *Leon*, the play shifted to state courts. The chess pieces started to move by themselves. Many state courts have rejected, in whole or in part, the good-faith exception. These courts hold that their state law, either statutory or constitutional, affords greater protection against unreasonable searches and seizures than the Fourth Amendment.

Nine state courts have held that their state constitutions forbid recognition of a good-faith exception.[57] The New York Court of Appeals was the first state court of last resort to reject the exception. In *People v. Bigelow*,[58] it rejected the notion that a good-faith exception would have little or no effect on future police misconduct. The court held that to allow the prosecution to use illegally seized evidence against a criminal defendant would frustrate the rule's purpose by "creating a positive incentive . . . to others to engage in similar lawless acts in the future."[59]

Two years later, in *State v. Novembrino*,[60] the New Jersey Supreme Court also rejected the good-faith exception, finding intolerable tension between the exception and the guarantee of the New Jersey Constitution that search warrants "shall not issue except upon probable cause."[61] The Court reasoned that adoption of the "good-faith exception [would] ultimately reduce respect for and compliance with the probable cause standard."[62]

Similarly, the New Hampshire Supreme Court recently held that the good-faith exception violated the New Hampshire Constitution.[63] The court reasoned that deterrence of police misconduct, although the main purpose of the rule, is not the only purpose. The rule also protects a citizen's right to privacy and ensures police compliance with the requirement of probable cause.[64] Consequently, the New Hampshire Court viewed the exclusionary rule "as a logical and necessary corollary to achieve the purposes for which prohibitions against unreasonable searches and seizures were constitutionalized."[65]

The Vermont Supreme Court, picking up on Justice Brennan's rejection of *Leon*'s cost-benefit analysis, also rejected the good-faith exception.[66] By comparison, the New Mexico Supreme Court focused not on deterrence or judicial integrity but on the effectuation of the constitutional right of an accused under the New Mexico Constitution to be free from an unreasonable search and seizure.[67] In rejecting *Leon*, the Pennsylvania Supreme Court relied on the right of privacy under the Pennsylvania Constitution.[68] The Idaho Supreme Court found that the federal good-faith exception was incompatible with the purposes of the exclusionary rule under the Idaho Constitution.[69] The Wisconsin courts reached a similar result under the Wisconsin Constitution.[70]

Six states have rejected the good-faith exception because of its incompatibility with state statutes.[71] For example, the North Carolina Supreme Court, without reaching the state constitution, relied on that state's statutorily created exclusionary rule to exclude physically seized evidence.[72] Thus, the court refused to recognize a good-faith exception to its statutorily created exclusionary rule.[73] The supreme courts of Georgia,[74] Massachusetts,[75] and Delaware[76] have reached similar results.

Although the Iowa Supreme Court recognizes the good-faith exception under the Iowa Constitution, it refused to apply the exception when police officers seized evidence under a warrant issued in violation of statutory law.[77] Likewise, Texas and Illinois have modified *Leon*'s good-faith exception. Texas, for example, requires a finding of probable cause before permitting admission of illegally seized evidence under a good-faith exception.[78] The Texas approach differs from that of the U.S. Supreme Court, which permits admission of illegally seized evidence if the officer reasonably believed in the existence of probable cause. Although Illinois adopted the good-faith exception as described in *Leon*, the Illinois courts have rejected subsequent expansions of the exception.[79]

Ordinarily, a state court of last resort has the final word on interpreting a state constitution, subject always to the power of the people to adopt a constitutional amendment. Similarly, a judicial interpretation of a state statute generally enjoys finality, subject to the legislature's power to amend the statute. State courts and legislatures work more closely than their federal counterparts to the ultimate source of power in a democracy, the people.[80] Through a constitutional amendment, voters can override a judicial interpretation of a state constitution. No one understood that possibility better than Chief Justice Burger.

In 1982, the voters of both California[81] and Florida amended their respective state constitutions to ensure that the state judiciaries did not exclude evidence that was admissible under federal law. In Florida, for example, voters adopted a constitutional amendment requiring the Florida courts to construe Florida law "in conformity with the Fourth Amendment to the United States Constitution as interpreted by the United States Supreme Court."[82]

In a concurring opinion in *Florida v. Casal*,[83] written the following year, Chief Justice Burger endorsed the reaction of the Florida voters. He wrote:

> With our dual system of state and federal laws, administered by parallel state and federal courts, different standards may arise in different areas. But when state courts interpret state law to require more than the Federal Constitution requires, the citizens of the state must be aware that they have the power to amend state law to ensure rational law enforcement. The people of Florida have now done so with respect to Art. I, Sec. 12 of the State Constitution. . . .[84]

The Chief Justice's concurring opinion sheds light on his evaluation of the priorities of federalism, law and order, and fundamental rights. The opinion countered Justice Brennan's call for state courts to circumvent decisions of the U.S. Supreme Court by relying on their state constitutions.

State legislatures and voters have counteracted state-court decisions providing expanded protection for criminal defendants. In New Jersey, the New Jersey Supreme Court held that the New Jersey Constitution prohibited the imposition of a death sentence when a defendant has been convicted of causing only serious bodily injury resulting in death, as opposed to purposely and knowingly causing death.[85] Several years later, the voters approved a constitutional amendment explicitly permitting imposition of the death penalty "on a person convicted of purposely and knowingly causing death or purposely and knowingly causing serious bodily injury resulting in death."[86] Similarly, the New Jersey Legislature has passed legislation limiting the state supreme court's proportionality review in death penalty cases "to a comparison of similar cases in which a sentence of death has been imposed" rather than to all cases in which the death penalty could have been imposed.[87]

A sympathetic reading of *Michigan v. Long* is that the opinion merely instructs state courts that they may insulate their opinions from Supreme Court review by stating that the courts were relying exclusively on state law. Such a reading would go no further than identifying the Court's view of the role of state courts in the federal system.

Some fear that through decisions such as *Michigan v. Long* and *Leon*, however, the U.S. Supreme Court hopes to prevent state courts from heeding Justice Brennan's call to grant expanded protection of fundamental rights under state constitutions. Chief Justice Burger's concurrence in *Casal* fed that fear.[88] That concurrence reflects not so much an endorsement of the role of state courts in the federal system as one of law and order over fundamental rights.

Leon is discussed not to persuade the reader that the U.S. Supreme Court was right or wrong in that decision but to show how that decision produced a reaction from state courts and how that state-court reaction then precipitated a counterreaction—much like the moves in chess games. Even so constrained, however, the issue extrapolates to fundamental concerns about federalism and state courts, concerns about the design of the chessboard, and the rules of the game.

Reaction to those concerns will vary depending on numerous considerations, including views of the federalist system, the role of state courts in a constitutional democracy, and the relative roles of law and order and fundamental rights at the close of the twentieth century.

Those considerations lead to further questions about the extent to which fifty independent state-court systems can substitute for the federal courts in the protection of fundamental rights. Other questions concern the "common ideal of American constitutionalism"[89] and the role of state courts in giving voice to "the values and principles of the national community."[90] State courts may have different perceptions from those of the U.S. Supreme Court on fundamental values and rights. It is entirely proper for state court opinions to reflect those perceptions. The U.S. Supreme Court, which necessarily addresses the needs of a nation, may take a minimalist approach to protecting fundamental rights. A state supreme court, concerned about only an individual state, may perceive the need for greater protection. In relying on the state constitution as the source of that protection, a state supreme court does not insult the U.S. Supreme Court. Instead, the state court honors its role as a player in the federalist system.

VI

Decisions of the Supreme Court, including those that restrict the protection of fundamental rights, can become self-fulfilling prophecies. Lawyers, judges, and the public, even when they disagree with the Court's decisions, profoundly respect the Court as an institution. Decisions of the Supreme Court not only reflect the tensions of the time, but they guide others in determining how to resolve those tensions. Even if the Court is perceived as infallible only because it is final,[91] the perception of infallibility, or something close to it, survives. As a practical matter, a state court that reaches a decision on a state ground contrary to a decision of the U.S. Supreme Court on a parallel federal ground must justify its decision to the legal community and to the public. In an era of constant public concern about crime, a state court's justification for granting enhanced protection to the rights of criminal defendants better be persuasive. Ultimately, judicial action, like legislative or executive action, depends on public acceptance.

In the third quarter of this century, the Warren Court sought to inspire confidence in the criminal justice system by protecting the constitutional rights of criminal defendants. Marking the last quarter has been increased public concern about violent crime. For some, however, emphasis of that concern has undermined confidence in the system. The predicament is in striking the appropriate balance among respecting a defendant's constitutional rights, protecting public safety, and preserving confidence in the criminal justice system.

As the moves and countermoves of Chief Justice Burger and Justice Brennan demonstrate, courts possess latitude in construing constitutional rights. Like federal courts, state courts may respond to the perceived needs of the time. Both the perception of those needs and the appropriate judicial response to them, however, may differ in state courts.

Still, the federal system and public opinion can cause state courts to reflect before disagreeing with the U.S. Supreme Court. Reflection need not stop the process; it can lead to decisions that are more principled and useful.[92]

In a constitutional democracy, the majority has access to the other two branches of government at both the state and federal levels. Courts, therefore, bear the unique responsibility of protecting the constitutional rights of the minority from the majority. Decisions such as *Leon* raise the question whether state courts bear a special responsibility to protect the rights of society's outcasts, including criminal defendants.

VII

A recent study suggests that state supreme courts may be reluctant dragons. The study concludes that state courts continue to rely on federal law and are slow to develop state constitutional law. In an article in *Judicature*, the publication of the American Judicature Society, entitled *State Supreme Court Commitment to State Law*,[93] Professor Michael Esler estimates that state supreme courts based their decisions primarily on state grounds in only 22 percent of their cases.[94] In addition, in 98 percent of the decisions based on state law, the state supreme courts deferred to precedents of the U.S. Supreme Court.[95]

Professor Esler points to a number of political, legal, and institutional theories to explain the reluctance of state supreme courts to expand state constitutional doctrines, especially in the area of criminal procedure. First, powerful organizations often support police and other law enforcement officials in favoring vigorous law enforcement over protection of the rights of criminal defendants.[96] Second, electoral pressures and the proximity of state court judges to their constituents sensitize those judges to public opinion, which is generally unsympathetic to the rights of the accused.[97] This is especially so in states in which judges must run for election or retention.[98]

Because state law may expand, but not contract protection under federal law, some perceive that state supreme courts base their decisions on state law solely to effect more liberal results.[99] *Michigan v. Long*'s plain-statement requirement has made state courts more accountable for decisions that expand the rights of criminal defendants.[100] The requirement reminds state court judges that if their decisions stray too far from prevailing public opinion, the voters may reject those decisions or restrict them by amending their state constitutions.[101]

Third, Professor Esler suggests that practical considerations impede state court activism. The incorporation of federal guarantees against the states led states to rely on those guarantees.[102] In addition, many state judges may be unwilling to devote the time and resources necessary to develop state law.[103] Finally, records of state constitutional proceedings may be difficult to find or nonexistent, thereby impeding the ability of state courts to ascertain the intent of the framers of the state constitution.[104]

Interestingly, however, during the hearings on his confirmation as Chief Justice to succeed Warren Burger, William H. Rehnquist acknowledged the independence of state supreme courts:

> I do not think the [United States Supreme Court] is necessarily the final arbiter of the law of the land. It is the final arbiter of the U.S. Constitution and of the meaning of Federal statutes and treaties. But we still live in a somewhat pluralistic society where the States' highest courts are the final arbiters of the meaning of their State constitutions.[105]

In *Arizona v. Evans*,[106] the U.S. Supreme Court recently reassessed the impact of *Michigan v. Long*. The case arose from the arrest of Isaac Evans on charges of illegal possession of marijuana. A Phoenix police officer stopped Evans after he observed him driving the wrong way down a one-way street. When asked to present his driver's license, Evans told the officer that his license had been suspended. A computer inquiry, taken via a terminal in the officer's car, confirmed that Evans's license was suspended. The inquiry also indicated an outstanding misdemeanor warrant for Evans's arrest. Consequently, the officer placed Evans under arrest. While being handcuffed, Evans dropped a hand-rolled cigarette that smelled like marijuana. A search of Evans's automobile revealed a bag of marijuana under the passenger's seat. The trial court subsequently learned that the previous warrant for Evans's arrest had been quashed, but due to a court clerk's error, the information remained in the computer system.

Evans argued that the marijuana should be suppressed as "the fruit of an unlawful arrest."[107] He further argued that the good-faith exception to the exclusionary rule did not apply because police error, not judicial error, caused the invalid arrest.

The trial court granted the motion to suppress. A divided panel of the Arizona Court of Appeals reversed, holding that "the purpose of the exclusionary rule would not be served by excluding the evidence obtained."[108] The Arizona Supreme Court reversed. Rejecting any distinction between clerical errors made by law enforcement personnel or by court employees, the Arizona Supreme Court sustained the exclusion of the evidence.[109] The Court stated that exclusion would "hopefully serve to improve the efficiency of those who keep records in our criminal justice system[,]" as well as deter future police misconduct.[110] The U.S. Supreme Court reversed, holding that the exclusionary rule did not apply when an unlawful arrest was made pursuant to clerical errors of court employees.[111]

Despite dissents from Justices Ginsburg and Stevens calling for the overruling of *Michigan v. Long*,[112] the Court applied the plain-statement requirement to determine whether the Arizona Supreme Court's decision rested on adequate and independent state grounds. Speaking for the Court, Chief Justice Rehnquist affirmed the Court's commitment to *Michigan v. Long*, stating that under that decision, "state courts are absolutely free to interpret state constitutional provisions to accord greater protection to individual rights than do similar provisions of the United States Constitution."[113] Thus, the Rehnquist Court, like the Burger Court, believes that state supreme courts should be the final arbiters of their state constitutions, but that those courts must be accountable for their decisions. Accordingly, the Rehnquist Court believes that the plain-statement rule will ensure "that state courts will not be the final arbiters of important issues under the federal constitution; and that [the United States Supreme Court] will not encroach on the constitutional jurisdiction of the states."[114]

VIII

Chief Justice Burger and Justice Brennan have retired from the Court and left our imaginary chess game. Will the chess pieces, the individual state courts, continue the game on their own? Some scholars, pointing to a lack of doctrinal consistency in state-court opinions, have concluded that state constitutional law is a failure, a conclusion that suggests the game should end.[115]

Other scholars and courts believe the game should continue. They defend state constitutionalism as "a process of giving voice to the state court's understanding of the values and principles of the national community."[116] Still others legitimize state constitutional law by relying on objective factors to justify a deviation from U.S. Supreme Court opinions interpreting federal law.[117] Admittedly, the consistent application of established principles would make the game more predictable and inspire greater confidence in its ultimate outcome. Judicial federalism, like federalism generally, however, is not as tidy as one might wish. The logic of applied federalism is less coherent than that of a chess game.

For the foreseeable future, state courts relying on state law occasionally may disagree with results reached by the U.S. Supreme Court under federal law. One recent commentary argues that the New Federalism has led to a "tidal wave of state court opinions that diverge from the standards established under the federal constitution."[118] The article points out that many state courts in a variety of situations have rejected federal Fourth Amendment analysis in favor of more protective state constitutional standards. In New Jersey, moreover, the protection extends beyond search and seizure to other areas of constitutional law. For example, the New Jersey Supreme Court has granted greater protection not only to privacy rights in curbside garbage[119] and telephone toll-billing records[120] but also to the privilege against self-incrimination[121] and the right to counsel.[122]

Although Chief Justice Burger and Justice Brennan have left the scene, the chess pieces and the kibitzers remain. The game continues. To this extent, we have yet to see the final effect of the Burger Court on state constitutional law. Notwithstanding its blemishes, state constitutional law plays a vital role in the federalist system. Without the Burger Court, state constitutional law may not have come so far so fast. The next moves are up to the state courts and the kibitzers.

Notes

1. 463 U.S. 1032 (1983).
2. 468 U.S. 897 (1984).
3. Compare Brennan, "State Constitutions and the Protection of the Individual," 90 *Harv. L. Rev.* 489 (1977) (arguing that state courts should expand on the individual liberties protected by the federal Constitution through interpretation of state constitutions); Kahn, "Interpretation and Authority in State Constitutionalism," 106 *Harv. L. Rev.* 1147 (1993) (advocating vigorous state constitutionalism); Kauger, "Reflections on Federalism: Protections Afforded by State Constitutions," 27 *Gonz. L. Rev.* 1 (1991) (arguing that state courts should remain the primary guardians of civil liberties and equal rights); Pollock, "State Constitutions as Separate Sources of Fundamental Rights," 35 *Rutgers L. Rev.* 707, 722 (1983) (urging state courts to develop a principled theory for reliance on state constitutional law); Utter, "State Constitutional Law, the United States Supreme Court, and Democratic Accountability: Is There a Crocodile in the Bathtub," 64 *Wash. L. Rev.* 19 (1989) (arguing that because state courts are less insulated from public opinion, state court opinions have greater democratic legitimacy than U.S. Supreme Court opinions); Williams, "In the Supreme Court's Shadow: Legitimacy of State Rejection of Supreme Court Reasoning and Result," 35 *S.C. L. Rev.* 353 (1984) (recognizing the legitimacy of state constitutional law) with Diehm, "New Federalism and Constitutional Criminal Procedure: Are We Repeating the Mistakes of the Past," 55 *Md. L. Rev.* 223, 234–37 (1996) (suggesting that New Federalism may lead to incoherent and inconsistent body of law); Gardner, "The Failed Discourse of State Constitutionalism," 90 *Mich. L. Rev.* 761 (1992) (arguing that state constitutional law has failed to produce a coherent and intelligible body of law).
4. See Murdock v. City of Memphis, 87 U.S. (20 Wall.) 590, 636 (1875) (holding Congress only conferred jurisdiction on the Supreme Court to decide questions of federal law and, consequently, if a state court's opinion rested on at least one independent state ground, alone sufficient to decide the case, the Supreme Court would affirm the decision "without inquiring into the soundness of the decision on such other matter or issue"); see also Jourdan, "Tennessee Judicial Activism: Renaissance of Federalism," 49 *Tenn. L. Rev.* 135, 136–40 (1981) (providing a brief historical perspective and legal basis for the doctrine of adequate and independent state grounds).
5. See, e.g., Lynch v. New York *ex rel.* Pierson, 293 U.S. 52 (1934); Eustis v. Bolles, 150 U.S. 361 (1893); Klinger v. Missouri, 80 U.S. 257 (1871).
6. See, e.g., California v. Krivda, 409 U.S. 33 (1972); Herb v. Pitcairn, 324 U.S. 117 (1945); Minnesota v. National Tea Co., 309 U.S. 551 (1940).
7. See, e.g., Texas v. Brown, 460 U.S. 730 (1983); Oregon v. Kennedy, 456 U.S. 667 (1982); Johnson v. Risk, 137 U.S. 300 (1890).
8. 463 U.S. at 1041. Specifically, the Court held:

> If a state court chooses merely to rely on federal precedents as it would on the precedents of all other jurisdictions, then it need only make clear by a plain statement in its judgment or opinion that the federal cases are being used only for the purpose of guidance, and do not themselves compel the result that the court has reached. Id.

9. Id. at 1041.

10. Id. at 1040–41.

11. Id. at 1042.

12. See, e.g., Mills v. Rogers, 457 U.S. 291 (1982) (holding that the substantive rights provided by the federal Constitution define only a minimum and that state law may recognize liberty interests more extensive than those independently protected by the federal Constitution); Pruneyard Shopping Center v. Robins, 447 U.S. 74 (1980) (holding that states were free to provide in their own constitutions greater individual liberties than those recognized under the federal Constitution).

13. See, e.g., Gormley, "Ten Adventures in State Constitutional Law," *Emerging Issues St. Const. L.* 29, 37 (1988) (suggesting that the U.S. Supreme Court's decision in *Long* was an attempt to expand Supreme Court review "over potentially unpalatable state constitutional decisions").

14. See, e.g., Esler, "State Supreme Court Commitment to State Law," 78 *Judicature* 25, 30 (1994), discussed more fully infra notes 80–91 and accompanying text.

15. 447 U.S. 74 (1980).

16. Id. at 88.

17. See Right to Choose v. Byrne, 450 A.2d 925 (N.J. 1982).

18. See Committee to Defend Reprod. Rights v. Myers, 625 P.2d 779 (Cal. 1981).

19. 448 U.S. 297 (1980). For an expanded discussion of state-court rejection of the Supreme Court's reasoning in *Harris v. McRae*, see Williams, supra note 3, at 362–74.

20. Id. at 326.

21. See Brown v. Board of Educ., 347 U.S. 483 (1954).

22. See Gideon v. Wainright, 372 U.S. 335 (1963).

23. See Miranda v. Arizona, 384 U.S. 436 (1966).

24. See Mapp v. Ohio, 367 U.S. 643 (1961).

25. See Michigan v. Long, 463 U.S. 1032 (1983).

26. See United States v. Leon, 468 U.S. 897 (1984).

27. See Utter, supra note 3, at 28–29 (discussing state courts' traditional role as the primary protectors of individual rights).

28. Id. at 29.

29. Id. at 29–30; see also Diehm, supra note 3, at 234–37.

30. See generally Brennan, supra note 3.

31. See, e.g., Utter, supra note 3, at 29 & n. 66; see also Diehm, supra note 3, at 224.

32. See infra notes 57–79 and accompanying text.

33. See, e.g., People v. Hellis, 536 N.W.2d 587, 594 (Mich. Ct. App. 1995) (holding that the language and history of article I, section 11, of the Michigan Constitution provides no justification for rejecting a good-faith exception to the exclusionary rule, as enunciated in *Leon*); Ex parte Morgan, 641 So. 2d 840, 843 (Ala. 1994) (applying good-faith exception to exclusionary rule, as enunciated in *Leon*, to permit inclusion of illegally seized evidence); State v. Dillon, 1994 WL 510444, at *2–*3 (Tenn. Crim. App. Sept. 19, 1994) (permitting admission of evidence seized pursuant to officer's good-faith reliance on a subsequently invalidated search warrant).

34. 232 U.S. 383 (1914).

35. The Court held that letters seized from a defendant in violation of the Fourth Amendment could not be used against him at trial. Id. at 398. The Court reasoned:

> If letters and private documents can thus be seized and held and used in evidence against a citizen accused of an offense, the protection of the 4th Amendment, declaring his right to be secure against such searches and seizures, is of no value, and,

so far as those thus placed are concerned, might as well be stricken from the Constitution.

Id. at 393. See also Morrissey, "State Courts Reject *Leon* on State Constitutional Grounds: A Defense of Reactive Rulings," 47 *Vand. L. Rev.* 917, 924 (1994).

36. 367 U.S. 643 (1961).

37. Id. at 655.

38. See, e.g., Ball, "Good Faith and the Fourth Amendment: The 'Reasonable' Exception to the Exclusionary Rule," 69 *J. Crim. L. & Criminology* 635 (1978) (discussing whether a good-faith exception to the exclusionary rule is supported by "historical and decisional antecedents" and assessing the potential effect of a good-faith exception on the interpretation of Fourth Amendment rights); Bernardi, "The Exclusionary Rule: Is a Good Faith Standard Needed to Preserve a Liberal Interpretation of the Fourth Amendment?," 30 *DePaul L. Rev.* 51 (1980) (urging the adoption of a good-faith exception to the exclusionary rule and rejecting criticisms of the exception); Robertson, "Reason and the Fourth Amendment—The Burger Court and the Exclusionary Rule," 46 *Fordham L. Rev.* 139 (1977) (analyzing the development of the exclusionary rule under the Burger Court and setting forth several possible avenues the Burger Court might take to further limit the scope of the exclusionary rule, including the adoption of a good-faith exception).

39. In his dissent in Bivens v. Six Unknown Named Agents of Fed. Bureau of Narcotics, 403 U.S. 388 (1971), Chief Justice Burger stated:

> I submit that society has at least as much right to expect rationally graded responses from judges in place of the universal "capital punishment" we inflict on all evidence when police error is shown in its acquisition. Yet for over 55 years, and with increasing scope and intensity . . . our legal system has treated vastly dissimilar cases as if they were the same. Our adherence to the exclusionary rule, our resistance to change, and our refusal even to acknowledge the need for effective enforcement mechanisms bring to mind Holmes' well-known statement: "It is revolting to have no better reason for a rule of law than that so it was laid down in the time of Henry IV. It is still more revolting if the grounds upon which it was laid down have vanished long since, and the rule simply persists from blind imitation of the past."

Id. at 419–20 (Burger, C.J., dissenting) (quoting Holmes, "The Path of the Law," 10 *Harv. L. Rev.* 457, 469 (1897)).

40. 468 U.S. 897 (1987).

41. Id. at 903.

42. Id. at 902.

43. Id. at 904.

44. Id.

45. Id. at 913.

46. Id. at 907.

47. Id. at 922.

48. Id.

49. Id. at 906.

50. Id. at 928–29 (Brennan, J., dissenting).

51. Id. at 929.

52. Id. at 938–39 (arguing that "the exclusion of illegally obtained evidence was compelled not by judicially fashioned remedial purposes, but rather by a direct constitutional command").

53. Id. at 953–54. Justice Brennan argued:

The flaw in the [majority's] argument . . . is that its logic captures only one comparatively minor element of the generally acknowledged deterrent purposes of the exclusionary rule. To be sure, the rule operates to some extent to deter future misconduct by individual officers who have evidence suppressed in their own cases. But what the Court overlooks is that the deterrence rationale for the rule is not designed to be, nor should it be thought of as, a form of "punishment" of individual police officers for their failures to obey the restraints imposed by the Fourth Amendment. Instead, the chief deterrent function of the rule is its tendency to promote institutional compliance with the Fourth Amendment requirements on the part of law enforcement agencies generally.

Id.

54. Id. at 949–55 (arguing that the Court's assessment of the "costs" of the exclusionary rule has generally been exaggerated and that the Court failed to recognize the institutional effect the exclusionary rule has had on law enforcement training and procedures).

55. Id. at 956–58.

56. See, e.g., Kamisar, "The 'Police Practice' Phases of the Criminal Process and the Three Phases of the Burger Court," in *The Burger Years, Rights and Wrongs in the Supreme Court 1969–1986*, 143, 161 (Herman Schwartz ed., 1987). Professor Kamisar disagreed with the Burger Court's decision to undertake a cost-benefit analysis when determining whether to apply the exclusionary rule. Id. He believed that proper application of the exclusionary rule should not rest on the empirical proposition that it deters police misconduct. Id. Professor Kamisar argued, rather, that application of the exclusionary rule should rest on a "principled basis," as set forth in earlier Supreme Court decisions. He explained:

[The principled basis for the exclusionary rule in earlier Supreme Court decisions] was to avoid "sanctioning" or "ratifying" the unconstitutional police conduct that produced the proffered evidence, to keep the judicial process from being contaminated by partnership in police misconduct, to prevent the government whose agents violated the Constitution from being in any better position than the government whose agents obeyed it, and ultimately, to assure the police and the public alike that the Court took constitutional rights seriously.

Id. See also Morrissey, supra note 35, at 919 (asserting that "a number of compelling reasons militate in favor of state court rejection of *Leon*," and urging more state courts to reject *Leon's* good-faith exception).

57. See infra notes 58 through 70 and accompanying text; see also State v. Marsala, 579 A.2d 58 (Conn. 1990).

58. 488 N.E.2d 451 (N.Y. 1985).

59. Id. at 458.

60. 519 A.2d 820 (N.J. 1987).

61. Id. at 854 (citing N.J. Const. art. I, ¶ 7).

62. Id.

63. See State v. Canelo, 653 A.2d 1097 (N.H. 1995).

64. Id. at 1105.

65. Id.

66. See State v. Oakes, 598 A.2d 119 (Vt. 1991).

67. See State v. Gutierrez, 863 P.2d 1052 (N.M. 1993).

68. See Commonwealth v. Edmunds, 586 A.2d 887 (Pa. 1991).

69. See State v. Guzman, 842 P.2d 660 (Idaho 1992).

70. See State v. Grawien, 367 N.W.2d 816 (Wis. Ct. App.), pet. denied, 362 N.W.2d 428 (Wis. 1985).

71. See infra notes 72 through 79.

72. See State v. Carter, 370 S.E.2d 553 (N.C. 1988) (interpreting N.C. Gen. Stat. § 15A-974).

73. Id. at 562.

74. See Gary v. State, 422 S.E.2d 426 (Ga. 1992) (interpreting Ga. Code Ann. § 17-5-30).

75. See Commonwealth v. Upton, 476 N.E.2d 548 (Mass. 1985) (interpreting Mass. Gen. L. ch. 276 §§ 1, 2A, 2B).

76. See Mason v. State, 534 A.2d 242 (Del. 1987) (interpreting Del. Code Ann. tit. 11, § 2308).

77. See State v. Beckett, 532 N.W.2d 751 (Iowa 1995) (interpreting Iowa Code § 808.3).

78. See Davis v. State, 831 S.W.2d 426 (Tex. Ct. App. 1992) (interpreting Tex. Code Crim. Proc. Ann. art. 38.23 (Supp. 1992)), *pet. discretionary review refused.*

79. See People v. McGee, 644 N.E.2d 439 (Ill. App. Ct. 1994) (rejecting the U.S. Supreme Court's expansion of the good-faith exception as enunciated in Illinois v. Krull, 480 U.S. 340 (1987)).

80. Utter, supra note 3, at 34 (contending that state court decisions are "dramatically more vulnerable to democratic influences").

81. On June 8, 1982, the California voters adopted Proposition 8, which amended Cal. Cons. art. I, § 28(d) to read, "Relevant evidence shall not be excluded in any criminal proceeding. . . ." For a review of some of the reasons the voters adopted Proposition 8 and for a review of the California courts' subsequent treatment of the amendment, see Trask and Searight, "Proposition 8 and the Exclusionary Rule: Towards a New Balance of Defendant and Victim Rights," 23 *Pac. L.J.* 1101 (1992).

82. Fla. Const. art. I, § 12 (amended Nov. 2, 1982). For an excellent historical analysis of Florida constitutional law, see Hawkins, "Florida Constitutional Law: A Ten-Year Retrospective on the State Bill of Rights," 14 *Nova L. Rev.* 693 (1990).

83. 462 U.S. 637 (1983).

84. Id. at 639 (Burger, C.J., concurring).

85. See State v. Gerald, 549 A.2d 792, 807 (N.J. 1988).

86. N.J. Const. art. I, § 12 (amended Nov. 3, 1992).

87. See N.J. Rev. Stat. § 2C:11-3(e) (amended 1992).

88. See supra notes 83 through 84 and accompanying text.

89. Kahn, supra note 3, at 1166.

90. Id. at 1168.

91. See Brown v. Allen, 344 U.S. 443, 540, *pet. for reh'g, denied,* 345 U.S. 946 (1953) (Jackson, J., dissenting) ("We [the Justices of the Supreme Court] are not final because we are infallible, but we are infallible only because we are final.").

92. Chief Judge Kaye of the New York Court of Appeals argues that state courts have an advantage over federal courts in protecting individual rights. She states that although federal courts must rely on constitutional grounds when protecting individual rights, state courts may rely on state constitutional grounds or the common law. Chief Judge Kaye contends that state courts' ability to rely on the common law to protect individual rights permits those courts cautiously to expand individual rights while permitting state legislatures to "correct" unpopular decisions by statute. Kaye, "State Courts at the Dawn of a New Century," 70 *N.Y.U. L. Rev.* 1, 17 (1995).

93. Esler, "State Supreme Court Commitment to State Law," 78 *Judicature* 25 (1994).

94. Id. at 28.

95. Id. According to Esler, only eight states consistently utilized state law, basing at least

half of their decisions on state law ground: Alaska, Arkansas, Florida, New Jersey, New York, South Dakota, Tennessee, and Texas. Id. at 29.

96. Id. at 29–30.

97. Id. at 30.

98. Id.

99. Id.

100. Id.

101. Id.

102. Id. at 31.

103. Id.

104. Id.; see also Abrahamson, "Reincarnation of State Courts," 36 *Sw. L.J.* 951, 964 (1982) (contending that state courts' reluctance to expand individual rights is due to deference of state court judges to decisions of the U.S. Supreme Court, habit of judges and lawyers of looking only to federal law, and the difficulty facing those that "strike out on their own to analyze the state constitution").

105. Kauger, supra note 3, at 2 (quoting *Nomination of Justice William Hubbs Rehnquist: Hearings Before the Senate Comm. on the Judiciary*, 99th Cong., 2d Sess. 141 (1986)).

106. 115 S. Ct. 1185 (1995).

107. Id. at 1188.

108. Id. (quoting State v. Evans, 836 P.2d 1024, 1027 (Ariz. App. 1992).

109. Id. at 1189.

110. Id. (quoting State v. Evans, 866 P.2d 869, 872 (Ariz. 1994)).

111. Id. at 1193–94.

112. Id. at 1197–1203 (Ginsburg and Souter, JJ., dissenting) (arguing that Long's "plain statement" rule impedes states' ability to serve as laboratories for testing solutions to novel legal problems).

113. Id. at 1190.

114. Id. (quoting Minnesota v. National Tea Co., 309 U.S. 551, 557 (1940)).

115. See, e.g., Gardner, supra note 3; Diehm, supra note 3.

116. Kahn, supra note 3, at 1168.

117. See, e.g., Williams, supra note 3.

118. Diehm, supra note 3, at 238.

119. See State v. Hempele, 576 A.2d 793 (N.J. 1990).

120. See State v. Hunt, 450 A.2d 952 (N.J. 1982).

121. See State v. Hartley, 511 A.2d 80 (N.J. 1986).

122. See State v. Sanchez, 609 A.2d 400 (N.J. 1992).

· 18 ·

THE BURGER COURT IN ACTION

BERNARD SCHWARTZ

A 1995 book on the Rehnquist Court was entitled, *The Center Holds.*[1] Just after the Court's 1995 swing to the right, a commentator stated, "[T]he title is just one letter off. 'It should be, The Center Folds.'"[2]

The comment may well be true of the Rehnquist Court, but it is certainly not true of the Burger Court. In a 1985 interview, then-Justice William H. Rehnquist compared the Burger and Warren Courts. Rehnquist stated that the impact of the Court had been diminished under Chief Justice Warren E. Burger. "I don't think that the Burger Court has as wide a sense of mission. Perhaps it doesn't have any sense of mission at all."[3]

Certainly the Warren Court did have Rehnquist's "sense of mission" when it virtually rewrote the corpus of our constitutional law; concepts and principles that had appeared unduly radical became accepted rules of law. The Warren Court led the movement to remake constitutional law in the image of an evolving society. In doing so, the Justices had to perform the originative role that the jurist normally is not called on to exercise in more stable times—a role usually considered more appropriate for the legislator than for the judge.

From this point of view, the Warren Court was the paradigm of the result-oriented Court, which used its power to secure the result it deemed right in the cases that came before it. Employing the authority of the ermine to the utmost, Warren and his colleagues never hesitated to do whatever they thought necessary to translate their own conceptions of fairness and justice into the law of the land. The same was plainly not true of the Burger Court. Yet, if the Burger Court did not have any "sense of mission" comparable to its predecessor, that was not true of the entire Court—only of the centrist majority that pointed the way during most of the Burger tenure.

Rehnquist, who also said, "I don't know that a court should really have a sense of mission,"[4] clearly was a Justice who did, and that was true of some of the others as well. We can refer to a 1986 analysis by Justice Harry A. Blackmun, which found a tripartite division within the Burger Court. Blackmun said that he had always put "on the left" Justices William J. Brennan and Thurgood Marshall and "on the right" Chief Justice Burger and Justice Rehnquist. "Five of us," Blackmun concluded, were "in the middle"—Justices Potter Stewart, Byron R. White, Lewis F. Powell, John Paul Stevens, and himself.[5]

There is no doubt that the two Justices at each of the Burger Court's polar extremes were judges with an agenda. Stated broadly, Justices Brennan and Marshall, those "on the left," saw it as their duty to preserve and, if possible, extend the Warren Court's liberal jurisprudence. To them, the primary role of the courts was to serve as protectors of individual rights, and they consistently voted to ensure the effectiveness of that role. At the other pole, Chief Justice Burger and Justice Rehnquist had the opposite judicial agenda. They sought what Rehnquist called "a halt to . . . the sweeping rules made in the days of the Warren Court"[6]—and not only a halt but a rollback of much of the Warren jurisprudence. The Burger-Rehnquist conservative program included enlargement of government authority over individuals, a check to the expansion of criminal defendants' rights, and limitations on access to federal courts.

The actions of the polar Justices were based on more or less fixed juristic principles that served as the foundation for the jurisprudential edifices they sought to construct. They adhered rigidly to those principles in most cases, which enabled Court watchers to state with confidence how they would vote in almost all cases. Because their positions were normally fixed, it was rash to predict that they would vote differently in any important case. I was once told that the Brennan law clerks had confidently predicted that Rehnquist would vote with their Justice in the *Bakke* case.[7] One finds it hard to see the basis for their belief, given Rehnquist's reflex toward the right in cases involving racial classifications. At any rate, the Court community quickly saw where Rehnquist stood when, in line with his consistent position in such cases, he circulated a lengthy memorandum asserting that the special-admissions program at issue in *Bakke* was invalid.[8]

But if the four polar Justices habitually cast their votes in accordance with their basic liberal or conservative principles, that was not true of the Justices "in the middle." They were essentially pragmatists who considered cases on their individual facts and voted now with one polar core, now with the other. In certain fields, to be sure, the center Justices had a defined position. Thus, Justices White and Powell more often voted with the conservative bloc in criminal cases whereas Justices Blackmun and Stevens were to be found with Justice Brennan in many cases involving infringements upon personal rights—particularly those growing out of the right of personal autonomy that Justice Blackmun had enshrined in his *Roe v. Wade* opinion.[9]

Despite these tendencies, the center Justices did not have anything like a defined juristic *Weltanschauung*. And that was true as well of the Burger Court as an institution. As its decisions oscillated between the polar blocs, or somewhere between the two extremes, the Justices in the middle held the balance—tilting it at times in one direction, at times in the other, ensuring that the Court would not be a mere reflection of either polar bloc. "I, with others," said Justice Blackmun, "have been trying to hold the center. I think we've been fairly lucky in how we've come out."[10]

The Lost Leader

One who knew Warren Burger years before he was elevated to Olympus must agree with Justice Blackman's assessment: "The Chief," says Blackmun, who grew up with him, "has a great heart in him, and he's a very fine human being when you get to know him, when the tensions are off. One has to remember, too, that he's under strain almost constantly."[11]

However reluctantly, one must conclude that Burger was miscast in the role of leader of the Court—a harsh but fair description of a man who devoted so much of his life to the bench and worked as hard as he could to improve the judicial system, and one who also could be warm and charming in his personal relationships. Yet his personality was in many ways contradictory—as summarized by a reporter, "[A]t once gracious and petty, unselfish and self-serving, arrogant and insecure, politically shrewd yet stupid and heavy-handed at dealing with people."[12]

Of course, it was more than these personality contradictions that damaged Burger's effectiveness as a leader of the Court. A major part of his failure may be attributed to the manner in which he presided at conferences and assigned opinions. But an important factor was his inadequacy as a judge. One who examines the decision process in important cases must reluctantly conclude that Burger was out of his depth. Although the picture in some accounts of his intellectual inadequacy is certainly overdrawn, most of his colleagues could run intellectual rings around the Chief Justice.

"When Warren E. Burger succeeded Earl Warren as chief justice of the United States in 1969," Anthony Lewis has written, "many expected to see the more striking constitutional doctrines of the Warren years rolled back or even abandoned. . . . In these, it was often said, the Warren Court had made a constitutional revolution. Now a counter-revolution was seemingly at hand."[13] That the counterrevolution did not occur was, in large part, the result of the new Chief Justice's ineffective leadership.

Chief Justice Burger began his tenure with a definite program to overrule the principal Warren Court decisions. According to Justice William O. Douglas's *Autobiography*, the new Chief Justice "announced in Conference . . . the precedents we should overrule. *Miranda*,[14] *Gideon*,[15] . . . *Reynolds v. Sims*[16] and many others were on the list."[17] Yet, though, as Douglas put it, "Burger worked hard on it,"[18] he was never able to secure the rollback in Warren Court jurisprudence that headed his agenda.

To the contrary, the intended counterrevolution only confirmed most of the Warren Court jurisprudence. It can, indeed, be stated as a fact that no important Warren Court decision was overruled during the Burger tenure. Some of them were narrowed by Burger Court decisions; others were, however, not only fully applied but even expanded.

We can see this even in the field of criminal justice, where Chief Justice Burger was most eager to disown the Warren heritage—in then-Justice Rehnquist's phrase, to make "the law dealing with the constitutional rights of accused criminal defendants . . . more even-handed now than it was when I came on the Court." It was, after all, to "the area of the constitutional rights of accused criminal defendants" that Rehnquist primarily referred when he referred to the "sweeping rulings of the Warren Court."[19]

The transformation of constitutional law in the criminal justice field during the Warren years culminated in the celebrated *Gideon-Mapp-Miranda* trilogy.[20] The latter two in particular were decisions for which the Warren Court was widely criticized—denounced for putting "another set of handcuffs on the police."[21] Testifying before a Senate subcommittee just after *Miranda*, Truman Capote plaintively asked, "Why do they seem to totally ignore the rights of the victims and potential victims?"[22]

Though the Warren criminal cases became a major issue of Richard M. Nixon's presidential campaign, the Justices appointed by Nixon did not tilt the Court to the point of repudiating them. In fact, one of the Warren criminal trilogy was substantially expanded by the Burger Court. In *Gideon*, Chief Justice Warren had told the conference that it was "better not to say [the right to counsel applies in] 'every criminal case,' if we don't have to here." Warren told the others, "maybe it's best just to decide this case."[23] The Court followed Warren's suggestion to limit the *Gideon* decision to the case at hand and held only that there was a right to assigned counsel in the felony case at issue, without addressing the question of how far the new right extended.

The Burger Court not only followed *Gideon*, it expanded it to every case in which imprisonment may be imposed as a penalty, regardless of whether the crime involved is classified as a felony, misdemeanor, or even petty offense.[24] *Gideon* also only upheld the right to counsel at the criminal trial.[25] The Burger Court extended the right to counsel to preliminary hearings[26]—that is, before any formal accusation and trial—and gave practical effect to the right of the accused to represent himself if he so chose and knowingly and intelligently waived the right to counsel.[27]

Chief Justice Burger was strongly opposed to *Mapp* and *Miranda*, but he was not able to secure the votes needed to overrule those cases. Early in the Burger tenure, indeed, a majority of the Justices indicated that they were dissatisfied with the *Mapp* exclusionary rule. Before a majority could act on the dissatisfaction, however, two of the *Mapp* opponents retired. Justice Powell, one of the replacements, was not prepared to overrule *Mapp*, though he was willing to narrow the exclusionary rule.[28] *Mapp* was not overruled, but the later Burger years saw a narrowing of the exclusionary rule, culminating in the good-faith exception[29] and cost-benefit cases[30] toward the end of Burger's tenure.

Miranda had a similar fate in the Burger Court. The Chief Justice himself was anything but a partisan of *Miranda*. In a 1977 case, when the Court refused to act on the request of twenty-two states to overrule *Miranda*'s procedural ruling,[31] the Chief Justice circulated a memorandum stating, "I will probably write separately focusing on the utter irrationality of fulfilling Cardozo's half-century old prophecy—which he really made in jest—that some day some court would carry the Suppression Rule to the absurd extent of suppressing evidence of a murder victim's body."[32]

Despite his disapproval of *Miranda*, the Chief Justice never succeeded in overruling that decision. The most the Burger Court did was to narrow *Miranda*, though that hardly affected the essentials of its doctrine. In the end, Burger himself realized that *Miranda* still remained as a pillar of defendants' rights.[33]

The other Warren Court landmarks also served as foundations of the Burger Court jurisprudence. *Griffin v. Illinois*[34]—in many ways the Warren watershed case in the Court's effort to ensure economic equality in the legal process—was extended to include the right of an indigent defendant to the psychiatric assistance needed for an effective defense[35] and even, outside the criminal law field, to invalidate court fees that prevented indigents from bringing divorce proceedings.[36]

Brown v. Board of Education[37] and its Warren Court progeny were applied by the Burger Court in the *Swann*[38] and *Keyes* cases,[39] which held in them that the courts possessed broad remedial power to ensure desegregation, including extensive busing. The *Brown* principle was expanded to uphold affirmative action programs to aid minorities.[40] No Justice, not even Rehnquist, who had once probably taken a different view,[41] questioned the antidiscrimination premise that underlay *Brown*. In fact, the most important thing about the Burger Court decisions in this area was that, as an opinion was to conclude in the last Burger term, "we have reached a common destination in sustaining affirmative action against constitutional attack."[42]

The same was true in the other areas of Warren Court jurisprudence, including the First Amendment,[43] reapportionment,[44] other aspects of equal protection,[45] and judicial review in operation.[46] In all these areas, the central premises of the Warren Court decisions were not really challenged by its successor. The core principles laid down in the Warren years remained as securely rooted in our public law as they were when Chief Justice Burger first took his seat.

Chief Justice Burger's inadequacy as a leader was, however, evident in some of the most important cases decided during his tenure. A striking example may be seen in *United States v. Nixon*[47]—apart from *Roe v. Wade*,[48] the *cause célèbre* of the Burger Court. The Chief Justice's draft opinion there was so inept that it had to be completely rewritten by the other Justices. The final opinion was described by a Justice as an "opinion by committee," instead of one written by its nominal author.[49]

There was a comparable situation in the last important case decided by the Burger Court: *Bowsher v. Synar*.[50] The Burger draft opinion contained a far more expansive view of presidential power than the other Justices were willing to accept. It was only after the Chief Justice revised his draft in accordance with the Justices' suggestions that the draft could come down as the *Bowsher* opinion. Similarly, in the *Swann* school-busing case,[51] the Chief Justice's opinion had to be substantially revised before it could come down as the opinion of the Court. His draft was not supported by the law or the rationale behind the decision itself.

Truly, Warren Burger as head of the Court was the paradigm of Robert Browning's *Lost Leader*.

We Are All Activists Now

The Burger Court was a fragmented tribunal, with the balance, as indicated above, usually held by the center moderates. But that did not prevent it from being an activist Court. To the contrary, "the entire record of the Burger Court . . . is one of activism."[52] Yet the Justices "decide[d] without much self-conscious concern for whether this is a proper role for the Court."[53] In Anthony Lewis's neat phrase, "We are all activists now,"[54] at least so the jurisprudence of the Burger Court tells us.

One thing to be learned from the Burger years "is that the great conflict between judicial 'restraint' and 'activism' is history now."[55]

The statistics bear out the conclusion that the Burger Court record was, indeed, one of judicial activism. One measure was its willingness to strike down legislative acts. The Warren Court invalidated 21 federal and 150 state statutes; the Burger Court struck down 31 federal and 288 state laws.[56] The laws invalidated were at least as significant as those ruled unconstitutional by the Warren Court. The federal statutes that failed to pass constitutional muster in the Burger years included laws governing election financing and judicial salaries,[57] granting eighteen-year-olds the vote in state elections,[58] establishing bankruptcy courts,[59] as well as laws based on gender classifications in the military[60] and in various social security programs.[61] In addition, the Burger Court struck down the legislative veto, a method used by Congress to control executive action in nearly 200 statutes,[62] and a law designed to deal with the endemic budget deficit.[63] "If deference to Congress be the acid test of judicial restraint, the litmus of the Burger Court comes out much the same color as that of its predecessor."[64]

Yet it is not numbers alone than mark the Burger Court as an activist one. More important than quantity was the quality of the decisions rendered. The Burger Court was as ready as its predecessor to resolve crucial constitutional issues and to do so in accordance with its own conceptions of what the law should be. *United States v. Nixon*[65] brought the Court into the center of the Watergate vortex, and its decision led directly to the first resignation of a President. Nor was there any doubt among the Justices on the propriety of their exercise of power to resolve the crisis. The *Nixon* decision process demonstrates the willingness of the Justices to mold the crucial constitutional principles to accord with their individual policy perceptions. The impact of judicial review was definitely broadened by *Nixon* and the Burger Court's other separation-of-powers decisions.[66]

The Warren Court's activism was manifested in the number of new rights recognized by it, but its "rights explosion" was more than equaled by that under its successor. Few decisions were more far-reaching in their recognition of new rights than *Roe v. Wade*.[67] The right of privacy had first been ruled a constitutional right by the Warren Court in *Griswold v. Connecticut*.[68] It may be doubted, however, that the *Griswold* Court would have included the right to an abortion within this new right. At the *Griswold* conference, Chief Justice Warren stated, "I can't say . . . that the state has no legitimate interest (that could apply to abortion laws)"[69]—implying that he thought abortion laws were valid.

In *Roe*, however, the majority had no hesitation in extending the right of privacy to include the right to an abortion. More than that, the *Roe* decision process and opinion lend substance to Justice Stewart's criticism in a letter to Justice Blackmun, author of the *Roe* opinion, of "the specificity of its dictum—particularly in its fixing of the end of the first trimester as the critical point for valid state action. I appreciate the inevitability and indeed wisdom of dicta in the Court's opinion, but I wonder about the sedirability of the dicta being quite so inflexibly 'legislative.'"[70] One familiar with the interchanges between the Justices on the line between valid and invalid state action in abortion cases, with the Blackmun drafts moving from a two-pronged time test to the tripartite approach followed in the final opinion, cannot help but feel that the Justices were acting more like a legislative committee than a court. Their drawing of lines at trimesters and viability was, for Stewart, "to make policy judgments" that were more "legislative" than "judicial."[71]

The decision in *Roe v. Wade* may be taken as the very archetype of the activist decision: The decision was not based on principles worked out in earlier cases but on "policy judgments" made on an ad hoc basis which led to recognition of a new right. Even here the Justices were influenced more by pragmatism than principle. "Too many wealthy women were flouting the law to get abortions from respected physicians. Too many poor women were being injured by inadequately trained mass purveyors of illegal abortions. Concerns of that sort, rather than issues of high principle, are what appeal to the centrist activists of the Burger Court."[72]

The hallmark of the activist Court is the *Roe*-type decision that creates a new right not previously recognized in law. The Burger Court recognized new rights for women and those dependent on public largesse. During the Burger years, the law on sexual classifications was completely changed.[73] Though the Court did not go as far as Justice Brennan had wished,[74] virtually all legal disabilities based on sex were placed beyond the legal pale.

Even more significant in some respects was the recognition of legal rights in the field of government largesse. Until the Burger Court, no one had any "right" to the largesse dispensed by government. This was true regardless of the nature of the given largesse—whether it was a job, a pension, welfare aid, veterans' or disability benefits, a government contract, or any other benefit to which the individual had no preexisting right.[75] The result was to place those dependent on public largesse in a legal status subordinate to that of others in the community. If the governmental benefaction was a mere "gratuity" or "privilege," it could be withheld or revoked without adherence to the procedural safeguards that would otherwise be required by the Due Process Clause.[76]

Such a legal approach may have been rendered obsolete by the reality of twentieth-century society. But it was not until the Burger Court that the law started to make the Welfare State itself a source of new "rights" and to surround those rights in public benefactions with legal safeguards comparable to those enjoyed by the traditional rights of property. The landmark case was *Goldberg v. Kelly*,[77] where due process was held to require "a full 'evidentiary hearing'" before welfare benefits might be terminated. As the Court put it there, "It may be more realistic today to regard welfare entitlements as more like 'property' than a 'gratuity.' . . . Such benefits are a matter of statutory entitlement for persons qualified to receive them."[78]

Goldberg v. Kelly was soon applied to other cases involving government largesse: unemployment compensation, public housing, public employment, and government contracts.[79] In all these cases, the "privileges" of not too long ago were transformed into virtual "rights" entitled to the full procedural protection afforded to traditional property rights. Because of the Burger Court, the law was beginning to resolve the basic issue of fair dealing by government with those dependent on it.

Rootless Activism

The Burger Court opinions are full of essays on the virtue of judicial restraint.[80] Typical is an oft-quoted statement of the Chief Justice:

[T]he Constitution does not constitute us as "Platonic Guardians" nor does it vest in this Court the authority to strike down laws because they do not meet our standards of desirable social policy, "wisdom," or "common sense." . . . We trespass on the assigned function of the political branches under our structure of limited and separate powers when we assume a policymaking role, as the Court does today.[81]

There are similar statements in the opinions of other Justices.

Despite this, we have just seen that the Burger Court was definitely an activist Court. But there was a fundamental difference between the activism of the Burger Court and that of its predecessor. Chief Justice Warren and his supporters (notably Justice Brennan) acted on the basis of overriding principles derived from their vision of the society that the Constitution was intended to secure.

In particular, the Warren Court acted on the basis of two broad principles: nationalism and egalitarianism. It preferred national solutions to what it deemed national problems and to secure such solutions was willing to countenance substantial growth in federal power.[82] Even more important was the Warren Court's commitment to equality. If one great theme recurred in its jurisprudence, it was that of equality before the law—equality of races, of citizens, or rich and poor, of prosecutor and defendant. The result was what Justice Abe Fortas once termed "the most profound and pervasive revolution ever achieved by substantially peaceful means."[83] More than that, it was the rarest of all political animals: a judicially inspired and led revolution. Without the Warren Court decisions giving ever wider effect to the right to equality before the law, most of the movements for equality that have permeated American society would never have gotten off the ground.

Yet the Warren Court was more than the judicial counterpart of the Platonic philosopher-king. To Warren and his supporters, the Supreme Court was a modern Court of Chancery, a residual "fountain of justice" to rectify individual instances of injustice, particularly where the victims suffered from racial, economic, or similar disabilities. The Warren Justices saw themselves as present-day chancellors, who secured fairness and equity in individual cases, fired above all by a vision of the equal dignity of man, to be furthered by the Court's value-laden decisions.[84]

No similar vision inspired the activism of the Burger Court. Instead of consciously using the law to change the society and its values, it rode the wave, letting itself be swept along by the consensus it perceived in the social arena—moving, for example, on gender discrimination when it became "fashionable" to be for women's rights.[85] From this point of view, the Burger Court's activism has been well termed a "rootless activism,"[86] which dealt with cases on an essentially ad hoc basis, inspired less by moral vision than by pragmatic considerations.[87]

The rootless activism of the Burger Court was a direct consequence of the divisions already stressed between the Justices. Because of it, "the hallmark of the Burger Court has been strength in the center and weakness on the wings.[88] The balance of power was held by the Justices "in the middle."[89] In Burger's last term, however, the center's grip started to weaken. As Justice Blackmun put it just after the Chief Justice retired, "I think the center held generally . . . [but] it bled a lot. And it needs more troops. Where it's going to get them, I don't know."[90]

The shift toward the right did not occur until the end of the Burger tenure. Before that, the balance was with the pragmatic Justices who did not decide cases in accordance with a preconceived ethical philosophy. This was particularly true when Justices Stewart and Powell were the key swing votes. The Stewart reply, when he was asked whether he was a "liberal" or a "conservative," is most relevant. "I am a lawyer," Stewart answered. "I have some difficulty understanding what those terms mean even in the field of political life. . . . And I find it impossible to know what they mean when they are carried over to judicial work."[91]

Justices who felt this way had the lawyer's aversion to making fundamental value choices. Judicial policymaking was as frequent a feature during the Burger years as in the Warren years. But the policy choices were, in the main, made by Justices who, as relatively moderate pragmatists, were motivated by case-by-case judgments on how to make a workable judicial accommodation that would resolve a divisive public controversy. Inevitably, their decisions did not make for a logically consistent corpus such as that constructed by the Warren Court. In most areas of the law, the Burger Court decisions reflected less an overriding calculus of fundamental values than lawyerlike attempts to resolve the given controversy as a practical compromise between both sides of the issues involved.[92]

In the Warren Court, the leadership had come from the left, and constitutional doctrine was, in the important cases, made by Chief Justice Warren and his liberal supporters, notably Justice Brennan. Under Warren's successor, Brennan was shunted to one of the extremes that now more often played a lesser role. The Burger Court's activism was molded more by the moderate Justices "in the middle." As such, it was "inspired not by a commitment to fundamental constitutional principles or noble political ideals, but rather by the belief that modest injections of logic and compassion by disinterested, sensible judges can serve as a counterforce to some of the excesses and irrationalities of contemporary governmental decision-making."[93]

Thus judicial activism itself became a centrist philosophy, primarily practical in nature, without an agenda or overriding philosophy. Its essential approach was to adapt the answer of Diogenes, *Solvitur gubernando*,[94] and more or less on a case-by-case basis. Fundamental value choices were more often avoided than made. In its operation, "the Burger Court . . . exhibited a notable determination to fashion tenuous doctrines that offer both sides of a social controversy something important."[95]

The Burger years appear to have marked a legal watershed. After the Warren Court's rewriting of so much of our public law, the Burger Court was bound to be primarily a Court of consolidation. Transforming innovation, in the law as elsewhere, can take place only for so long. In historical terms, indeed, the Burger Court's main significance was its consolidation and continuation of the Warren heritage. Its role in this respect seems all the more important now that the Burger Court itself has given way to the Rehnquist Court.

In William H. Rehnquist the Court once again has a strong Chief Justice.[96] The Rehnquist Court, too, has been an activist Court, but its activism has been tilted toward the right. More than that, under the leadership of the conservative activist who now sits in the center chair, it has been shaping a new constitutional case law that is starting to be the reverse image of that fashioned under Chief Justice Warren. The law, like other institutions, has its epochs of ebbs and flow.[97] In the face of the Rehnquist flood tide, the Burger Court "in retrospect," as David J. Garrow puts it, "may be an almost liberal Supreme Court."[98] Its critics may yet look back on its receding period with more than a little nostalgia.

Notes

1. Simon, *The Center Holds: The Power Struggle inside the Rehnquist Court* (1995).
2. *Legal Times*, July 31, 1995, at A23.
3. *N.Y. Times* (Magazine), March 3, 1985, at 35.
4. Id.
5. *N.Y. Times*, March 8, 1986, at 7.
6. Supra note 3.
7. Regents of Univ. of Cal. v. Bakke, 438 U.S. 265 (1978).
8. See Schwartz, *Behind* Bakke: *Affirmative Action and the Supreme Court* 71 (1988).
9. 410 U.S. 113 (1973).
10. *N.Y. Times*, March 8, 1986, at 7.
11. *N.Y. Times* (Magazine), Feb. 20, 1983, at 20.
12. *Wash. Post* (national weekly ed.), July 7, 1986, at 8.
13. Foreword, in *The Burger Court: The Counter-Revolution That Wasn't* vii (Blasi ed., 1983).
14. Miranda v. Arizona, 384 U.S. 436 (1966).
15. Gideon v. Wainwright, 372 U.S. 335 (1963).
16. 377 U.S. 533 (1964).
17. Douglas, *The Court Years 1939–1975: The Autobiography of William O. Douglas* 231 (1980).
18. Id. at 232.
19. Supra note 3 at 34, 35.
20. Gideon v. Wainwright, 372 U.S. 335 (1963); Mapp v. Ohio, 367 U.S. 643 (1961); Miranda v. Arizona, 384 U.S. 436 (1966).
21. Schwartz, *Super Chief: Earl Warren and His Supreme Court* 593 (1983).
22. Weaver, *Warren: the Man, the Court, the Era* 233 (1967).
23. Schwartz, supra note 21, at 460.
24. Argersinger v. Hamlin, 407 U.S. 25 (1972);
25. The Warren Court also extended the right to counsel to criminal appeals. Douglas v. California, 372 U.S. 353 (1963). However, according to Ross v. Moffitt, 417 U.S. 600 (1974), the right only extends to the first appeal as of right, not to further appellate proceedings.
26. Coleman v. Alabama, 399 U.S. 1 (1970).
27. Faretta v. California, 422 U.S. 806 (1975).
28. See Schwartz, *The Ascent of Pragmatism: The Burger Court in Action* 359 (1990).
29. United States v. Leon, 468 U.S. 897 (198).
30. INS v. Lopez-Mendoza, 468 U.S. 1032 (1984).
31. Brewer v. Williams, 430 U.S. 387 (1977).
32. Warren Earl Burger, memorandum to the Conference, Dec. 29, 1976. A toned-down version of this statement is contained in the Burger dissent in Brewer v. Williams, 430 U.S. 387, 416 (1977).
33. See Rhode Island v. Innis, 446 U.S. 291, 304 (1980).
34. 351 U.S. 12 (1956).
35. Ake v. Oklahoma, 470 U.S. 68 (1985).
36. Boddie v. Connecticut, 401 U.S. 371 (1971)
37. 347 U.S. 483 (1954).
38. Swann v. Charlotte-Mecklenburg Bd. of Educ., 402 U.S. 1 (1971).

39. Keyes v. Denver School Dist., 413 U.S. 189 (1973).

40. Regents of Univ. of Cal. v. Bakke, 438 U.S. 265 (1978).

41. See Schwartz, "Chief Justice Rehnquist, Justice Jackson, and the *Brown* Case," 1988 Sup. Ct. Rev. 245, 246–47.

42. Wygant v. Jackson Board of Educ., 476 U.S. 267, 302 (1986).

43. See Schwartz, supra note 28, at 130–86.

44. E.g., Board of Estimate v. Morris, 489 U.S. 688 (1989).

45. Schwartz, supra note 28, at 215–81.

46. Id. at 40–63.

47. 418 U.S. 683 (1974). For a fuller treatment of the case and the draft opinions there, see Schwartz, *The Unpublished Opinions of the Burger Court* ch. 5 (1988).

48. Supra note 9.

49. Schwartz, supra note 28, at 84.

50. 478 U.S. 714 (1986). For a fuller treatment and the Burger draft, see Schwartz, "An Administrative Law 'Might Have Been'—Chief Justice Burger's *Bowsher v. Synar* Draft," 42 *Admin. L. Rev.* 22 (1990).

51. Supra note 38. For a fuller treatment and the Burger draft, see Schwartz, *Swann's Way: The School Busing Case and the Supreme Court* (1986).

52. *The Burger Years: Rights and Wrongs in the Supreme Court 1969–1986*, xx (H. Schwartz ed., 1987).

53. Supra note 13 at ix.

54. Id.

55. Id.

56. Caplan, *The Tenth Justice* 268 (1987).

57. United States v. Will, 449 U.S. 200 (1980); Buckley v. Valeo, 424 U.S. 1 (1976).

58. Oregon v. Mitchell, 400 U.S. 112 (1970).

59. Northern Pipeline Const. Co. v. Marathon Pipe Line Co., 458 U.S. 50 (1982).

60. Frontiero v. Richardson, 411 U.S. 677 (1973).

61. The cases are listed in supra note 13, at 306 n. 14.

62. INS v. Chadha, 462 U.S. 919 (1983).

63. Bowsher v. Synar, 478 U.S. 714 (1986).

64. Supra note 13 at 200.

65. Supra note 47.

66. United States v. Will, 449 U.S. 200 (1980); Buckley v. Valeo, 424 U.S. 1 (1976); INS v. Chadha, 462 U.S. 919 (1983); Bowsher v. Synar, 478 U.S. 714 (1986).

67. Supra note 9.

68. 381 U.S. 479 (1965).

69. Schwartz, supra note 21, at 577.

70. See Schwartz, supra note 28, at 307.

71. Id.

72. Supra note 13 at 212–13.

73. Frontiero v. Richardson, 411 U.S. 677 (1973); Schwartz, supra note 28, ch. 3.

74. Schwartz, supra note 28, at 224.

75. The cases are summarized in Schwartz, *Administrative Law* § 5.12 (3d ed. 1991).

76. Id.

77. 397 U.S. 254 (1970).

78. Id. at 262.

79. The cases are summarized in Schwartz, supra note 75, § 5.16.

80. Supra note 13 at 198.

81. Plyler v. Doe, 457 U.S. 202, 242 (1982).

82. Funston, "The Burger Court and Era," in 1 *Encyclopedia of the American Judicial System* 190 (R. Janosik ed., 1987).

83. Fortas, "The Amendment and Equality Under Law" in *The Fourteenth Amendment Centennial* 34 (Schwartz ed., 1970).

84. Compare supra note 13 at 212.

85. Compare 55 U.S.L.W. 2225 (1986).

86. Supra note 13 at 198.

87. Compare id. at ix.

88. Id. at 211.

89. Supra note 5.

90. *N.Y. Times*, Sept. 25, 1986, at B10.

91. Schwartz, supra note 21, at 320.

92. Compare supra note 13 at 216.

93. Id. at 211.

94. Compare Pound, *Administrative Law* 56 (1942).

95. Supra note 13 at 216.

96. Schwartz, supra note 28, at 413.

97. Cardozo, "A Ministry of Justice," 35 *Harv. L. Rev.* 113, 126 (1921).

98. Schwartz, supra note 28, book jacket.

· 19 ·

INTERNATIONAL IMPACT

FINN BACKER

This book contains essays on the U.S. Supreme Court from 1969 to 1986, the years of the Burger Court. As we all know, the Supreme Court of the United States is the guardian of the U.S. Constitution. The history of the international impact of the Supreme Court can therefore be seen, first and foremost, in terms of the Constitution and how it has been interpreted by the Supreme Court at any given time in the over 200 years of its existence.

It has been amply demonstrated by all that has been said and written on the subject that we are dealing with an ongoing dynamic process of interpretation. The Constitution undergoes changes in content and meaning as it continues to develop in the process of interpretation by the Supreme Court. The Constitution is, in other words, not only the highest law of the land, only occasionally amended, but also a dynamic interpretation of this law that reflects changing ideas and changing needs in the society.

The object of this essay is to examine whether, and if so, what impact, the Supreme Court under Warren Burger's leadership, through its interpretation of the Constitution, has exerted abroad. This is not a simple subject. The question clearly implies a comparison with the decisions of the Warren Court. The Burger Court has consolidated, but not carried further, the accomplishments of the great liberal period in the Supreme Court's history under Earl Warren's leadership. The results from this period have become a source of law that has contributed, directly and indirectly, to the development of law throughout the world.

It takes a while, however, for the results of U.S. Supreme Court practice to be fully appreciated and to exert influence in other countries—with different governmental structures, different legal systems, and different kinds of constitutions. It is therefore hardly to be expected that the impact from the Warren Court and the Burger Court can be clearly distinguished from each other. There is reason to believe that the reforms could, in any case, not continue at the same tempo as before. The changes that came during the period of the Warren Court were so great that they could not be absorbed fully or immediately either in the United States or elsewhere.

Outside the United States the decisions of the Supreme Court are of significance in terms of the ideas from which they derive and the practical conclusions which the Supreme Court draws from these ideas. The practice of the Supreme Court affects the general political and ideological climate and may lead to discussion about whether change is necessary or desirable, and whether the American solutions are applicable. What will emerge from such a process is, however, more uncertain. The result may be a change in court practice, but more often it may be new laws. It is possible too, that conditions are so different in another country that American solutions are rejected as irrelevant.

I. Judicial Review in America

Ever since the decision in *Marbury v. Madison*[1] in 1803, judicial review has been a characteristic feature of the U.S. Supreme Court. The Supreme Court can review the constitutionality of laws—not only the laws of the individual states but also federal laws. No such tradition has existed in most European countries. There is, of course, good logic in Chief Justice Marshall's opinion of 1803—that the Constitution is the fundamental law and that, in case of conflict between it and another law, the Constitution takes precedence. Undeniably, this represents a curtailment of democracy in a more absolute sense, in that a group of nonelected persons—judges (who are not elected in European countries)—shall have the power to make the final decision on how far the Constitution reaches, and not just content themselves with refusing to recognize laws that are clearly unconstitutional.

Judicial review as such predates *Marbury v. Madison* by about 200 years. Scholars have traced the origins of the idea to the beginning of the seventeenth century in England, and it was elaborated also in colonial times in America.[2]

In England in 1610, Sir Edward Coke decided Dr. Bonham's case in the Court of Common Pleas, asserting in his opinion that "when an act of parliament is against common right and reason or repugnant, or impossible to be performed, the common law will control it, and adjudge such act to be void."[3]

The Bonham Case was invoked in America in 1761 by James Otis in the *Writs of Assistance Case* in Massachusetts.[4] On the basis of Coke's statement in the Bonham Case and the principle of "natural rights," he argued that British officers had no power under the law to use search warrants that did not stipulate the object of the search. Precedents for the practice of judicial review can be found both in the state courts and in the lower federal courts, where judges had refrained from following laws they considered contrary to the provisions of the state or federal constitution.[5]

The principle of judicial review was a subject of contention among the prominent men of the time, both during and after the framing of the Constitution. Supreme Court Justice James Iredell, who was a proponent of judicial review during the Constitutional Convention, developed an institutional foundation for judicial power in *Calder v. Bull*.[6] He rejected the idea of basing decisions of the Court on "laws of nature." He proposed instead that the only basis for invalidating a statute passed by Congress or by a state legislature, is that it violated a provision of the written Constitution in a "clear and urgent case."[7]

At the Virginia Ratifying Convention in 1788, John Marshall stated: "If Congress were to make a law not warranted by any of the powers enumerated, it would be considered by the judges as an infringement of the Constitution which they are to guard. . . . They would declare it void."[8] *Marbury v. Madison* can in a sense be considered a "practical application" of these words.

The power of the Supreme Court to rule on the constitutionality of a law is, as we know, not explicitly spelled out in Article III, Section 2, of the Constitution. As pointed out in a short reference in the *Encyclopedia Britannica*, the success of the practice of judicial review "rested ultimately on the Supreme Court's own ruling, plus the absence of effective political challenge to it."[9]

II. Judicial Review in Europe

In most European countries it has been accepted doctrine that the legislature determines its own competence, and that it is not the task of the ordinary courts to scrutinize the legislature. It should also be mentioned that in a country like Great Britain, which does not have a written constitution, Parliament's older laws—which deal with such matters as the position of the monarchy, the state church, and the union between England and Scotland—are not necessarily considered to be of a higher order than the current laws.

For most of the continental European countries the situation has been radically changed in the period since World War II.[10] We have witnessed a flowering of the idea of constitutionalism, where the activities of the legislature can also be critically examined. There is no doubt that American thinking on judicial review has played a part here—along with experiences with totalitarian states before and during the war. The solution that has been chosen is, however, unlike the American model.

Most of the continental European countries have established special courts which can rule on the constitutionality of laws. This has generally happened in connection with the introduction of new constitutions, which contain explicit provisions on individual rights. Here also there is a visible American influence. The first of the new constitutional courts was established in Germany in 1951. It is also this court which has the widest competence of the European constitutional courts.

The period in which most of these constitutional courts were established coincides with the period of the Warren and Burger Courts in the United States. The development is still in progress now in Eastern Europe. It is rather doubtful that the Burger Court has had an independent impact on the developments in Europe.

III. The European Convention on Human Rights (1950)

The United Nations adopted a Universal Declaration of Human Rights in 1948. This declaration is not a treaty, and it was not binding on the member states in a legal sense. Later—in 1966—the United Nations adopted *two* conventions, one on civil and political rights and another on economic, political, and cultural rights. By this time the Convention for the Protection of Human Rights and Fundamental Freedoms (the Convention on Human Rights), which was adopted in 1950, had been in effect for several years.

The European Convention concerns political and civil rights but later was expanded by several protocols. This is a much more powerful instrument for promoting human rights among the nations in the Council of Europe than is the case with the United Nations convention. In effect, this Convention embraces practically all the countries of Western Europe. It has been binding on a relatively large group of closely knit nations for many years. Perhaps even more important, the Convention has established two effective enforcement agencies, the Commission and the Court of Human Rights. Thus, it is no longer the single member state which determines the extent of its obligations under the Convention. Today, all states of importance in Western Europe have recognized the compulsory jurisdiction of the Court of Human Rights. In recent years a number of countries in Eastern Europe have demonstrated a desire to join the Convention, and some have indeed done so.

A member state may, for political or other reasons, not wish to lodge a complaint against another member state. The control and enforcement system of the Convention can, therefore, not be fully effective unless the individual victim of an alleged violation can himself petition the Commission and, through the Commission, the court. Such a right for the individual requires a declaration from the state against which a complaint has been made, that it recognizes the competency of the Commission to receive such petitions. All member states of importance have now made such declarations. The right of the individual to petition, together with acceptance of the Court's jurisdiction, represents a strong force in the struggle for human rights.

The full significance of this Convention has emerged in the last two decades, after most of the member states—actually in the same period covered by the Warren and Burger Courts—had recognized the competency of the court and the right of the individual to press a claim. The court has, in its interpretation of the Convention, adopted a rather "activist" policy, which can best be compared with the policy the U.S. Supreme Court follows in its interpretation of the U.S. Constitution. Even a judge in the Supreme Court of a member nation often has the feeling of being the object of judicial review at an even higher level.

During the past twenty-five years there has been an ever-increasing number of individual petitions. Today nearly all the complaints to the Commission are petitions from individuals. Although only a very small percentage of the complaints results in a decision against a member state, the absolute number of such decisions has increased over the years. Many such decisions concern cases against such member states as Great Britain and France, which have good traditions as democracies. Rolv Ryssdal, former Chief Justice of the Norwegian Supreme Court, and for several years now the president of the Court of Human Rights, has pointed out that this does not necessarily indicate that there are more frequent violations in these countries than in others. On the contrary, it is probable that citizens in democratic countries are more aware of their rights, and act to protect them.

In Norway, there has, in the last few years, been a noticeable increase both in the number of references made to the Convention and in the number of individual petitions. This seems to coincide with increasing knowledge of the Convention among both lawyers and laymen. The first decisions against Norway came just a few years ago.[11] More recently, in another case, the Court of Human Rights declared

that the procedure followed by the Norwegian Supreme Court in a particular criminal case was a breach of the Convention.[12] There is perhaps reason to believe that
the number of such decisions will increase in the years to come.

IV. Judicial Review in Scandinavia

A. *Denmark and Sweden*

None of the Scandinavian countries has established a special court to review the
constitutionality of laws.[13] In Denmark, Norway, and Sweden it is generally accepted that the ordinary courts can carry out this function. Sweden is the only
country in Scandinavia that has explicit provisions (from 1979) in its constitution
with instructions for setting aside laws that are unconstitutional. So far, it seems that
no law has been set aside.

In Denmark it has been assumed, at least since around 1920, that the courts
can review the constutionality of a law. An important decision from 1921 is based on
this assumption, but the claim that the constitution was violated was not upheld.
The Danish Supreme Court pointed out that the right to review must be exercised
with restraint. A decision from 1976 is, to my knowledge, the closest the court has
come to setting aside a law. In accordance with the law, the government decided to
transfer some medieval manuscripts from the Danish foundation that owned them
to the University of Iceland. The law contains no provisions for compensation, and
no ordinary compensation was awarded. A certain sum was nevertheless paid.

B. *Norway*

In Norway the story is quite different.

In 1975, Professor Carsten Smith, now Chief Justice of the Norwegian Supreme Court, examined 170 cases in which the constitutionality of a law was challenged.[14] This study shows that in the period from 1890 to the middle of the 1970s,
the Supreme Court set aside twenty-five different provisions, in whole or in part. A
more comprehensive study from 1992, using somewhat different methods, was carried out by Professor Eivind Smith.[15] This study uncovered 132 cases in which the
constitutionality of a law was challenged. From 1931 to 1984, the court found nineteen or twenty laws unconstitutional. From 1985 to the present in some five cases
the question of constitutionality was raised; three of these cases are from 1996, and
the decision in the last two cases has not yet been made.[16]

Because we are talking about constitutionality, let me say a few words about
the Norwegian Constitution of 1814. It is the second oldest written constitution still
in force. Only the Constitution of the United States is older. There have, of course,
been changes in the Norwegian Constitution, but it has never undergone a systematic or radical revision. It came into being under very difficult circumstances in
about a month in the spring of 1814. It was modeled on the many new constitutions
of the time, but it was the French Constitution of 1791 which left the strongest imprint.

The Norwegian Constitution is based on the principle of a separation of powers[17] with independent courts. It does not contain a bill of rights, but there are some isolated provisions on civil rights. The most important and frequently cited are Article 97, that no *ex post facto* laws shall be enacted, and Article 105, that in the event of expropriation, the citizen is entitled to full compensation.

There are provisions to the effect that no one may be convicted unless he or she has broken a law or punished without having been sentenced.[18] There are also provisions against arbitrary arrest and illegal search of one's home.[19] Freedom of the press is guaranteed to a certain extent.[20] In recent years a provision on religious freedom was also added.[21]

The Norwegian Supreme Court was established in 1815, and its practice naturally became the standard for the other courts. At the beginning of the nineteenth century, judicial theory generally held that the courts could *not* review the constitutionality of laws. There is some uncertainty about just how early the Supreme Court of Norway decided that it could engage in such review. It is clear, however, that the practice goes back more than 100 years, and that it was influenced by the American system. There is indeed reason to believe that Norway was the first country in Europe that took up American ideas in this area.

The theoretical basis for this practice was first presented in Professor Torkel Halvorsen Aschehoug's work on the Norwegian Constitution, published in 1885. Aschehoug examined the rules on judicial review in other countries and warmly recommended the American solution.[22] In 1890 the Supreme Court, for the first time, set aside a law *express verbis*, on the basis of Article 97.[23] At the time many people believed that this decision was inspired by Aschehoug's recent work. Aschehoug himself, however, claimed that the Norwegian Supreme Court had, in fact, in a number of cases as long ago as 1822, reviewed the constitutionality of laws.[24]

Newer research, based partly on the voting protocols of the supreme court, seems to confirm this claim and to indicate that the court, as early as 1840, had begun to examine the question of judicial review. It is difficult to verify this claim because the individual opinions of the judges were kept secret until 1862. The decisions of the supreme court have been reported since 1836 in the *Norwegian Court Gazette*.[25]

Among others, there is a case from 1866, in which Chief Justice P. C. Lasson based his opinion on the same line of reasoning that Chief Justice Marshall enunciated in 1803.[26] Three judges argued that because Parliament seemed to have overlooked the constitutional question, the supreme court must intervene to correct the error. Judge Lasson, whose opinion would be decisive, preferred to go beyond the particular case and to discuss the principle of review. He presented his view in a most unequivocal manner: The case had been presented in terms of both private and constitutional law. Judge Lasson found that the matter to be decided here was clearly a constitutional question: "[I]nasmuch as the courts cannot be compelled to judge according to both laws at the same time, they must necessarily prefer the constitution."[27]

Later the right to judicial review was loudly proclaimed as a conservative device to hinder democratic development. In leftwing circles, this view prevailed for a long time. Today almost everyone seems to have a more "relaxed" attitude to the practice. This may be a result of the knowledge that judicial review was practiced before Aschehoug published his book, as well as of the greater recognition of human rights.

In the period between 1890 and 1930, the court made a series of decisions to set aside laws. On the whole, the power of judicial review was used in a conservative manner to protect established business interests against new encroachments. There is a certain parallel to developments in the United States.

During this period, in 1926, the plenum law, which explicitly assumes the right of the Norwegian Supreme Court to practice judicial review, was passed.[28] In its present form this law provides that if two or more judges in a section (of five judges hearing a case) wish to consider the question of constitutionality, the case must be heard by the entire court.

In the period after 1931, there was relatively little activity involving judicial review. In connection with the "legal settlement" after the war, several Norwegian traitors and German war criminals claimed that the laws under which they were convicted were in conflict with Article 97 of the Constitution. This argument did not win support, perhaps not surprising when one takes into account the special conditions during the German occupation and the legal settlement that followed.

After the war, there were several important cases in which businessmen and others unsuccessfully claimed that provisions in the constitution were being violated by the very far-reaching economic regulatory laws which were then in force. Compensation was, in fact, not granted when land was regulated for purposes of protection or preservation of natural resources. In practice this might make a property worthless.

Even though the Norwegian Supreme Court insisted that it had the right to exercise judicial review power, many people began to wonder whether this was idle talk, and whether the court would ever again have the courage to set aside a law. In 1976, however, the Norwegian Supreme Court, in a 10–7 vote, handed down a plenum decision which in effect set aside the most far-reaching provisions in a law of 1973.[29] The explicit purpose of this law was indeed to limit compensation in connection with expropriation.

The issue in this particular case was what would be full compensation for land to be used for new roads. The court decided that what in the law was a discretionary power for the commission of appraisers could and should be used in most cases when the market value of the property is higher than its present use indicates. In 1984, the law was repealed and replaced by a new law which takes into consideration the objections of the Norwegian Supreme Court.

This is considered a milestone case because it "revived" the right to judicial review. The case is noteworthy also in another sense: Unanimously, and clearly influenced by the American "preferred position theory," the court expressed the opinion that the constitutional provisions protecting the individual's personal freedom and security must have greater force than provisions protecting economic rights.

The writer for the majority found that Parliament's understanding of the relationship between the particular law and the Constitution must weigh heavily when economic rights are concerned, and that the courts must be cautious in questioning the legislature's judgment. He would hesitate to declare the law unconstitutional when there was reasonable doubt. But if judicial review has any real meaning, the courts must use it when they, as in this case, found beyond reasonable doubt that the law would lead to results that violated the constitution. The writer for the minority voiced the opinion that in cases involving economic rights, the legislature itself must, in principle, decide its relation to the constitution. In cases in which there are differences of opinion concerning the understanding of constitutional provisions, the court has no authority to question the decisions of the legislature.

These opinions reveal how much more careful we are in exercising judicial review in Norway than in the United States, even though the Norwegian system resembles the American in some ways. In conclusion, we can ascertain that the idea of judicial review gained a foothold in Norway and, probably also in other parts of the world, during the period of the Burger Court. This development started much earlier. It would be difficult to demonstrate that the practice of the Burger Court had a direct impact on developments, but it is a contributing factor in the more general American influence, which has been both lasting and significant.

V. Influence in Special Areas

At this point I would like to discuss the influence of certain specific decisions of the Burger Court. It must be clear that I am most familiar with conditions in Norway and the other Scandinavian countries, and that it has not been possible to carry out a thorough international comparison.

A. Roe v. Wade

The case that stands out by far as the most important, or at least the most talked about, is *Roe v. Wade*.[30] In many European countries the right to requested abortion in the first trimester of pregnancy is established by law. This development occurred for the most part during the period when Warren Burger was Chief Justice. From what has been written about *Roe v. Wade*, it seems that the decision is somewhat accidentally based on the Fourth Amendment. The case could well have been decided on the basis of other provisions in the Constitution.

The difference between the situation in Europe and in the United States is that no one in Europe, as far as I know, has derived the right to self-determined abortion from a country's constitution. The question has been resolved on a more practical level. Many countries, including Norway, have constitutional provisions, comparable to the Fourth Amendment, that prohibit arbitrary search of one's home and similar acts. However, not even the most eager activists for self-determined abortion would ever dream of invoking such a provision in their cause. On the contrary, opponents of self-determined abortion have sought support for their cause in the constitution.

In Germany, they were successful, as indicated by a decision of the German constitutional court on February 25, 1975.[31] The abortion law allowed requested abortion during the first twelve weeks of pregnancy. The German Constitution guarantees the right to life and bodily integrity (Article 2, nr. 2). The court declared that this right applies to the fetus as well as to the mother. The abortion law could therefore not grant the mother an unconditional right to abortion at the expense of the fetus. On this ground, the law was declared unconstitutional. To balance the conflicting interests, the court proposed instead a system of medical and social conditions. In the new law from 1976, the legislature followed these instructions.

The Norwegian Supreme Court dealt with the same question in 1983,[32] but in an indirect fashion. The abortion law was, however, not set aside. In 1978, after a change in abortion law, women have a right to requested abortion during the first twelve weeks of pregnancy.

A priest in the Norwegian state church declared that because of the new law he would no longer perform the administrative duties of his position. The state instituted legal procedures for dismissal. The priest claimed that the new law was contrary to Articles 2 and 4 in the Norwegian Constitution (rules concerning the state church). According to the constitution, the King is obliged to profess his faith in the state religion, and to protect and enforce it. He is thus prevented from participating in a legislative process which results in a law that violates the teachings of the church. The King had (formally) been an accessory to the government's bill, and had sanctioned the law that had been enacted. It was also claimed that the new law violated Article 3 of the United Nations Declaration of Human Rights, and Article 2 of the European Convention on Human Rights (on respect for life), as well as unwritten legal principles of a constitutional nature.

None of these arguments received support, and the priest was discharged from his position. With regard to the constitution, the supreme court remarked that the state church system could not impose restrictions on the exercise of ordinary legal authority in areas not concerned with the state church. The King is bound by constitutional provisions concerning the state church only when he exercises authority as the highest steward of that church.

It is rather doubtful that the Norwegian revision of the abortion law in 1978 was inspired by *Roe v. Wade*. But the revision was, without doubt, influenced by general developments in other countries. The 1983 decision, like the decision in *Roe v. Wade* and later decisions on the right to self-determined abortion, did not soothe tempers just because the supreme court had had its say. The question of self-determined abortion is still a "burning" issue in Norway, as in the United States.

B. Other Decisions of the Burger Court

It is very difficult to compare the other well-known decisions of the Burger Court with developments on the other side of the Atlantic. The United States is very far ahead of us in the protection of various forms of individual rights. This must be at least partially related to the differences in social and political needs and, even more so, legal traditions. The many decisions on desegregation, racial discrimination, and affirmative action can be viewed against a background of racial and ethnic mixture in American society and to the provisions in the U.S. Constitution and other laws to hinder discrimination. In most European countries, the need for such provisions has traditionally been smaller. But the situation has been partly changed because of immigration from the Third World during the last few decades.

1. DISCRIMINATION   Even though we have had more immigration in Norway as well, little has been done to combat discrimination. We have joined the United Nations Convention Against Discrimination of 1965. In the Penal Code, there are now provisions against encouraging racial hatred and against discrimination in the form of refusing to provide goods or services.[33] But that is all. We do not, for example, have a Racial Relations Act such as the British have had since 1976.[34] Provisions against discrimination in employment, modeled on provisions that already exist in other European countries, have been suggested in a bill presented to the Parliament. It is, however, difficult to know what the fate of the bill will be.

In one area, however, much has been done in Norway, namely, in the area of gender equality. A law of 1978[35] contains directions on a rather far-reaching form of affirmative action in favor of women, in reality a quota system. Not everyone is completely happy with this law, but its validity has never been challenged, not even by those who have studied the divided decision of the Burger Court in the *Bakke* case.[36]

It is my belief that the European countries, to an increasing degree, will appreciate American experiences in the area of racial discrimination as the problem becomes more pressing in Europe. The period when one could feel morally superior in relation to practice in the United States and did nothing to prevent the occurrence of similar situations is definitely over.

2. CRIMINAL CASES   With regard to the practice of the Burger Court in criminal cases, many European judges are somewhat relieved that the activist policy of the Warren Court has not gone further, and also that it has not been significantly reversed. At least in Norway, where few human rights are guaranteed in the constitution, we are accustomed to think that it is the ordinary laws, and not the constitution, that determine what rights the accused shall have and the significance of procedural errors that may have occurred. It is also the ordinary laws that determine when the public shall be excluded from a trial. The criminal procedure law has for many years contained a provision that gives the accused the right to defense counsel paid by the state. In other words, the fact that a constitution does not include guarantees of human rights does not necessarily mean that such rights do not exist.

We can say that in comparison with the United States, rights are less absolute, and the consequences of violation will generally be judged more concretely. We do not have any prohibition against a person being "put twice in jeopardy" (as in the Fifth amendment), and the "exclusionary rule" is enforced much less consistently. The key question is how the rights of the accused can be further strengthened at the same time that the victim's interests and the need for an efficient administration of justice are given rightful consideration in the system. Confidence in the courts is perhaps not increased if a person who is patently guilty of serious punishable acts is acquitted because of a procedural error.

Defense attorneys naturally exert pressure to extend the rights of the accused and to maximize the significance of procedural errors. They seem to have found inspiration for this in American court practice, probably more from popular television series than from a study of the practice of the U.S. Supreme Court. In Europe, developments are leading, in a cautious manner, in the direction of greater rights for the accused. This is due less to what is happening internally in any one country than to the way in which the European Court of Human Rights interprets Article 6 (on fair trial) of the European Convention of Human Rights. In the long run, no member country will escape learning that it has violated human rights in the true sense. Sometimes this may appear to be tiresome procedural nit-picking, more than enforcement of human rights, but then again it depends on the eyes that see.

3. FREEDOM OF SPEECH AND PRESS   In reading the Burger Court decisions on freedom of speech and press under the First Amendment, one is struck by the strong position that these freedoms enjoy in the United States. The freedoms are more protected in the United States than in Norway, in spite of the fact that many countries, including Norway, have constitutional provisions safeguarding these rights. It may not, however, be quite clear where the balance between the various considerations should lie. Many Europeans will have some reservations about accepting constitutional protection of "commercial speech," which follows from the decision in *Virginia State Board of Pharmacy v. Virginia Consumer Council*.[37] In Norway, for example, there is a prohibition against both alcohol and tobacco advertising.[38]

Looking at the U.S. Supreme Court decisions concerning the conflict between freedom of speech and the provisions about protection of the American flag—for instance, the Burger Court's 1974 decision in *Spence v. Washington*[39]—it should be mentioned, as a kind of curiosity, that in Norway there is no provision on protection of the Norwegian flag. That has been considered superfluous. There are, however, provisions on protection of foreign flags.[40]

As a conclusion to this section, it should be noted that the press also enjoys a strong position in Norway, and that it is exerting pressure to improve its position. There is good reason to believe that the effort will be successful. In fact, at the request of the press, a committee will consider liberalization of the law on defamation.

4. *UNITED STATES V. NIXON*   After *Roe v. Wade*, *United States v. Nixon*[41] is the best known decision of the Burger Court abroad. This decision shows that not even the President of the United States is exempt from ordinary laws, even though the Court to a great degree recognized presidential privilege. There are parallels to such privilege in many other countries. There has been some speculation about whether a matter like Watergate would have surfaced at all and grown to such dimensions in another country, where exposure of top political leaders is less likely than in the United States.

The decision has, in any case, set a good example for other countries. When it was probable that the tapes that were to be delivered contained evidence of a criminal act, the Court actually had no choice. In many cases, the person in the highest position would know how to cover his tracks better. At that stage, it would be a question of willpower, persistence, and resources for the person who wishes to reveal the facts. It is my impression that the United States is far ahead of the rest of the world in this respect. The politically inspired need to expose an opponent can, naturally, also result in a negative effect. All in all, international developments seem to be heading toward a tougher climate for politicians who have something to hide—and the United States will lead the way.

VI. Conclusion

This examination of the international impact of the Burger Court may not have yielded much concrete material. In other countries, jurists rarely refer to an American court decision or to the practice of the U.S. Supreme Court in a given period as decisive for the solution that was chosen. On the other hand, a review of foreign law is frequently included when a draft of a new law is being prepared. From this material, it is difficult to determine how much weight has been given to foreign laws and principles. To evaluate the influence of the Burger Court abroad, one must make assumptions based on standpoints taken abroad after the Burger Court made its decision. It can often be seen that the U.S. Supreme Court has based its decision on ideas that have had an impact in other countries.

The United States plays a significant role as the source for ideas in the political, social, and legal spheres that later gain support all over the world. But this is not the fate of all American ideas, and as a rule, there will be some adjustment or remodeling. The impact of the Burger Court must be viewed in this context.

Notes

1. 1 Cranch 137 (U.S. 1803).
2. The following paragraphs are based on *The Oxford Companion to the Supreme Court of the United States* 464–70 (Hall ed., 1992).
3. See id. at 464.
4. "Lechmere's Case, 1761," in 1 Schwartz, *The Bill of Rights: A Documentary History* 184 (1971).
5. See supra note 2 at 522.
6. 3 Dall. 386 (U.S. 1798).
7. See Powell, "Summary of *Calder v. Bull*," in supra note 2 at 114–15.
8. See id. at 465.
9. 5 *Encyclopedia Britannica* 626 (15th ed. 1978) (an unsigned article on judicial review).
10. A good survey can be found in Favoreu, "Constitutional Review in Europe," in *Constitutionalism and Rights: The Influence of the United States Constitution Abroad* (Henkin and Rosenthal eds., 1990).
11. See the decision of the European Court of Human Rights, Aug. 29, 1990, in the "Arne-saken" (Arne case), E.V. Norway, Series A. nr. 181-A.
12. Decision of the Court of Human Rights, Feb. 19, 1996, Case of *Botten v. Norway* (150/1994/579), not yet available in Series A.
13. The material concerning Denmark and Sweden is based on Eivind Smith, *Hoyesterett og folkestyre* [The Supreme Court and Democracy] 26–31 (Oslo: University Press, 1993).
14. See Carsten Smith, "Domstolene og rettsutviklingen" ["The Courts and the Development of Law"], in *Lov og rett* [*Law and Justice*] 292 ff, particularly 300 (1975).
15. See Smith, supra note 13, at 205, 236–38.
16. These two cases, State of Norway, represented by Rikstrygdeverket (National Social

Security Administration) v. Borthen and Thunheim v. State of Norway (Rikstrygdeverket), were decided on November 8, 1996. The Supreme Court found that the constituion had not been violated in either case. In the *Thunheim* case, there was one dissenting vote, namely, mine.

17. Kongeriget Norges Grundlov, given i Rigsforsamlingen paa Eidsvold den 17de Mai 1814 [Constitution of the State of Norway, adopted at Eidvoll, May 17, 1814].

18. See supra note 17, art. 96.

19. See supra note 17, art. 99, para. 1; art. 102.

20. See supra note 17, art. 100.

21. See supra note 17, art. 2, para. 1.

22. T. M. Aschehoug, *Norges Nuvarende Statsforfatning* [The Present Constitution of Norway], vol. III, 352 (Christiania: 1885).

23. See *Retstidende* [*Norwegian Court Gazette*], 1890, at 455 ff.

24. See Aschehoug, supra note 22, vol. III, 354 ff.

25. Supra note 23.

26. The decision was published in *Ugeblad for Statistik og Statsokonomi* [Weekly Magazine for Statistics and State Economy], vol. VI, 165 ff.

27. See supra note 25; Carsten Smith, "Om domstolenes provelsesrett. Foredrag seminar for Gudmund Sandvik 13.3.1995" ["On the Right of the Courts to Judicial Review. Lecture Seminar for Gudmund Sandvik, March 13, 1995"].

28. Lov av 25. juni 1926 nr. 2, Om forandring i lovgivningen om Hoiesterett [Law of June 25, 1926 nr. 2 concerning changes in the legislation about the supreme court].

29. *Retstidende* [*Norwegian Court Gazette*], 1976, at 1.

30. 410 U.S. 113 (1973).

31. This decision is reported in Eivind Smith, Rettslig handtering av normer i Europa og i Norge [Legal treatment of norms in Europe and in Norway]; Tidssrift for rettsvitenskap [*Journal of Jurisprudence*], 1983, at 77 ff. The case is discussed id. at 110. The German decision is also reported in the Norwegian judgment from 1983, referred to infra note 32.

32. *Retstidende* [*Norwegian Court Gazette*], 1983, at 1004.

33. Alminnelig borgerlig straffelov (referert til som Straffeloven) av 22. mai 1902 nr. 10 [General civil penal code of May 22, 1902, nr. 10, referred to as the Penal Code], arts. 135a, 349a.

34. The law from 1976 is the third on this subject. The first, rather limited law, is from 1965. See Juss, "The Constitution and Sikhs in Britain," 2 *B.Y.U. L. Rev.* 481–523, particularly 521–22 (1995).

35. Lov av 9, juni 1978 nr. 45 Om likestilling mellom kjonnene [Law of June 9, 1978, on Equality between the Sexes].

36. Regents of Univ. of Cal. v. Bakke, 438 U.S. 265 (1978).

37. 425 U.S. 748 (1976).

38. Lov av 2. juni 1989 nr. 27 om omsetning av alkoholholdig drikk m.v. § 9-2 [Law of June 2, 1989, on the sale of alcoholic beverages etc. (alcohol law), art. 9 para. 2]. Lov av 9. mars 1973 nr. 14 om vern mot tobakkskader § 2 [Law of March 9, 1973, on the Prevention of Smoking Injuries, art. 2].

39. 418 U.S. 405 (1974).

40. Straffeloven § 95 forste ledd [Penal Code art. 95, para. 1). See also supra note 33 for full reference.

41. 418 U.S. 683 (1974).

20

THE BURGER COURT
A Critique

JOSEPH M. MCLAUGHLIN

If the two centuries in the life of the Supreme Court be imagined as a mosaic, where do the seventeen Burger tiles fit? It is difficult to address this question intelligently without first erecting an historical scaffolding from which to evaluate the seventeen-year Burger reign. The distinguished political historian Robert G. McCloskey has supplied three handy epoch's in the Court's history, and they provide a useful vantage point.[1]

The first period, lasting from about 1790 to 1865 (from Jay through Taney), of course, included the tenure of Chief Justice John Marshall. McCloskey sees this period as "the struggle to promote the principle of national union"[2] when the Court molded the contours of federalism.[3] The shapeless relationship between state and federal sovereignty was chiseled in such landmarks as *McCulloch v. Maryland*[4] and *Gibbons v. Ogden*.[5] But it took a tragic civil war to determine that we were one nation, a federal union created not by the individual states but by the citizens in whom sovereignty ultimately resided. (It is a curious footnote of history that the term "the United States of America" took a plural verb before the Civil War and a singular verb thereafter.)[6]

McCloskey's second period, from about 1885 to 1935, saw the country's transition from an agricultural to an industrial economy and focused on what McCloskey described as "business-government relationships."[7] Supreme Court litigation primarily involved property rights, pitting robber barons and corporations of the Gilded Age against government attempts to rein them in.[8] It was the salad days of *Lochner v. New York*,[9] substantive due process, and liberty of contract.[10] It ended with the famous court-packing proposal that came a cropper with *West Coast Hotel Co. v. Parrish*[11] and its grudging concession that states had extensive power to regulate what used to be regarded as sacred, constitutionally protected property rights.

McCloskey's third era coincides with the Court's preoccupation with civil rights, beginning as early as 1925 in *Gitlow v. New York*,[12] in which the Court expressed little doubt that freedom of the press was among the liberty interests protected by the Due Process Clause from state encroachment.[13] Presumably, other

First Amendment rights were also protected, thus furnishing the *mise en scène* for the great incorporation debates that were to follow.[14]

Civil rights claims had been elbowing their way to prominence even before 1937. One year before, for example, *Grosjean v. American Press Co.*[15] struck down a Louisiana law that had the practical effect of imposing a tax only on newspapers critical of Huey Long. A year later, in *DeJonge v. Oregon*,[16] the Court invalidated a statute that made it a crime to attend a Communist meeting. Justice Cardozo declared in *Palko v. Connecticut*[17] that First Amendment liberties are on "a different plane of social and moral values" and that freedom of thought and of speech is "the matrix, the indispensable condition, of nearly every other form of freedom. . . . [N]either liberty nor justice would exist if they were sacrificed."[18] Justice Stone expanded on that theme and planted in the famous footnote four of *United States v. Carolene Products Co.*,[19] the doctrinal seeds of the "preferred freedoms" that flowered in the Court's civil liberties orientation for the next half-century. It reached full maturity in "rights triumphalism" during the Warren era, as the Court trumpeted its duty to defend civil liberties — even if much of the public, many states, and the Court's sister branches remained unsupportive, indeed, resistant. The result, in McCloskey's words, was "government by judiciary,"[20] a notion repugnant to conservatives in the Edmund Burke tradition.

Yet it was not so much the unrestrained policymaking of the Warren Court that set it apart; it was the consistently *liberal* political bent of its policies. Whereas business interests and other conservative political forces were the protegés of the past legal system, the Warren Court's clients were society's underdogs — racial minorities, political dissenters, and criminal defendants. The Warren Court became the paradigm of legal liberalism, which historian Laura Kalman has recently defined as "confidence in the ability of courts to change society for what judges believe is the better."[21]

The Burger Years: 1969–86

A Republican sat in the White House for all but four years of the Burger era. Republican Presidents made six consecutive appointments to the Supreme Court. Richard Nixon and Ronald Reagan shared a common philosophy about the Supreme Court, emphasizing the need for "strict constructionists," advocates of judicial restraint who would "interpret" rather than "make" law. Both wailed that liberal Justices were acting as "superlegislators," imposing their own personal views on the American public in the name of constitutional interpretation. To them the nine Justices were reminiscent of the *bel canto* countertenors of a bygone era. Those famous castrati often took the score as a mere outline for their vocal fripperies. Composers could not dictate to these idols. They could only harbor the wistful hope of hearing something resembling what they had written.

The Nixon-Reagan message was truculent: path-breaking, liberal social policy announcements by the Supreme Court must end, and they intended to use their control over judicial nominations to achieve that goal. Given this presidential rhetoric, conservatives understandably expected the Burger Court to come up with the antidote for the Warren Court's liberal activism. They were to be disappointed.

Indeed, in a memorandum recently declassified after a quarter-century under seal, President Nixon revealed that he would have supported a constitutional amendment barring federal courts from integrating public schools and housing.[22] He feared that "ultra liberal" rulings from the four Justices he had appointed (including Justice Rehnquist) would integrate the nation against its will.[23]

The Burger Court disappointed conservative expectations in two ways. First, the Nixon, Ford, and Reagan appointees did not topple the columns erected by the Warren Court. What Alpheus Thomas Mason wrote as early as 1974 was still true when Warren Burger retired in 1986: "The three major pillars of the Warren Court's constitutional edifice—Race Relations, Reapportionment, and Rules of Criminal Procedure—though somewhat eroded, are still virtually intact."[24]

Second, although the Burger Court admittedly chipped away at Warren Court precedents in such constitutional areas as criminal procedure and obscenity, it actually strengthened other Warren Court doctrines. In the bargain, it practiced its own brand of liberal activism in some areas in which the Warren Court had done little or nothing—most notably in abortion, sex discrimination, busing, and affirmative action. Addressing a new slate of social controversies that emerged in the 1970s and 1980s, many Burger Court decisions fit comfortably into the Warren Court mold. That is why, more than a decade after the beginning of the Burger era, the Court remained a festering wound for President Reagan. He still lamented its policies on abortion, school desegregation, school prayer, and affirmative action, much as Nixon had decried Warren Court policies on criminal procedure. At the end of the Nixon-Reagan era, American constitutional jurisprudence still did not reflect the values and preferences of conservatives on social issues.

The enigma of the Burger Court may be that it never developed a truly consistent philosophy. Without question, however, it was an activist Court. One index of judicial activism is a willingness to declare acts of Congress unconstitutional. The Warren Court struck down, on average, barely more than one federal statute each term; the Burger Court invalidated federal laws at twice that rate.[25]

Another earmark of an activist Court is its willingness to establish new rights, especially those not explicit in the text of the Constitution. The Warren Court, for instance, had hinted at its intent to disinter substantive due process when the Justices, although unable to fashion a coherent theory, began to develop a constitutional right to privacy in *Griswold v. Connecticut*.[26] But it was the Burger Court that gave full throat to substantive due process and a right of privacy when in *Roe v. Wade*,[27] the Justices gave constitutional protection to a woman's right to have an abortion.

Burger Era Activism

Four areas focused on during the Burger years bear special scrutiny: (1) racial discrimination, (2) sex discrimination, (3) religion, and (4) criminal procedure.

Racial Discrimination

The Burger Court sang from the same choir book of liberal constitutional policies as the Warren Court. Hindsight is always 20-20, but the racial discrimination cases of the Warren era had been easy to decide: They involved blatant, indeed brutal, discrimination, and the intent to discriminate had been explicit.[28]

The problems became more subtle, and the answers less obvious, once the issues moved north of the Mason-Dixon line and beyond de jure discrimination. The Burger Court faced the subtler forms of racial discrimination surrounding de facto school segregation, institutional racism, and, most explosively, affirmative action.

For the most part, the Burger Court rejected cross-district busing and rigid affirmative action quotas, and its record demonstrated little sympathy for fair housing principles. Yet, in the areas of school desegregation and affirmative action, the Burger Court echoed the philosophical call of the Warren Court.[29]

Affirmative action, as a core concept, did not emerge until the 1970s. The Burger Court's record was especially noteworthy and it was a virtual appendix to the Warren text. *Regents of the University of California v. Bakke,*[30] *United Steelworkers v. Weber,*[31] and *Fullilove v. Klutznick*[32] might well have been penned by the Warren Court, but they were the handiwork of the Burger Court. Constitutional rights, at least since the Taney Era, had historically been judicially recognized only on the basis of an *individual's* right; in the affirmative action decisions, however, the Burger Court advanced a conception of constitutional rights premised on *classes* (i.e., on racial and ethnic identities). From a so-called conservative Court, this was an unexpected shock.

Sex Discrimination

Whereas the civil rights revolution for racial minorities emerged in the 1950s and 1960s, the women's right movement did not come to a boil until the Burger era. On sex discrimination the Burger Court crafted an important and decidedly liberal body of law. Those policy initiatives were consistent with the spirit of Warren Court reforms, extending greater constitutional protection to a politically weak and historically mistreated group.

Although the Burger Court might be faulted for its failure to make sex a suspect classification or for not going far enough in specific reforms, it hacked at the roots of sex discrimination and stereotyping in such cases as *Frontiero v. Richardson,*[33] *Craig v. Boren,*[34] and *Roberts v. United States Jaycees.*[35] Its legacy in this area reflects a sympathy for the social and economic policies central to the women's movement of the 1970s and the 1980s. Indeed, both conservatives and liberals would probably agree that there is no more extreme example of liberal judicial activism in modern times than the Burger Court's decision in *Roe v. Wade.*[36]

Religion

Evangelical Christianity has deep roots in American life, running at least to Plymouth Rock. It has been prominent in causes from Abolition to Prohibition. The Warren Court's decision restricting school prayer and Bible reading in the classroom[37] reignited the religious right as the 1960s began. Indeed, a case can be made that it was the born-again movement, personified by Jimmy Carter, and the rise of the Moral Majority that brought Ronald Reagan to the White House.

During the Burger era, there was a dramatic revival of religious fundamental-ism in this country. Powerful religious figures led a vocal and well-financed initia-tive to play a leading role in the nation's political life. That movement lamented the "immoralities" that it found infecting national life. The religious right believed that Supreme Court decisions on criminal defendants' rights, obscenity, school prayer, and abortion had eroded the nation's moral fiber.

These critics allied themselves with the resurgent conservative wing of the Re-publican Party especially during the tenure of Ronald Reagan. Although the wall of separation that the Court had recognized in *Everson v. Board of Education*[38] was as-saulted, again the record of the Burger Court was not notably conservative. The Court banned various forms of public financial support to sectarian elementary and secondary schools,[39] and in *Wallace v. Jaffree*[40] it declared unconstitutional a state statute authorizing public schools to set aside one minute of silence for meditation or voluntary prayer. However, despite the prominence of religious fundamentalism during the Burger era, the Court's policies on school prayer and other controversial establishment clause issues did not take a noticeable turn to the right.

Criminal Procedure

The most sulphurous attacks on the Warren Court were launched against its crimi-nal justice decisions, and, not surprisingly, this is where the Burger Court went the furthest in rejecting the Warren Court's legacy.

The transformation in criminal justice under the Warren Court was revolu-tionary. "More than that," Professor Bernard Schwartz observed, "it was the rarest of all political animals: a judicially inspired and led revolution."[41] Furthermore, as Richard Funston noted, "no area of Burger Court decision-making suggested a greater disjunction with its predecessor than [criminal defendants' rights]."[42] Fun-ston also summarized rather neatly the most important Burger Court decisions on criminal procedure:

> [The] right to counsel was limited to post-indictment lineups. The warrantless use of "bugged" informers was upheld. The emerging doctrines of the right to con-frontation were stunted. Full-scale arrest searches of persons stopped for mere traf-fic violations were approved. The end of the road in extending the procedural safeguards of criminal trials to juvenile proceedings was apparently reached. State-ments obtained in violation of *Miranda* were admitted for purposes of impeaching the credibility of the defendant who had testified in his own behalf. Even acknowl-edged violations of constitutional rights were dismissed as harmless errors, having no significance on the outcome of the trial and not worthy of appellate notice.[43]

Confrontation Jurisprudence

In few areas of criminal procedure has the Court—whether under Warren, Burger, or Rehnquist—so abysmally failed to settle on a first principle than in its hearsay Confrontation Clause jurisprudence. Not that it has lacked opportunities. On each occasion, however, it has shuddered, like Dracula before a cross, murmuring some-thing like, "We have no occasion in the present case to map out a theory of the

Confrontation Clause that would determine the validity of all such hearsay 'exceptions' permitting the introduction of an absent declarant's statements."[44] Several times the Court has disavowed "any intention of proposing a general answer to the many difficult questions"[45] surrounding hearsay and confrontation.

The shotgun marriage of the hearsay rule and the right of confrontation has always been an unhappy union, and at this point all that can realistically be expected is a state of peaceful coexistence. The common-law hearsay rule generally excludes out-of-court statements by a person not now under oath and subject to cross-examination. Similarly, the Confrontation Clause of the Sixth Amendment grants to a criminal defendant the right to confront "the witnesses against him." There are however at least thirty exceptions to the hearsay rule (depending on definitional nuances, not relevant here) in which statements that are clearly hearsay are nonetheless admissible in a criminal case. Do these exceptions pass muster under the Confrontation Clause?

The Burger Court, of course, was not writing on a clean slate. When he became Chief Justice, Burger inherited a slim portfolio of confrontation jurisprudence: (1) the Confrontation Clause applied to the states via incorporation through the Due Process Clause of the Fourteenth Amendment[46]; (2) the core value of the Confrontation Clause was its guarantee of the right to cross-examine witnesses[47]; and, apparently, (3) this meant that if the declarant was still alive and able to be called as a witness, the Sixth Amendment demanded that he be called rather than offering his out-of-court hearsay declaration.[48]

Fairly quickly the Burger Court had to wrestle with two related but distinct questions: May a state create new exceptions unknown when the Sixth Amendment was adopted? And for that matter, which of the old common-law exceptions remained valid after the enactment of the Confrontation Clause?

The Burger Court's first major foray into Confrontation Clause jurisprudence occurred in *California v. Green*.[49] California passed a statute[50] permitting a prior inconsistent statement of a witness to be introduced as substantive evidence, thereby abrogating the common-law rule limiting such testimony to its impeachment value. The California Supreme Court overturned Green's conviction[51] in the belief that the Warren Court's decision in *Barber v. Page*,[52] with its emphasis on unavailability of the declarant-witness and the opportunity for the defendant to cross-examine the witness at the time he first utters the statement, required it to hold that "[b]elated cross-examination before the trial court . . . 'is not an adequate substitute for the right to cross-examination contemporaneous with the original testimony before a different tribunal.'"[53] The Supreme Court reversed.

Justice White, writing for the majority, was unwilling to accept the total constitutionalization of the hearsay rule that some had inferred from the Warren Court opinions:

> While it may readily be conceded that hearsay rules and the Confrontation Clause are generally designed to protect similar values, it is quite a different thing to suggest that the overlap is complete and that the Confrontation Clause is nothing more or less than a codification of the rules of hearsay and their exceptions as they existed historically at common law. Our decisions have never established such a congruence; indeed, we have more than once found a violation of confrontation

values even though the statements in issue were admitted under an arguably recognized hearsay exception. The converse is equally true: merely because evidence is admitted in violation of a long-established hearsay rule does not lead to the automatic conclusion that confrontation rights have been denied.[54]

Chief Justice Burger, while accepting White's reasoning, weighed in with a concurrence emphasizing the importance of allowing states to develop their own rules of evidence, free from the strictures of the Confrontation Clause. Burger's concurrence was based on old-time notions of federalism—that letting states act as laboratories in developing rules of evidence would furnish guides to other states and perhaps even to Congress.

Less than six months after *Green*, a profoundly divided Court decided *Dutton v. Evans*.[55] Even more than *Green*, *Dutton* illustrated the Burger Court's drive to blunt the Warren Court's penchant for making the Confrontation Clause congruent with the hearsay rule. Like *Green*, *Dutton* involved testimony admissible under a state hearsay exception that would not have been admitted under its federal counterpart. In *Dutton*, Evans, Williams, and Truett were charged with murdering three Georgia police officers. At Evans's trial, the prosecution offered the testimony of a man named Shaw, who was in prison with Williams. Inmate Shaw testified that while discussing his trial, inmate Williams had barked, "[I]f it hadn't been for that dirty son-of-a-bitch, Alex Evans, we wouldn't be in this now."

The trial court admitted Williams's declaration under a Georgia co-conspirator hearsay exception that admitted not only statements made in the course of and in furtherance of the conspiracy (the common-law and federal rule) but even statements made after the conspiracy in an effort to conceal it. The Fifth Circuit agreed with Evans that the Georgia co-conspirator exception, in expanding on its federal counterpart, "authorize[d] practices repugnant to the sixth amendment."[56] The Supreme Court reversed.

Justice Stewart wrote the Court's opinion, joined by Chief Justice Burger, Justice White, and the latest Nixon appointee, Justice Blackmun. Simply because the state rule of evidence went further than its federal counterpart, Stewart explained, does not brand the state rule unconstitutional per se. He reminded us that the responsibility of a federal court in reviewing the constitutionality of a state hearsay exception is not to judge which of the two approaches, state or federal, is the better rule of evidence but whether the state exception violates the Sixth Amendment. Justice Harlan added a significant concurrence. Justices Black, Douglas, and Brennan, joined Justice Marshall in an indignant dissent.

This case, Justice Stewart stated, provided a paradigm of why federal courts should analyze state exceptions apart from the Federal Rules of Evidence. The Court's previous attempts to define the limits of the co-conspirator exception were undertaken solely "in the exercise of its rule-making power in the area of the federal law of evidence"[57] and were never intended to constitutionalize that exception. Stewart conceded that although "it seems apparent that the Sixth Amendment's Confrontation Clause and the evidentiary hearsay rule stem from the same roots . . . this Court has never equated the two, and we decline to do so now."[58]

Moving from the general to the particular, Justice Stewart turned to consider whether admitting Williams's statement, made in prison, about Evans's participation in the conspiracy, violated the Confrontation Clause. Extrapolating from *California v. Green*, Justice Stewart concluded that a hearsay exception would survive a Confrontation Clause attack if the exception bore some "indicia of reliability."[59] Although Evans was obviously denied the chance to confront Williams, Justice Stewart dismissed as "wholly unreal" the theoretical possibility that Evans could have conducted effective cross-examination. At best, the most effective cross-examination, Stewart contended, could only hope to impeach Williams's identification of Evans as a co-conspirator. For Stewart, the surrounding circumstances, particularly the fact that the statement was made against Williams's penal interest and was made spontaneously, furnished sufficient "indicia of reliability" to guarantee reliability.

The two concurring opinions, by Justices Blackmun and Harlan, range over a broad spectrum but exhibit the same determination to minimize the role of the Confrontation Clause in appraising hearsay exceptions.

Justice Harlan, in his concurrence, executed a 180-degree course change from his earlier view on the relationship between the Confrontation Clause and the hearsay rule and, in the process, he made a major contribution to the debate. Six months earlier in *Green*, Harlan had filed another concurrence, arguing that the Confrontation Clause mandated a rule of preference *requiring* the government to produce witnesses when available. After further consideration in *Dutton*, Harlan now abandoned this view.

A strict rule of preference regarding availability, he explained, "would be unduly inconvenient and of small utility to a defendant."[60] Such a view would bar evidence long deemed reliable, such as business records, official statements, learned treatises, and trade reports. Indeed, if adopted, the earlier Harlan approach would have gutted Rule 803 of the Federal Rules of Evidence which sets forth twenty-four exceptions to the hearsay rule that may be invoked even when the declarant is available to be called. Instead, Harlan now urged Wigmore's awkwardly worded view:

> The Constitution does not prescribe what kinds of testimonial statements (dying declarations, or the like) shall be given infra-judicially—this depends on the law of Evidence for the time being—but only what mode of procedure shall be followed—i.e., a cross-examining procedure—in the case of such testimony as is required by the ordinary law of Evidence to be given infra-judicially.[61]

Justice Harlan's new interpretation of the Confrontation Clause as merely a regulation of trial procedure with no necessary connection to the rules of evidence allowed him to smash the Warren Court's identification of the Confrontation Clause with the rule against hearsay—an equation that "once made . . . carrie[d] the seeds of great mischief for enlightened development in the law of evidence."[62] Instead, Harlan argued that the litmus test of constitutionality was more appropriately performed not under the Confrontation Clause but under the Due Process Clause. One benefit of such an approach would be to encourage states to reform their rules of hearsay without having to worry about the Federal Rules of Evidence, for, as Harlan had already said in *Green*, "it could scarcely be suggested that the Fourteenth Amendment takes under its umbrella all common-law hearsay rules and their exceptions."[63]

Though one can only speculate whether the presence of former Chief Justice Earl Warren at the *Dutton* argument would have made the four-Justice dissent a majority, Justice Marshall criticized the plurality for reaching "a result completely inconsistent with recent opinions of this Court, especially *Douglas v. Alabama*, and *Bruton v. United States*."[64] These cases, Marshall explained, established a "clear" precedent that absent the opportunity for cross-examination, incriminating testimony is constitutionally inadmissible under the Confrontation Clause. Marshall decried Justice Stewart's reliance on indicia of reliability, explaining:

> [I]f "indicia of reliability" are so easy to come by, and prove so much, then it is only reasonable to ask whether the Confrontation Clause has any independent vitality at all in protecting a criminal defendant against the use of extrajudicial statements not subject to cross-examination and not exposed to a jury assessment of the declarant's demeanor at trial. I believe the Confrontation Clause has been sunk if any out-of-court statement bearing an indicium of a probative likelihood can come in, no matter how damaging the statement may be or how great the need for the truth-discovering test of cross-examination. Our decisions . . . require more than this meager inquiry.[65]

In footnote seven, Justice Marshall focused on the plurality's reluctance to equate the Confrontation Clause with the rule barring hearsay. From *Pointer* to *Bruton*, this brief footnote is the first serious discussion of the controversy from members of the old Warren Court majority whose opinions often assumed an identity between the two doctrines. Though dismissing the plurality's concerns as "a prospect more frightening than real," Marshall did little to alleviate them. To him, the notion that the Confrontation Clause, as applied in Warren Court opinions, constitutionalized the hearsay rule was a canard resulting from the mistaken belief that the Warren Court adopted the traditional definition of hearsay—an-out-of-court statement presented for the truth of the matter stated—for confrontation purposes.

> Rather, the decisions, while looking to availability of a declarant . . . recognize[d] that cross-examination is included in the right of an accused in a criminal case to confront the witnesses against him and that admission in the absence of cross-examination of certain types of suspect and highly damaging statements is one of the "threats to a fair trial" against which the Confrontation Clause was directed.[66]

Justice Marshall, however, says nothing about how he would determine which statements were "suspect and highly damaging." We are left staring down a well with no bottom.

Clearly, the Burger Court intended to reel in the constitutional protection that the Warren Court had cast deep into the roiling waters of the criminal justice system. Now the rule seemed to be that the Confrontation Clause neither guaranteed cross-examination nor barred hearsay. Instead, it simply guaranteed a mode of trial that included a general right to confront adverse witnesses who actually appeared in court and nothing more. This limited reading seemed to be rooted in notions of federalism. Giving the Confrontation Clause an unlimited role would suffocate the evolution of hearsay reform within the states. But exactly how the Burger Court intended to decide whether the admission of hearsay violated the Confrontation Clause remained vague.

In sum, Justice White's opinion in *Green* suggested that all that was required to satisfy the Confrontation Clause was cross-examination, whether contemporaneous or belated. Stewart seemed to require even less. The presence of "indicia of reliability" would satisfy the Confrontation Clause, though he refrained from establishing a standard for such indicia. Justice Harlan's approach was the most comprehensive. He would have confined the Confrontation Clause to a simple guarantee that the accused have a right to cross-examine those witnesses who do, in fact, testify at trial. For Harlan the admissibility of hearsay would be determined by the rules of evidence regulated solely by the flywheel of the Due Process Clause.

What is clear about all these approaches is that the Burger Court reeled in the Confrontation Clause and relaxed the standard for what constituted reliable evidence. Both the indicia of reliability test and the due process test were highly subjective analyses that were void of the absolute guarantees that the Warren Court seemed to suggest.

Ten years after *Green* and *Dutton*, the Burger Court returned to this nettlesome problem, and yet again, the Court demonstrated that it was no slave to consistency. In *Ohio v. Roberts*,[67] the defendant was charged with check forgery and possession of stolen credit cards. At a preliminary hearing, the defendant claimed that Anita Issacs told him he could use the credit cards, which belonged to her parents. When the defendant called Anita to testify at the preliminary hearing, she denied the defendant's story. At trial, the defendant continued to maintain that Issacs had given him permission to use the cards. To rebut this argument, the prosecutor, after demonstrating Anita Issacs's unavailability (there were five unanswered subpoenas), introduced her former testimony given at the preliminary hearing. The Ohio Court of Appeals reversed the conviction because the prosecutor had not sufficiently demonstrated Issacs's unavailability.[68] The Supreme Court of Ohio affirmed the reversal but did so on the different ground that the opportunity to cross-examine Issacs at the preliminary hearing failed to afford the defendant his constitutional right to confrontation for purposes of the trial.[69] The U.S. Supreme Court reversed.

Justice Blackmun, writing for Chief Justice Burger and Justices Stewart, White, Powell, and Rehnquist, rejected the conclusions of the Ohio courts, both in their evaluation of the reliability of the testimony and in their assessment of unavailability. Most significantly, Blackmun tried his hand at establishing a "general approach" for determining the constitutionality of evidence admitted under a hearsay exception:

> [W]hen a hearsay declarant is not present for cross-examination at trial, the Confrontation Clause normally requires a showing that he is unavailable. Even then, his statement is admissible only if it bears adequate "indicia of reliability." Reliability can be inferred without more in a case where the evidence falls within a firmly rooted hearsay exception. In other cases, the evidence must be excluded, at least absent a showing of particularized guarantees of trustworthiness.[70]

Applying his new approach, Justice Blackmun first concluded that the prosecutor had successfully demonstrated that the witness was unavailable for purposes of the Confrontation Clause. Quoting from *Green*, Blackmun argued that "the lengths to which the prosecution must go to produce a witness . . . is a question of reasonableness."[71] The prosecutor's attempts to determine Issacs's whereabouts through interviews with her mother and the issuance of five subpoenas to her last known address demonstrated a reasonable effort to produce her. Although the dissent argued that the prosecutor should have been required to investigate other leads that Issacs had been in San Francisco one year earlier, Blackmun dismissed this cavil with the comment that "[o]ne in hindsight, may always think of other things."[72]

Turning his attention to whether the prior testimony bore sufficient indicia of reliability, Justice Blackmun found the defense counsel's examination of Issacs at the preliminary hearing to be "replete with leading questions" sufficiently testing the witness's memory, motive, and veracity. This was sufficient to guarantee to "the trier of fact a satisfactory basis for evaluating the truth of the prior statement."[73] Thus, Anita Issacs's prior testimony fulfilled both prongs of the Court's new test and was fully admissible as substantive evidence.

Although Justice Blackmun modestly suggested that his approach to the admissibility of hearsay under the Confrontation Clause was not new but was culled from the Court's prior opinions, his test, especially the first prong dealing with availability, seemed to deviate from the Burger Court's ad hoc review of Confrontation Clause cases and to establish a significant burden for the state to overcome before it could introduce hearsay. Blackmun explained the availability test as follows:

> [I]n conformance with the Framers' preference for face-to-face accusation, the Sixth Amendment establishes a rule of necessity. In the usual case (including cases where prior cross-examination has occurred), the prosecution must either produce, or demonstrate the unavailability of, the declarant whose statement it wishes to use against the defendant.[74]

This broad rule of necessity, paradoxically, seems to revert to Justice Harlan's concurrence in *Green*, holding that the Confrontation Clause required prosecutors to produce available defendants—despite Harlan's disavowal of this view just six months later in *Dutton*. The unavailability requirement seemed to have been resurrected like Lazarus. And it bore the same stench. If the majority meant what it said, then it would invalidate, in one fell swoop, most of the hearsay exceptions because rule 803 makes them admissible even if the declarant is available (e.g., excited utterances, business records, and physical condition). Rather than reversing the Warren Court's penchant for excluding hearsay, this would have expanded the exclusionary trend.

Fortunately, this seemingly clear holding that a showing of unavailability was normally required did not survive long. In *United States v. Inadi*,[75] the Burger Court revisited the question and, almost indignantly, denied that a showing of unavailability was usually required. Explaining that *Roberts* did not mandate "a wholesale revision of the law of evidence, nor does it support such a broad interpretation of the Confrontation Clause,"[76] *Inadi* limited the *Roberts* unavailability prong to the specific hearsay exception (former testimony) involved in *Roberts*. Justice Powell explained:

> *Roberts* must be read consistently with the question it answered, the authority it cited, and its own facts. All of these indicate that *Roberts* simply reaffirmed a long-

standing rule, foreshadowed in *Pointer v. Texas*, established in *Barber*, and refined in a line of cases up through *Roberts*, that applie[d] unavailability analysis to prior testimony. *Roberts* cannot fairly be read to stand for the radical proposition that no out-of-court statement can be introduced by the government without a showing that the declarant is unavailable.[77]

Why should the requirement of unavailability be limited to the former testimony exception? Justice Powell explained that former testimony "seldom has independent evidentiary significance of its own, but is intended to replace live testimony."[78] It is therefore a less reliable form of the same evidence. Accordingly, the Confrontation Clause and the law of hearsay, both favoring the best evidence available, require that a declarant be unavailable before former testimony can be admissible. Exceptions permitting the use of co-conspirator statements, under *Inadi*, however, work the other way around. "Co-conspirator statements derive much of their value from the fact that they are made in a context very different from trial, and therefore are usually irreplaceable as substantive evidence."[79] The distinction is comprehensible, but it strikes one as contrived.

From this tour of the cases, the conclusion is inescapable that neither the Warren Court, which ignited the fire, nor the Burger Court, which stoked it, settled on a workable rationale to govern the relationship between the hearsay rule and the Confrontation Clause. The Rehnquist Court has inherited the problem but, in Alfred North Whitehead's memorable phrase, has left the darkness unobscured. Justice Harlan's game attempt to channel the debate away from the Confrontation Clause and into the Due Process Clause gave promise as the notion of due process is far more elastic than the confrontation language which is too blunt an instrument to address the myriad problems presented by hearsay. Unhappily, Justice Harlan won no converts on his Court, and although Justices Thomas and Scalia later signed on to it in *White v. Illinois*,[80] Chief Justice Rehnquist responded dismissively that the argument "comes too late in the day to warrant reexamination of this approach."[81] The Court still wanders in the desert of confrontation, awaiting its Moses.

Separation of Powers

A minor—but important—theme of the Burger Court was a renewed emphasis on the constitutional separation of powers.

For example, a problem that had plagued the nation for more than fifty years was how to deal with the recurring encroachment by Congress on the constitutional functions assigned to the executive branch. This invasion was manifest in what had become known as the "one-house veto," a device whereby Congress would impose specific executive duties upon the executive branch and then provide that either house of Congress could override (read, veto) the executive action by the passage of a resolution negating the decision of the executive department that made it.

It began modestly with one act in 1932; by 1983 there were 295 veto-type procedures existing in 196 different federal statutes. Not surprisingly, the enactment of such statutes occurred most frequently when the White House and the Congress were controlled by different political parties. It was thus transparent that Congress was trespassing on the powers assigned to the executive branch, an evil that the Constitutional Convention had sought to prohibit. Specifically, the framers of the Constitution sought to prevent the "accumulat[ion], in a single body, [of] all the most important prerogatives of sovereignty . . . [which] should create in reality that very tyranny which the adversaries of the new Constitution either are, or affect to be, solicitous to avert."[82]

The courts for fifty years had been reluctant to act. In 1983, however, the Supreme Court took on *INS v. Chadha*,[83] in which the House of Representatives, pursuant to a one-house veto provision, had passed a resolution vetoing an immigration judge's decision to suspend the deportation of an alien, a power the judge had by statute. The one-house veto issue was ripe for decision, and the majority opinion written by Chief Justice Burger administered the coup de grace to the long-standing practice. In an opinion remarkable for its clarity and directness in dealing with the complex issues, the Chief Justice concluded:

> With all the obvious flaws of delay, untidiness and potential for abuse, we have not yet found a better way to preserve freedom than by making the exercise of power subject to the carefully crafted restraints spelled out in the constitution.[84]

And what decision of the Burger Court was more historic than its unanimous decision in *United States v. Nixon*.[85] During the Watergate investigation, the Special Prosecutor issued a subpoena duces tecum for certain tapes and documents relating to conversations and meetings between the President and others, including many government officials. As several Presidents before him had successfully done, President Nixon claimed executive privilege. Denying Nixon's claim of absolute executive privilege in refusing to turn over White House tapes to congressional Watergate investigators, the Chief Justice delivered the opinion for the Court. History will certainly regard it as one of the most significant opinions of any Justice.

The Supreme Court rejected a jurisdictional challenge that the dispute between the Special Prosecutor and the President was "intra-executive" in nature and, therefore, the courts lacked authority to review the President's claim. Most significantly, it ruled that there was no absolute right to executive privilege, pointing out that the three departments of government "were not intended to operate with absolute independence."[86] It further observed:

> To read the Art. II powers of the President as providing an absolute privilege as against a subpoena essential to enforcement of criminal statutes on no more than a generalized claim of the public interest in confidentiality of nonmilitary and nondiplomatic discussions would upset the constitutional balance of "a workable government" and gravely impair the role of the courts under Art. III.[87]

Then, most significantly, the Court held "that 'the public . . . has a right to every man's evidence,' except for those persons protected by a constitutional, common-law, or statutory privilege,"[88] Finally, the Court ruled:

> We conclude that when the ground for asserting privilege as to subpoenaed materials sought for use in a criminal trial is based only on the generalized interest in confidentiality, it cannot prevail over the fundamental demands of due process

of law in the fair administration of criminal justice. The generalized assertion of privilege must yield to the demonstrated, specific need for evidence in a pending criminal trial.[89]

Federalism

If one were to search for an *ideé fixe*, to borrow a concept from Berlioz, flowing quietly, but inexorably, through the Burger years, it would be an obsession with federalism. Nowhere was the Burger Court's struggle more passionate than its quest to reinvigorate the notion of federalism.

The Tenth Amendment states: "The powers not delegated to the United States by the Constitution, nor prohibited by it to the States, are reserved to the States respectively, or to the people." Two very different meanings can be given this provision. One is that the Tenth Amendment permits Congress to legislate *only* when the Constitution says it may, whereas states may legislate *unless* the Constitution says they may not. The other perspective, a "states' rights" view, is that the Tenth Amendment reserves a sacrosanct zone of activities to the states and that a law is unconstitutional if it infringes upon state sovereignty even if the law otherwise lies within the scope of Congress's powers.

Through the 1800s, the former view was generally followed. In this century, until 1937, the latter perspective controlled. From 1937 until the 1990s the Court went back to the original view, with the result that from 1937 until 1992, there was only one case in which the Court found a federal law to violate the Tenth Amendment. That was in *National League of Cities v. Usery*,[90] where five Justices, including Burger, agreed that the tenth Amendment was a barrier to Congress's effort to apply the Fair Labor Standards Act to state and municipal governments. Nine years later, however, the Court in *Garcia v. San Antonio Metropolitan Transit Authority*[91] expressly overruled *Usery*. If the states were distressed over acts of Congress, the Court suggested, they would have to seek legislative, not judicial, relief. In a short dissent in *Garcia*, Justice Rehnquist predicted that in time, the second position emphasizing states' rights would again be adopted.

The Rehnquist prediction came true in *New York v. United States*[92] in 1992. A federal law, the Low-Level Radioactive Waste Disposal Act required that all states clean up their own radioactive wastes by 1996. The law provided that states failing to do so would automatically take title to the wastes and become liable for any harms caused by them. By a 6–3 decision, the Court held that the law violated the Tenth Amendment because it conscripted state governments, forcing them to pass laws or regulations. Justice O'Connor, writing for the majority, said that it was irrelevant that the law served a vital environmental need. She concluded, simply, that federal laws compelling state legislative or regulatory activity violate state sovereignty.

It is unclear how far the Court will go in using the Tenth Amendment to limit congressional power. Tenth Amendment challenges to many federal laws, such as the Motor Voter Bill and the Brady Handgun Control Bill, are now pending in the Supreme Court. What is clear is that the conservative Justices have succeeded in resurrecting federalism as a significant constraint on Congress's powers.

For much of this century, state constitutional law remained a backwater port visited only by academic gnomes. The real action was on the federal level, and the focus of scholarship was on the U.S. Supreme Court. Until the mid-1980s, most law schools had even banished state constitutional law from the curriculum.

With Warren E. Burger at the helm of the Court and the concomitant rise of federalism as a legitimate and indeed pervasive constitutional doctrine, "rights" activists shifted their battlefield from the Supreme Court back to the state courts. In areas as diverse as privacy, criminal defendants' rights, and state funding of education for school districts, state courts became the engines of change, promoting greater rights for state citizens than those bestowed by the Supreme Court and, in some cases, restoring rights abrogated by the Supreme Court.

A Critique

The 1970s and 1980s are generally regarded as conservative years in American politics. The New Frontier and the Great Society were history for sure, and perhaps even the New Deal consensus itself. Democratic liberalism went on the defensive in a political era dominated by two conservative Republican Presidents, Richard Nixon and Ronald Reagan. Not surprisingly, new political tides were ultimately reflected in new Supreme Court appointments. "The Supreme Court," as James Bryce noticed, "feels the touch of public opinion."[93]

A broader look at the Burger Court's record, however, reveals that it turned out to be anything but a tribunal bent on returning to a golden age of "judicial restraint." Although the Court did curb some judicial innovation—in the area of equal protection, for example—those who had expected, and even hoped, that the Burger Court would make a 180-degree turn from the Warren Court surely have looked on the years between 1969 and 1986 with profound disappointment.

Considering the new forests into which the Burger Court ventured—abortion, the death penalty, prison conditions, commercial speech, and sex discrimination, among them—it seemed to have taken its cue from its predecessor and perpetuated the process of "judicializing" or "constitutionalizing" yet more areas of American life.[94] Anthony Lewis clearly was correct in 1983 when he wrote that the doctrines of the Warren Court are, in many respects, "more securely rooted now than they were in 1969." Indeed, Lewis added, "the reach of earlier decisions on racial equality and the First Amendment has been enlarged."[95]

Despite trenchant criticisms he had often leveled in his dissenting opinions, Justice William Brennan also conceded that the Burger Court had not "unraveled the work of the Warren Court"[96] but had, in fact, produced the decision that legalized abortion, the first case to strike down the death penalty in a number of states, and affirmative action rulings. If change had been inevitable with the advent of the Burger era, there was, as Brennan phrased it, still "room for the old dog."[97]

At the turn of the century, shortly before Warren Burger's birth in 1907, American jurisprudence trumpeted the values of a laissez-faire economic policy, unregulated capitalism, and vested property rights. When Chief Justice Burger resigned, these values had been reenshrined. The Burger Court era was characterized by the conservative political, economic, and social thought that came to be called "Reaganism." Its major values were conservative notions of limited government, individuality, equality of opportunity, and access to the system. Defining moments included the election of Republican Presidents from 1968 forward (save 1976), budget cuts for social programs, and a steady stream of conservative "moralistic" rhetoric that set the tone for the period.

The Burger Court poured a foundation for a new era in the Supreme Court's history. Consistent with McCloskey's notion of historical epochs during which tectonic constitutional plates shift for several decades and then new seismic explosions occur, in time the Burger Court may come to be viewed as a bridge spanning the Warren Court's liberalism and the Rehnquist Court's conservatism.

Notes

I wish to acknowledge the invaluable research assistance of Philip Pallone, Georgetown University School of Law, Class of 1998.

1. McCloskey, *The American Supreme Court* 134 (1960).
2. Id. at 79.
3. See Calabresi, "'A Government of Limited and Enumerated Powers': In Defense of *United States v. Lopez,*" 94 *Mich. L. Rev.* 752, 799 (1995) (noting that federalism guarantees were developed by such well-known cases as *McCulloch v. Maryland* and *Gibbons v. Ogden*); Dailey, "Federalism and Families," 143 *U. Pa. L. Rev.* 1887, 1888 n. 23 (1995) (explaining that early Supreme Court decisions such as *McCulloch* and *Gibbons* expressed "loyalty to the concept of federalism"); Massey, "Etiquette Tips: Some Implications of 'Process Federalism'," 18 *Harv. J.L. & Pub. Pol'y* 175, 177 (1994) (stating that Supreme Court chose to enforce principles of federalism beginning with *McCulloch v. Maryland*); Scheiber, "American Federalism and the Diffusion of Power: Historical and Contemporary Perspectives," 9 *Toledo L. Rev.* 618, 628–31 (1978) (recognizing that Supreme Court strictly adhered to principles of federalism prior to Civil War).
4. 17 U.S. (4 Wheat.) 316 (1819).
5. 22 U.S. (9 Wheat.) 1 (1824).
6. See Wills, *Lincoln at Gettysburg* 145 (1992).
7. McCloskey, supra note 1, at 134.
8. See, e.g., Allegeyer v. Louisiana, 165 U.S. 578 (1897). The Court held that substantive due process is violated by a state ban on marine insurance policies by out-of-state companies. This is the first Supreme Court decision to strike down a state statute using substantive due process. The *Lochner* era primarily focused on protecting property rights.
9. 198 U.S. 45 (1905) (striking down statute which limited number of hours bakery workers could work each week).
10. Id. at 64. (relying on substantive due process to invalidate state statute that is found to be restrictive of an individual's liberty to contract).
11. 300 U.S. 379 (1937) (holding state statute valid that provided for establishing minimum wages for women).
12. 268 U.S. 652 (1925) (holding state statute punishing those who advocate overthrowing the government constitutional).
13. Id. at 666 (recognizing that "freedom of speech and of the press—which are protected by the First Amendment from abridgment by Congress—are among the fundamental personal rights and 'liberties' protected by the due process clause of the Fourteenth Amendment from impairment by the States").

14. Id. The Supreme Court began the process of incorporation by its decision in *Gitlow*.

15. 297 U.S. 233 (1936) (declaring a state license tax applicable only to newspapers with circulation of more than 20,000 copies per week unconstitutional).

16. 299 U.S. 353 (1937).

17. 302 U.S. 319 (1937).

18. Id. at 326–27.

19. 304 U.S. 144 (1938).

20. McCloskey, supra note 1, at 10. See also Boudin, *Government by Judiciary* (1932).

21. Kalman, *The Strange Career of Legal Liberalism* (1996).

22. See Weiner, "Nixon Aide Called Dole too Loyal as Party Chief," *Austin Am. States-man*, Oct. 18, 1996, at A5 (stating that recent memo was released revealing Nixon's support for a constitutional amendment barring federal courts from integrating public schools and housing for fear that the four Supreme Court justices he had appointed would integrate the nation against its will).

23. N.Y. *Times*, Oct. 18, 1996, at A24.

24. Mason, "The Burger Court in Historical Perspective," *Pol. Sci. Q.* 89 (1974).

25. See Howard, "Chief Enigma," 81 A.B.A. *J.* 66, 67 (Oct. 1995).

26. 381 U.S. 479 (1965) (holding that Connecticut statute forbidding use of contraceptives violates the right of marital privacy lying within the penumbra of specific guarantees established by the Bill of Rights).

27. 410 U.S. 113, 153 (1973) (recognizing a right to privacy in the Fourteenth Amendment's concept of personal liberty).

28. See, e.g., Runyon v. McCrary, 427 U.S. 160 (1976) (holding that 42 U.S.C. § 1981 prohibits private, nonsectarian, commercially operated schools from denying admission to prospective Negro students); Lau v. Nichols, 414 U.S. 563 (1974) (holding that failure of San Francisco school system to provide English-language instruction to Chinese students violated section 601 of the Civil Rights Act of 1964); Keyes v. School Dist. No. 1, Denver, Co., 413 U.S. 189 (1973) (holding that a school district's segregation based on certain ethnic neighborhoods establishes a prima facie case of intentional segregation and the district court must determine whether this prima facie case can be rebutted by respondent's argument that such segregation was not racially motivated); Swann v. Charlotte-Mecklenburg Bd. of Educ., 402 U.S. 1 (1971) (stating in response to desegregation resistance that today's objective is to eliminate from the public schools all vestiges of state imposed segregation that was held violative of equal protection guarantees established by *Brown v. Board of Education*).

29. See, e.g., Jones v. Alfred H. Mayer Co., 392 U.S 409, 412 (1968). Petitioners claimed that respondents refused to sell them a home solely because one of the petitioners was black. The Court held that Congress had the power to enact 42 U.S.C. § 1982, conferring on all citizens the same right "as is enjoyed by white citizens" to purchase, lease, sell, hold and convey real and personal property. In so doing, the Court discussed the Thirteenth Amendment, stating as follows:

> Negro citizens North and South, who saw in the Thirteenth Amendment a promise of freedom—freedom to . . . "buy and sell when they please"—would be left with "a mere paper guarantee" if Congress were powerless to assure that a dollar in the hands of a Negro will purchase the same thing as a dollar in the hands of a white man.

Id. at 443; see Cooper v. Aaron, 358 U.S. 1, 9–11 (1958). In *Cooper*, the school board requested that the school desegregation plan be suspended due to tensions existing at the school. The district court granted the request. The court of appeals reversed and the Supreme Court affirmed its holding. The Supreme Court stated that state support of segregated schools through this arrangement cannot be "squared with the Fourteenth Amendment's command that no state shall deny to any person within its jurisdiction the equal protection of the laws." The Court held that a student's right not to be segregated based on his race was "so funda-mental . . . that it is embraced in the concept of due process of law." Id.; see Brown v. Board of Educ., 347 U.S. 483, 495 (1954). The Court held, in this landmark decision, that public school segregation of white and black children based on their race denies black chil-dren the equal protection of the laws guaranteed by the Fourteenth Amendment. The "sepa-rate but equal" doctrine promulgated by the Court in *Plessy v. Ferguson* was declared uncon-stitutional.

30. 438 U.S. 265 (1978) (holding program taking race into account in making admis-sions decisions violated Equal Protection Clause).

31. 443 U.S. 193 (1979) (holding that affirmative action plan reserving 50 percent of openings for blacks was within discretion left by title VII to private sector).

32. 448 U.S. 448 (1980) (upholding validity of "Minority Business Enterprise" program, requiring 10 percent of federal funds to be used for local public works projects to be ex-pended on minorities).

33. 411 U.S. 677 (1973) (holding that military statutes providing that spouses of male members are dependents for purposes of benefits but that spouses of female members are not dependents unless they are dependent for over one-half of their support unconstitutional).

34. 429 U.S. 190 (1976) (holding a statute requiring males to be twenty-one to buy beer and females to be eighteen to buy beer a gender-based discrimination that denied males equal protection of the laws).

35. 468 U.S. 609 (1984) (holding that compelling a male civic organization to accept women as regular members did not abridge the males' freedom of association).

36. 410 U.S. 113 (1973) (holding Texas criminal abortion statute unconstitutional).

37. Engel v. Vitale, 370 U.S. 421 (1962).

38. 330 U.S. 1 (1947) (holding that provision in New Jersey Constitution authorizing re-imbursement to parents of bus fares paid for transporting their children to non-public schools did not violate the First Amendment).

39. See, e.g., Lemon v. Kurtzman, 403 U.S. 602 (1971).

40. 472 U.S. 38 (1985).

41. Schwartz, "The Warren Court and Era," in *Encyclopedia of the American Judicial System* 168 (R. J. Janosik ed., 1987).

42. Funston, "The Burger Court and Era," in *Encyclopedia of the American Judicial System* (R. J. Janosik ed., 1987).

43. Id. at 180.

44. California v. Green, 399 U.S. 149, 162 (1970).

45. United States v. Inadi, 475 U.S. 387, 392 (1986).

46. Pointer v. Texas, 380 U.S. 400 (1965).

47. Douglas v. Alabama, 380 U.S. 415 (1965).

48. Barber v. Page, 390 U.S. 719 (1968).

49. 399 U.S. 149 (1970) [hereinafter *Green II*].

50. Cal. Evid. Code § 1235 (West 1996). The statute provided that "[e]vidence of a statement made by a witness is not made inadmissible by the hearsay rule if the statement is inconsistent with his testimony at the hearing. . . ."

51. People v. Green, 451 P.2d 422 (Cal. 1969).

52. 390 U.S. 719 (1968).

53. *Green*, 451 P.2d at 425.

54. *Green II*, 399 U.S. at 155–56 (citations omitted).

55. 400 U.S. 74 (1970).

56. Evans v. Dutton, 400 F.2d 826, 828 (5th Cir. 1968).

57. *Dutton,* 400 U.S at 82.

58. Id. at 86.

59. Id. at 89.

60. Id. at 96 (Harlan, J., concurring).

61. Id. at 94 (Harlan, J., concurring) (quoting 5 J. Wigmore, *Evidence* § 1397, at 131 (3d ed. 1940) (footnote omitted)).

62. Id. at 95 (Harlan, J., concurring).

63. *Green II,* 399 U.S at 174.

64. *Dutton,* 400 U.S. at 100 (Marshall, J., dissenting).

65. Id. at 110.

66. Id. at 105–06 n. 7 (citations omitted).

67. 448 U.S. 56 (1980).

68. See Ohio v. Roberts, 378 N.E.2d 492, 494 (Ohio 1978).

69. 378 N.E.2d 492 (Ohio 1978).

70. *Roberts,* 448 U.S. at 64.

71. Id. at 74 (quoting *Green II,* 399 U.S. at 189 n. 22).

72. Id. at 75 (1980).

73. Id. at 73 (quoting Mancusi v. Stubbs, 408 U.S. 204, 216 (1972)).

74. Id. at 65.

75. 475 U.S. 387 (1986).

76. Id. at 391.

77. Id. at 394.

78. Id. at 394.

79. Id. at 387–88.

80. 502 U.S. 346 (1992).

81. Id. at 353.

82. See *The Federalist* No. 22 (Alexander Hamilton).

83. 462 U.S. 919 (1983).

84. Id. at 959.

85. 418 U.S. 683 (1974).

86. Id. at 707.

87. Id.

88. Id. at 709 (quoting Branzburg v. Hayes, 408 U.S. 665, 688 (1972)).

89. Id. at 713.

90. 426 U.S. 833 (1976).

91. 469 U.S. 528 (1985).

92. 505 U.S. 144 (1992).

93. 1 Bryce, *The American Commonwealth* 242 (1917 ed.).

94. See Dworkin, *Taking Rights Seriously* 82–92 (1977).

95. Lewis, *The Burger Court: The Counter-Revolution That Wasn't* vii (Blasi ed., 1983).

96. Leeds, "A Life on the Court: A Conversation with Justice Brennan," *N.Y. Times* (*Magazine*), Oct. 5, 1986, at 26.

97. Id. at 77.

21

THE LEGACY OF THE BURGER COURT

JOHN J. GIBBONS

This is the last essay in this book. Inevitably, some of what is said here has already been discussed, but some of those thoughts seem worthy of reiteration.

This essay discusses the legacy of the Burger Court. Professor Schwartz chose the topic, and I have been wondering, ever since he did so, just what it encompassed. If there is a legacy of the Supreme Court between 1969, when Chief Justice Warren E. Burger was sworn in, and 1986, when he retired, it is not at all clear that it is a Burger legacy. Certainly, the Chief Justice did not leave his imprint on the Court as an institution in the way that John Marshall did. Unquestionably, there was a Marshall legacy. Certainly, perhaps for the reasons mentioned by Professor Tushnet, Chief Justice Burger did not exercise the kind of leadership of his colleagues that his immediate predecessor, Chief Justice Earl Warren, exercised— leadership that earned him the accolade of "Super Chief."[1] Of the thirteen Chief Justices who proceeded Chief Justice Burger, perhaps only Marshall, Taney, and Warren exercised such influence over their colleagues that the Court for their eras became forever associated with their name. One does not hear, for example, of the Ellsworth Court, or the Waite Court, or the Vinson Court. Even the eleven years when the distinguished Chief Justice Charles Evans Hughes presided are more likely to be referred to as the Court of the Nine Old Men.

Still, in the pantheon of Chief Justices, Warren Burger's place is certainly higher than many of his predecessors, and perhaps the seventeen years during which he presided will in the future commonly be referred to as the Burger Court, if for no other reason than persistent media usage during those years.

In thinking about the legacy of the Court in that period, one is tempted to focus, as most of the essays in this book have focused, on those decisions that dealt with individual rights—the clash between claims of individual autonomy and the collective society represented by the state or national governments. That focus is appropriate because the protection of individual liberty is the Court's most important function.

There is another group of cases, however, that do not resolve disputes between individuals and governments but, rather, disputes among competing political organizations. This group of cases includes federalistic disputes between national and state policies, and separation of powers disputes among the three branches of the federal government.

Many commentators on the Court's work have noted the conflict between majoritarian democracy and judicial review. When such a conflict is resolved in favor of individual autonomy rather than the regime in power, the case for judicial review is strongest. In those cases the Court is perceived as standing above the political battlefield, acting as the neutral and dispassionate guarantor of prepolitical human rights recognized explicitly or implicitly in the Constitution, or guaranteeing individual participation in the political process as it exists. When the Court intervenes in the clash of interest-group politics, by imposing its views of a proper structure of political institutions, it ceases to be neutral and dispassionate but becomes an active participant on the political battlefield. In these federalistic and separation-of-powers cases some political organization could lay down the rule of law that is challenged without in any way interfering with protected individual liberties. Thus, the Court takes sides in a dispute over which group of politicians should have the power to make the decision.

It is not meant to suggest that the resolution of many such structural disputes has no practical effect on individual rights. Quite the opposite is true, as Dean Belsky's essay makes plain. If, for example, the Court for structural federalistic reasons withholds a federal judicial remedy for the vindication of individual liberty interests against the states, many fewer individuals will have those rights vindicated. Turning the decision on the Court's perspective as to the respective roles of the state and federal governments in a political structure, however, simply disregards the individual rights issues underlying the dispute.

What this essay proposes to examine briefly is the Burger Court's performance in resolving these political structure, or political power, cases in three areas: (1) its treatment of the respective roles of the national and state governments in regulating commerce; (2) its treatment of the role of the national judiciary in effectively enforcing individual rights against the states; and (3) its treatment of the respective roles of the Congress and the President in controlling the rulemaking authority of federal administrative agencies. In each of these areas the legacy of the Court in the Burger era is significant.

I. In Commerce Clause Jurisprudence, the Picture Is That of Dual Sovereignty Revived

As we all know, Commerce Clause jurisprudence involves, first, the power of Congress to regulate and second, the power of states to regulate in the absence of preemptive congressional regulation. Back in the dark ages of dual sovereignty, it was frequently asserted by the Court that federal and state political power were mutually exclusive. If the Court assigned legislative competence to the states, the Tenth Amendment stood as a barrier to federal legislation.[2] If it assigned legislative competence to Congress, even in the absence of federal legislation the dormant or unexercised Commerce Clause prevented state legislation.[3] By the 1970s, however, the Court had long since abandoned its effort to impose on an unruly and increasingly national political process its own version of the allocation of legislative competence in economic matters. If Congress saw the need for legislation, that ended the inquiry.[4] State law could coexist with federal law only if it survived express or implied preemption.[5] The dormant Commerce Clause still played a role, but it had become a nonconstitutional role, a federal common-law role, in the sense that a dormant Commerce Clause pronouncement was held to be subject to congressional override.[6] This arrangement was a sensible one because it left resolution of disputes over economic policy for ultimate resolution by the political process at the national level, whereas the former dual-sovereignty structure imposed by the Court in many instances foreclosed the operation of that process.

On June 24, 1976, however, the Burger Court decided two Commerce Clause cases which were clear departures from the sensible arrangement that was just described. One was a dormant Commerce Clause case and the other an exercised commerce power case. The dormant Commerce Clause case is *Hughes v. Alexandria Scrap Corp.*[7] The exercised Commerce Clause case is *National League of Cities v. Usery*,[8] which Chief Justice Abrahamson's essay discusses in some detail.

In *Alexandria Scrap*, a 6–3 majority introduced into dormant Commerce Clause jurisprudence for the first time a distinction between state regulation of commerce engaged in by others and direct participation by the state in commerce. The Court held, with no significant exposition of its reasons, that the state's participation in the market was not subject to dormant Commerce Clause scrutiny, even though a political organization having taxing power and thus not dependent on profits participated in the market in a manner distinctly different from any other market participant.

The *Alexandria Scrap* opinion says nothing about the power of Congress to overrule its holding and subject state market participants to federal economic legislation. In *National League of Cities*, however, the individual cities and states were participants in the market for labor, and Congress had subjected them to a garden-variety Commerce Clause enactment, the Fair Labor Standards Act of 1938.[9] Harking back to Chief Justice Chase's 1869 reference to "an indestructible Union . . . of indestructible States,"[10] the Court held that application of the Fair Labor Standards Act to the participation of states and local governments in the market for labor violated the Tenth Amendment. In so holding, the Court overruled *Maryland v. Wirtz*,[11] a case decided toward the end of the Warren Court. On the other hand, it declined to overrule its own year-old precedent in *Fry v. United States*,[12] upholding application to the states of the Economic Stabilization Act of 1970, which temporarily froze wages of state and local government employees. This interesting distinction meant that the Tenth Amendment served as a bar to federal Commerce Clause regulation that increased the cost of state-purchased labor but did not serve as a bar to federal Commerce Clause regulation that stabilized such cost. Hence, the net effect of *National League of Cities* was to deprive public-sector labor unions of their legislative victory in Congress but to preserve for state and local governments the benefits of a wage freeze imposed by Congress. There was no cross-reference between the *Alexandria Scrap* and *National League of Cities* opinions, but the Tenth Amendment underpinnings of the former, although not explicit, seem plain enough. And if one put together what states could do as market participants and what Congress could not do to regulate their market activities, the role of the states as political decision makers was increased, whereas that of the national government was diminished.

Thus, as of June 24, 1976, six Justices of the Burger Court were ready to restore a nineteenth-century version of court-imposed structural relationships in the federal union. In doing so they were ready to disregard the vast changes in the national economy, population, transportation and communication infrastructure, monetary system, and external affairs that had caused their predecessors to abandon dual sovereignty years earlier. June 24, 1976, was certainly among the more weird days in the Court's modern history.

What subsequently happened to the *Alexandria Scrap* and *National League of Cities* efforts at reviving dual sovereignty is interesting. The *Alexandria Scrap* market participant rule seemed to thrive for a while. In *Reeves, Inc. v. Stake*,[13] the Burger Court in 1980 upheld a South Dakota policy of discriminating against out-of-state purchasers in the sale of cement manufactured in a state-owned plant. A few years later, in *White v. Massachusetts Council of Construction Employers, Inc.*,[14] it sustained against a dormant Commerce Clause challenge a City of Boston executive order mandating discrimination against nonresidents of that city in purchasing construction labor. But the next year, in *South-Central Timber Development v. Wennicke*,[15] the Court, over dissents by Justices Rehnquist and O'Connor, refused to apply the doctrine to a competitive bid requirement, imposed by the State of Alaska, conditioning the sale of timber that it owned on an undertaking to process the timber locally. Two years later, in *Wisconsin Department of Industry v. Gould, Inc.*,[16] a unanimous Burger Court rejected the effort of Wisconsin to avoid the implied preemption of the National Labor Relations Act (NLRA) by relying on the market participant doctrine. A Wisconsin statute prohibited the state from doing business with companies found to have violated the NLRA three times within a five-year period. The Wisconsin statute applied only to business of the state itself. "[T]he 'market participant' doctrine," said the Court, "reflects the particular concerns underlying the Commerce Clause, not any general notion regarding the necessary extent of state power in areas where Congress has acted."[17] There is no reference in *Gould* to *National League of Cities* or to the Tenth Amendment, and no real explanation for the distinction for purposes of that Amendment between a federal Commerce Clause statute and a federal common-law rule derived directly from the Commerce Clause.

Trying to reconcile, for students in constitutional law, the outcomes in this handful of market participant cases has proved to be a daunting task. Naturally one tries to avoid stating that the Court's federalism exercise in inventing and applying the doctrine is nothing more than a concealed way of achieving a preferred economic outcome in a given case. But what other more elevated principle can actually be derived from the opinions?

Although the market participant doctrine has not been extended beyond court-imposed dormant Commerce Clause rules, *Alexandria Scrap* has not been overruled. As Chief Justice Abrahamson points out, *National League of Cities'* subsequent history is different. The Burger Court struggled over most of the decade following that decision to determine the reach of the newly resuscitated Tenth

Amendment as a limit on congressional power. In 1981, a divided Court rejected a Tenth Amendment challenge to several federal statutes regulating strip mining.[18] In 1982 it unanimously rejected a Tenth Amendment challenge to the application of the Railway Labor Act[19] to the Long Island Railroad, owned and operated by the State of New York.[20] That same year a divided Court rejected a Tenth Amendment challenge to portions of the Public Utility Regulatory Policies Act of 1978,[21] directing state utility commissioners to consider federally suggested regulatory standards.[22] In 1983, a divided Court rejected a Tenth Amendment challenge to the 1974 amendment that extended the Age Discrimination in Employment Act to state employees.[23]

Finally, in 1985, Justice Blackmun apparently had enough of the revival of dual sovereignty. In *Garcia v. San Antonio Metropolitan Transit Authority,*[24] he wrote an opinion for five Justices expressly overruling *National League of Cities*. The Court held that the Fair Labor Standards Act did bind the states in their purchase of labor if Congress said so. The states, he reasoned, must find protection against a burdensome Commerce Clause in the political structure of the federal government, and the Court should not intervene to set aside decisions made by the political branches in this structure. The majority thus appeared to adopt the sensible arguments made by Professor Herbert Wechsler in 1961 and Professor Jesse Choper in 1980 that state interests were adequately safeguarded by the structural aspects of the national political system.[25] Four Justices dissented vigorously, and Justice Rehnquist predicted that the principle of the *National League of Cities* case "will, I am confident, in time command the support of a majority of this court."[26] The position of the four dissenters must be counted as a part of the Burger Court's legacy. The dissenters insisted that the revival of dual sovereignty is alive and well. We can see in post-Burger Court decisions such as *New York v. United States*[27] and *United States v. Lopez*[28] that they were right. The revival of nineteenth-century versions of the Tenth Amendment as an enforceable limit on the legislative powers of the national government is a clear and, in my opinion, an unfortunate legacy of the Burger Court. The Court left the heights of dispassionate arbiter between governments and individuals and descended to become a participant in the battles of intergroup political action in state capitols and in Washington, D.C.

II. Turning to the Protection of Individual Rights against the States, the Picture Is one of Federal Judicial Power Curtailed

The Warren Court made two major substantive constitutional-law advances. The first was the overruling of *Plessy v. Ferguson*[29] and thus the dismantling of the constitutional arrangements respecting race which the Court had endorsed after 1877.[30] The second was the application to the states of most of the individual rights features of the Bill of Rights.[31] Neither of these substantive advances could be made effective in the absence of effective employment of the judicial power of the United States. Deployment of that power required effective federal review of state criminal judgments, as well as effective use of federal civil injunctive and declaratory remedies. To accomplish the former, it was necessary both to eliminate state procedural bars to the consideration of federal claims as barriers to federal review and to increase federal judicial capacity. To accomplish the latter, it was necessary to reconsider several cases decided at the outset of World War II that had made federal injunctive remedies against the enforcement of state law largely ineffective.[32]

The Warren Court did both. It eliminated the state procedural bar rule in *Fay v. Noia*[33] and *Henry v. Mississippi*.[34] *Henry v. Mississippi* held that such a bar was no obstacle to Supreme Court review of a final state court judgment in a criminal case. As, however, the Supreme Court's appellate jurisdiction was a scarce resource, it was the elimination of the state procedural bar rule in habeas corpus cases that actually made the judicial power of the United States effective. The availability in district courts of habeas corpus review vastly increased federal judicial resources available for review of state criminal convictions. As to the injunctive remedy, the Warren Court restored its effectiveness in *Dumbrowski v. Pfister*,[35] recognizing the appropriateness in many cases of federal injunctions against the enforcement of unconstitutional state laws.

Very early, the Burger Court commenced curtailment of the availability of federal injunctive relief. On February 23, 1971, it handed down decisions in six cases that narrowly circumscribed the circumstances in which a federal court could grant injunctive or declaratory relief against state criminal statutes.[36] This group of cases, in which the lead opinions were announced in *Younger v. Harris*, in a technical sense are only interpretations of federal remedial statutes. Thus, in theory they could be modified by federal legislation. What is significant about the cases, however, is the repeated references to the "comity" that the national sovereign acting through its courts owes to the state sovereigns acting through their courts. The opinions resonate with Tenth Amendment rhetoric. The Justices appeared to accept the very dual sovereignty arguments that Justice Story had rejected in *Martin v. Hunter's Lessee*[37] in 1816 and Chief Justice Marshall had rejected in *Cohens v. Virginia*[38] in 1835.

The *Younger v. Harris* rule was initially applied only to pending criminal charges, but in 1975 it was extended to some criminal prosecutions filed after the commencement of a federal declaratory judgment suit[39] and to civil proceedings "in aid of a closely related to criminal statutes."[40] In 1976, the rule was extended to actions of state executive officials.[41] A year later, the *Younger v. Harris* rule was extended to state contempt proceedings[42] and to civil attachment proceedings brought by a state.[43] Thus, its revival of dual sovereignty led the Burger Court to a drastic curtailment of the remedial powers of the lower federal courts, leaving litigants in many instances with no opportunity for Article III review in any forum but the Supreme Court itself. And if the Supreme Court declined review of rejections of federal claims, as was likely in most cases considering its limited adjudicatory capacity, the Burger Court confirmed in *Allen v. McCurry*[44] that state law determined the judgment preclusion effect of the state court judgment.

Younger v. Harris and its progeny are, of course, possible, if not always persuasive interpretations of the jurisdictional and remedial statutes they apply. Theoretically, they remain subject to legislative reconsideration. But what is disquieting is that the comity and federalism arguments used in justification for those interpretations placed the Burger Court on one side (the winning side, as it happens) of a political debate over the degree to which federal power should be used to control the actions of state actors. The Court added legitimacy to the states' rights side of the debate by suggesting that recognition of state sovereignty was a constitutional imperative driving the interpretation of federal remedial statutes.

The habeas corpus story is similar. In *Fay v. Noia*,[45] and *Henry v. Mississippi*,[46] Justice Harlan had urged that the federal government is constitutionally required to recognize the adequacy of state *procedural* bars to the consideration of federal claims, unless those bars are so arbitrary or irrational as to amount to an independent denial of due process. The Burger Court did not adopt that extreme limitation on congressional authority. But from the beginning, driven by the same Tenth Amendment comity rhetoric as drove the injunctive and declaratory remedies cases, the Burger Court undertook a reinterpretation of the habeas corpus statute. First it held that a guilty plea was a bar to the consideration of federal claims in habeas corpus.[47] It applied the guilty plea procedural bar to a habeas corpus claim that the state had excluded African Americans from the jury that indicted the defendant.[48] It applied the guilty plea procedural bar to a claim of a prisoner who, while pleading guilty, had consistently proclaimed his innocence.[49] It applied a state simultaneous-objection-by-counsel rule to bar consideration of a habeas corpus claim that a trial of a defendant in prison garb violated due process.[50] It applied a state rule requiring pretrial objection to the composition of a grand jury as a bar to consideration in habeas corpus of a federal claim in habeas corpus that the composition was illegal.[51] It applied a state simultaneous objection rule as a bar to consideration of a claim that a confession used to convict a defendant was involuntary.[52] And in *Stone v. Powell*[53] it virtually freed the states to disregard the Fourth Amendment by holding that Fourth Amendment claims could not be considered in habeas corpus as long as the state provided a procedural opportunity to litigate an exclusionary rule contention. All this reinterpretation of the *Fay v. Noia* interpretation of the habeas corpus statute was done with the same states rights arguments that were relied on in dismantling the injunctive and declaratory remedies against the states, and that were relied on by the *National League of Cities* majority as a reason for curtailing congressional power under the Commerce Clause.

Throughout the Burger Court years, there were repeated proposals in Congress to curtail by legislation the remedial powers of the Article III courts over state courts. Then, although not in more recent times, Congress fairly consistently rejected the states rights lobbying efforts. The Burger Court, however, in restating the federal law of remedies against the states, rather consistently gave states what they were unable to obtain by legislation. Today, of course, in statutes such as the Prison Litigation Reform Act[54] and the 1996 amendments to the habeas corpus statute,[55] Congress has gone further in curtailing the remedies against states that violate federal constitutional rights than the Burger Court ever thought of going. It can at least be asked whether the states' rights rhetoric of that Court did not contribute to the political climate that produced this recent unfortunate legislation. In my opinion, it did. The Burger Court became, in my view, a more effective lobbiest for the curtailment of federal power to enforce individual rights against state actors than the frequently clamorous state attorneys general.

III. Federal Executive Power Increased

Turning from the Burger Court's "federalism" legacy, let us consider what that Court left us about separation of powers. By 1969, this nation had undergone more than a century of evolution in the structure of political organs of the national government. The first important delegation by Congress of rulemaking authority to an administrative agency was the legislation in 1887 that created the Interstate Commerce Commission. From that time forward, the utility of delegation of rulemaking authority—delegation of the power of legislation—was never in doubt. True, there was not a great deal of such delegation until the vast expansion of federal legislation that occurred during the 1930s and in World War II. But the practice of delegating legislative powers to administrative agencies was well established long before the New Deal.

This practice can be referred to as an evolution in the structure of political organs of the national government because, plainly, it was. There is no reference in the text of the 1787 Constitution, or in any constitutional amendments, either to administrative agencies or to delegation of legislative powers. Instead, there is a peculiarly rigid structure in which the legislative function is divided between a two-house legislative branch and an executive, not responsible to that branch but holding veto powers over its enactments, subject, of course, to override by supermajorities.

When that structure was set out in 1787, parliamentary government had not fully evolved, but in Great Britain, at least, the principle of parliamentary supremacy over the Crown was firmly established. For reasons good and sufficient at the time, the framers rejected parliamentary supremacy in favor of a structure having not only federalistic limitations but also separation-of-powers limitations within the national government.

In Great Britain and other parliamentary democracies, the parliamentary system eventually evolved to the point that what we regard as executive powers—powers over how the laws are carried into execution—were entrusted to the majority in parliament. To that majority is also given the task of filling in the interstices of legislation written, necessarily, in general terms. In the United States, however, the very structure of the national government prevented a similar evolution. Parliamentary majorities, and hence executive ministers, are responsible to parliament. The President of the United States and his executive branch officers are not.

American politicians, however, have at least since the 1880s been pragmatic problem solvers. The problem to be solved was the impossibility, in our divided scheme for legislative enactments, of agreeing on every foreseeable issue to which a given piece of legislation might apply, or in any system, of actually foreseeing every such issue. The solution was the invention of administrative agencies, to which could be delegated the details of application of more generalized legislative enactments in specific instances. It was a rather neat solution that introduced needed flexibility into a political structure spelled out in the 1787 Constitution that, if literally imposed, simply would not work. Certainly it had not worked prior to the Civil War.

The ingenious invention of delegated rulemaking authority, however, presented its own problem. In a parliamentary system the government—the majority—can be delegated vast authority because it remains responsible to the democratically chosen members. How does a legislature ensure that holders of delegated authority remain accountable? American politicians, once again pragmatic problem solvers, devised two ingenious methods. The first, which was in the Burger Court relatively uncontroversial, was the enactment of judicial review provisions such as Section 10 of the Federal Administrative Procedure Act. Judicial review of agency action is a means of ensuring that agencies holding delegated legislative powers will remain within the bounds of the authority delegated to them. That method has been largely effective, but not entirely so. In 1984, the Burger Court in *Chevron USA, Inc. v. Natural Resources Defense Counsel*[56] watered down judicial oversight by ruling that it would defer to any reasonable agency interpretation of the statute the agency was charged with enforcing.

The second oversight method, which in the Burger Court proved to be very controversial, is the legislative veto, dealt with by that Court in *INS v. Chadha*.[57] There are other Burger Court separation-of-powers cases, but *Chadha* is clearly the most interesting one because, as Justice White pointed out in his dissent, it invalidated at least fifty-five major federal statutes containing one-house or two-house legislative veto provisions. Others have identified nearly 200 such statutes. Moreover, the position of the executive branch with respect to those statutes was well-known. A succession of Presidents had opined for years that they were unconstitutional. Furthermore, beginning with the Ford administration, the White House had begun, through the Office of Management and Budget, to exercise executive oversight of agency rulemaking. Just as the Constitution makes no explicit reference to delegated rulemaking authority, it makes no reference to oversight of that delegated legislative activity by unelected officials in the Office of Management and Budget, many of whom are not even subject to Senate confirmation. Moreover, for much of the Burger Court era the executive and legislative branches were controlled by different political parties. Thus, *Chadha* arrived on the scene at a time of considerable tension between the branches, especially over the alleged burden of federal regulation of the environment and of workplace safety, and at a time that the executive branch was vigorously pressing its own policy agenda on the administrative agencies.

Chadha was a contrived lawsuit in which both sides wanted the same outcome. It fell well outside the conventional rules about justiciability in the Article III Courts. The Burger Court nevertheless welcomed it, brushing aside questions of justiciability and eliminating in one fell swoop a significant and evolving method of legislative oversight over delegated rulemaking authority; a method that the Congress still resorts to despite the Supreme Court's *Chadha* pronouncement. The next year, in *Chevron*, the Court reduced the level of judicial oversight as well. Clearly, the elimination of legislative oversight, combined with the reduction of judicial oversight, had the intended effect of increasing executive branch power.

The tendency of the Burger Court to maximize executive branch power at the expense of Congress may be seen in other cases as well. In *Bowsher v. Synar*,[58] the Court considered provisions of the Balanced Budget and Emergency Deficit Control Act of 1985 that required an executive branch agency, the Office of Management and Budget, and a legislative branch agency, the Congressional Budget Office, to estimate the amount of the deficit for the next fiscal year. These agencies

were required to report to the Comptroller General who would issue a report speci-
fying budget reductions. That report triggered the issuance of a sequestration order
by the President, putting into effect the reductions submitted by the Comptroller,
unless Congress within a specified time, met the deficit goal in another way. Because the Comptroller General was an officer removable by Congress, the Burger
Court held the statute providing for his participation was, on separation-of-powers
grounds, unconstitutional. The Court's opinion makes clear that had the same
delegation of rulemaking authority been made to an executive branch official, the
Secretary of the Treasury, for example, or even to an independent agency, it would
have survived separation-of-powers scrutiny. The defect that the Court identified
was that the Comptroller General was removable for cause by a joint resolution of
Congress. Thus, said the Court, "[H]e may not be entrusted with executive powers."[59] Executive powers? Since when is the exercise of delegated rulemaking anything but legislative? And more puzzling still, because joint resolutions are subject
to presidential veto, how was congressional removal authority any different than
congressional authority to remove an executive branch official by impeachment?
Two-thirds is two-thirds in either context. Be that as it may, the Burger Court once
more took a position that increased executive branch authority while decreasing
legislative branch authority.

In *Chadha*, the Burger Court attempted to justify its active participation in the
political battle between an executive of one party and a legislature controlled by another by an appeal to "freedom." Acknowledging that the political structure created
in 1787 "imposed burdens on governmental processes that often seem clumsy, inefficient, unworkable," the Court continued:

> With all the obvious flaws of delay, untidiness and potential for abuse, we have not
> yet found a better way to preserve freedom than by making the exercise of power
> subject to the carefully crafted restraints spelled out in the Constitution.[60]

Despite this evocation of freedom, and perhaps of the reverence due the freedom-
loving founders, two things are plain. First, the Court never identified the manner
in which in *Chadha* the legislative veto or in *Bowsher* the role of the Comptroller
General threatened our freedoms. Second, both *Chadha* and *Bowsher removed*
checks on executive branch power. The suggestion that such checks are a threat to
freedom is counterintuitive. One would think that the branch that controls the
military is the branch over which checks ought to be placed in the interest of freedom.

Taken together, *Chadha* and *Bowsher* stand for these propositions:

1. The exercise of delegated rulemaking authority is an "executive" function, even
   though had Congress enacted the same rule, it would unquestionably be exercising a legislative function.
2. Neither by retaining veto authority, nor by maintaining removal authority over
   an officer to whom the delegation is made, may Congress participate in the
   oversight of delegated rulemaking.

The Burger Court's legacy with respect to separation of powers is a rigid textu-
alism, masking the reality that the Court became an active participant in a political

battle over policy differences between the two spheres of political power at either end of Pennsylvania Avenue. That legacy is unfortunate. Professor Wechsler and Professor Choper cogently warned that there was no good reason for the Court to spend its own limited political capital by exercising the antimajoritarian power of judicial review in resolving such disputes. As long as individual rights are not adversely affected, the Supreme Court should let the political process determine the evolution of American political structures. The Burger Court unwisely rejected that sound counsel.

Summary

In summary, the federalism jurisprudence of the Burger Court, in both its Commerce Clause aspect and its federal law enforcement against the states aspect, was seriously flawed. Its separation-of-powers jurisprudence was flawed as well. Both flawed legacies provide precedents that ten years later continue to have unfortunate effects. Would that one could predict improvement. The present Court is at least as committed to active participation in the political battles of the day as was its predecessor.

Notes

1. Schwartz, *Super Chief: Earl Warren and His Supreme Court—A Judicial Biography* (1983).
2. See, e.g., United States v. E.C. Knight Co., 156 U.S. 1 (1895).
3. See, e.g., Passenger Cases, 7 How. (48 U.S.) 283 (1849).
4. See, e.g., Wickard v. Fillburn, 317 U.S. 111 (1942).
5. See, e.g., Rice v. Santa Fe Elevator Corp., 331 U.S. 218 (1947); Hines v. Davidowitz, 312 U.S. 52 (1941).
6. Prudential Ins. Co. v. Benjamin, 328 U.S. 408 (1946).
7. 426 U.S. 794 (1976).
8. 426 U.S. 833 (1976).
9. 52 Stat. 1060, 29 U.S.C. §§ 211 et seq.
10. Texas v. White, 7 Wall. (74 U.S.) 700, 725 (1869).
11. 392 U.S. 183 (1968).
12. 421 U.S. 542 (1975).
13. 447 U.S. 429, 436-437 (1980).
14. 460 U.S. 204 (1983).
15. 467 U.S. 82 (1984).
16. 475 U.S. 282 (l986).
17. Id. at 289.
18. Hodel v. Virginia Surface Min. & Reclamation Ass'n, 452 U.S. 264 (1981).
19. 44 Stat. (pt. 2) 577, *as amended*, 45 U.S.C. §§ 151, et seq.
20. United Transp. Union v. Long Island R.R. Co., 455 U.S. 678 (1982).
21. Pub. L. No. 96-617 § 113, 92 Stat. 3117, 16 U.S.C. § 2623 (1978).
22. FERC v. Mississippi, 456 U.S. 742 (1982).
23. EEOC v. Wyoming, 460 U.S. 226 (1983).
24. 469 U.S. 528 (1985).
25. See Wechsler, "The Political Safeguards of Federalism—The Role of the States in the Composition and Selection of the National Government," in *Principles, Politics, and*

Fundamental Law 49 (Wechsler ed. 1961); Choper, *Judicial Review and the National Political Process* (1980).

26. 469 U.S. at 580.
27. 505 U.S. 144 (1992).
28. 115 S. Ct. 1624 (1995).
29. 163 U.S. 537 (1996).
30. Brown v. Board of Educ., 347 U.S. 483 (1954).
31. See Mapp v. Ohio, 367 U.S. 643 (1961) (search and seizure); Gideon v. Wainwright, 372 U.S. 333 (1963) (counsel); Malloy v. Hogan, 378 U.S. 1 (1964) (self-incrimination); Pointer v. Texas, 380 U.S. 400 (1965) (confrontation); Klopfer v. North Carolina, 386 U.S. 213 (1967) (speedy trial); Washington v. Texas, 388 U.S. 14 (1967) (compulsory process); Duncan v. Louisiana, 391 U.S. 145 (1968) (jury trial); Benton v. Maryland, 395 U.S. 784 (1969) (double jeopardy).
32. See Beal v. Missouri Pac. R.R. Corp., 312 U.S. 45 (1941); Douglas v. City of Jeannet, 319 U.S. 157 (1943).
33. 372 U.S. 391 (1965).
34. 379 U.S. 443 (1965).
35. 380 U.S. 479 (1965). See also the Warren Court's interpretation of 42 U.S.C. § 1983, in Monroe v. Pape, 365 U.S. 167 (1961).
36. Younger v. Harris, 401 U.S. 37 (1971); Perez v. Ledesma, 401 U.S. 82 (1971); Dyson v. Stein, 401 U.S. 200 (1971) (per curiam); Byrne v. Karalexis, 401 U.S. 216 (1971) (per curiam).
37. 1 Wheat (14 U.S.) 304 (1816).
38. 6 Wheat (19 U.S.) 264 (1821).
39. Hicks v. Miranda, 422 U.S. 332 (1975).
40. Huffman v. Pursue, Ltd., 420 U.S. 592, 604 (1975).
41. Rizzo v. Goode, 423 U.S. 362, 366–68 (1976).
42. Juidice v. Vail, 430 U.S. 327 (1977).
43. Trainor v. Hernandez, 431 U.S. 434 (1977).
44. 449 U.S. 90 (1980).
45. 372 U.S. 391 (1963).
46. 379 U.S. 443 (1965).
47. McMann v. Richardson, 397 U.S. 759, 770 (1970); Parker v. North Carolina, 397 U.S. 790, 795–96 (1970).
48. Tollett v. Henderson, 411 U.S. 258 (1973).
49. North Carolina v. Alfred, 400 U.S. 25 (1970).
50. Estelle v. Williams, 425 U.S. 501 (l976).
51. Francis v. Henderson, 425 U.S. 536 (1976).
52. Wainright v. Sykes, 433 U.S. 72 (1977).
53. 428 U.S. 465 (1976).
54. Omnibus Appropriations Act for Fiscal Year 1966 tit. VII, Pub. L. No. 104–134, 110 Stat. 1321.
55. Antiterrorism and Effective Death Penalty Act of 1996, Pub. L. 104-132, 110 Stat. 1214.
56. 467 U.S. 837, 842–45 (1984).
57. 462 U.S. 919 (1983).
58. 478 U.S. 714 (1986).
59. Id. at 732.
60. 462 U.S. at 959.